MEDIA STUDIES

Media History, Media and Society

1 MEDIA STUDIES: VOLUME 1: MEDIA HISTORY, MEDIA AND SOCIETY

Part 1: History

Chapter 1: History of the South African Media – *David Wigston*
Chapter 2: The Media in Africa – *Fackson Banda*

Part 2: Media and Society

Chapter 3: Approaches to the Study of Mass Communication – *Pieter J. Fourie*
Chapter 4: The Role and Functions of the Media in Society – *Pieter J. Fourie*
Chapter 5: The Effects of Mass Communication – *Pieter J. Fourie*
Chapter 6: Media Culture – *Magriet Pitout*
Chapter 7: The Ideological Power of the Media – *Stefan Sonderling*
Chapter 8: The Public Sphere in Contemporary Society – *Pieter Duvenage*
Chapter 9: Globalisation, Information Communication Technology and the Media
 – *Pieter J. Fourie*

2 MEDIA STUDIES: VOLUME 2: POLICY, MANAGEMENT, AND MEDIA REPRESENTATION

Part 1: Media Policy

Chapter 1: The nature of media and communication policy – *Jo Bardoel & Jan van Cuilenburg*
Chapter 2: External media regulation in South Africa – *David Wigston*
Chapter 3: Internal media regulation in South Africa – *Marie van Heerden*

Part 2: Media Management

Chapter 4: Media and communication markets – *Jo Bardoel & Jan van Cuilenburg*
Chapter 5: Strategic media management – *Jo Bardoel & Jan van Cuilenburg*

Part 3: Representation

Chapter 6: Defining representation – *Julie Reid*
Chapter 7: News as representation – *Arnold S. De Beer*
Chapter 8: Media and identity – *Herman Wasserman*
Chapter 9: Media and race – *Lynnette Steenveld*
Chapter 10: Media and gender: feminist and masculinity studies – *Beschara Karam*
Chapter 11: Media and sexual orientation: the portrayal of gays and lesbians *Christo Cilliers*
Chapter 12: Media and environment – *Ian Glenn*
Chapter 13: Media and AIDS – *Corrie Faure*

Chapter 14: Media and violence – *Magriet Pitout*
Chapter 15: Media and terrorism – *Bert Kirsten*

3 MEDIA STUDIES: VOLUME 3: MEDIA CONTENT AND AUDIENCES

Section 1: Media Content And Content Analysis

Section A : Qantitative content analysis
Chapter 1: Quantitative content analysis – *David Wigston*

Section B: Qualitative content analysis
Chapter 2: Media semiotics – *Pieter J Fourie*
Chapter 3: Media, language and discourse – *Stefan Sonderling*
Chapter 4: Media and visual literacy – *Trudie du Plooy*
Chapter 5: Visual text analysis – *Trudie du Plooy*
Chapter 6: Narrative analysis – *David Wigston*

Section 2: Media Audiences

Chapter 7: Research theories in media audience studies: anthropological ethnography and uses and gratification theory – *Magriet Pitout*
Chapter 8: Questionnaire surveys in media studies – *Elirea Bornman*
Chapter 9: Field research – *Magriet Pitout*
Chapter 10: Measuring media audiences – *Elirea Bornman*

4 MEDIA STUDIES: VOLUME 4: PRODUCTION PLANNING AND MEDIA ETHICS

Part 1: Media Production And Planning

Chapter 1: Newspaper production planning – *Corrie Faure*
Chapter 2: Television production planning – *David Wigston*
Chapter 3: Radio production planning – *David Wigston*
Chapter 4: Educational broadcasting planning – *David Wigston*
Chapter 5: Website production planning – *Bert Kirsten*
Chapter 6: An introduction to film theory – *Pieter Fourie*
Chapter 7: Film production planning – *Beschara Karam*

Part 2: Media ethics

Chapter 8: What is ethics? – *Corrie Faure*
Chapter 9: Professional ethics and codes of conduct – *Marie van Heerden*
Chapter 10: Ethical issues in the media – *Marie van Heerden*

MEDIA STUDIES

Media History, Media and Society

Second Edition

Pieter J. Fourie (Editor)

This volume is part of a four-volume series

Volume 1: Media Studies: Media History, Media and Society
Second edition

First published in 2001 as *Media Studies: Institutions, Theories and Issues*
Reprinted 2001
Reprinted 2003
Reprinted 2004
Reprinted 2005
Reprinted 2006
Reprinted 2007
Second edition 2007

Juta & Co.
Mercury Crescent
Wetton, 7780
Cape Town, South Africa

© 2007 Juta & Co. Ltd

ISBN: 978 0 702 17692 0

All rights reserved. No part of this publication may be reproduced or transmitted in any form or by any means, electronic or mechanical, including photocopying, recording, or any information storage or retrieval system, without permission in writing from the publisher.

Typeset in 10.5 pt on 14 pt Minion Pro

Project Manager: Sarah O'Neill
Editor: Christina Scott
Proofreader: Alexandra le Feuvre
Indexer: Jan Schaafsma
Design and layout: Charlene Bate
Cover designer: Pumphaus Design Studio
Printed in South Africa by Creda Communications

The authors and the publisher have made every effort to obtain permission for and to acknowledge the use of copyright material. Should any infringement of copyright have occurred, please contact the publisher, and every effort will be made to rectify omissions or errors in the event of a reprint or new edition.

Contents

About the authors   xiii

Introduction   xxi
Pieter J. Fourie

PART 1: HISTORY

Chapter 1: A History of the South African Media   3
David Wigston
1.1 Introduction   4
1.2 Broadcasting   6
    1.2.1 From 1919 to 1936: The establishment of radio in South Africa   6
    1.2.2 From 1936 to 1948: The South African Broadcasting Corporation   8
    1.2.3 From 1948 to 1960: Post-World War II expansion   10
    1.2.4 From 1960 to 1971: A period of transformation   12
    1.2.5 From 1971 to 1981: A period of challenge   14
    1.2.6 From 1981 to 1992: The rationalisation of broadcasting   17
    1.2.7 From 1992 to 2000: A period of restructuring   19
    1.2.8 From 2000 to the present: The ambiguities of post-apartheid broadcasting   26
1.3 The Press   28
    1.3.1 The English press   28
    1.3.2 The Afrikaans press   33
    1.3.3 The development of a black press   36
    1.3.4 The alternative press   40
    1.3.5 The press during the apartheid years   44
    1.3.6 Key developments in the press since democratisation   52
1.4 Summary and conclusion   54

Chapter 2: The Media in Africa   59
Fackson Banda
2.1 Introduction   60
2.2 The media in Africa: The colonial period   61
    2.2.1 The beginnings of the media in Africa   63
    2.2.2 The functions of the media in colonial Africa   65
2.3 Post-colonial media in Africa   70

	2.3.1 Post-colonial media: state control	70
	2.3.2 Post-colonial functions of the media: nation building	71
	2.3.3 Media/cultural imperialism	73
2.4	African media in the age of globalisation	74
2.5	Challenges	82
2.6	Summary and conclusion	84

PART 2: MEDIA AND SOCIETY

Chapter 3: Approaches to the Study of Mass Communication

Pieter J. Fourie

Section 1: Mass communication culture/ defining mass communication/what is theory? — 91

3.1	Introduction: mass communication cultures	91
	3.1.1 The oral communication culture	91
	3.1.2 The written and printed communication culture	92
	3.1.3 The electronic communication culture	94
3.2	Defining mass communication	95
	3.2.1 Questions related to a definition of mass communication	97
3.3	What is theory?	103
	3.3.1 The value of theory	103
	3.3.2 The goals of theory	104
	3.3.3 The building blocks of theory	105
	3.3.4 Evaluating theory	110
	3.3.5 Goals of mass media theory	112

Section 2: Theoretical approaches — 115

3.4	Theoretical approaches to the study and research of mass communication	115
	3.4.1 Categorising theories	115
	3.4.2 The positivistic approach	117
	3.4.3 The critical approach	124
	3.4.4 Meaning production theory	146
	3.4.5 Technological determinism	151
	3.4.6 The information society approach	154
	3.4.7 The poststructuralist/postmodern approach	157
	3.4.8 Postcolonial theory and the Afro-centric approach	174
	3.4.9 Normative theory	178
3.5	Summary	180

Chapter 4: The Role and Functions of the Media in Society 184
Pieter J. Fourie

Section 1: News and information 185
4.1 The functions of the media 185
    4.1.1 Functionalism 185
    4.1.2 The political functions of the media: The case for pluralism 188
    4.1.3 Normative theory 190
        4.1.3.1 The authoritarian theory 191
        4.1.3.2 The libertarian theory 192
        4.1.3.3 The social responsibility theory 194
        Case study 4.1: Public Service Broadcasting in South Africa 195
        4.1.3.4 The Soviet communist theory 197
        4.1.3.5 The development theory 198
        Case study 4.2: The Media Development and Diversity Agency 199
        4.1.3.6 The democratic-participant theory 199
        Case study 4.3: Civic journalism 200
    4.1.4 Rethinking normative theory 201
    4.1.5 New thinking about normative theory 203
        4.1.5.1 The postmodern perspective 203
        4.1.5.2 The postcolonial perspective 207
        4.1.5.3 Revisiting normative media theory in South Africa 209

Section 2: Entertainment 216
4.2 The entertainment function 216
    4.2.1 A rhetorical perspective 216
    Case study 4.4: Rhetorical motifs in popular television genres 217
    4.2.2 A behavioural perspective 219
    4.2.3 A sociological perspective 222
    4.2.4 Entertainment as a value judgement 224
4.3 Summary and conclusion 224

Chapter 5: The Effects of Mass Communication 227
Pieter J. Fourie

5.1 Introduction 228
5.2 Categorising media effects 229
5.3 An overview of effect theories 232
    5.3.1 Short-term theories 232
    5.3.2 Long-term theories 237

5.4	Stereotyping	247
	5.4.1	What is a stereotype?	248
	5.4.2	The characteristics and working of stereotypes	256
	5.4.3	The origin of stereotypes	258
	5.4.4	The need to contextualise media representations	260
	5.4.5	Changing stereotypes	263
5.5	A cautionary note about effect theories and research	264
5.6	Summary	267

Chapter 6: Media Culture 269

Magriet Pitout

6.1	Introduction	270

Section 1 271

6.2	Culture and communication	271
6.3	High, popular and mass culture: theoretical perspectives	272
6.4	Cultural studies	274
	6.4.1 Theoretical assumptions of cultural studies	275
6.5	Conceptual definitions	276
	6.5.1 What is culture?	276
	6.5.2 Ideology	278
	6.5.3 Hegemony	279
	6.5.4 Hall's theoretical model of preferred reading	281
	6.5.5 Polysemy	283
	6.5.6 Intertextuality	284

Section 2 285

6.6	Social and cultural forms of expression	285
	6.6.1 Religion	285
	6.6.2 Sport	289
	6.6.3 Architecture and the built environment	292
	6.6.4 Music	293
6.7	Research	297
6.8	Future developments	298
6.9	Case studies	298
	Case study 6.1: Critical reflections on Mel Gibson's "The Passion of the Christ"	298

Case study 6.2: The "Da Vinci Code"   300
Case study 6.3: A brief history of South Africa's architecture and the built environment   302
6.10 Summary   303

Chapter 7: The Ideological Power of the Media   306
Stefan Sonderling
7.1 Introduction   307
7.2 A popular view of ideology   308
7.3 Theories of ideology   309
    7.3.1 Neutral theory of ideology   309
    7.3.2 Critical theories of ideology   310
7.4 Ideological struggles and conflicts of interpretations   318
    7.4.1 Preferred reading   318
    7.4.2 Discursive practices   319
    Case study 7.1: The professional ideology of journalists   319
    Case study 7.2: How the mass media promote ideology   321
7.5 Summary   322

Chapter 8: The Public Sphere in Contemporary Society   324
Pieter Duvenage
8.1 Introduction to Habermas   325
8.2 Transformation of the public sphere   328
    8.2.1 The historical argument   328
    8.2.2 Practices and institutions in the public sphere   329
    8.2.3 The decline of the public sphere   332
8.3 Criticism of the early Habermas   334
8.4 Public reason and communicative action   337
    8.4.1 Stage 1   337
    8.4.2 Stage 2   338
    8.4.3 Stage 3   339
    8.4.4 Stage 4   339
8.5 The public sphere: a recent statement   342
    8.5.1 Democracy and the public sphere   342
    8.5.2 Mass-communication and considered public opinions   344
    8.5.3 Pathologies of political communication   347
8.6 Unconcluding remarks   348

Chapter 9: Globalisation, Information Communication, Technology and the Media   350

Pieter J. Fourie

9.1 What is globalisation? A theory and some characteristics   351
    9.1.1 Giddens' theory of globalisation   351
9.2 The impact of globalisation on the media   362
    9.2.1 Economic trends   363
    9.2.2 A new regulatory paradigm   369
9.3 From the NWICO to the GII and the WSIS   373
    9.3.1 The New World Information and Communication Order   374
    9.3.2 The Global Information Infrastructure Project (GII)   380
    9.3.3 The World Summit on the Information Society (WSIS)   382
    9.3.4 Criticism of the Global Information Infrastructure Project and the World Summit on the Information Society   383
    9.3.5 A yardstick for ICT policy monitoring   387
9.4 Researching globalisation, the information society and ICT   392
    9.4.1 International (global) communication research: media imperialism   392
    9.4.2 New media research: The internet – access, its nature, uses and impact on culture and democracy   396
9.5 Summary   405

References   410
Index   428

About the Authors

Fackson Banda holds the SAB Ltd Chair in Media and Democracy as well as the pan-African UNESCO Chair in Communication within the School of Journalism and Media Studies at Rhodes University, South Africa. He worked as executive director of the Panos Institute Southern Africa, Zambia. Before joining Panos, Prof. Banda was a practising broadcast journalist. He taught subjects in mass communication at the University of Zambia's Department of Mass Communication. A published scholar, Prof. Banda is currently involved in teaching courses at the undergraduate and postgraduate levels, focusing on media policy and institutions as well as mass media theory and society. His research interests include political economy, communication and human rights, media policy, African media debates and postcolonial theory, among others.

Pieter Duvenage is currently teaching philosophy and media studies at a number of tertiary institutions in Johannesburg and Pretoria. He is the author of, amongst others, *Habermas and Aesthetics* (Polity, 2003).

Pieter J. Fourie is professor in communication science at the University of South Africa where he teaches media studies. He is the author and editor of a number of works in the field of South African media studies, including the first publication in South Africa in the field of visual communication and semiotics *Beeldkommunikasie: Kultuurkritiek, ideologiese kritiek, en 'n inleiding tot die beeldsemiologie* (McGraw-Hill, 1983) and *Aspects of film and television communication* (Juta, 1988.) He is editor of the research journal *Communicatio: South African Journal for Communication Theory and Research* and serves on the editorial boards of a number of research journals. In 2003 he was awarded the Stals Award of the Suid-Afrikaanse Akademie vir Wetenskap en Kuns for his contribution to the development of communication science in South Africa. He is a National Research Foundation rated researcher.

Magriet Pitout was until recently associate professor in the Department of Communication Science, Unisa where she specialised in media studies, popular culture and research methodology. She retired at the end of 2006 and is now teaching media studies and public relations at different tertiary institutions.

Stefan Sonderling is a senior lecturer in the Department of Communication Science at the University of South Africa. He lectures in communication theory, postcolonial and Afro centric communication theory, media studies, language and society, and development communication. He has also worked as a photojournalist on a number of South African newspapers and as a television camera reporter for SABC television news.

David Wigston is a senior lecturer in the Department of Communication Science at the University of South Africa. He specialises in teaching research methodology and media studies, particularly broadcasting. He is a regular contributor to the Department's highly successful annual Winter School in research methodology for post-graduate students.

A Brief South African Media Map (2007)

Population figures
45.6 million: Black African: 79%; White: 9.6%; Coloured: 8.9%; Indian: 2.5%

Languages: isiZulu: 23.8%; isiXhosa: 17.6%; Afrikaans: 13.3%; Pedi: 9.4%, English, 8.2%; Setswana: 8.2%; seSotho: 7.9%; xiTsonga: 4.4%; Other: 7.2%. (cf. Koenderman 2007: 6–7.)

Access to media (all races)
Daily newspapers: 24.7% (of all adults of the population (16+) over 12 months)
Weekly newspapers: 30.9%
Weekly magazines: 17.5%
Monthly magazines: 26.6%
Any (AMPS) newspaper/magazine: 51.8%
Radio (Last seven days): 92.7%
Television (Last seven days): 78.8%
Internet users: 5.1 million
Personal computers per 1 000 people: 88
Broadband subscribers per 1 000 people: 1.3
Internet (Accessed last four weeks): 6.4%
Telephone main lines: 4.729 million
Mobile subscribers: 33.96 million
Population covered by mobile: 96%
(cf. Koenderman, 2007:15.)

Some important Acts bearing on external and internal media regulation
- The Constitution of the Republic of South Africa (Act no. 108 of 1996) (Section 16 Freedom of Expression, Section 32 Access to Information, Section 14 Right to Privacy, Section 36 Limitations of Rights)
- Independent Communications Authority of South Africa (Icasa) Act, 2000 (Act no. 13 of 2000)
- Broadcasting Act, 1999 (Act no. 4 of 1999)
- Broadcasting Amendment Act, 2002 (Act no. 64 of 2002)
- Telecommunication Act (Act no. 103 of 1996)

- Telecommunications Amendment Act, 2001 (Act no. 64 of 2001)
- Electronic Communications and Transactions Act, 2002 (Act no. 25 of 2002)
- Films and Publications Act, 1996 (Act no. 69 of 1996)
- National Film and Video Foundation Act, 1997 (Act no. 73 of 1997)

Important regulatory bodies, monitoring bodies and media organisations

State Regulatory Bodies

Independent Communications Authority of South Africa (Icasa)
Universal Service Agency (USA)
State Information Technology Agency (Sita)
Broadcasting Monitoring Complaints Committee (BMCC)
Film and Publication Board
National Film and Video Foundation

(Industry self-regulation)/Media organisations

Broadcasting Complaints Commission of South Africa (BCCSA)
Office of the Press Ombudsman and Appeal Panel
Print Media South Africa (PMSA)
South African National Editors' Forum (SANEF)
Advertising Standards Authority of South Africa (ASA)
Community Press Association
Forum of Black Journalists
National Association of Broadcasters (NAB)
Foreign Correspondents' Association of South Africa
Media Development Diversity Agency (MDDA)

Monitoring Bodies

Freedom of Expression Institute (FXI)
Media Institute of South Africa (MISA)
Media Monitoring Project (MMP)

The South African media system

Broadcasting

Public service broadcasting (South African Broadcasting Corporation)
15 public radio stations (e.g. radiosondergrense, SAfm, Thobela FM, Lesedi)
Three commercial radio stations (e.g. 5fm, Metro)

Together these radio stations broadcast in 11 languages and reach a daily adult audience of 19 million

Channel Africa Network (4 language services broadcasting throughout Africa)
Three full-spectrum free-to-air television channels (TV1, TV2, TV3)
One satellite pay-TV channel (Channel Africa)

Together public television reaches an estimated daily audience of 18 million with 4 million licensed television households.

Commercial broadcasting
- 12 radio stations (e.g. 702, 567 Cape talk)
- M-Net television channel – analogue/digital pay television service with a number of niche channels broadcasting to 50 countries across Africa
- e.tv – free-to-air television channel
- DStv – digital satellite pay television with over 70 channels and a subscriber base of ± 1.1 million

Community broadcasting
More than 90 community radio stations licensed by Icasa in 2006

Print media

The major publishing houses/groups arc: Johnnic Communications; Independent News and Media (Pty) Limited; Associated Magazines; Naspers including Media 24 and MIH; Caxton Publishers and Printers Limited; M&G Media Limited; Natal Witness Printing and Publishing Company (Pty) Limited; Primedia Publishing Limited; Ramsay, Son and Parker (Pty) Limited; Kagiso Media

The major distribution groups are: Newspaper Circulation Services, Magazine Circulation Services; Media 24 (Nasionale Nuus-Distribueerders); Allied Publishing; RNA Distributors.
- Twenty-one (21) daily newspapers (2006): e.g. *Beeld, Cape Times, Volksblad, The Mercury, Daily Dispatch, Star, Pretoria News, Cape Argus*
- Nine (9) National Sunday newspapers (2006): e.g. *Rapport, Sunday Times, Sunday Independent*
- 360 newspapers targeted at regional, community, country and local communities (cf. Koenderman 2007:24)
- Over 400 consumer magazines (cf. Koenderman 2007:25)
- Over 650 business-to-business journals and annuals (ibid:27)
- 100s of knock-and-drop (freebies) neighbourhood newspapers totalling 4.5 million newspapers per week

- Print media circulation: 26 million (2005)/Average of 1 605 million copies of urban dailies sold daily in 2005

News agencies

South African Press Association (SAPA) plus foreign agencies operating in South Africa: Agence France-Presse, Associated Press, Deutsche Presse Agentur, Reuters, United Press International.

Growth of media opportunities 1975–2007 (Koenderman 2007:16)

	1975	2007
TV stations	Nil	71
Radio stations	7	124
Daily newspapers	22	20
Major weekly newspapers	19	28
Consumer magazines	180	670
Community newspapers and magazines	N/A	425
DStv audio services (including international radio stations)	–	65
Internet web pages	–	+10 Billion

Internet and telecommunications

The are five main telecommunications service providers in South Africa: Telkom, Neotel, Vodacom, MTN, and Cell C.

Internet users: 5.1 million
Personal computers per 1 000 people: 88
Broadband subscribers per 1 000 people: 1.3
Internet (Accessed last four weeks): 6.4%
Telephone main lines: 4.729 million
Mobile subscribers: 33.96 million
Population covered by mobile: 96%
(Cf. Koenderman, 2007:15.)

Cinema

The two main distributors are Ster-Kinekor and Nu-Metro. Ster-Kinekor has 473 screens. As an example of cinema attendance and advertising cost Koenderman (2007:30) refers to Sandton Cine Complex: The complex consists of 11 individual movies screens owned by Ster-Kinekor. Together the complex has 1 745 seats and in an average week in 2006 12 859 tickets were sold. A 30-second ad spot in 2007 shown on the 11 screens in this complex costs R13 270 per week. More than a thousand producers are registered and in 2004 the film industry contributed R1.4 billion to the R7.7 billion entertainment industry (comprising film and television production, cinema, and interactive industries). In 2003, 24 feature films were produced.

Advertising

The South African advertising industry is dominated by large international groups such as FCB, Lobedu Leo Burnett, Grey Worldwide, Young & Rubicam, and J. Walter Thompson. Altogether there are 77 active agencies. The top five spenders on advertising during 2004 were: Unilever (R418.2 million; 55 million), National government (R394.5 million; 51.9 million), Shoprite Checkers (R327 million; 43 million), MTN (cell phone) (R294.1 million; 38.7 million), Pick 'n Pay (R258.9 million; 34 million). Adspend: R17.1 billion spend on advertising in 2005 of which R15.5 billion advertsing in the traditional media: print, television and radio, with the rest on cinema and a growing proportion on the Internet and outdoor advertising.

Sources:

Burger, D. 2007. *South African Yearbook 2006/2007.* Chapter 6: Communications. Government Communication and Information System (GCIS), Pretoria. p. 132–154.

Koenderman, T. 2007. *Tony Koenderman's Ad Review.* South African Media Facts in Association with Finweek and in partnership with OMD. Sandton: Johannesburg.

Introduction

Pieter J. Fourie

What is media studies?

No simple description will do. Suffice it to say that it is the systematic, critical, and analytical study of the media (television, radio, press, video, film, Internet) as one of the most important producers and disseminators of symbolic meanings (content) to the public, a group, an organisation and/or the individual. Media studies investigates the owners of the media, the producers of media content, the media content itself, and the users (readers, listeners, viewers) of media. It investigates the (power) relationships between the media and politics, media and culture, media and economy, media and society, and between the media and the public as well as the relationships between media and democracy, and freedom of expression as a prerequisite for democracy. Each word in the above description lends itself to further description and unravelling when applied to specific aspects of media analysis, as will become apparent throughout this book.

Why media studies?

Here we briefly offer eight reasons.

The omnipresence of the media and the media's role in society, culture, the economy, politics and education – in short, the media's impact on everyday life – can no longer be underestimated. It justifies serious academic investigation.

In the humanities and social sciences the media have become just as important as an object of academic study as the traditional canons of literature, philosophy, "high" art, and the theories of sociology, politics, and anthropology. After all, the media are the flagship of late 20th and early 21st century culture. As today's dominant symbolic form of expression through which everyday existence is described and documented, the media call for serious academic scrutiny.

The central role of the media and information and communication technology in globalisation and the impact of the "new" information revolution on every aspect of society, have pushed the importance of media studies to the fore. We are experiencing an information revolution similar to that of the invention of the printing press and thereafter the telegraph, with the same profound consequences for the way in which politics, economics, education, culture, religion, the judiciary, public administration and many forms of public communication are conducted.

The growth of the media industry itself has given new importance to media studies. The fact that the media have become a major economic role-player is evidenced by listings on stock exchanges and the coverage of the media by the media on the pages of their business sections, in radio and television programmes and on the Internet, in newspaper editorial articles and articles about its power and importance as a pillar of democracy. This has made the media itself a story and a culture in itself for itself. In short, the media's prominent self-reflection – reporting about itself – has contributed to a public awareness of the centrality of the media in present day society, economy, politics and culture.

The media form the backbone of the marketing, advertising and public relations industries. Without the media, these industries will fail to grow and play a role as important financial institutions and providers of jobs. At the same time their role as the main generators and communicators of our present-day consumer culture would be sized down remarkably. As a result, a sound knowledge of how the media work, think and disseminate meaning is fundamental to these industries.

From a communication science perspective, the most important reason for media studies is the recognition of the media as fundamental to democracy. To empower the media to sustain and develop democracy, to understand the complex relationship between the media and the state, and to develop a critical understanding of the media as complex political and ideological agents, demands a sound knowledge of media institutions and their practices. It requires the ability to critically analyse media content against the background of scientifically tested theories and methods.

Given the increasing complexity of the communications and media industry, the workers in this industry (journalists, broadcasters, filmmakers, programme-makers, public relations officers, advertisers, communication consultants and directors in organisations), themselves recognise the need for critical research-oriented knowledge of the nature and working of the media. They, after all, are the people producing the meanings with which we have to deal with on a daily basis when we read newspapers, watch television, listen to the radio, surf the Internet, etc. They are the people responsible for framing our ways of thinking about everyday matters, about the world, our society and communities, the market and its products, about other people, and even our thinking about ourselves. For media workers, a critical understanding of how the media work may help contribute to a more responsible approach to what they are busy with, whether this may be the writing of newspaper and magazine articles, the writing, development, production and presentation of films, television and radio programmes, Internet websites and pages, advertisements, and so on. Eventually, a critical understanding of the media may lead to an improvement in the quality of our present-day media culture and its products.

Finally, a reason for the importance of media studies relates to the media users or media audiences themselves. There is an increased awareness amongst a growing population of media users of the role of the media in their lives and the need to understand this role. Who are the media people and institutions, how do they operate, and what is the content and quality of these products that play such an important role in how we define ourselves, our society, our world and, eventually, our perceptions of reality? In short, there is a growing awareness amongst the public of the need to understand the media as one of the most important disseminators of meaning in today's society.

Structure and content of this book

With the above as a motivation for media studies, this book was first published in 2001. It is now revised and presented in four volumes to introduce the reader to theory and research related to:
- the nature and practices of the media as a powerful institution;
- the political economy of the media;
- the functions and effects of the media;
- the media as a producer and disseminator of meaning;
- media policy;
- media management;
- media and/as representation;
- the analysis of media content;
- the nature of media audiences;
- media production planning;
- media ethics.

These topics form the core of the four volumes of this book, which are:
- *Media Studies, Volume 1: Media history, media and society*
- *Media Studies, Volume 2: Policy, management, and media representation*
- *Media Studies, Volume 3: Media content and audiences*
- *Media Studies, Volume 4: Production planning and media ethics*

In this, the first volume, which has two parts with nine chapters, the focus is on media history and the relationship between media and society.

Part 1: Media history

In the first part, a brief history of African and South African media is given. The authors' point of departure is that knowledge of the history of the media in Africa and in South Africa is crucial for an informed discussion of the present and the future of the media.

South African media history

In the first chapter, David Wigston gives a brief overview of the history of the South African media (press and broadcasting). In consecutive parts, he deals with the origins and development of the South African Broadcasting Corporation, economic and political factors that have influenced the South African media environment, stages in the development of the South African press, and with present issues in South African broadcasting and in the press.

Media in Africa

This is followed by Fackson Banda's chapter on the media in Africa. It is impossible to give (in the space of a single chapter) a complete overview of the history of the media in Africa, or a media-map of what constitutes the media in every African country today. Banda therefore focuses on broad periods, influences on and challenges to the media in the colonial period, the post-colonial period and, at present, in the era of globalisation. Under challenges, he deals with the deregulation of the African media landscape, the privatisation and commercialisation of state media, communitarianism, and the impact of new information and communication technologies (ICTs) on the media in Africa.

Both Wigston and Banda introduce important concepts related to media regulation and the relationship between the media and society. Concepts such as colonial, post-colonial, globalisation, modernisation, privatisation and commercialisation are introduced and further dealt with in consequent chapters of this book, such as the chapters on the functions of the media, media and ideology, and media and globalisation.

Part 2: Media and Society

In this part, the complex relationship between the media and society is introduced by focusing on the following: different theoretical approaches to the study of this relationship; theories about the functions or role of the media in society and its power and effects; the nature of media culture and of the media as an ideological instrument; the quality of the media as a public sphere, or as a space for public discourse; and finally, the relationship between the media and globalisation, including the impact of information and communication technology on the media.

Media theory

Given its length, chapter three is divided into two sections. In section one, Pieter J. Fourie introduces three broad public communication cultures, a working definition of mass communication, a discussion of what theory is, and mass communication theory in the context of sociological theory. In the second part, he introduces eight theoretical approaches, summarising what these approaches are about, what they emphasise, and what they seek to achieve towards an understanding of mass communication and the media as social phenomena. The approaches introduced are (1) the positivistic and (2) critical approaches, (3) meaning production theory, (4) technological determinism, (5) the information society approach, (6) the poststructuralist/postmodernist approach, (7) postcolonial theory and the Afrocentric approach, and (8) normative media theory.

Functions of the media

The second chapter in this section, chapter 4, deals with the functions or the role of the media in society. Fourie distinguishes between the media's information, surveillance, political and entertainment functions. As far as the first is concerned, he looks at a number of normative theories, for example, the liberal and social responsibility theories, and a revision of these theories, also from an African perspective. As far as entertainment is concerned, he asks: What is entertainment? He then seeks to answer this question from a rhetorical perspective, arguing that all entertainment seeks to answer basic questions about own and cultural identity, knowledge, behaviour, and survival.

Effects of the media

Some of the main effect theories are introduced in chapter five. Fourie distinguishes between short-term and long-term theories. In the first, the media are seen to have an immediate and strong effect on behaviour (such as political behaviour: how we vote). In the second, the emphasis is more on how the media have an effect over a longer period of time on how people perceive (see) and think about other people, topics, issues, reality and so on. The emphasis is thus on the role of the media in the production of meaning. This chapter ends with an in-depth treatment of the concept of stereotyping. This is done because of the media's potentially strong influence on the ways in which we see and experience things in stereotypical ways – supposedly usually negative stereotypes about race, gender, and sexual orientation.

Media and culture/media and ideology

In both chapters six (media and culture) and seven (media and ideology), the respective authors, Magriet Pitout and Stefan Sonderling, emphasise the ideological nature and role of the media in society. A distinction is made between high, popular and mass culture. The cultural studies approach in media studies and some of its main assumptions are introduced. This approach is closely associated with the analysis of ideology in which the media is primarily seen to be an ideological instrument. Concepts such as "ideology", "hegemony", "polysemy", "intertextuality", "preferred reading", "discursive practice", and different theories about ideology are introduced in these chapters. The media's representation of cultural forms such as religion, sport, architecture and the built environment, and music are also briefly discussed.

The media as public sphere

As argued by Pieter Duvenage, the *public sphere* is a major issue in communication and media studies and specifically in mass communication. The aim with this chapter is to provide the reader with a good theoretical grasp of this important concept and to do so with close reference to one of the most important communication theorists of our time – Jürgen Habermas. In chapter eight, Duvenage thus provides us with a brief sketch of Habermas's intellectual background; an introduction to Habermas's treatment of the concept "public sphere" in his influential early work *The Structural Transformation of the Public Sphere* (1962); an introduction to critical perspectives on Habermas's work; and an introduction to Harbermas's treatment of the concepts of "public reason" and "communicative action".

Globalisation, ICT and the media

In the final chapter, Pieter J. Fourie situates the media in the era of globalisation. He briefly explains the difference between pre-modern, modern and postmodern (or late modern) times. He describes some of the characteristics of globalisation and looks at its impact on the media. In this regard, he specifically refers to dominant economic, policy and managerial trends closely associated with globalisation and the development of information and communication technology (ICT), such as concentration, convergence, liberalisation, privatisation, internationalisation, and commercialisation. How have these trends contributed to a new media environment requiring new ways of media regulation? He deals with movements such as the New World Information and Communication Order (NWICO), the Global Information Infrastructure project (GII), and the World Summits on the Information Society (WSIS). How have and how are these movements dealing with matters such as media control, access, quality and participation? Fourie ends the chapter with an introduction to a number of ways in which globalisation and ICT and their impact on the media are researched. He specifically looks at the research fields of international (global) communication, media policy research, and research about the communicative nature of the Internet: its uses, and its impact on culture, identity and democracy.

Context

From the above description it is clear that this volume is concerned with questions, theories and research about the nature of the media as a powerful institution in society and about the media as a producer and disseminator of meaning. In volumes 2, 3 and 4 the focus is on the political economy of the media, media policy and management, media content, audiences, production and ethics. In volume two, we deal with media policy, media management, and media representations, including the representation of gender, race, sexual orientation, media and violence, media and terrorism, media and identity, the media and the environment, media and AIDS, and the media and news. Volume three is about approaches to the analysis of media content, including semiotic analysis, narrative analysis, visual text analysis, quantitative content analysis and audience analysis. Anthropological, ethnographic and uses and gratification theory are explained and research methods such as survey and field research as well as methods for measuring media audiences are introduced. Volume four deals with media production planning and media ethics.

In the four volumes the authors thus cover a variety of approaches to the central topics in critical media studies. We use the term "critical" to distinguish our approach from the more practical approaches in which the emphasis is on media production techniques. Ours is critical in the sense of trying to understand the media from various theoretical perspectives as major producers of meaning and as key role-players in people's understanding and experience of politics, economics, society, and culture, and in understanding their own lives and experiences of reality. Furthermore, our approach is analytical in the sense of trying to provide the reader with the theoretical background on the basis of which critical questions and hypotheses about key issues related to the media can be formulated and investigated with applicable analytical instruments.

South Africa hosts one of the most advanced media sectors in sub-Saharan Africa. With a media history that stretches back to the late 18th century it is, today, a sector driven by a highly skilled and professional work force, advanced technology, and a well-established regulatory system. I trust that this volume as well as the subsequent volumes will contribute to the reader's and student's better understanding of this exciting world of the media.

Department of Communication Science
University of South Africa
Pretoria
July 2007

PART 1

History

chapter one

A History of the South African Media

David Wigston

LEARNING OUTCOMES

At the end of this chapter you should be able to:
- identify the most important events in the development of the media in South Africa;
- describe how key events helped to shape the media;
- explain the relationships between society and the media;
- identify and describe issues and possible trends in the development of the media;
- determine possible solutions to contemporary media-related problems from the past;
- evaluate the role played by regulation in the development of the media in South Africa.

Media Studies: Volume 1

THIS CHAPTER

SOUTH AFRICA HAS what is probably the most advanced media sector in sub-Saharan Africa. With a media history that stretches back to the late 18th century it is today a sector driven by a highly skilled and professional work force, advanced technology and a well-established regulatory system. The question arises, what factors contributed to this situation? To answer this question we need to look closely at the nature, processes involved and various relationships associated with broadcasting and the press over the decades.

This is the context of this chapter, where we map out the organisation, various processes and inter-relationships associated with broadcasting and the press in South Africa. However, we need to keep in mind that the social, economic and political forces that shape the structure of the media are not static but dynamic, constantly evolving and changing over a period of time with the result that the media map itself is also constantly shifting. To track these changes and to understand the *status quo* of the media in South Africa requires us to take a historical approach. Thus we explore in this chapter, albeit very briefly, how broadcasting and the press of today have been shaped by various political and economic events during the past.

The most important topics dealt with in this chapter are:
- why the history of the media is important;
- the origins and development of the SABC;
- economic and political factors that have influenced the media environment;
- the various stages in the development of the press;
- various issues in broadcasting and the press.

1.1 INTRODUCTION

Why do we need to study the history of the media? While the answer to this question is simple, the process of arriving at that answer is by no means simplistic. Our understanding of the nature and structure of the present media environment is largely influenced by what happened in the past. Thus, if we are to consider the structure and organisation of various institutions within today's media environment, we need to deliberate on the reasons for and the roles played by those institutions within a certain context. In order for us to achieve this, we need to give serious attention to the historical development of the media in South Africa.

Studying media history is not without its difficulties. No useable model has yet emerged enabling us to undertake an all-encompassing historical

study of the media environment since media history is a fairly recent phenomenon in communications research. Press models cannot be used to describe broadcasting structures or vice versa, as their respective roles have been largely determined independently of each other by politics and economics. Similarly, the relationship between the state and broadcasting is very different from that between the state and the press. Broadcasting has been dominated by the state controlled South African Broadcasting Corporation (SABC) since 1936 while the press has been dominated by commercial enterprises which has resulted in a sometimes rough and rocky relationship with the government, both past and present.

Before we start with the history of the media in South Africa we need to consider the approach we are going to take in order to look at the historical development. There are two broad approaches that can be used when studying media history. Ideally we need to engage in what Dahl (1978:132) terms "deep-drilling" as this does more justice to the subject than adopting an all-embracing episodic approach that is more chronological in nature. "Deep-drilling" implies looking at the resulting interactions between technology, politics, economics and culture at a particular point in time in order to try and untangle the shifting relationships between the media institutions, the government and the public. This approach can provide us with a better understanding of the distinctive qualities of the media. A major drawback of such an approach is that it is very detailed and as such, does tend to break up the continuity of development.

With the above in mind, and because of the constraints of time and space, and as this is probably your first encounter with the history of the South African media, we follow the episodic approach in this chapter. Keep in mind, while working through this chapter, that an obvious weakness in adopting an episodic approach is the exclusion of detailed institutional and political history as well as management analyses, audience research and gate-keeping studies. Obviously, we needed to take some decisions regarding what we included and excluded in this brief history of South African broadcasting and the press. Thus, if you are familiar with the particular history of broadcasting and the press in South Africa, you may disagree with us regarding the emphasis of certain events over others. But then you need to keep in mind that the purpose of this brief history is an introductory one, and we hope that it will inspire you to further your own in-depth investigations.

Media Studies: Volume 1

1.2 BROADCASTING

South African Broadcasting Corporation

The historical development of broadcasting in South Africa is also largely the history of the South African Broadcasting Corporation (SABC), simply because the SABC monopolised the airwaves at its inception. Not until fairly recently was any other form of broadcasting permitted. We can divide the history of broadcasting in South Africa into several periods. These periods are based on those originally devised by Tomaselli, Tomaselli and Muller (1989:24), whose list extends from 1924 up to 1971, where four specific periods are identified. To provide a broader and more comprehensive overview of the history of broadcasting in South Africa, we have added to this original list.

Keep in mind that when we delimit historical periods in the development of the media, we cannot be too categorical about the exact date when a period begins or ends. Determining the specific year in which any particular period begins or ends is usually an arbitrary decision. Periods tend to merge with one another rather than begin or end abruptly. Therefore, when we consult other authors on the historical development of broadcasting, we may find that they may have differing opinions about the grouping of periods and the importance of events during those periods. With this point in mind, let us consider the key events in each period associated with broadcasting in South Africa.

1.2.1 From 1919 to 1936: The establishment of radio in South Africa

The early development of broadcasting in South Africa followed a similar pattern to that in the United Kingdom. Radio began with a few enthusiastic amateur radio hams, followed by several experimental broadcasts and only later by regular programming on a more organised basis.

Amateur broadcasts

We can identify three prominent amateurs who offered broadcasts following the lifting of security restrictions on the use of radio following World War I (1914–1918). They are:
- John Samuel Streeter, who broadcast gramophone concerts on a weekly basis, first from Sea Point and then from Observatory, Cape Town;
- Reginald Hopkins, who broadcast pianola music together with messages from his home in Wynberg, Cape Town;

A History of the South African Media

- Arthur Sydney Innes, who broadcast programmes of gramophone recordings from his radio station, known as 2OB, located in Observatory, Johannesburg.

The programmes provided by these amateur operators were popular and reportedly heard well into the rural Karoo. However, listeners had to build their own receivers in order to hear the programmes. As the popularity of radio as a means of entertainment grew, so too did the realisation that radio was becoming more than just a pastime for a few select enthusiasts. Radio moved into the next important stage in its development.

Experimental broadcasts

A series of sixteen concerts were broadcast from South African Railways headquarters in Johannesburg, beginning 18 December 1923 (Rosenthal 1974:30). The aim of these concerts was to raise funds for the Empire Exhibition. Each of the Railway broadcasts lasted two hours. As few people owned receivers, arrangements were made for group listening at the Railway Institutes (subsidised social and mutual aid societies for employees) located to the east of Johannesburg in Witbank, Germiston and Pretoria. The American electrical engineering company, Western Electric, provided the transmitting and receiver equipment as they viewed the experimental broadcast as a business opportunity to promote their receivers. Although intended for a specific audience, the broadcasts could be heard throughout the country by those who had access to receivers.

| Railway broadcasts

The first regular broadcasts

Following the popularity of the amateur and experimental broadcasts, the government called for applications for licences to provide regular and sustained radio broadcasts. However, the licences were limited to one per metropolitan area. Regular broadcasts began in Johannesburg on 1 July 1924, when the Associated Scientific and Technical Societies (AS&TS) took over the equipment used for the railway broadcasts and began broadcasting as Station JB. Licences were also granted to the Cape Peninsula Publicity Association which began broadcasts from Cape Town on 15 September 1924, and the Durban City Corporation, which followed with broadcasts on 10 December 1924. The three radio stations tried various schemes to raise capital and improve their financial positions, such as the sale of advertising on air. Despite these efforts, the three

| Station JB

stations only remained operational for some two years before being forced to consider closure, largely due to a lack of financial sustainability.

The African Broadcasting Company

In 1927 the Johannesburg real estate and cinema chain millionaire Isidore William (IW) Schlesinger took over the broadcasting operations of the three fledgling radio stations with the consent of the government, amalgamating them to form the African Broadcasting Company (ABC). This brought about the centralisation and standardisation of production. However, the use of telephone land-lines to distribute signals to Durban and Cape Town resulted in sub-standard quality programmes, while the growth in income from listeners' licences was dismal. A crisis point was reached in March 1929 when expenditure soared in order to improve programme quality and pay artists a reasonable fee (previously men received between £1 and £6 and women a box of chocolates) (Rosenthal 1974:122).

To avert yet another financial crisis, the Blue Free Voucher Scheme was introduced. This was an arrangement between ABC and the retailers of radio sets, whereby ABC stopped leasing radio sets to listeners while the dealers offered new sets at a discount. Part of the discount went to paying the licence fee. The scheme was highly effective in generating income but by 1935 the ABC was again in financial difficulty. At the same time, the government considered broadcasting as too important to be left to commercial organisations. An investigation by Sir John Reith, governor of the British Broadcasting Corporation (BBC), resulted in the Reith Report. It recommended that the ABC be developed as a public corporation modelled on the BBC, free of government control or political motivation. An emphasis was to be placed on high quality programming. Also, the technological difficulties of broadcasting to the whole of South Africa had to be resolved.

1.2.2 From 1936 to 1948: The South African Broadcasting Corporation

Formation of the SABC

Reith's report was debated in Parliament and resulted in the Broadcasting Act, no. 22 of 1936, which was passed on 1 August 1936, the same day on which the South African Broadcasting Corporation (SABC) began

A History of the South African Media

to function as an entity. One major difference between the organisation of the SABC and the BBC was that the SABC was not subject to regular commissions of inquiry. An amount of £150 000 was advanced by the financial institution Sanlam as capital for the new SABC.

> South African Broadcasting Corporation

Broadcasts in Afrikaans

Up to this point, programming was predominantly in English, but section 14 of the Broadcasting Act of 1936 provided for Afrikaans broadcasts. Providing programmes for Afrikaans listeners by means of a bilingual service proved problematic. At this time, the majority of Afrikaners lived in rural areas and medium-wave signals did not reach these areas of the country satisfactorily. To try and resolve the problem a short-wave service was introduced. This effort to provide a service for Afrikaans listeners (this short-wave service) was however technically inferior and quickly became a point of contention. The signal would fade suddenly and was subject to severe distortion by summer thunderstorms, while the listener was required to make several frequency changes during the course of the day. The division of time between English and Afrikaans was also in a ratio of 8:2. The minimal amount of time devoted to Afrikaans-language programmes, in addition to technical problems, did not encourage listeners to tune in (Tomaselli *et al* 1989:37).

> bilingual service

The 1938 re-enactment of the Great Trek (when tens of thousands of Boer farmers, descendants of refugees from religious intolerance in Europe, left the British-controlled Cape for the inland regions in the 1830s and 1840s) was a stimulus in the development of Afrikaans broadcasting. Audience demand for coverage of the event quickly revealed the many shortcomings in the organisation of a nation-wide service. The solution, it was felt, was to split the service. And so, in 1938, the short-wave service carried only Afrikaans programming, becoming known as the B Programme (what is today known as *radiosondergrense*, or Radio Without Borders), while the medium-wave service continued with English programming, under the somewhat superior sounding moniker of the A Programme (today's SAfm).

> B Programme

From these developments, we infer that from its very beginnings, the development of the SABC was shaped not only by the geography of the country and the limitations of technology, but also the ideology of the time which saw the Union government under domination of the United Party led by General Jan Smuts. From the perspective of today,

it is largely presumed that tight government control of broadcasting was always the doing of the apartheid-era and far more hard-line Nationalist Government following World War II (1939–1945). But history tells us that it was, in fact, the United Party-led government, which united white English and Afrikaans-speakers and was in power from 1933 to 1948, which initiated this policy.

1.2.3 From 1948 to 1960: Post-World War II expansion

Introduction of news services

As with the growth of radio in the United States and Britain, there was a strained relationship between the fledgling radio stations and the South African press over the presentation of news. In an agreement with the press, Station JB could only broadcast news that had already appeared in print. The SABC in 1936 reached an agreement with the South African Press Association (SAPA), itself a closed association formed by mainstream newspapers, to provide four news bulletins a day. The SABC had no control over the content or organisation of these bulletins until the SABC created an internal news department in 1950. This also signalled the end of relaying news bulletins from the BBC in London. The first SABC-produced news bulletin was aired at 07:00 on 17 July 1950. As the news department expanded, so the number of bulletins offered was increased, reaching six per day three months later in October 1950.

The Schoch Commission

By 1946, as with the ABC and its predecessors, the SABC was beginning to experience financial difficulties. Two methods were tried to relieve the financial burden: one was to exempt the SABC from paying income tax; a second was to reduce the Post Office share of the licence fee to one percent. These moves were to little avail, and the only way out was to consider a move to commercialisation and sell advertising time on air. The revenue received from the sale of advertising on one station would then subsidise the remaining stations. The Schoch Commission was appointed in 1946 to investigate the matter, as well as a number of other broadcasting issues.

The resulting report was presented to the government in February 1948 and recommended that commercial broadcasting be established independently of the SABC. The commercial station would be taxed at ten percent of its gross revenue, which would be used to subsidise the

A History of the South African Media

SABC. The SABC would then continue to produce quality programmes reflecting high culture. Other than from advertising agencies and the SABC, there was little enthusiasm for the introduction of a commercial service (Tomaselli *et al* 1989:42–44). In the meanwhile, a Nationalist Government with a pro-Afrikaaner and stronger pro-racial segregation agenda had been voted into power in 1948 and it saw things differently. Rather than permitting the introduction of independent broadcasting, the recommended commercial service was to be part of the SABC. The purpose now was not to provide additional income as originally intended, but rather to expand the transmitter network and provide for additional Afrikaans programming (Tomaselli *et al* 1989:37).

Thus Springbok Radio was launched on 1 May 1950 as a bilingual commercial service. Springbok Radio soon proved to be highly popular with listeners, and is particularly remembered among English-speakers for the abundant number of soap operas, comedy shows, quiz shows and dramas that made up its programme schedule. However, with the coming of television to South Africa in the late seventies, many of these programmes moved to the newer medium, resulting in an audience loss for Springbok Radio. Unable to compete with television, Springbok Radio closed down in late 1985. But by then commercial radio had become firmly established as part of the South African broadcasting environment.

> Springbok Radio

Here we need to consider the long term implication of the decision not to implement the recommendations of the Schoch Commission. Had the government accepted the recommendations in 1948, then the structure of broadcasting in today's South Africa would be very different. Whereas the Schoch Commission strongly recommended the decentralisation and the commercialisation of radio, the government opted to follow a centralised monopolistic policy which resulted in the strong position of the SABC today.

Programming for black listeners

Back in 1936, the Reith Report made special mention of the provision of programming for language groups other than English and Afrikaans. Yet at no point was this ever given consideration by the government. It was only during the course of World War II that an initial unsuccessful attempt was made at providing night-time programming for some black listeners. This was done using telephone lines to compounds in the gold mines, hostels and major townships. There was also an additional morning broadcast three times a week on the English and Afrikaans medium-wave services. This service was really a pro-English propaganda exercise as a war-time contingency measure (Tomaselli *et al* 1989:39–41). Following the end of the war in 1945 the service was withdrawn as it was costly to maintain, while income from black listeners could not provide sufficient revenue to keep the service going.

redifussion service

Starting in 1949, a half-hour programme was transmitted daily on the English and Afrikaans medium-wave services in isiZulu, isiXhosa and seSotho, three of the biggest languages in South Africa. In August 1952 a rediffusion service (relaying of programmes by cable from a central receiver) was installed in Orlando, a working-class blacks-only residential area formed in 1935 far south of Johannesburg, later to become part of Soweto. Loudspeakers were hired out to subscribers and installed in their homes. Sixteen hours of programming were provided daily. Over the next seven years the service was extended to neighbouring townships. The service peaked in 1956 with fourteen thousand subscribers and then declined as forced removals to newer, more remote townships took place (Tomaselli *et al* 1989:51–53). The SABC was keen to extend the service to all townships, but was prevented from doing this by the government. Tomaselli *et al* (1989:52) offer three possible reasons for this.

- the installations were expensive to set up and maintain;
- the implementation of FM services was imminent;
- it gave an image of permanency when the black townships were considered merely a temporary phenomenon.

There was also conflict between the SABC director-general Gideon Roos and the more conservative SABC board over the issue. As an interim measure, the daily half-hour programme on the medium-wave services was extended to a full hour.

1.2.4 From 1960 to 1971: A period of transformation

Introduction of FM

FM transmissions

Radio Highveld

In order to provide listeners with better reception and more channels, plans were begun in 1960 for the introduction of FM (frequency modulation) services throughout the country. FM transmissions would provide for improved radio reception over a distance of about 60 kilometres from the transmitter and each transmitter would allow for six radio channels, sufficient for the three existing stations (the English and Afrikaans Services and Springbok Radio) while also allowing for the

A History of the South African Media

creation of three new radio stations. However, the cost was enormous (R40 million was provided by the government) and this almost crippled the SABC financially. The network required the installation of some 500 new transmitters, complete with towers for the antennas, across the country (de Villiers 1993:130). On 25 December 1961, the three existing services began FM broadcasts from the SABC tower (now the Sentec tower, located in Brixton, Johannesburg), followed shortly by isiZulu and seSotho services. The first regional radio service, Radio Highveld, was started in Johannesburg on 1 September 1964, and offered bilingual programming in English and Afrikaans. This was followed by Radio Tsonga and Radio Venda on 1 February 1965, Radio Good Hope on 1 July 1965 in Cape Town and Radio Port Natal (later to become East Coast Radio) on 1 May 1967 in Durban. These three regional stations operated according to a strict programme formula that consisted mainly of middle-of-the-road music, advertising and abbreviated news bulletins. Initially these channels brought in many new listeners without any loss to the existing radio services.

Station automation

In 1969 the three regional stations, Radio Highveld, Radio Good Hope and Radio Port Natal, were fully automated. Announcements, advertisements and music were all pre-recorded well in advance of the broadcast date, each on separate tapes which were then played automatically throughout the day and night in a predetermined order. The sequence was regulated by means of inaudible pulses on the recording tape. Theoretically, station automation reduces the costs of running a radio station. An automated radio station requires exceptionally few personnel thus cutting costs by reducing salaries and expenses. Some 115 SABC staff members were made redundant by station automation, which helped to reduce the financial burden brought about by the introduction of FM broadcasts. But the SABC's decision to introduce station automation also had an ideological benefit. Automation allows for greater control of programme content by station management. This meant that all programme content could be checked to comply with policy before being broadcast. This coincided with a new programming policy that actively promoted national interests. The end result was blandness in programme quality that ultimately cost the SABC dearly in terms of listener numbers, particularly when independent stations such as Capital Radio, Radio Bop and Radio 702 came on air.

Media Studies: Volume 1

African language services

Radio Bantu

The first full-scale radio stations aimed at black listeners came into being with the introduction of FM transmissions. The first service in seSotho and isiZulu were broadcast in Johannesburg on 1 January 1962 and was known collectively as Radio Bantu. From 1 July 1962 services were also presented in North Sotho and seTswana, while on 1 February 1963 isiZulu transmissions were introduced in Natal. On 1 June 1963, isiXhosa began broadcasting from Grahamstown. As the FM network expanded throughout the country, so programming on the medium-wave services was phased out. Programming consisted primarily of traditional, choral and jazz genres until the early 1960s when jive was added. Discussions were limited to topics lacking overt political content. News was patronisingly insular in that content emphasised local news almost to the exclusion of international events. The SABC made the presumption that an emphasis on local items best served the needs of black listeners (Tomaselli *et al* 1989:73). In 1960 the Bantu Programmes Control Board was created, through which all programme content was controlled by thirty-five white staff with a knowledge of black languages, in order to prevent any disparaging comments from being made on air regarding government policies (Tomaselli *et al* 1989:60).

1.2.5 From 1971 to 1981: A period of challenge

Introduction of television

Meyer Commission

During the 1950s and 1960s, the Nationalist Government vehemently opposed the introduction of television on moral and ethical grounds. In 1971 the Meyer Commission was appointed to investigate the possibility of introducing television to South Africa. In an apparent about-turn, one of the findings of the Commission was that in a country with a diverse culture and multiplicity of languages, television should be used "to advance the self-development of all its peoples and to foster their pride in their own identity and culture" (Mersham 1993:175). As this thinking was in line with the government's ideology of separate development for different races, the proposals of the Meyer Commission were accepted and on 27 April 1971 the government announced that the SABC was to provide a television service.

The SABC's first test broadcasts began on 5 May 1975 and a regular service was introduced on 5 January 1976. The service initially provided 37 hours of programming a week on one channel in English and Afrikaans. A

A History of the South African Media

boycott by the British actors union, Equity, as a protest against apartheid severely restricted the programming that was available to the SABC. As a result, the English service was dominated by American programmes such as *Dallas* and *Santa Barbara* while the Afrikaans service was sustained by American and German programmes which were dubbed in Afrikaans. Advertising began in January 1978. A second service, known as TV2/3, began on 1 January 1982, splitting later into two separate channels on 30 March 1985. Gradually additional stations came on air: Bop-TV (provided from the city of Mmbatho in the so-called independent Tswana-speaking homeland of Bophuthatswana, but available in Johannesburg) on 31 December 1983, M-Net (an over-the-air subscription service based on entertainment content on 1 October 1986, Trinity Broadcasting Network (a religious television service in the Ciskei) (now part of the Eastern Cape) on 3 December 1986, and e.tv much later on 1 October 1998.

The coming of independent radio

Prior to democratisation in 1994, any radio service other than that provided by the SABC has always had to come from beyond South Africa's borders. An extremely popular service was provided from Lourenço Marques (now Maputo) in neighbouring Mozambique. Known simply as LM Radio, the service started broadcasting in 1934, predating the formation of the SABC by two years. LM Radio was well known for its use of the top-40 music format, which was introduced in the 1960s in order to target the teenage and young adult market, which it did with a great deal of success despite being limited to short wave transmissions. It was simply a case of providing the market with what it wanted. Sunday listenership was particularly high as observance of the sabbath was strictly enforced by the SABC at the time. For example, although advertising was allowed on the commercial services, no jingles, sound effects or music could be used and music that was played had to be in keeping with the day. A second similar across-the-border service, Swazi Music Radio, or SMR, was started from Swaziland in the 1970, but only lasted about five years before closing down.

| LM Radio

The government's policy of creating the so-called independent national states of Transkei, Bophuthatswana, Venda and Ciskei created an unintended loophole that permitted additional independent radio services to begin broadcasting to South Africa. Simply put, South African legislation was not valid in these so-called independent states, which meant that the draconian

| Capital Radio

| Radio 702

15

laws which protected the SABC monopoly were not binding in these states. As a result, stations such as Capital Radio, Radio 702, Radio Bop and Radio Thohoyandou came on the air, providing their transmitter sites were located in one of the independent homelands. Radio 702 and Capital Radio made a major impact on radio listeners in urban areas as they presented opportunities for hearing alternative points of view not heard on SABC stations. In addition, Capital Radio and Radio 702 made big inroads into SABC radio audiences simply by providing better quality programming.

When originally setting up the "independent homelands" the possibility of creating an opening for independent radio services had not been considered by the government. Once done it was a *fait accompli* – any closing of the loophole would be tantamount to admitting to the sham of the so-called independence enjoyed by the homelands. None the less, this arrangement irked the South African authorities as news content could not be overtly controlled as with the SABC. Thus, the authorities periodically had to make use of dirty tricks to silence the independent stations, particularly Capital Radio. Although Capitol Radio's programming came from studios located in the small town of Port St John on the south-east coast of the country, news bulletins and a daily one-hour news commentary between 18:00 and 19:00 originated from Johannesburg because of logistical needs and was fed to the transmitter site in Herschel via land line. On several occasions the land line would go down, either before or during a news bulletin, for no apparent reason.

Figure 1.1 Although the SABC was an autonomous corporation responsible to Parliament, content, particularly that of the news, was manipulated by the National Party (*Rand Daily Mail*, 1 June 1981)

A History of the South African Media

1.2.6 From 1981 to 1992: The rationalisation of broadcasting

This ten-year period saw two major investigations into South African media, each putting forward differing points of view. It is also during this period that we can see the beginnings of major changes to the broadcasting environment in South Africa. For example, in anticipation of future developments, the SABC embraced Thatcherite policies modelled along the lines of conservative British Prime Minister Margaret Thatcher by commercialising the corporation through a division into various business units, and M-Net begins broadcasting.

The Steyn Commission, 1981

The Steyn Commission of 1981 was an extensive investigation into all forms of media. The resulting report was highly criticised for pandering to government ideology. Yet the Steyn Commission made four important recommendations regarding broadcasting:

- government control of the SABC needed to be relaxed in order to ensure the autonomy and impartiality of the broadcaster;
- the SABC board should be opened to all interest groups and not be limited to white members only, while the board would no longer be responsible to any particular minister but rather to the head of state;
- The Department of National Education should work in close collaboration with the SABC in order to realise the full potential of broadcasting in education;
- the creation of independent radio within South Africa should be allowed. This last recommendation was not received favourably as the government considered independent broadcasting to be detrimental to the national interest.

| Steyn Commission |

These recommendations *vis-à-vis* broadcasting were, however, not accepted by the government. The country had to wait another ten years for the Viljoen Commission before any meaningful changes could be made to the broadcasting environment in South Africa.

The introduction of a subscription service

One of the biggest and most surprising changes to the broadcasting scene during this period was the arrival of M-Net, which began broadcasting on 1 October 1986 as the first over-the-air subscription television service in the southern hemisphere. M-Net was a direct result of growing concern by the major newspaper groups over the rampant commercialisation of

| M-Net |

the SABC. This translated into a considerable loss of advertising revenue for the press. The ad spend (the amount of money advertisers spend on advertising) in the press dropped from 86 percent in 1977 to 51 percent in 1990, while that for radio and television rose from 17 percent to 44 percent for the same period.

A proposal for a subscription television service, managed and owned by a consortium formed by the major English and Afrikaans newspaper groups, was put to the government in 1984 by the management of Nasionale Pers (now Naspers). Here we need to keep in mind the support originally provided by the Afrikaans press for the government. Thus, as a *quid pro quo*, the government approved the proposal, provided the channel limited itself to providing entertainment programmes and did not broadcast news. Effectively the new service was then not in competition with the SABC as an information provider, over which the government exerted a strong influence. The name "M-Net" was selected as an acronym for "media-network", indicating the original ownership of the service by the various press groups.

The Viljoen Commission, 1991

Viljoen Commission

With the coming of 1989, the political order in place for four decades started to change. Hardline National Party leader PW (Pieter Willem) Botha suffered a stroke and eventually reluctantly made way for a party colleague considered more of a reformer, FW (Frederik Willem) de Klerk, who introduced a number of sweeping reforms, such as the unbanning of the African National Congress (ANC). Within this scenario, the Viljoen Commission in 1991 investigated the future of broadcasting in South Africa. The major recommendations made by the Commission were the following:

- the setting up of an Independent Broadcasting Authority to regulate broadcasting;
- commercial broadcasting should be subject to fewer restrictions than public broadcasting;
- ownership of radio and television stations should be limited;
- the SABC should become a public service broadcaster;
- the deregulation of broadcasting should begin with the introduction of community radio services.

The Viljoen Commission also had its critics. From its very inception, the Commission was labelled as being unrepresentative of the broader

A History of the South African Media

South African community. This led to concerns that, as with the Steyn Commission earlier, the findings would be within the ideology of the government and that the strong bias towards the promotion of the Nationalist Government by the SABC would continue. However, these fears were allayed when the report clearly indicated that dramatic changes were on the cards.

1.2.7 From 1992 to 2000: A period of restructuring

The beginnings of community radio

Following the release of the Viljoen Commission report, there was extensive lobbying for the restructuring of broadcasting. Following a period of hiatus, a number of new stations came onto the air with a limited geographic range and for a limited period of time, usually about three weeks, with a temporary broadcast licence issued by the Department of Home Affairs. These stations were usually linked to some or other cultural or commercial event, such as the Rand Easter Show in Johannesburg. The first radio station to operate legally under the new dispensation was that of Festival FM which broadcast for only ten days, from 09:00 until 18:00 as part of the Grahamstown National Arts Festival in the Eastern Cape, beginning 27 June 1991.

The temporary status of community broadcasting continued until 1995 when the Independent Broadcasting Authority (IBA) finally issued a number of temporary licences that allowed stations to broadcast for a period of one year. Some ninety stations went on air, covering a wide range of interests from religious and campus stations to wildlife and community development.

> community broadcasting

The establishment of a regulatory authority for broadcasting

An area of concern in the run-up to the first democratic elections of 1994 was the partisanship of the SABC towards the Nationalist-led government and the creditability of the SABC as a news and information provider. A solution was to distance the SABC from the government through the creation of an independent broadcasting regulator. Thus it was that the Independent Broadcasting Authority (IBA) was an outcome of the Multi-Party Negotiation Forum, held at the World Trade Centre (now Caesars, a hotel and casino complex) during 1993. The regulatory authority was officially established by the passing of the IBA Act, no. 153 of 1993 by parliament on 18 October 1993 to commence work on 30 March 1994.

> Independent Broadcasting Authority

Media Studies: Volume 1

(The IBA Act has since been repealed by the Electronic Communication Act, no. 36 of 2006.)

Figure 1.2 Corruption on the part of some IBA officials did much to dent the credibility of the IBA (*Sowetan*, 22 April 1997)

Independent Communications Authority of South Africa

The IBA was heavily criticised for being exceedingly slow in concluding its investigations for the Triple Inquiry Report and then in issuing licences. The IBA countered that it intended to be thorough in its work. But the IBA was required to establish policy as well as regulate that policy. This was seen by many as a serious conflict of interest that affected the objectivity of the Authority in its activities. The Authority was also dogged by a number of scandals involving impropriety in the activities of some key personnel. All told, these aspects had a negative impact on the Authority's credibility which further delayed the issuing of new licences. An end to the many problems that dogged the IBA was seen in the creation of a new regulatory authority that was formed by amalgamating with the South African Telecommunications Regulatory Authority (Satra) to form the Independent Communications Authority of South Africa (ICASA).

The Triple Inquiry Report

Triple Inquiry Report

The role of the IBA was to generate policy regarding broadcasting, to issue broadcast licences and to regulate and monitor the activities of broadcasters. However, the IBA was placed in a unique position in that any previous regulations were *ad hoc*, scattered within various pieces of legislation. The first task that faced the IBA was to constitute a formalised regulatory structure, beginning with the establishment of criteria for licence applications before it could actually start to function as a regulator.

A History of the South African Media

Thus it was that the Triple Inquiry Report was eventually published some two years later in 1995. The report concerned itself with three basic broadcasting issues:
- the protection and viability of public broadcasting – *inter alia* it was recommended that the SABC's financially lucrative regional radio stations be sold off to generate much needed capital;
- establishing the percentage of local content – recommending that local content form at least half of all programming by the year 2000. This target was never reached and became the subject of further discussion in 2001;
- establishing criteria regarding cross-media ownership – the idea here was to create a diversity within the broadcasting environment where no one person could own more than one television station, two FM and two medium-wave radio stations. However, a newspaper could not have an interest in both a radio and television station at the same time. Further limits were placed on newspaper ownership of radio and television stations. For example, a newspaper that exceeded 15 percent of the total distribution within its circulation area could not have any financial interest in a radio or television station in that area.

Additionally, the report recommended that radio stations owned by the former so-called TBVC states (Transkei, Bophuthatswana, Venda and Ciskei) were to merge with the SABC, or be sold, or that the frequency be considered for a community station.

The three tier system

There are three classes of broadcasting licence, known as the three tier system, but the distinction between each class was problematic as the description of each type was spread over two pieces of legislation, the IBA Act, no. 153 of 1993 and the Broadcasting Act, no. 4 of 1999. Each class is briefly outlined below. The repeal of the IBA Act in 2006 has resolved this dilemma.

> three tier system

Public broadcasting is supposed to emphasis quality programming and is defined in legal terms as a service provided by the SABC or any other statutory body or person The mandate of the public broadcaster is to serve the various cultural and language groups that make up the country. Programming is expected to reflect the diverse cultural and linguistic nature of South Africa and to include significant amounts of educational, news and public affairs programming, including national, developmental

> Public broadcasting

and minority sports. Of the three SABC channels, the multilingual SABC 1 and 2 are considered to be public service channels while the English-language SABC 3 is considered to be a public service commercial channel. In reality there is little distinction in the terms of programming offered by these three channels.

Commercial broadcasting

Commercial broadcasting is defined as a service operated for profit and need to provide a diverse range of programming in all official languages. Currently only two television services are considered commercial services, M-Net and e.tv. Programming, as described in the legislation, is vaguely described as "diverse" and must be provided in all official languages reflecting the culture, characters, needs and aspirations of the audience. News and information programmes must be provided on a regular basis. M-Net, being a subscription service, is subject to a different set of regulations from that of e.tv, which is a free-to-air service.

Community broadcasting

Community broadcasting refers to a broadcasting service which:
- is fully controlled by a non-profit entity and carried on for non-profitable purposes;
- serves a particular community;
- encourages members of the community it serves to participate in the selection and provision of programmes to be broadcast;
- may be funded by donations, grants, sponsorships or advertising or membership fees.

Community services can operate either on a long-term licence issued for four years or on a short-term licence for a month. Two types of community are also defined, a geographic community or a community of interests. At any given time there are about one hundred community radio stations in operation. The first community television licence was issued to Soweto Community Television, which began transmissions on Sunday 1 July, 2007 for a period of one year.

Restructuring of the SABC

SABC

As part of the new dispensation for broadcasting in South Africa, and in order to meet the challenge brought about by many new competitors, the SABC entered into a lengthy phase of restructuring in order to fulfil its new role as that of the nation's public broadcaster. Previously, albeit theoretically, the SABC was considered an independent autonomous body responsible to parliament. This was changed when the Corporation became SABC (Pty) Ltd with the state as the sole shareholder. At the same time, the

A History of the South African Media

organisation was also split into two divisions which were termed as a public service division and a public service commercial division. The idea was that the commercial services, such as Metro FM, 5FM and SABC1 would generate funds in order to cross subsidise the public service division.

Despite a much-hoped-for turnaround, the SABC experienced yet another financial crisis, aggravated largely over the preceding decade by a culture of non-payment of television licence fees. Piracy peaked at 57 percent of all viewers during 1997, resulting in a revenue loss of some R900 million a year (South African Broadcasting Corporation 1999:9). In addition the Astrasat project, an analogue free-to-air satellite service that began operating during July 1996, was finally abandoned in February 1998 as a dismal failure, resulting in a write-off of R143 million.

As part of the restructuring process, six of the SABC's seven highly successful and lucrative regional commercial stations had to be sold to the private sector. It was hoped that the income generated from the sale of these radio stations could be used to offset the SABC's financial difficulties. But it was a bitter pill for the SABC to swallow when the income from the sale of these radio stations went to the Treasury instead.

With the assistance of outside consultants, McKinsey and Associates, the SABC managed to turn around its financial deficit and recorded a budget surplus of R122 million by the end of March 1999 (South African Broadcasting Corporation 1999:9). But this turnaround came at a price – local content dropped while the use of English was increased to attract a more affluent audience in order to maximise advertising revenue (Duncan, 2000), contradicting its public service mandate. The SABC still had to deal with the problem of credibility, particularly as a provider of news, which it has never managed to resolve successfully, notwithstanding having a large and efficient news department. In addition, the matter of low staff morale, inadequate labour relations and faulty human resources administration was a thorny issue as the SABC underwent a period of transformation. The broadcaster continues to be rocked by scandals, including that of corruption and maladministration, which has resulted in a rapid turnover of management.

The role of black empowerment in broadcasting

In April 1998 the Independent Broadcasting Authority (IBA) awarded the first free-to-air commercial television licence in South Africa to the Midi group, a consortium of previously disadvantaged groups. The new station,

e.tv

to be known as e.tv, was almost constantly awash with criticism and controversy starting with allegations of political interference in allocation of the licence (Kobokoane 1999a:1). Broadcasts started on 1 October 1998 and by the end of its first week of operation, the station was highly criticised for reneging on its promise to provide indigenous programming. Instead it broadcast American material (Pokwana 1998:23). This resulted in a threat by the then IBA to withdraw e.tv's licence for violating its licence agreement (Hlophe 1999:6).

Figure 1.3 Resolving the financial woes of the SABC meant abandoning some public broadcasting principles (*City Press*, 6 March 1997)

A further dispute arose between e.tv and the IBA over the station's delayed start of news bulletins. The news service was scheduled to begin on 1 December 1998. The delay was attributed to the non-arrival of equipment. The news service finally took to the air on 1 February 1999, strategically placed one hour before the flagship English-language news bulletin presented on SABC 3 at 8 pm. No sooner was the news service up and running when strained relations between e.tv journalists and management threatened to shut down the news service. Claims surfaced that contracts did not comply with labour laws; editorial positions were filled by incompetent staff and quality control was considered inefficient (Malefane 1999:8). Despite this, e.tv news was seen as refreshingly informal compared with that offered by the SABC (Banda 1999:3; Hagen 1999:1; Wrottersley 1999:5). A strong plus was the fact that viewers quickly came to regard e.tv as truly independent and objective in its news coverage compared to the SABC (Klein 1999a:3).

A History of the South African Media

Figure 1.4 e.tv's initial financial problems and licence contraventions placed the IBA in a compromising position (*Sowetan*, 4 December 1998)

Before the issue regarding licence conditions had been resolved, a financial crisis in February 1999 brought the station to the brink of bankruptcy – e.tv's monthly expenditure of R15 million could not be offset by advertising revenue of R7 million (Klein 1999b:3). The previously disadvantaged minority shareholders had failed to come forward with their share of the capital (Kobokoane 1999a:1). This scenario created a dilemma for the IBA: if the station's licence was revoked, it would strike a severe blow to black empowerment. But if the IBA made concessions to e.tv over its licence it would face the wrath of those who lost bids for the licence and who knew full well that e.tv could never fully comply with its intentions (Moerdyk 1999a:15). The IBA created a problem for itself by insisting on such stringent operating conditions for the new station and not allowing market forces to determine issues such as advertising and programming (Moerdyk 1999a:15).

As a result of their inability to raise the necessary capital, minority shareholders forfeited their holdings to HCI, who now held a much larger share of Midi TV. This solution was unacceptable to the IBA. Subsequently HCI proposed the creation of a special purposes vehicle to hold the shares owned by minority groups until such time as they could raise the capital. This proposal put pressure onto the IBA, who was bound to uphold legislation but could not let the Midi group disintegrate, to accept the proposal. Despite all the tensions and problems e.tv has proved a success with a rapid growth in ratings. It has firmly entrenched itself within the

South African media environment, gaining a loyal viewership, and is posing a serious threat to the SABC's dominance of free-to-air services.

1.2.8 From 2000 to the present: The ambiguities of post-apartheid broadcasting

The role of the SABC as the public broadcaster

Despite efforts to shake off the stigma of being a crisis-ridden organisation, criticism of the SABC has compounded over the years since democratisation in 1994. This is despite the SABC's independence being guaranteed by law, drawing up an editorial charter and being reviewed by an independent regulator. Yet the broadcaster continues to:

> *"stumble from controversy to controversy over its relationship with the government and the ruling party" (Harber 2006:18).*

News and current affairs programming is poor, dull and disappointing. The reason, says Harber (2006:18), lies in the organisation culture and news values at work in the news room. A major stumbling block would seem to lie in the Editorial Charter which emphasises upward-referral, where decisions are not taken by senior journalists or editors but need to be handed on upwards to higher levels of authority in the organisation. The fact that the SABC chief executive is also the executive head of news is seen as a serious conflict of interests (Tabane 2006:4). There have also been reports about nepotism, breaches of policy and interference by the board regarding operating decisions. Some of the controversial issues relating to the SABC during 2005 and 2006 include:

- alleged censoring of a broadcast of the public booing Deputy President Phumzile Mlambo-Nguka's address at a Women's Day rally;
- cancelling of a documentary critical of President Thabo Mbeki just hours before being aired;
- the blacklisting of political analysts critical of President Thabo Mbeki and the government.

Gumede (2006:14) suggests that these controversies point towards a broad decline in the ethics of the SABC. These controversies also point to a weakness on the part of the regulator which is supposed to hold the SABC accountable for the service it provides. Gumede further adds that the SABC's problems are a direct result of the fact that the members of the SABC board and top management really have no idea of what a public broadcasting service should look like. As a result the SABC is steadily sliding away from being a public service broadcaster to that of a state broadcaster.

Figure 1.5 Despite a supposed guarantee of editorial independence, the SABC is still seen as a government mouthpiece (*Mail and Guardian* 19 October 2006)

Changes to broadcasting regulation

In 2005 the SABC was granted a licence to begin two new regional television channels focusing on marginalised indigenous languages. The use of English on these two channels is meant to be limited to unavoidable situations, such as where interviewees can only express themselves in English. The aim of the two channels is to ensure that languages such as tshiVenda, xiTsonga, siSwati and isiNdebele received more broadcast time. The two channels will also include programming in Afrikaans. SABC 4 is meant to cover Limpopo, North West, Gauteng, the Free State and Northern Cape. SABC 5 is meant to reach Mpumalanga, eastern Limpopo, Gauteng, KwaZulu-Natal, Eastern and Western Cape. At the time of writing, these two stations are still to go on air. In 2004, ICASA announced that it was making seven new commercial radio licences available for what the regulator termed as "secondary markets". However, hearings into the granting of the licences were delayed pending the passage of the ICASA Amendment Act and the Electronic Communications Act in 2006. These acts, together with a more detailed discussion of the regulation of broadcasting can be found in volume Two of *Media Studies*.

1.3 THE PRESS

Unlike broadcasting, which closely allied itself to government ideology, there has always been a strained relationship between the press and the government in South Africa. The resulting tension has manifested itself in the form of constant threats of restrictive legislation. However, the degree of this tension has ebbed and flowed according to political developments in the history of South Africa, beginning literally with the arrival of Dutch colonial administrator Jan van Riebeeck at the Cape of Good Hope in 1652. Roelofse (1996:70–71) identifies five enduring themes that run through the history of the press in South Africa:
- tension and conflict between government and the press;
- divisions in the press based on language;
- further divisions in the press based on race;
- the state sees the press as a threat to peace and security;
- efforts by journalists to circumvent undemocratic laws.

Roelofse (1996:70) indicates that it is difficult to identify distinct periods for the press as we did for broadcasting. Rather, we need to divide the history of the press into four distinct strands, each of which follows its own developmental pattern. These strands are:
- the English press;
- the Afrikaans press;
- the black press;
- the alternative press.

1.3.1 The English press

The early years in the Cape Colony

Locally produced newspapers did not appear in South Africa until a century and a half after the occupation of the Cape by van Riebeeck in 1652, simply because the Dutch East India Company, which controlled the site, perceived the press as a potentially revolutionary instrument. News and views had to be channelled through newspapers published far away in the Netherlands (Fourie 1994:291). It was only after the Dutch reluctantly ceded the Cape to British military rule in 1795 (a reprisal for the Dutch alliances with British enemies) that the first local publication began. The *Cape Town Gazette and African Advertiser/Kaapsche Stads Courant en Afrikaansche Berigte* was first published on 16 August 1800 by Alexander Walker and John Robertson, who were also renowned for being corrupt slave-dealers. The paper appeared mainly in English and

A History of the South African Media

was printed on a government-owned press at the Castle, the centre of community and military life in Cape Town. Little but official notices and advertisements were printed in this newspaper which was strongly controlled by the British governor between 1814 and 1826, Lord Charles Somerset. Private newspapers were prohibited except for those published by missionaries in the hinterland (Diederichs 1993:73).

The struggle for freedom of the press

The first non-government newspaper was *The South African Commercial Advertiser*, which first appeared on 7 January 1824 in Cape Town, owned by George Greig but with Thomas Pringle and John Fairbairn as the editors. These three tenacious settlers broke the twenty-two year monopoly of the government press (de Kock 1982:53). Although this paper was published mainly in English, it also made provision for Dutch news and advertisements. The paper consisted of eight pages of which four were filled with advertisements (de Kock 1982:42). The paper was soon closed down by the governor of the Cape Colony, Lord Charles Somerset who feared reports of his spurious activities.

The South African Commercial Advertiser

Some two months after starting the *Commercial Advertiser*, Thomas Pringle and John Fairbairn, now honoured as South Africa's first journalists, also started a bilingual periodical known as *The South African Journal and Het Nederduitsch Zuid-Afrikaansch Tydschrift* with the Reverend Abraham Faure. The first edition appeared on 5 March 1824. *The Journal* was immediately unpopular with the authorities as the content tackled constitutional matters such as the curbing of despotic power and in later issues the freedom of the press. By mid-May 1824, Pringle and Fairbairn were warned that they could only continue publication provided they stopped criticising the authorities. Pringle, refusing to submit to authority, closed down *The Journal*.

The South African Journal

The *Commercial Advertiser* was revived again on 31 August 1825 by Greig after a drawn-out battle with the colonial office in London. But it didn't exist for long, as the British government suspended publication 19 months later when Fairbairn depicted outgoing governor Lord Somerset as vindictive. And so the struggle to secure the freedom of the press continued. Only when Lord Somerset was out of the way did it became possible to make press freedom a reality, and on 30 April 1829, Ordinance no. 60 was signed, a document that provided liberty and political rights to the press. Roelofse (1996:72) identifies three factors that eventually

Lord Somerset

Commercial Advertiser

influenced the granting of press freedom from strict colonial government control.
- Lord Somerset's departure from the Cape on 5 March 1826;
- the appointment of General Richard Bourke, who favoured a free press, as governor;
- John Fairbairn's dogged pursuit of matters relating to the press with the British government.

1820 Settlers

A second event that strongly influenced the development of the press in South Africa was the arrival of 5 000 British settlers in 1820, one of the largest settler movements by English speakers in colonial-era Africa, who brought both printing presses and expertise with them. As a result, by the end of the nineteenth century, there was hardly a town of any size that did not have its own newspaper. Many of the editors of these smaller newspapers lived in the frontier towns, as the settlers had been brought in to entrench colonial claims against isiXhosa-speaking farmers and pastoralists in the Frontier Wars. Unlike Fairbairn and Pringle who explored more philosophical issues of press freedom, the new wave of publishers championed the cause of both British settler and Dutch farmer alike (Diederichs 1993:74). The English left an indelible stamp on the development of the press in South Africa in their efforts to establish press freedom.

The Newspaper Press Union

Following the early years of struggle for press freedom in the Cape, direct government control no longer posed a threat to the press by the 1880s. But in its place there was indirect control through subtle pressure. A new libel law had been passed that posed a serious threat to the freedom of the press. Government advertising was withheld and high tariffs for telegraphic services were charged, essentially tying off the main artery that supplied the newspapers with the news. In addition, the government exploited the continual petty squabbling among newsmen in order to keep the press fragmented. The press also had to face a number of logistical problems such as long distances, poor infrastructure and a limited audience of literates who had to be served in two languages (de Kock 1982:108–109). All that was fought for by Pringle and Fairbairn was in danger of disappearing.

Joseph Dormer

The only way the press could protect their hard-won liberty and not be done out of their earnings was to unite in a common front. Organised

A History of the South African Media

by Joseph Dormer of the *Cape Argus* and RW Murray from the *Cape Times*, twenty-six newspapermen met in Grahamstown in what is now the Eastern Cape, on 27 November 1882. Here the Newspaper Press Union (NPU) was formed with the purpose of promoting and protecting the common interests of the South African press. The NPU undertook to fight for the amendment of libel legislation and to establish a protective fund to help newspapers that ran into financial difficulties.

Further developments of the press in South Africa

The first newspaper in Natal (now the province of KwaZulu-Natal) was *De Natalier*, a four-page weekly, mostly in Dutch with some smatterings of English, that appeared on 15 March 1844, edited by Charles Etienne Boniface, who had left the Cape hastily when faced with a charge of libel at *De Zuid-Afrikaan*. The newspaper did not last very long, closing in 1846 following libel action. The newspaper was quickly replaced by *The Natal Witness*, then a bilingual weekly paper, which today, as the Pietermaritzburg daily *The Witness* is the oldest newspaper in South Africa still in publication (Cutten 1935:40; Leahy & Voice 1993:90), predating *The Cape Argus* and *The Cape Times*. While many smaller newspapers sprung up in the British colony of Natal in the period 1850 to 1859, most were defunct by 1860 (Cutten 1935:41–42). Few of these country newspapers in Natal showed the characteristic bilingualism evident in the Cape and Transvaal newspapers. Of the more important Natal newspapers, Durban's English-language morning daily *The Natal Mercury* (now *The Mercury*) appeared in 1852, while the afternoon daily *The Daily News* began in Durban under the name *Natal Mercantile Advertiser* on 3 January 1878.

| The Natal Witness/ The Witness |
| The Natal Mercury/ The Mercury |
| The Daily News |

The first publication to appear inland in the Transvaal, then beyond British control and run as an Afrikaans republic, was not a newspaper but the *Government Gazette*, published by Cornelis Moll in Potchefstroom, then the capital of the Zuid-Afrikaanse Republiek (ZAR), on 25 September 1857 (Cutten 1935:50; Diederichs 1993:74). The name was changed two years later to the *Gouvernements Courant der ZAR*. However, the first Transvaal newspaper, *De Oude Emigrant*, was established on 15 October 1859, also in Potchefstroom. Three years later *De Emigrant* began, edited by AF Schubert following the collapse of *De Oude Emigrant* nine months earlier, which was blamed for bringing journalism into disrepute with its insulting articles (Cullen 1935:50). From 1863 the *Staats Courant* was published from a building on Church Square in Pretoria.

| Government Gazette |
| De Oude Emigrant |

Media Studies: Volume 1

Transvaal Argus

The *Transvaal Argus* was set up in 1866 with Fredrich Jeppe as editor in Potchefstroom. Two years later it was renamed the *Transvaal Advocate*. As this paper was published in English and came out before the discovery of gold triggered massive population movements in the region, its circulation was limited and constantly suffered from economic problems and soon collapsed (Cullen 1935:51–52). The first Transvaal newspaper of any significance appeared on 8 August 1873 with *De Volkstem* (The Voice of the People in Dutch later altered to *Die Volkstem* in Afrikaans in 1922) which aside from a break in 1880 during the Anglo-Boer War, continued publication until 1951 (Leahy & Voice 1993:90; Cullen 1935:54).

Diggers' News

The Mining Argus

Within a short time gold was discovered and the mining camp of Johannesburg sprung up in 1886. A number of newspapers appeared that had close ties with the mining industry. The first is considered to be the *Diggers' News*, sold at sixpence a copy from the printing works in Market Street from 24 February 1887. It consisted of four pages mostly filled with advertisements. A day later *The Mining Argus* appeared. The offices of the bi-weekly *Argus* consisted of a stretch of canvas over a wooden frame. Copy was sent to Pretoria by horseback for the paper to be printed but during the journey, some of the copy often got lost, resulting in a loss of revenue for advertisements not printed. *The Standard and Transvaal Mining Chronicle* also began in March 1887 and later amalgamated with the *Digger's News*, to be followed by *The Transvaal Observer*.

The Star

The Johannesburg English-language daily *The Star* originated in Grahamstown, then one of the country's biggest cities, as *The Eastern Star* and moved to the Witwatersrand region after the discovery of gold, appearing as an evening newspaper renamed *The Star* on 3 April 1889. *The Star* was to become the biggest daily in South Africa and continued to have the biggest circulation up to 1991, when briefly overtaken by the township-focused English-language daily *The Sowetan*. Both are now competing with a new tabloid competitor, *The Daily Sun*, which appears to have brought new readers into the newspaper-reading world.

The Friend

The Friend of the Sovereignty and Bloemfontein Gazette was the first newspaper in the Free State, beginning publication 10 June 1850. Four years later, when the Free State achieved independence as a Boer republic, the paper changed its name to *The Friend of the Free State*, later shortened to simply *The Friend*. This newspaper had the distinction of being edited, for a short period during the British occupation, by none other than the famous Anglo-Indian author Rudyard Kipling and went on to have 130

A History of the South African Media

years of publication. *A Gouvernements Courant* was published in 1857, followed five years later on 29 October 1862 by *De Tijd* (The Time), the first Dutch newspaper in the Free State, which continued publication for thirteen years. The publication of newspapers in the Free State did not reach the same levels of development as with the Cape, Natal or Transvaal, and it was not until 11 March 1876 that a third newspaper appeared under the title *De Express en Oranje Vrijstaats Advertentieblad*. *De Express* was eventually closed down by the military authorities in 1900 because of its strong connection with the English during the Second Anglo–Boer War (1899–1902) then raging (Cullen 1935:47). Other newspapers that started up in the Free State included *The Daily News* which started July 1882, *De Burger*, *The Independent* and *Fakkel* but few lasted for very long or made a significant impact.

1.3.2 The Afrikaans press

The beginnings of the Afrikaans press

Unlike some of the English press, the Afrikaans press appeared to remain passive for a long time. Roelofse (1996:74) claims that for the Dutch-speaking Afrikaner, the concept of freedom stemmed from the authority of and obedience to the state (as long as that state did not include the hated British colonisers) while for the English, freedom was located within the individual while the state functioned in order to serve their interests. Roelofse (1996:74) claims that as a result of these differing views, the English may have placed a higher value on freedom of the individual than did the Afrikaner. This distinction continued to influence the approaches adopted by the press right through the 20th century.

The Dutch/Afrikaans press was established largely as a reaction to the liberal views of Fairbairn in the *South African Commercial Advertiser*, particular regarding issues such as slavery, the tensions between the Dutch farmers and the amaXhosa and the work of missionaries. However, the founder of the Afrikaans press was not of Dutch descent, but an eccentric hunchback Portuguese Jew, Josephus Suasso de Lima, who had been sacked from the Dutch East India Company for the misuse of documents. In 1826 de Lima established a weekly newspaper *De Verzamelaar* (The Collector) at the Cape which had, according to Roelofse (1996:74), no real historical significance other than being the first publication exclusively in Dutch. Publication continued for some 22 years, dogged by financial difficulties (de Kock 1982:94).

De Verzamelaar

De Zuid-Afrikaan

The first newspaper to speak for Dutch/Afrikaner interests, *De Zuid-Afrikaan* (The South African) began on 9 April 1830 by Christoffel Joseph Brand, an advocate unpopular with the local authorities for his ability to successfully defend cases against the government in the law courts. The paper was formed largely as a reaction to the indifference of the English press to the Afrikaner's needs and the attempted anglicisation of the Afrikaaner by the government. John Fairbairn of the *Commercial Advertiser* clashed bitterly with *De Zuid-Afrikaan* over issues such as the right to own slaves, which Fairbairn opposed, and the rights of the *Voortrekkers,* literally "those who trek ahead," who fled the British-run Cape Colony in the 1840s and 1850s to move into the interior of the country.

Die Afrikaanse Patriot

Die Afrikaanse Patriot (The Afrikaner Patriot) promoted Afrikaans as a language, being the mouthpiece of the *Genootskap van Regte Afrikaners* (Association of Genuine Afrikaners), later known as the Afrikanderbond. The first issue appeared in Paarl in the Western Cape on 15 January 1876. Although there were only fifty subscribers for the first edition of the monthly newspaper, it drew an immediate reaction from the community. The paper was harshly criticised for promoting what was then considered a "kitchen" language (de Kock 1982:90). The Synod of the Dutch Church forbade children to read it and teachers were reprimanded for writing articles for publication. The *Cradocksche-Afrikaner* said of it scathingly "Semi-educated Griquas will surely be delighted with this paper" (Cullen 1935:36). Because of the intense opposition to written Afrikaans, subscribers and contributors had to write, in a clandestine fashion, via *De Zuid-Afrikaan* in Cape Town (de Kock 1982:91). The paper was the effort of the Reverend Stephanus Jacobus du Toit, founder of the Genootskap, and his older brother Daniel François du Toit who later edited *Die Afrikaanse Patriot* for a short period. The paper was by no means a propaganda sheet but a complete newspaper supplying news and market prices in addition to letters, prose and poetry (de Kock 1982: 90–91). In its second year, the paper became a weekly and by the third year subscriptions rose to 3 000 when it gained support from Afrikaners living in the *Zuid-Afrikaanse Republiek* (South African Republic) after the British annexed it. However, the newspaper lost a great deal of its readership after 1892 as a result of du Toit's support of English mining magnate Cecil John Rhodes against Transvaal president Paul Kruger. Influential members of the Genootskap resigned and withdrew their capital in an attempt to change the policy of the paper, without much

A History of the South African Media

success, and eventually the paper went out of business in 1904 (Cullen 1935:3; de Kock 1982:91). Today, *Die Afrikaanse Patriot* is considered to have played an important part in the establishment of Afrikaans as a language (Diederichs 1993:74).

There are a number of crucial differences between the development of the Afrikaans and English press during the nineteenth century, which had an enduring effect well into the twentieth century (Roelofse 1996:75). The Afrikaans newspapers were:

- not the result of professional journalist practice – the editors were in most cases ministers of religion committed to Calvinistic ethics rather than professional journalists, such as Abraham Faure and SJ du Toit;
- not primarily considered as commercial ventures; the Afrikaner cause weighed more heavily than profits and as a result many of the early Dutch and Afrikaans newspapers folded;
- seen as cultural and political crusaders, where promotion of the Afrikaans language, political independence and the perceived threat of black nationalism became enduring themes;
- committed to Africa and the role of the Afrikaner in South Africa; whereas the English press reported diligently on British affairs, the Afrikaans press focused on the affairs of Afrikaners and South Africa.

Formation of the Afrikaans press groups

The development of the Afrikaans press during the first half of the twentieth century is deeply intertwined with politics. Apart from the establishment of the National Party, 1915 is significant in that it saw the beginnings of three major Afrikaans-language newspapers. *Het Volksblad* was the first to appear in March as a weekly publishing out of Potchefstroom, which became a daily on its move to Bloemfontein in 1925 (Muller 1987:120). As the paper was not nationally distributed, it did not make much impact politically. | *Het Volksblad*

Four months later, in July 1915, *De Burger* appeared in Cape Town, later to become *Die Burger* (The Citizen) and the flagship title in the Naspers Group. It was also considered the Cape voice of Afrikaner nationalism as the paper was originally established by wealthy professional men who needed a means to air their political views as well as a potential business enterprise for their capital, under the leadership of JHH de Waal. De Nasionale Pers Beperk was registered as a company in May 1915 for | *Die Burger*

| *Die Vaderland*

35

this purpose. As a result of *De Burger's* efforts at promoting Afrikaner nationalism, the paper did not receive a warm welcome from the powerful anglicised minority within Cape Town, where there was a call in 1917 for an advertising boycott of the paper. The third paper to appear in 1915 was the bi-weekly *Ons Vaderland* (Our Fatherland) in Pretoria, with General James Barry Munnik Hertzog and his two main supporters, TJ Roos and NC Havenga as the main shareholders. The paper changed its title to *Die Vaderland* (The Fatherland) in December 1931.

Die Transvaler

While returning from the National Party congress held at Middleburg in 1935, Hofmeyer and Malan devised a scheme to launch a new newspaper, *Die Transvaler*, (The Transvaaler) which was to provide a northern counterbalance to the highly influential *Die Burger* with the first edition appearing in October 1937. Oddly, the first editor to be appointed was a social psychology professor who hailed from the Cape, Hendrik Verwoerd. According to Muller (1987:125) this was Hofmeyer's big mistake. In the very first editorial, the new editor rebuked the Jewish community for meddling in Afrikaner financial affairs and suggested that all Jews be deported. Such outspoken views antagonised some of the founders, who resigned from the board after two years, but also the English and largely Jewish entrepreneurs in the Transvaal. The result was an advertisement boycott of the newspaper, similar to that experienced by *Die Burger*, resulting in financial losses. Verwoerd went on to become the architect of the all-encompassing racial policy of apartheid, or apartness. Thus we find, on the eve of World War II, *Die Burger*, an influential newspaper in the south of the country serving nationalist and capitalist interests, while up north *Die Transvaler* was beginning to find its republican feet under the editorship of Verwoerd (Muller 1987:126).

1.3.3 The development of a black press

Newspapers for black readers appeared soon after Ordinance no. 60 in 1829 granted press freedom to the Cape Colony (see section 1.3.1 *The struggle for freedom of the press* above). Hachten and Giffard (1984:145) identify four periods in the historical development of the black press in South Africa:
- 1830–1880: The missionary period
- 1880–1930: The independent élitist period
- 1930–1980: The white-owned period
- 1980–1995: The multiracial period

Roelofse (1996:82) has suggested that since 1995 the black press has moved into a fifth period in which the mainstream, traditionally white newspaper groups started a process of restructuring to bring about black empowerment.

From 1830 to 1880: The missionary period

The origin of the black press in South Africa is closely linked to the establishment of mission stations in the Eastern Cape and the work between missionaries and black residents. Not only did the missionaries teach literacy; they also provided the skills and equipment necessary for publishing. In the process they also transferred the basic tenets of Western culture, reflected in the first black newspapers (Johnson 1991:16). Initially, publications were limited to spelling and religious books, such as *Morisa Oa Molemo*, produced by the London Missionary Society in the Tswana language at Kuruman in the 1830s. The first newspaper intended for black readers was *Umshumayeli Wendaba* (Publisher of the News), printed at the Wesleyan Mission Society in Grahamstown from 1837 to 1841. The Lovedale Missionary Institute produced *Ikwezi* (Morning Star) between 1844 and 1845, with *Indaba* (The News), a bilingual Xhosa/English newspaper following in 1862. *The Kafir Express*, also a bilingual paper, appeared in 1870. The Xhosa section, *Isigidimi Sama Xosa* (The Xhosa Messenger) became a separate newspaper in 1876, and is considered important as it was the first newspaper to be edited by black journalists.

From 1880 to 1930: The independent élitist period

Commenting on the implications of the work of the missionaries, Johnson (1991:16) says a widening gap soon emerged between those who had received a missionary education and the rural-based majority who had not, resulting in the formation of a minority black élite infused with Western values who felt a need for newspapers independent of missionary control. The central figure here can be considered the 25-year-old John Tengo Jabavu who in 1884 resigned his position as editor of *Isigidimi Sama Xosa* to found *Imvo Zabantsundu* (African Opinion) at King William's Town, the first newspaper written, owned and controlled by black citizens of South Africa (Cullen 1935:81). The paper rapidly developed into an influential expression of black opinion, promoting principles of non-violence and working together with liberal whites in an effort to bring about reforms, but soon ran into problems, including

John Tengo Jabavu

Media Studies: Volume 1

financial difficulties and internal tensions, and experienced intense competition from *Isigidimi* (Johnson 1991:17).

AK Soga

While *Imvo* was in decline, a new paper emerged in November 1897, *Izwi la Bantu*, which strongly opposed Jabavu on the issue of an organisation to represent black rights. With AK Soga as editor, *Izwi* was considered far more radical than *Imvo* demonstrating a socialist approach towards capitalism and urging black readers to improve their lot. *Ilanga Lase Natal* (The Natal Sun) was the first important newspaper to emerge for Zulu readers; started in 1903 by John Dube. In 1912 Dube was elected the first chairman of the South African Native National Congress (SANCC), which later was to become the African National Congress (ANC) in 1923.

Abantu-Batho

Pioneering black journalists were involved in the beginnings of the SANCC with the exception of John Tengo Jabavu who was considered too radical at the time, focussing in his writing on the growing threat of Afrikaner nationalism and the need for equal rights and public education. One of the first activities of the newly formed organisation was the establishment of a newspaper to serve as a mouthpiece, *Abantu-Batho* (The People) (Johnson 1991:19). Other publications from this period were also associated with the establishment of political movements. For example, Mahatma Ghandi, a lawyer in South Africa before he led India's fight for independence from Britain, launched the paper *Indian Opinion* in 1903 as an immensely popular weekly in Durban (Hachten & Giffard 1984:146).

From 1930 to 1980: *The white-owned period*

Bantu World

The World

Despite their important contribution to political awareness, most black newspapers lacked capital, equipment, skilled workers and a reliable distribution network. Bertram Paver, an ex-farmer and itinerant salesman saw potential profits to be made from the aspiring black market (Johnson 1991:21). The Bantu Press Ltd was formed and inaugurated a national newspaper *Bantu World* in April 1932. The establishment of *Bantu World* is important as it represents a move from a local to a national black press in addition to redefining the role and strategy of the press. *Bantu World* was modelled as a tabloid on the British *Daily Mirror*. While Paver tried to avoid the image of white control over a black staff, a new controlling factor began to emerge: economics (Johnson 1991:21). Fourteen months later the Bantu Press was taken over by the Argus Company, which continued to control the company until 1952, quickly becoming the

first media monopoly with publications throughout southern Africa: ten weekly newspapers, in addition to handling advertising for twelve different publications in eleven languages (Hachten & Giffard 1984:147). By 1962, *The World* had become a daily. From then until its banning on 19 October 1977, it was a significant voice in journalism. Shortly after the Soweto uprising against deliberately poor education in June 1976, Percy Qoboza was appointed as the first black editor without white supervision.

The next important development came in May 1951 when Jim Bailey, the son of mining magnate Abe Bailey, started the *African Drum*, followed in March 1955 by the *Golden City Post*. With these titles, Bailey started a new trend in journalism, using a formula of sport, sex and crime to establish a popular press which appealed to the broad mass of literate black South Africans. In October 1951, the *African Drum* was shortened to *Drum* and moved from Cape Town to Johannesburg, under the editorship of Anthony Sampson and Tom Hopkinson, who brought Fleet Street experience from Britain to the publication. Roelfose (1996:83–84) identifies a number of significant contributions made by *Drum*:

- it became the forerunner of the alternative press active during the final years of apartheid, in that it fearlessly conducted investigative journalism and addressed the social and political grievance of black South Africans;
- it focused world attention on South Africa by exposing abuses such as exploitation of blacks on many white farms, the appalling prison conditions and the Sharpeville massacre of 1960;
- it restored pride in the black population by focusing on sociocultural issues;
- it highlighted the contributions made by world-class black musicians and writers to South African culture;
- it developed modern and colourful English for black urbanites.

In addition to providing a lasting impact on black journalism, by 1969 *Drum* had a weekly circulation of 470 000, larger than most of South African periodicals (Hachten & Giffard 1984:149). Although *Drum* was never banned, unlike many of its journalists, the periodical was withdrawn in 1965. It reappeared later in a milder form, without the aggressive reporting of political issues that had earlier been so meaningful to urban blacks (Hachten & Giffard 1984:149).

> *Drum*

1980–1996: The multiracial period

With urbanisation, many of the so-called white newspapers found, as the 1960s moved into the 1970s, that they gained a substantial black readership with the introduction of regular township editions. Black journalists who were originally hired for the township editions or as stringers (freelance newspaper correspondents) now began to move into more regular positions on the major newspapers. Papers such as the *Rand Daily Mail* took the lead in integrating more news about the townships into all parts of the paper. When the *Rand Daily Mail* closed in 1985, almost 80 percent of its readers were black (Roelofse 1996:84).

Another victim of the political turmoil of the apartheid years was the *Post*, which closed at the end of the 1970s because its registration had lapsed following industrial action and the government's unwillingness to agree to re-registration. This ironically led to the birth of South Africa's largest daily newspaper for some time, the *Sowetan* (Roelofse 1996:84–85). The Argus group produced a knock-and-drop (local newspaper delivered free to suburban homes) newssheet known as the *Sowetan Mirror*, which was distributed in the townships. This newssheet absorbed some of the thirty journalists who lost their jobs due to the closure of the *Post*. On 2 February 1981, the tabloid was transformed into a daily tabloid to fill the void left by the *Post*, edited by Joe Latekgomo, former deputy-editor of the *Post* (Hachten & Giffard 1984:152). The *Sowetan* was sold by the Argus group to the black business group New Africa Investments Limited (NAIL) in 1994 thus initiating the start of black economic empowerment.

1.3.4 The alternative press

An alternative press usually becomes active when the political, economic, social or cultural views of certain social groups are excluded from the popular media market. Although the alternative press particularly came to the fore in the late 1970s after two Argus newspapers, *World* and *Post*, were closed by the government, the alternative press in South Africa has a much longer history. The emergence and development of the alternative press tends to parallel the struggle against apartheid. Louw (1989:26–27) and Johnson (1991:24) identify three distinct phases in the historical development of the South African alternative press. These periods are:

- From the 1930s to the 1960s
- From the 1960s to the late 1970s
- From the 1980s to the mid 1990s

A History of the South African Media

From the 1930s to the 1960s: A period of opposition and resistance

This first phase was a complex period in the development of resistance, where alternative publications reflected on the development of political movements against a background of ongoing internal conflict and political apathy. During the 1930s white control of the press targeting the black market was consolidated while the ANC entered a period of inertia following the adoption of a policy to shun militancy. The result was a dwindling of black-owned newspapers, such as *Inkundla*, to represent an independent liberal voice. Despite being viewed as a radical left publication by the authorities of the time, *Inkundla* was actually moderate in its views, providing a mix of politics, sport, the arts and general-interest features. However, the paper did openly support the ANC and played a key role in the election of Albert Luthuli as the President of the ANC. *Inkundla* closed in 1951 and is considered as a transition journal because it was independent, relatively liberal, but with a wide and sympathetic coverage of the ANC.

> *Inkundla*

Other publications from this period include *Fighting Talk* (1942–1963) which campaigned for soldiers' rights and warned of the advances of Nazism. *The Guardian* began publication in 1937, became the *New Age* in 1954, which in turn became *Spark* in 1962, closing in 1963, and promoted the cause of the ANC. This publication is a good example of a radical newspaper (Johnson 1991:27). In turn, *The African Lodestar* (1949) promoted the multiracial Communist-oriented Youth League within the African National Congress, that eventually split, with some members leaving to form the Pan Africanist Congress (PAC) in 1959.

From the 1960s to the late 1970s: A period of rising black consciousness

The alternative press emerged again in the late 1960s as part of an expression of rising black consciousness, taking the form of massive labour strikes such as in 1973 which were part of the opposition to white domination. Reaction from the state came in the form of repressive tolerance where leaders were allowed to release tensions as long as it was restricted to rhetoric (Johnson 1991:28). The rise of black consciousness, both as an ideology and strategy, prompted the re-emergence of independent non-commercial alternative publications, such as the *SASO Newsletter* of the South African Students Organisation

> Steve Biko

(SASO), which was founded in Durban during 1970, and was crucial in spreading black consciousness ideology. The *Newsletter* was aggressive, bringing racial issues to the foreground of the black political agenda and set the trend for similar publications such as *Black Review*, which started in 1972 and *Black Viewpoint*, which was edited by Steve Biko, a SASO founder and black consciousness author who was to die after being brutally assaulted by police.

It is ironic that the very success of the rising black consciousness was its own undoing. As the uprising spread across the country, it brought mass participation (Louw 1989:27). According to Louw (1989:27), this phase was primarily characterised by a top-down approach to resistance, where intellectuals became leaders and the alternative press started to play a significant role in the mobilisation of black people. The passive attitude of the government changed dramatically, leading to the banning of organisations, publications and leadership, which created another vacuum.

From the 1980s to the mid 1990s: The climax of the alternative press

The re-emergence of the alternative press during the 1980s was related to the emergence of the Mass Democratic Movement (MDM) and the United Democratic Front (UDF) in 1983, while the ANC was still banned or in exile. Unlike the second phase, this phase was marked by a bottom-up style of resistance to apartheid where the alternative press was to play an important part in this resistance. The Nationalist government, however, viewed the alternative press as part of the total onslaught concept and blamed outside influences for corrupting the people (Hachten & Giffard 1984:3). Louw and Tomaselli (1991:7–13) distinguish between three categories of alternative press.

The progressive-alternative press

This category is also known as the people's media as it expressed the struggle at community level as part of the great national struggle. Community issues were central to the purpose of the alternative press, which formed part of the process of popular resistance. Examples of publications here are *Grassroots*, *Saamstaan* (Stand together) and *Al Qalaam*, which publishes to this day.

A History of the South African Media

The left-commercial press

As resistance grew, it was still generally ignored by the conventional press, which preferred to report on the activities of the so-called leaders installed by the government to "run" the black homelands, none of which were recognised internationally as functioning states. To accommodate this deficiency, a left-commercial press emerged after 1983 as a hybrid development of the capitalist and progressive-alternative presses. Coverage focused on national news and finance was gathered through the sale of advertising space but with a heavy reliance on assistance from sympathetic donors and from journalists who were prepared for work for very little. Titles included the *New Nation,* formed in Johannesburg in 1986, *South* in Cape Town and *New Africa* in Durban, both during 1988. Not even the states of emergency could prevent their development, simply because the emergency had become a way of life where activists exploited legal loopholes (Louw & Tomaselli 1991:9–10). When leaders were detained, new ones simply took their place.

| New Nation |
| South |

In many respects, according to Louw and Tomaselli (1991:10), the experiences of the left-commercial press is similar to that of the Afrikaans press which mobilised Afrikaner nationalism during the 1930s. At one stage *New Nation* and *South* were banned for periods of between one and three months. Circulation figures were not very high, averaging about 20 000 per issue, although *New Nation* did have a readership of 67 000 but the newspapers were influential beyond their size.

The independent social-democrat press

The aims of the social-democrat press were financial independence and support of broad democratic ideals while maintaining their independence from any specific political movement. The ideal of accuracy in reporting was also important. Whereas most publications grew out of the various resistance groups, the *Weekly Mail* grew out of the closure of the *Rand Daily Mail* in 1985. Former *Rand Daily Mail* journalists found themselves stigmatised and unable to find gainful employment. The solution was to start a newspaper of their own and in this way the *Weekly Mail* under Anton Harber and Irwin Manoim pioneered a commercially viable leftist-press (Louw & Tomaselli 1991:12–13).

| Weekly Mail |

The *Vrye Weekblad*, under the editorship of Max du Preez, appeared on 4 November 1988 and was the only left-wing Afrikaans alternative newspaper and soon became known as a newspaper that did not hesitate

| Vrye Weekblad |

to criticise the shortcomings of the government of the day, despite the restrictions on the press, sometimes with dire consequences. For example, in 1992 *Vrye Weekblad* had 37 criminal charges, eight libel suits and five urgent court interdicts against it (Faure 1995:127).

Mail & Guardian

Following widely-based reforms announced in February 1990, the position of the alternative press, which had often carried exclusive news of the struggle, gradually deteriorated. The mainstream press now started to cover news of the recently unbanned political parties and trade unions. The alternative press therefore lost their exclusivity. Another setback came in the withdrawal of overseas funding following the dismantling of apartheid. This made it even more difficult for alternative newspapers to survive, since their working class readers are, on the whole, poor and there is little incentive to attract advertisers. Clearly some adjustments had to be made. The *Weekly Mail* merged with Britain's *The Guardian* from 3 April 1992 to become the *Mail & Guardian*. The *Vrye Weekblad* changed in May 1992 from a weekly newspaper to a fortnightly glossy news magazine with the emphasis on providing background and depth with little success, and finally closed down on 2 February 1994 (Diederichs 1993:86).

1.3.5 The press during the apartheid years

Relationship with the government

Whereas in most countries, the press is usually categorised according to various political affiliations, the South African press, from its very beginnings in the Cape Colony, has been organised in terms of race and language. Thus we find the English press, the Afrikaans press, the black press in both English and indigenous languages, the Indian press and so on. Roelofse (1996:85) writes:

> "while race has since the beginning of our press history been one of the defining characteristics of the South African press, race and racism reached its zenith in the period 1948 to 1990 – the apartheid era."

On coming to power in 1948, the Nationalist government immediately implemented various policies that strengthened the position of the Afrikaaner, most of who lived in the urban areas and who were desperately poor. The government also made moves to neutralise the rising aspirations of black South Africans, who were perceived as a

serious threat. This was achieved through a form of social engineering that became known worldwide as apartheid. When the National Party came to power, a broader and fundamentally political classification of the South African press became established. Newspapers were either pro-government or in opposition. Within this scenario, any efforts at editorial independence were bound to fail, as the government labelled newspapers as either supportive or oppositional.

Given the close bond between the Afrikaans press and politics established during the first half of the twentieth century it is not surprising that under apartheid the Afrikaans press found itself in a unique and privileged position. Not only did journalists from the Afrikaans newspapers find themselves at Nationalist Party meetings, but they were also given special treatment at Party congresses as civil servants responsible for the distribution of information. In the end, this proved to be self-defeating, as Roelofse (1996:87) writes:

> *"Their close links, however, worked against good journalism in that they did not expose or investigate graft or corruption, even when they knew something about it. They became victims of self-censorship in exchange for favours from prominent people in government."*

A crucial aspect in the successful control of South African society lay in the use of propaganda so that any attack on government policies was considered unpatriotic or even treasonable. World-wide condemnation of apartheid resulted in the fact that South Africa remained high on international news agendas for a sustained period of time, with negative consequences. This resulted in efforts by the government to control the flow of information in order to sustain the apartheid system (see the discussion in the next section). By the mid-1970s the National Party felt it had become necessary to counter the negative information regarding South Africa that was being distributed worldwide. At the same time, it was felt that something had to be done about the unpatriotic and rebellious English press. Gradually, there emerged a strategy for controlling the press, based on propaganda and political action such as Roelofse (1996:87–88) delineates:

- declaring a commitment to press freedom in parliamentary debates;
- accusing the press of being disloyal towards South Africa and of being in collusion with South Africa's enemies, usually the communists;
- threatening the press with legal action unless the press sorted itself out;

Media Studies: Volume 1

- appointing commissions of inquiry, usually pro-government, to investigate the press;
- discussing possible regulatory legislation with press owners;
- encouraging the press to draw up codes of conduct and to set up control bodies.

Through this strategy, the government could lay claim to placing a high premium on press freedom while at the same time getting the press to regulate itself through the application of self-censorship. This resulted in a great deal of uncertainty in newspapers as to what could be printed and what could not. In the end, newspapers decided to play it safe and ignored news that would provoke the ire of the government. As a result, news in the mainstream press regarding rising black aspirations went unreported

Figure 1.6 There were many attempts during the 1970s to bring the English press into line with government thinking (*Cape Times*, 14 November 1980)

The Citizen

The information scandal

During 1978 and 1979 the apartheid government was rocked by a major scandal when the press revealed that the Department of Information had engaged in a clandestine propaganda exercise to "sell apartheid to the world" (Hachten & Giffard 1984:230). Using millions of rands of taxpayers' money illegally, the Department had, without approval of the government, begun a campaign to influence public opinion on a global scale. To this end, the Department had: established a pro-government English morning tabloid aptly titled *The Citizen*; subsidised a news magazine *To the Point*; tried to buy out the South African Associated Newspapers (SAAN) media

A History of the South African Media

group, the *Washington Star* newspaper in the US and; had a fifty percent stake in United Press International Television News (UPITN) in an effort to manipulate the flow of news on South Africa.

The scandal was quickly dubbed Muldergate by the press, as Dr CP Mulder, then tipped as the next Prime Minister, was the minister responsible for the Department of Information. The event saw the end of his political career as well as that of John Vorster who was obliged to retire as Prime Minister (Roelfose 1996:90). The scandal led to the introduction of legislation which required newspapers to seek permission from the Advocate General before they could expose corruption in state administration. In this way the government tried to muzzle the press but the move drew such a sharp reaction that the legislation was amended. The Information Scandal is important in that it marked a turning point in the cosy relationship between the Afrikaans press and the apartheid government. Roelofse (1996:60) writes:

| Muldergate

> "It destroyed the blind faith of a significant number of Afrikaners traditionally loyal to the cause of the National Party, the so-called *verligtes* (a person who is considered enlightened, broad-minded, receptive to new ideas and change)."

The event also split the Afrikaans press, with the Cape-based Nasionale Pers condemning the government openly, while Perskor attempted to protect the National Party leadership.

> "In fact", writes Roelofse (1996:91), "on the very morning of the day Dr Connie Mulder's involvement in the affair was admitted, Die Transvaler carried a front page lead denying his involvement. Beeld and Die Burger did not make the same mistake."

Following the scandal, the Afrikaans press began to express misgivings about the government and apartheid with an increasing frequency, producing cracks in the apartheid system that ultimately led to self-destruction.

The Steyn Commission of Inquiry

With criticism against apartheid policies on the increase following the Information Scandal, the government felt some response was needed, particularly given the importance of the media, especially the press, in supporting apartheid. With press–government relations at a low ebb, the

| Steyn Commission

Steyn Commission of Inquiry into the media was appointed in June 1980 as a further attempt to control the flow of news and information. This was seen by the government as a legitimate way of dealing with a troublesome and disloyal press. The brief of the Commission was to:

> *"inquire into and report on the question of whether the conduct of, and the handling of, matters by the mass media meet the needs and interests of the South African community and the demands of the times, and, if not, how they can be improved" (Hachten & Giffard 1984:77).*

This mandate of the Commission was later expanded to propose legislation to implement its recommendations. The Commission was led by a senior judge, Marthinus Steyn, and produced an extensive report of nearly 1 400 pages on 1 February 1982. It was without surprise that the Commission found many shortcomings in the media (Jackson 1993:23). The following were some of the recommendations (Hachten & Giffard, 1984:83–84):

- professionalisation of the media by registering journalists. Any journalist convicted of subversive activity would automatically be disqualified – a move which would have silenced most black journalists;
- establishing a press council to set norms and standards for objectivity and fairness, particularly when reporting on matters relating to the peace, order and safety of the country, thus effectively prohibiting any reporting on the rising black consciousness;
- breaking up the major press groups, particularly that of Argus and SAAN, under the guise that these monopolies were a threat to press freedom.

From its very beginnings, the Commission was controversial. Journalists, even from the Afrikaans press, refused to be associated with the inquiry. It is not with surprise that the final report was met with indignation by both pro- and anti-government newspapers. The English press rejected the report, in which nearly two-thirds was devoted to a description of the political environment, including Soviet Union's global aspirations to see communism dominate the world and black consciousness as part of the onslaught against the country. The report was quickly shown up as being seriously flawed in its selective use of data, factual inaccuracies and plagiarism.

A History of the South African Media

Figure 1.7 The Steyn Commission was seen as an attempt to restrain the Press' attacks on apartheid policies (*Rand Daily Mail*, 16 April 1980)

Oddly, the government did little to implement the draconian recommendations, despite the fact that the proposals supported the government point of view. Hachten and Giffard (1984:85) speculate that intervention by the conservative Ronald Reagan administration in the United States of America persuaded the government to rethink the Commission's recommendations. A second factor that persuaded the government to think otherwise was the fact that, as with the Information Scandal a few years earlier, the English and Afrikaans press stood together in their condemnation of the report. However, legislation was introduced in June 1982 establishing a new media council that forced all newspapers to join the Newspaper Press Union. A key aspect of the new legislation required all newspapers to be subject to the media council of the National Press Union in the event that government determined that disciplinary measures were necessary, or have their registration cancelled. This move was seen as an attempt to bring right-wing newspapers, such as *Die Afrikaner* and *Die Patriot*, under some sort of control (Hachten & Giffard 1984:85).

media council

Pressures on the press

Over the last quarter of the twentieth century, the South African press probably underwent greater challenges and changes than during any other period in the history of the media in South Africa. Jackson (1993:6–10) sums up the sources of pressure on the press, both political and economic, during the period from 1976 to 1990, which are discussed in the following section.

Media Studies: Volume 1

Pressure from the government

State of Emergency

The most specific challenge was the declaration of the State of Emergency by the government on 21 July 1985. However, it was the second State of Emergency that followed on 12 June 1986 that was the most restrictive on the press. Effectively, it placed large areas of the country off-limits to the press. The purpose was to control what the government saw as incorrect or distorted images from being disseminated abroad. In reality it controlled the flow of accurate information to the South African public. Special powers were granted to the ministers of law and order and home affairs to close any newspaper they wished, either temporarily or permanently. The State of Emergency was only lifted on 2 February 1990 by President FW de Klerk.

Figure 1.8 Following government restrictions on the press, there was a great deal of uncertainty regarding what could or could not be published (*The Star*, 22 December 1986)

"Tell me, does Pretoria have to clear this before we can publish it?"

Pressure from television

M-Net

advertising

Beginning in January 1978 the SABC started to accept advertising on television and this move had a major impact on the finances of the press, highly dependent on the income from the sale of advertising space. Advertisers turned to the newer medium of television with the result that newspapers' share of total adspend dropped dramatically from 46.1 percent in 1975 to 26.6 percent in 1987. Television on the other hand accounted for 30 percent, to which radio added another 11.6 percent (Jackson 1993:7). To counter the effect of loss of advertising revenue to television, the four major newspaper groups joined forces and launched a television service of their own on 1 October 1986 on a subscription basis known as Electronic Media Network, or simply M-Net for short.

A History of the South African Media

Pressure from the economic downturn

Compounding the loss of advertising revenue to television, the economic downturn of the mid-1980s led to further cuts in advertising spending. In addition to a spiralling inflation problem, sales tax was introduced in the country for the first time. The result was a 26 percent drop in income from advertising.

While the number of literate black South Africans was on the increase, the proportion of white readers continued to drop, with the result that by the end of the 1980s the majority of readers of papers like *The Star* and the *Rand Daily Mail*, were black. Despite the large circulation figures, this aspect had disastrous effects on financial results because the *Rand Daily Mail*'s readership profile could not attract potential advertisers. The low income levels of blacks at that time made them less attractive than the high income represented by whites.

Rand Daily Mail

Pressure from the alternative press

The rise of the Mass Democratic Movement (MDM) in the 1980s saw a coalescing of many anti-government organisations with an associated increase in the politicisation of many South Africans who were a growing market for news and information. Apart from the fact that the major newspapers were unable to provide coverage of events and information relevant to this market, these potential readers viewed the major newspapers with suspicion as being too close to the government and too concerned about making profits and maintaining white readership to be concerned with labour and life in the townships. This led to the rise of an alternative press.

alternative press

While posing little threat to the dwindling advertising revenue, the alternative press emphasised the fact that the major newspapers were out of touch with reality in South Africa. A more significant threat imposed by the rising alternative press was the challenge it presented to the English press that had traditionally seen itself as the voice of the opposition in the country. More and more, the alternative press took over the function as critic of the government.

Pressure from the public

By the end of the 1980s there was a growing apathy in the reading public towards a constant diet of negative news. There was a feeling among some

Media Studies: Volume 1

readers that the press was making a bigger issue out of unrest situations of the times than necessary. In addition, the ceaseless attacks by the government on the English press had resulted in a form of disdain on the part of the public regarding the values of a free press. Simply put, the press had become stigmatised with a negative image as the bearers of bad news created from living in a society obsessed with secrecy and intolerance.

1.3.6 Key developments in the press since democratisation

The rise of tabloid journalism

<small>tabloids</small>

Following on the global trends, the South African market has seen the arrival of not only tabloid-sized newspapers but also a particular standard of journalism referred to as tabloid journalism. Tabloids first appeared in the market place during 2003 and have shown phenomenal success with titles such as *The Sun*, its Afrikaans counterpart, *Die Son* and the *Daily Voice*. These titles target low-income earners who previously have never read a newspaper (Bonorchis 2005:3). Tabloids have stirred a debate regarding the quality of journalism, in that they focus largely on sensationalism, sex, bizarre and gory stories and they lack coverage of politics and serious issues like HIV/AIDS. The counter-argument is that they do also carry some stories that are useful, such as features on life skills and managing one's finances and that their stories still to a large extent reflect the reality of many South Africans (Hoeane 2005:8). However the Media Monitoring Project (Addressing the state of the media 2007) remains sceptical, expressing concern over the tabloid's use of shocking visuals, inflammatory headlines, blatant sexism and xenophobia where ethical journalist practices are sidelined resulting in lower-quality news and an equally low regard for human rights.

Over-saturation of the market

<small>market forces</small>

The first five years of the 21st century saw a rise in the number of new newspaper titles and an increase in the niche marketing. Johannesburg now has more daily titles than the city of New York (Harber 2003:31). However, it has quickly become evident that the market is unable to sustain the increasing number of dailies. The role of politics, as a controlling force, has been exchanged for that of economics and the market place. A classic example is that of the *Sowetan*, which rose to become the top seller during the 1990s, but has now lost aspiring readers to *The Star* while new readers flock to the tabloid *Daily Sun* (Sowaga 2003:4).

A History of the South African Media

A corollary to the increased number of titles is the scarcity of journalist skills and trained professionals. As an example, during late 2003, no less than five newspapers were without editors, largely a result of affirmative action where editors hop between titles (Harber 2003:31).

> affirmative action

Two titles which failed during this period were that of *Nova* and *ThisDay*. In the case of *Nova*, which lasted less than five months, distribution, circulation and time constraints were to blame (Taunyane 2006:7). The newspaper was aimed at high income earners in the 20 to 40 age group, who lived in township developments across Gauteng and who were considered to be under-served by the market. Delivery of the paper proved to be the major problem; it proved impossible to penetrate the security devices and physically deliver the newspaper.

In the case of the Nigeria-owned *ThisDay* it simply ran out of money. Initially hailed as a paper of quality with insight and diverse analyses not carried by any other title, the paper underestimated its circulation by fifty percent and failed to attract advertisers. After a year of being in print, *ThisDay* suspended operations owing over R20-million.

Rise of regional newspapers in the vernacular

Despite the comments made above, three newspapers in KwaZulu-Natal are on offer in isiZulu, simply because they each follow differing strategies. The daily *Isolezwe*, which started publication in 2002, has reached daily sales of 97 370 copies (Taunyane 2006:4). The paper is aimed at young, broad-minded readers. The bi-weekly *Ilanga*, however, is more family orientated. Started in 1876, *Ilanga* is not only one of the oldest newspapers in South Africa but also one of the biggest sellers at over 100 000 copies (Taunyane 2006:4). A unique area of growth within the newspaper has been that of the classified section. This points a change in readers' spending patterns. Also with a lengthy history of more than 60 years is the weekly *UmAfrika*, which has now become more niche orientated, focusing on issues and in-depth features for the more sophisticated reader. *UmAfrika* can be placed in the same category as the *Mail & Guardian* in terms of its profile. Despite a healthy readership, these titles cannot draw advertisers. This is attributed to the fact that most advertisers simply do not understand the market. But this is beginning to turn around with the biggest advertisers being the major supermarket chains, the local government and MTN (Taunyane 2006:4). The success of these three newspapers in isiZulu begs the questions: why are there

no mainstream newspapers in the other South African languages such as isiXhosa and seSotho? (Bloom: 2007).

1.4 SUMMARY AND CONCLUSION

The main reason why we need to examine the history of broadcasting and the press in South Africa lies in the need to provide a context for understanding the status quo. The development of the media is a complex process which is dependent on numerous internal and external factors over an extensive period of time. But in order to understand the past as more than a series of random events we need to explain that past in terms of a particular theory. In so doing we can also challenge dominant views regarding the media by looking at power, subordination and ideology as central issues.

To try and find a deeper meaning within the events of the past, we can make use of a simplified adaptation of Stöber's (2004) theory of media evolution. Basically, Stöber (2004:483) considers the media as not only a product of technical innovation but also that of social institutionalisation. Stöber (2004:495) describes institutionalisation as the interaction between four sub-systems (technology, law and politics, culture and economy) which bring about change to the media derived from dissatisfaction with the status quo. Stöber's theory consists of three stages:

- Invention stage, where there is a fundamental change in the media, usually considered as an improvement for an original purpose.
- Innovation stage, which is initiated when a framework is established, within old laws, to legitimate the changes. Society is introduced to the new scenario through changes in media content. As soon as the new media dispensation is accepted, debates on new laws and policy begin. This stage is brought to an end with the establishment of new functions and economic models and legal regulation.
- Diffusion stage, which is the period of acceptance, or tolerance, of the new scenario.

The beginning and end of each stage cannot be identified with any precision as there is usually a gradual merging between the stages. Similarly, some stages proceed quickly; others are slow, while it is also possible for the process to stall altogether. Within the history of broadcasting in South Africa we can, so far, identify five distinct cycles. Dates are approximate.

A History of the South African Media

- Cycle 1: 1919–1927, where we have amateur and experimental broadcasts in the invention stage, followed by regular broadcasts and the formation of the ABC.
- Cycle 2: 1927–1936, where there was a need to resolve the financial instability of the initial radio stations through the formation of the African Broadcasting Corporation. Power is located within a single individual, IW Schlesinger, who also owned African Consolidated Theatres and African Consolidated Film and held a monopoly on film distribution throughout the country.
- Cycle 3: 1936–1948, which saw a fundamental change in order to resolve yet another financial crisis, while the government expressed concern over the cultural importance of radio. This led to the creation of the South African Broadcasting Corporation. Power is now located in the English-dominated United Party who held power in the government and who introduced stringent regulation of broadcasting.
- Cycle 4: 1948–1994, the longest cycle thus far. Cycle 4 was initiated by two factors: another financial crisis in broadcasting and a change in government where the Afrikaans-dominated Nationalist Party took over the reigns and initiated the policy of apartheid to promote Afrikaner culture. The innovation stage of this cycle was brought to an end with the passing of the Broadcasting Act of 1952, to be followed by a lengthy period of diffusion during which the process of development stalls.
- Cycle 5: 1994–today, where the invention stage was marked by the democratisation of the country which introduced a need for the diversification of broadcasting. The innovation stage began during 1996 with the establishment of the IBA and the Triple Inquiry Report which tried to establish a new policy for broadcasting. This second stage is still in process during which we have already seen, *inter alia*, the introduction of a new economic model known as the three-tier structure of broadcasting. We have also seen the introduction of several acts of parliament in an attempt to establish a meaningful regulation of the broadcasting environment.

In the case of the press, it is not as easy to identify distinct cycles as with broadcasting, simply because the press has not been subject to the same rigorous controls as broadcasting. Nevertheless the press is currently paralleling the development of broadcasting, also brought about by the fundamental change that came with democratisation. We can say that the press is also currently in a stage of innovation as we can see new economic models in the form of Black Economic Empowerment through the

growth of such companies as Primedia, Siswe Media and Kagiso Media. Within the Afrikaans press we see the emergence of a new function in the promotion of Afrikaans as a distinct culture. How long this innovation stage will last is difficult to predict. For example, the matter of Black Economic Empowerment still remains an unresolved issue. What we can say is that the current cycle of media development can be considered the most complex of all the cycles in the history of the South African media.

Can we use past history to predict the future? Stöber (2004:485) says no; future developments are always clouded. The process remains obscure as we do not know which of the four sub-systems will become the driving force for change. But on the value of analysing the history of the media Stöber (2004:485) adds that

> "Only when we look back do the historical developments seem to have been rational and straight-forward."

However, the current cycle will one day run its course, to be replaced by a new set of challenges requiring new inventions and innovations. How long the current cycle will be and what the next cycle will consist of is to become the history of the future.

LEARNING ACTIVITIES

- You have been appointed to teach a media studies class at a local community college. As part of the curriculum you are required to teach media history. However, you find that your students are staying away from your classes because they feel there is no value in studying the past. How would you motivate them regarding the value of history to our understanding of the current media environment?
- You are part of a team involved in running a stand promoting South Africa at an Expo in a city in the United States. Many of the visitors to the stand question you about the lack of diversity in South African broadcasting and press. It appears that their understanding of the South African media environment is based on dated propaganda from decades ago. How would you explain attempts by the media to accommodate the diverse number of cultures and languages that can be found in South Africa?
- As part of the same team mentioned in the activity above, and because of your knowledge of South African broadcasting and the press, you are asked to design a time-line comparing the development of the press with

A History of the South African Media

that of broadcasting and film in South Africa which can then be enlarged and displayed on the stand.
- You have been nominated as a candidate for the position of a councillor to serve on the (fictitious) South African Media Regulatory Council. You are required to appear before a panel of judges at a public hearing where your suitability for the position is to be evaluated. As part of the hearing you are expected to air your views on the relationship of the state with the media. Before you can do this, you need to establish the nature of the relationship of the present government with the media and how this has changed, if at all, from previous governments. In formulating your position on the matter, you need to take into account the influence and effect of the state on the development of the media in South Africa. Prepare notes that you can use at your public hearing.
- You have been appointed to host a group of Russian journalists visiting South Africa for the first time. As Russia experienced the collapse of Communism at about the same time as the democratisation of South Africa, these journalists have expressed a keen interest in how the broadcasting and press environment has changed as a result of political events in the country. Prepare a brief that you can hand to these visiting journalists in which you highlight important developments over the past decade and then conclude with a description of the current media environment in South Africa.
- As part of an investment team, and because of your detailed knowledge of South African media, you have been asked to address your colleagues in a seminar concerning the problems and issues regarding the status quo in broadcasting in South African, so that potentially awkward questions from foreign investors can be given meaningful answers.
- You are visiting a prominent university overseas as part of a cultural exchange programme. During a seminar, the topic of government repression of the Press during the 1980s comes up. It quickly becomes obvious to you that the audience has a limited and generalised view of events, in that they see it as an isolated incident within the broader context of the media history of South Africa. You feel strongly that the record needs to be set straight. Without being partisan, respond to the discussion by placing events of the 1980s within a deeper historical context by elaborating on the often-fraught relationship between the South African press and the government on one hand, and differences between the various press groups on the other, that can be traced back to the colonisation of the Cape and continue into the current day.

FURTHER READING

Relating to broadcasting

Louw, P.E. 1993. *South African media policy: debates of the 1990s.* Bellville: Anthropos.

Rosenthal, E. 1974. *You have been listening ... The early days of history of radio in South Africa.* Cape Town: Purnell.

Tomaselli, R., Tomaselli, K & Muller, J. 1989. *Currents of power: state broadcasting in South Africa.* Bellville: Anthropos.

Van der Merwe, C. 1995. *Electronic media management.* Johannesburg: Africa Growth Network.

Relating to the press

Hachten, W.A. & Giffard, C.A. 1984. *Total onslaught: the South African press under attack.* Johannesburg: Macmillan.

Mervis, J. 1989. *The fourth estate.* Johannesburg: Jonathan Ball.

Tyson, H. 1993. *Editors under fire.* Sandton: Random House.

Manoim, I. 1996. *You have been warned: the first ten years of the Mail and Guardian.* London: Viking.

Tomaselli, K., Tomaselli, R. & Muller J. 1987. *Narrating the crisis: hegemony and the South African press.* Johannesburg: Richard Lyon.

Tomaselli, K. & Louw, P.E. (eds). 1991. *The alternative press in South Africa.* Bellville: Anthropos.

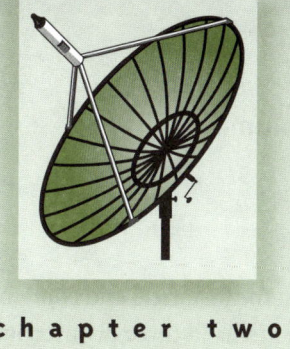

chapter two

The Media in Africa

Fackson Banda

LEARNING OUTCOMES

By the end of this chapter, you should be able to:
- pinpoint historical epochs characteristic of the media in Africa;
- interpret these historical epoch's implications for the present status of the media in Africa;
- analyse the impact of globalisation on the media in Africa.

Media Studies: Volume 1

THIS CHAPTER

THIS CHAPTER IS about the historical and contemporary development of the media in Africa. It places the media in three distinct but overlapping time periods. These are the colonial, post-colonial and globalisation epochs. The most important topics dealt with in this chapter are:
- the historical contextualisation of the media in Africa;
- the impact of globalisation on African media.

2.1 INTRODUCTION

Historical research on the media in sub-Saharan Africa, a region covering some 48 countries south of the Sahara desert, is patchy. This is understandable. Africa is a huge continent with a chequered history of colonial, cultural and political experiences. This lack of historical information on the media may also be true of Western societies. Curran (2002) argues that although pioneer historians of the press laid the foundations of modern media research, media history has since become marginalised.

Media-historical research in Africa has been varied. It has ranged from focusing on specific national contexts, such as Zambia (Kasoma 1986), to focusing on sub-regional contexts, such as South Africa, Namibia and Zimbabwe (Mosia, Riddle & Zaffiro 1994). In both cases, the analyses have tended to stick to particular media; in the former, it revolves around the press; and in the latter, it is centred on radio. This echoes Curran's observation about the often narrow historical research undertaken "within each of these specialisms" (Curran 2002:3). Some recent national-contextual historical research, however, has tended to encompass more media types – broadcasting, the press and film (Wigston 2001), including, in recent years, Internet platforms (Lesame 2005; Spitulnik 2002).

To understand media-historical research in sub-Saharan Africa, it is probably useful to use Curran's classification of British historical accounts of the media into six rival narratives, namely:
- the liberal narrative;
- the feminist narrative;
- the populist narrative;
- the libertarian narrative;
- the anthropological narrative;
- the radical narrative.

The Media in Africa

In liberal history, the winning of media freedom empowered the people. In populist history, the people demanded and obtained the media entertainment they wanted. In feminist history, the media responded to the increased liberation of women. In libertarian and anthropological historical accounts, the media came to promote greater social tolerance and to represent the nation in a more socially inclusive way. The radical narrative tells of the creation of a reason-based "public sphere" with a restricted membership – followed by a descent into manipulation and control (Curran 2002: 3–34).

Some African media history can be interpreted in terms of the above narratives. For instance, while hailing the liberation of most of Africa in the 1950s and the 1960s as entailing greater "press freedom and nationalism" *(the libertarian and anthropological interpretation)* (Ainslie 1966:7; Barton 1979:3), several accounts portray the post-colonial media situation as signalling the disappearance of press freedom *(the radical interpretation)* (Ainslie 1966:19; Hachten 1971:36–50; Barton 1979:ix). Later historical analyses were to tackle the question of communitarian or popular communication, with emphasis on community radio broadcasting (Fardon & Furniss 2000), hence demonstrating the "populist" narrative of media history.

This chapter concentrates on print and electronic media: newspapers, radio and television. The reason for this is that it is these media of mass communication which have, in most countries in Africa, received more historical-research attention.

2.2 THE MEDIA IN AFRICA: THE COLONIAL PERIOD

The status of contemporary African media is implicated in the colonial past (Hyden & Okigbo 2002:30). Faringer (1991:3) argues that today's press in English-speaking Africa appears to have roots in four different kinds of early newspapers, namely:
- official government gazettes;
- the missionary press;
- privately owned newspapers;
- the underground political, anti-colonial news sheets.

Colonialism, post-colonialism, African nationalism defined

Colonialism

Colonialism is increasingly becoming a discursive term lending itself to reinterpretations. Firstly, colonialism goes beyond the simple process of creating colonies. It is more effectively appreciated as a continuing legacy manifested in the way "sovereign" political communities emerged at the end of the Second World War.

Secondly, while it is important to think of colonialism as part of the experience of creating real or physical colonies, the effects of colonisation have had much more profound legacies that do not go away even when a given colony has moved on to a different form. Colonialism does not just end "officially" because there can be no reversion to pre-colonial societies. What passes as the end of colonialism has often been recognised as sovereignty or the gaining of independence but the communities that result are already grossly distorted as a consequence of colonialism (Yew 2002). It is for this reason, then, that Fieldhouse (1981:6) defines colonialism as "the state of subjection – political, economic and intellectual – of a non-European society which was the product of imperialism."

Thirdly, colonialism tends to reappear as neo-colonialism (Yew 2002; Young 2001). Imagination, language, culture, and even the mind can still be colonised by the West. These are important assertions because they raise the issue of how far we can truly distance ourselves from the embrace of colonial discourse (Yew 2002).

Postcolonialism

The discourse of post-colonialism is championed by such nationalist scholars as Frantz Fanon from the French-speaking Caribbean island of Martinique, Amilcar Cabral of the Portuguese colonies of Guinea Bissau and the Cape Verde islands, and Ngugi wa Thiong'o in the then British-controlled Kenya (in Brydon 2000). Postcolonialism is a concept that marks the realities of nations and peoples emerging into a new imperialistic context of economic and sometimes political domination (Young 2001: 57). As a social-justice project, postcolonialism attacks the status quo of economic imperialism but also signals an activist engagement with positive political positions and new forms of political identity (Young 2001:58).

Young recognises what Kwame Nkrumah characterised as "neo-colonialism" in his native Ghana:

> "not only were export and import trade, banking, insurance, transportation, and communications essentially in expatriate (i.e. mainly British) hands, but the country's major source of foreign exchange, cocoa, was securely tied up in a maze of international financing, marketing and processing arrangement" (Young 2001:45).

The Media in Africa

Although the formerly colonised territories gradually had their political sovereignty returned to them, they nevertheless remained subject to the effective control of the major world powers, the same group as the former imperial powers, prompting the question: "Was there merely a change in form rather than substance?" (Young 2001: 45).

This accords with the argument that the current status of African media is, in many ways, a reflection of the colonial media system.

African nationalism

It can be argued that "African nationalism" depicts a specific historical moment of struggle by African peoples to assert a postcolonial identity based on their cultural and historical experiences. African nationalism represents a movement for self-determination in an increasing number of African countries, from Nnamdi Azikiwe's Nigeria to Nelson Mandela's South Africa. In the years after the Second World War, "African nationalism" became more pronounced (Wikipedia 2006), largely because it was appropriated by many black Africans as an affirmation of their human rights.

To a large extent, African nationalism was also fired by the ideology of nationhood, complete with all the trappings of an independent nation state, such as a constitution, a currency, a flag, an anthem, a national identity card, a national air carrier, an official language and membership of the United Nations. A state or public broadcaster and other such symbols of nationhood were to define much of the postcolonial state, although most of them had their antecedents in the colonial system.

2.2.1 The beginnings of the media in Africa

In Anglophone Africa, the development of the media was directly or indirectly linked to the colonial objectives of the British Empire. As Mytton (1983:37) observes:

| Sierra Leone, Ghana

> "Africa's modern print and electronic media developed as the direct or indirect result of contact with Europe. Few African societies had a written language, and in those that did, printing was either unknown or underdeveloped. Arab traders brought literacy to West and East Africa, but the technology of printing came from Europe and the United States."

As Wilcox (1975:1) writes, the genesis of African journalism lay in the dry official publications of colonial governments. The press in Africa began with the publications owned or operated by officials of the British government. For instance, it began in Sierra Leone in 1801 with the publication of the *Royal Gazette*. Twenty-one years later, Ghana (then the Gold Coast) followed with the publication of the *Royal Gold Coast Gazette*. Ali Mazrui (in Wilcox 1975:1) gives an apt anecdote:

> "It is not for nothing that the word for newspaper in Swahili is 'gazeti'...The Adam and Eve of newspapers in Africa were government gazettes."

Nigeria

British colonialism sometimes barely tolerated the development of the native media. In 1862, for example, the governor of Nigeria said press liberty was a "dangerous instrument in the hands of semi-civilized Negroes" (Wilcox 1975:4). Such attitudes continued into the twentieth century. For instance, the Seditious Offences Bill, introduced in Nigeria in 1909, sought to punish publications ostensibly designed to inflame an excitable and ignorant populace which had "only recently emerged from barbarism and are still actuated by the old traditions of their race" (in Wilcox 1975: 4).

Zambia

Nonetheless, there was marked enterprise shown by Africans living in the British African states (Barton 1979:60; Hachten 1966:5–6). For instance, between 1950 and 1960, the *Central African Mail* in Northern Rhodesia (now Zambia) employed two African editors, Titus Mukupo and later Kelvin Mlenga (Mytton 1983:47).

Sénégal, Mali

While British colonialism tolerated private media initiatives by native Africans, French colonialism was even more reluctant. The earliest African paper of any significance in French West Africa was a weekly which appeared in 1907 in Sénégal as the organ of the local branch of the French Socialist Party (Barton 1979:60). In Mali, the French operated the radio services almost entirely in French and aimed at the colonial population without much consideration for the interests and needs of the African population (in Wilcox 1975:3).

In Francophone Africa, cultural imprints remain visible on the post-colonial media systems. As Michel de Breteuil, whose father Charles founded modern newspapers in French-speaking West Africa, including *Le Soleil* (The Sun) in Dakar, Sénégal, sums it up:

> "British colonialism was concerned with capitalism: French colonialism was concerned with culture" (in Barton 1979:59).

Like their French counterparts, the Portuguese territories of Angola and Mozambique were under iron-fisted colonial control (Hachten 1966:5).

The Media in Africa

2.2.2 The functions of the media in colonial Africa

The purpose of this section is to analyse the functions that the media in colonial Africa may have played. Five such functions can be synthesised from historical accounts of African media:
- colonialist expansion;
- African nationalism;
- "Palliative treatment" for the natives;
- colonialist federalism;
- capitalist expansion;
- missionary activity.

Colonialist consolidation

James S. Coleman (in Wilcox 1975:3) asserts that:

> *"during the period of stabilized colonial rule, the key structure in the socialization process – schools, religious organizations, media of communication, and governmental institutions – were concerned in various ways with rationalizing, perpetuating, and fostering loyalty or conformity to the colonial regime."*

Colonialism used the mass media to inculcate and entrench the belief that colonialism was a modernising practice meant to "develop" the natives (Gecau 1996). The colonial press was part of the campaign to spread and consolidate the ideology of Empire (Gecau 1996:194).

African nationalism

Native resistance sometimes led to the development of media to counter the surge of colonial consolidation. What Hachten (1971:143) calls "an African press for Africans" and what Barton (1979:13) dubs "a black press for black men" emerged in Sierra Leone, Ghana and Nigeria to publicise grievances, criticise British colonialism and support the struggle for African nationalism. James S. Coleman (in Hachten 1971:143–144) observes that African-owned newspapers served as a platform for the nationalist ideas of educated Africans. Nationalist newspapers had been a considerable influence in the awakening of racial and political consciousness in "the first wave of democracy on the African continent" (Hyden & Okigbo 2002:31). This was certainly true of Nnamdi Azikiwe, who trained in Ghana before becoming the founding editor of The *West African Pilot* in Lagos in Nigeria around 1937 and Kwame Nkrumah's *Accra Evening*

| Sierra Leone, Ghana, Nigeria |

News in Ghana about a decade later (Hachten 1971:146; Barton 1979:24). Interestingly, both Nnamdi Azikiwe and Kwame Nkrumah were to become presidents of their respective countries, although Nkrumah went on to ensure one-party rule and virtually total state control of the media through organisations like the Ghana News Agency, established in 1957; in contrast Nigeria, although enduring several military dictatorships, had a diverse media environment.

Kitchen (1956:73–81) notes that the indigenous African press was probably most advanced in the British West African territories of Nigeria and Ghana (the former Gold Coast) for the following reasons:
- the small size of the European population in the two countries ruled out the development of a strong colonial press;
- newspapers enjoyed a large degree of freedom from government control;
- the existence of economic opportunities for Africans permitted the development of substantial local capital for indigenous enterprises;
- many educated Africans had turned to journalism because it was a profession which had not been monopolised by Europeans.

Missionary activity

Iwe Ihorin

In 1859, African missionaries at Abeokuta in Nigeria produced the *Iwe Ihorin* (The Paper with the News) in the Yoruba language, and later a bilingual edition in Yoruba and English (Ainslie 1966:22; Bourgault 1995:154). Missionary activity contributed to the emergence of colonial African media, and subsequently to the nationalist media system.

"Palliative treatment" for the natives

radio

But colonial media may have also served as a tool for "anaesthetising" the natives with entertainment and supposedly developmental issues. The "saucepan special" was introduced in Zambia and other British colonies around 1949. It was the first popular mass-produced radio set in Africa. An unidentified listener at the time of the introduction of the "saucepan special" thanked the Colonial Broadcasting Officer for the "wireless sets" so the natives could listen to programmes on:

> "(1) agriculture, (2) building villages at a suitable place, (3) digging and building wells and dams, (4) latrines in villages, (5) care of children, (6) education of girls, (7) how to improve livestock and (8) many other things" (Mytton 1983:28).

The Media in Africa

In many circumstances radio may have been a "palliative" to make native Africans forget the injustices of colonial repression and the pain of racial subjugation. A native music industry developed in some colonies, including the federation of Northern Rhodesia (now Zambia), Southern Rhodesia (now Zimbabwe) and Nyasaland (now Malawi), which developed in partnership with radio broadcasting. In some countries, the lyrics held clues to rebellion.

Colonialist federalism

Colonial era print media, within narrow limits, could be intensely political. During the post-world-war economic boom, much of the white settler community in Northern Rhodesia, Southern Rhodesia and Nyasaland campaigned for a federal colonial territory. Although this was done in opposition to British colonial policy, which was pushing for the countries to become independent, and in the name of economic synergies, the view of many African nationalists was that the federation was meant to entrench a kind of neo-colonialism (Mwanakatwe 1994). Some sections of what Kasoma (1986) calls the "white press" were instrumental in agitating for the "federation" of the three territories. Roy Welensky, white trade unionist, campaigner for settler interests and later Prime Minister of the Federation, set up the *Northern News* in 1944 in part to push for the federation. When the federation collapsed in 1963 with the advent of independence in two of the three territories, he moved to Rhodesia (now Zimbabwe) and unsuccessfully campaigned against the white settlers" Unilateral Declaration of Independence and subsequent break with Britain (Mytton 1983:49).

Northern News

But not all colonial era white media shared identical viewpoints. Other settler media were opposed to the idea of a federation of the three territories. For example, Alexander Scott's *Central African Post* highlighted the views of African nationalists diametrically opposed to the proposed federation. However, this was not a permanent campaign. In 1954, Scott was to amend his earlier editorial policy and started supporting the idea of a federation made up of what was then Northern Rhodesia, Southern Rhodesia and Nyasaland (Kasoma 1986:42–43).

Given the fact that the pro-federation *Northern News* continued to thrive, it is reasonable to conclude firstly that Scott was compelled to "appease" the more affluent white readership supportive of the idea of a federated territory by joining ranks with the *Northern News*. Secondly, it is conceivable that his newspaper would have had difficulty attracting the white establishment advertising revenue, given its pro-native journalism. Thirdly, his editorial shift could have been influenced by the fact that he was aware of moves by the pro-federation South African Argus Group to buy off his *Central African Post*. Indeed, they bought it off, only to close it down in 1957 (in Banda 2003:30).

Capitalist expansion in post-war Africa

Nigeria, Ghana, Sierra Leone

As Hachten (1971) observes, a major development of the 1940s was the entry of foreign newspaper capital into West African journalism. The London *Daily Mirror* group used its financial and technical resources to establish three West Coast dailies – the *Daily Times* in Nigeria, the *Daily Graphic* in Ghana, and the *Daily Mail* in Sierra Leone. The policy of these papers was vigorous neutrality among the competing parties: objective reporting of news by African reporters and editors; constructive criticism; high-volume production and territory-wide distribution, using air transport for remoter areas. The papers were staffed editorially by Africans and were never identified with the colonial office. According to Hachten (1971:147), such papers were instrumental in establishing a more professional basis for the press and linking literate Africans with their new nationalist leaders. It was on such papers that libertarians like Kelvin Mlenga in Northern Rhodesia were to serve, compelling him to remark some years later as editor of the *Zambian Mail*:

> "It is my view that a newspaper owned and run by the State for the purpose of spreading Government propaganda is valueless. A newspaper must have freedom to disagree – sometimes quite violently – with Government policy ... If a Government wants to keep its finger on the pulse of public opinion, it is vital that there should be a free Press in the country" (in Ainslie 1966:19–20).

Anti-communism

The fear of communism in the colonial territories is evident in documents prepared by the British Colonial Office to call for the introduction of broadcasting services in the colonies. As Armour (1984:362) notes, in the 1940s the desire to take speedy counter-measures against communism provided a powerful inducement to provide funds from the United Kingdom specifically to develop broadcasting. Communism was undoubtedly linked in this project to the rising tide of African nationalism

The Media in Africa

as publishers such as Nnamdi Azikiwe, who founded the Zik media group, were having their impact outside Nigeria. Unsurprisingly, Charles Jeffries, Under Secretary of State in the Colonial Office, was to urge the Colonial Office to set aside a substantial sum of money for the development of broadcasting services in the colonies to ward off the threat of communist influence (in Armour 1984:362).

Colonial broadcasting thus assumed a fresh impetus, with the Colonial Office inviting the British Broadcasting Corporation (BBC) to conduct feasibility studies in the British colonial territories, including Kenya, the two Rhodesias, Nyasaland and Tanganyika (now Tanzania). For instance, the Central Africa Council had by 1945 agreed in principle that African broadcasting in the Rhodesias and Nyasaland should be from Lusaka and broadcasting for Europeans from Salisbury (now Harare) (Armour 1984:364).

One can discern here the Colonial Office's preoccupation with combating the ideology of communism, largely because it was seen as fanning nationalist sentiment and passion. In a sense, the very granting of independence to some colonies was a reflection of this fear. This is suggested by the report of the official Commission of Enquiry in the Gold Coast following the Accra riots of 1948 which recommended that:

> *"the Constitution and Government of the country must be so reshaped as to give every African of ability an opportunity to govern the country, so as not only to gain experience but also to experience political power" (in Armour 1984:363).*

Ghana became the first African British colony to gain independence in March 1957. The independence of Ghana "sent a shock wave through Africa" (in Armour 1984:363). It was not long before many other countries were to follow suit but it was only in 1980 that Southern Rhodesia (Zimbabwe) was to become independent, given the fact that the white settler population, under the leadership of Ian Smith, had launched a Unilateral Declaration of Independence in 1965 against the wishes of the British government, thereby prolonging the inevitable end of British colonial rule in sub-Saharan Africa. And South Africa did not have democratic elections until 1994. This brief historical review serves to remind us that:
- the cultural imprint of each colonising nation was indelibly left on the media systems inherited by the colonised societies;

- the roles of the media in the colonial period reflected the different discursive positions around which colonial society was organised, such as colonialist propensity for expansion, native resistance and missionary evangelisation.

2.3 POST-COLONIAL MEDIA IN AFRICA

To a large extent, the nationalist agenda of the anti-colonial period influenced much of the media in the post-colonial era. In some cases, the nationalist leaders who assumed the reins of political power at independence from colonial rule had published newspapers, such as Nnamdi Azikiwe of Nigeria and Kwame Nkrumah of Ghana (and perhaps here we should also include Roy Welensky, second and last prime minister in 1957 of the Federation of Northern and Southern Rhodesia and Nyasaland, who saw himself as pro-British but went against colonial policy to lobby for the federation for the white residents of the region). Such nationalists generally saw the media in the postcolonial state as vehicles for propagating their agenda of ethnic unification, national development and political consolidation. The continued ownership of broadcasting by the state, for example, was common evidence of this ideological viewpoint. The media were sometimes also seen as instruments for forging a pan-African identity in the face of "neo-colonialist" tendencies by the former colonisers.

2.3.1 Postcolonial media: state control

Many post-colonial governments" approach towards the media were located in the ideology of development communication, which stressed the transfer of the technology and the socio-political culture of modernity from the developed and industrialised North to the so-called Third World.

The new nations also aspired for political, economic and cultural self-determination (Servaes 1991) and so Kwame Nkrumah of Ghana, Julius Nyerere of Tanzania and Kenneth Kaunda of Zambia espoused the "revolutionary theory" of the press (Ainslie 1966:19–20; Wilcox 1975:19–21). Nkrumah articulated this in 1963 during the Second Conference of African Journalists. He told them that "the truly African revolutionary Press" existed in order to "present and carry forward our revolutionary purpose" and "establish a progressive political and economic system upon our continent that will free men from want and every form

The Media in Africa

of injustice" (in Ainslie 1966:19). This entailed greater state control of the media, a departure from the private ownership of media evident in the colonial period. Some nationalist leaders went so far as to articulate "philosophies" to justify state ownership of media (Wilcox 1975:21). For example, Kenneth Kaunda, Zambia's first president, serving from 1964 to 1991, propounded the philosophy of humanism which subjected all major societal institutions, including the media, to the custody of the state (Banda 2003:36; Kasoma 1986:104–105; Mytton 1983:58). This structure of media ownership has had several consequences:

- appointment of senior managerial and editorial executives by the ruling party;
- highly centralised editorial decision-making;
- a general lack of innovation and daring on the part of staff for fear of state reprisals;
- hierarchical reporting, with state functionaries being the central focus;
- marginalisation of oppositional voices from political parties and civil society;
- insufficient funds to create innovative content;
- the lack of a competitive edge.

2.3.2 Post-colonial functions of the media: nation-building

Wilcox (1975:24) elaborates the post-colonial functions of the media as follows.

Nation building

The nationalists needed the press to "build" the new nations through:

- helping to create a feeling of nationhood among the people traditionally divided by tribal loyalties;
- explaining the objectives of a new and frequently socialist society;
- spreading information about new and better ways of living and farming;
- obtaining cooperation in community and national projects;
- winning support for the party and its leadership.

National unity

The media were seen as instruments in forging and sustaining a unified national identity. President Jomo Kenyatta (1889–1978) of Kenya urged the press to:

"always seek to coalesce, rather than to isolate, the different cultures and aspirations and standards of advancement which make up our new nation" (in Wilcox 1975: 26).

An important part of this process – what Curran (2002) might call "the anthropological" role of the media – was the evolution of some politico-ideological slogans to rally the media around the project of national unity. The following slogans can be isolated: *African Personality* in Ghana; *Négritude* in Sénégal; *Harambee* (national unity) in Kenya and *Ujamaa* (togetherness) in Tanzania (Wilcox 1975:27; Friedland & Rosberg 1964; Senghor 2000). Other examples are *Humanism* in Zambia; and *Chimurenga* (revolution) in Zimbabwe.

Mass education

The postcolonial media were seen as a primary instrument of mass education. In countries where there was a lack of capital and teachers, it was argued, a government-owned and operated press was the only way that the masses could be educated and socialised into the modern sector. Given this orientation, radio became particularly useful for mass education because it capitalised on Africa's great oral tradition and did not require literacy. This was so in Tanzania, Togo, Ethiopia, Zambia and several other African countries (Bourgault 1995). Within the context of the "revolutionary press" ideology, journalists and politicians alike saw the media as forging national and continental unity, encouraging economic development and serving formal and social education, including adult literacy. Radio and television sets were thus sometimes installed as a matter of priority in schools and community centres (Ainslie 1966:18).

It is interesting to note that this functionalist approach is reminiscent of the original conceptualisation of public service broadcasting in the colonisers" own countries:
- providing citizens (as opposed to consumers in the market approach) with information that will allow them to participate fully in their societies;
- fostering their development, curiosity and education;
- tapping the best of a nation's cultural resources in literature, art, drama, science, history, etc.
- expressing national and regional cultural diversity (Fourie 2003:150).

Constructive criticism

African journalism was pressured to offer "constructive" or "responsible" criticism. The term is generally interpreted to suggest that the postcolonial ruling élites did not brook media content that portrayed them in a negative light. It also refers to the view that any unfavourable comment was a sign of disloyalty to the national character. Although Wilcox (1975:29) observes that constructive criticism is located in what is described as the traditional African value of respect for authority, it can be argued very forcefully that this was used as a pretext for disregarding the freedom of the media. In Zambia, for example, the then foreign affairs minister Simon Kapwepwe (1922–1980) said:

> *"My government upholds the freedom of the press but I would add a qualification ... the editorial columns of our newspapers ... should be constructive and responsible" (Wilcox 1975: 29).*

This dogmatic approach to a uniformity of media functions resulted in intolerance on the part of the nationalist leaders. It was all too easy to dismiss any genuine criticism of the politicians" performance as "destructive" to the national project of unity and reconstruction (Bourgualt 1995:153–179). The functions of post-colonial media, as seen by the nationalists, did not brook any suggestion inimical to national integration. In addition, the essentialist insistence on "national building" could work against ethnic diversity and difference.

2.3.3 Media/cultural imperialism

Many Africans had long been dissatisfied with what was seen as a deeply negative image projected by the major news agencies of the world. This was reinforced by the view that African culture was being undermined by content flows from the West in an unequal relationship sometimes characterised as "media/cultural imperialism". Media imperialism is sometimes described as the process:

> *"whereby the ownership, structure, distribution or content of the media in any one country are singly or together subject to substantial external pressures from the media interests of any other country or countries without proportionate reciprocation of influence by the country so affected" (Boyd-Barret 1977:116).*

Media imperialism is also interpreted as a series of targeted actions by the United States military-communication conglomerates to ensure

commercial, military and political hegemony throughout the world (Kunczik 1984). Such issues were behind the cry from several African countries in the 1970s for a New World Information and Communication Order (NWICO), the information counterpart of the arguments put forth for a New World Economic Order (Bourgault 1994:175).

The United Nations Educational, Scientific and Cultural Organisation (UNESCO) took up the debate and the Pan-African News Agency (PANA) was created in 1979 by the Organisation of African Unity (now the African Union) which consists of more than 50 independent states.

PANA aimed:

> *"to rectify the distorted image of Africa created by the international news agencies and to let the voice of Africa be heard on the international news scene" (in Bourgault 1994:175).*

The 1990s appears to have had a trend towards regional media/cultural imperialism which was particularly pronounced in Africa after the dismantling of the apartheid (segregation) regime in South Africa and the country's re-admission into the international community. South Africa transnationalised its media industry, as evidenced by Multichoice Africa, now providing much of the Digital Satellite Television (DStv) bouquet of channels to the rest of sub-Saharan Africa (Fourie & Oosthuizen 2001:436). However, the extent of the media penetration from South Africa requires more research (Ugboajah 1987). And according to Braman (1996), "cultural imperialism" can be eliminated in some kind of "interpenetrated globalisation" whereby the local can be the global and thus exist side by side with foreign forms of cultural expression. Meanwhile, South Africa's "expansionist-capitalist" agenda (Banda 2003:190) saw it liberalise the media market while retaining a complex multimedia and multilingual public broadcaster, the SABC, at home. While there was an inflow of foreign direct investment into the country (Tomaselli 2002), there was also an outflow of media investment from South Africa. Naspers-controlled television broadcaster MultiChoice International listed on the Dutch stock exchange as well as on the USA's Nasdaq (Banda 2006).

2.4 AFRICAN MEDIA IN THE AGE OF GLOBALISATION

Hyden & Okigbo (2002) place the media in Africa in what they call "the two waves of democracy". The first wave refers to the colonial period and the African-nationalist struggles for independence from colonial rule.

The Media in Africa

This initial wave was often effaced soon after independence, giving way to a "second wave" of post-colonialism that itself becomes implicated in Samuel P. Huntington's "third wave" (1991). Huntington contends that the "third wave" was a global movement towards democracy characteristic of the period from 1974 onwards which saw democratic regimes replace authoritarian ones in approximately thirty countries in Europe, Asia and Latin America. In other countries, considerable liberalisation occurred in authoritarian regimes. In still others, including several in Africa, movements promoting democracy gained strength and legitimacy (Huntington 1991:21–25). It was only in the 1990s that most countries in Africa began to experience the effects of the third wave as a reality. Indeed, some scholars refer to this process as Africa's "second liberation," to underscore the betrayed hopes surrounding the liberation from colonial rule in the 1950s and 1960s (Diamond 1999:ix).

Liberalisation: deregulation of the media landscape

Following the collapse of state socialism in much of Africa and the consolidation of capitalism worldwide in the 1990s, the process of media liberalisation unfolded from Nigeria to South Africa, with corresponding deregulatory policy and legislative changes. Against this backdrop, UNESCO called for a gathering of media practitioners and press freedom organisations in Windhoek in Namibia on May 3, 1991. This conference culminated in the Windhoek Declaration calling for an independent and pluralistic African press (Barker 2001:16), repudiating state ownership of media institutions and justifying liberalisation and privatisation (Moyo 2006).

Extracts from the Windhoek Declaration on Promoting an Independent and Pluralistic African Press

... Consistent with Article 19 of the Universal Declaration of Human Rights, the establishment, maintenance and fostering of an independent, pluralistic and free press is essential to the development and maintenance of democracy in a nation, and for economic development ...

By an independent press, we mean a press independent from governmental, political or economic control, or from control of materials and infrastructure essential for the production and dissemination of newspapers, magazines and periodicals ...

Media Studies: Volume 1

> By a pluralistic press, we mean the end of monopolies of any kind and the existence of the greatest possible number of newspapers, magazines and periodicals reflecting the widest possible range of opinion within the community …
>
> The welcome changes that an increasing number of African States are now undergoing towards multiparty democracies provide the climate in which an independent and pluralistic press can emerge …
>
> The world-wide trend towards democracy and freedom of information and expression is a fundamental contribution to the fulfilment of human aspirations …
>
> As a matter of urgency, the United Nations, and particularly the International Programme for the Development of Communication (IPDC), should initiate detailed research, in cooperation with governmental (especially UNDP) and non-governmental donor agencies, relevant non-governmental organisations and professional associations, into the following specific areas:
> 1. identification of economic barriers to the establishment of news media outlets, including restrictive import duties, tariffs and quotas for such things as newsprint, printing equipment, and typesetting and word processing machinery, and taxes on the sale of newspapers, as a prelude to their removal;
> 2. training of journalists and managers and the availability of professional training institutions and courses;
> 3. legal barriers to the recognition and effective operation of trade unions or association of journalists, editors and publishers;
> 4. a register of available funding from development and other agencies, the conditions attaching to the release of such funds, and the methods of applying for them; the state of press freedom, country by country, in Africa …
>
> May 3, 1991

Coupled with the political discourse of liberal democratisation (freedom of expression, press freedom and so on), many countries in Africa promulgated liberal-economic media policies. For example, in 1993 the recently-elected government of Frederick Chiluba (president from 1991 to 2001) passed the Zambia National Broadcasting Corporation (Licensing) Regulations to liberalise the broadcasting sector for private investment (Banda 2006:461) and commercialised its state media system, the Zambia National Broadcasting Corporation (ZNBC). Similar changes to open up the media, especially broadcasting, took place in Malawi, Mozambique and South Africa, among other nations (Tomaselli & Dunn 2001).

However some countries, such as Zimbabwe under ZANU-PF leader Robert Mugabe, experienced a reversal in the liberalisation process and re-regulated (reviving existing legislation from the colonial era or

reintroducing draconian regulations) the media industry through a series of heavy policy and legislative measures (Moyo 2005). For example, the enactment of the Access to Information and Protection of Privacy Act of 2002 first limited access to information held by government departments, statutory bodies and government agencies and secondly insisted on the registration of journalists and media services with the government-run Media and Information Commission. In fact, the closure of the *Daily News,* one of Zimbabwe's private newspapers, was a result of its refusal to register with the Commission (Forbes 2005:113).

An example of a more subtle form of re-regulation could be the unsuccessful 2006 motion by the South African Minister of Communications, Ivy Matsepe-Casaburri, to have a stronger say in the appointment of councillors of the country's communications regulatory agency – the Independent Communications Authority of South Africa (ICASA). Other examples of political pressure on the media include the mental, legal and physical harassment of journalists, the withdrawal of government advertising from privately owned media institutions and self-induced censorship (MISA 2006; Banda 2004).

The privatisation and commercialisation of state media

Ruling political élites have generally not favoured "privatising" their broadcast media for fear of ceding more communicative ground to alternative voices, often represented by the opposition political parties and critical civil-society groups. A related issue here is the setting up of nominally independent broadcasting regulatory authorities (Banda 2003). The independence of the Malawi Communications Regulatory Authority (MACRA), the Independent Communications Authority of South Africa (ICASA), the Independent Broadcasting Authority (IBA) in Zambia and the Broadcasting Authority of Zimbabwe (BAZ) has remained a contested issue, although the intensity of this varies from country to country. The need for an independent broadcasting regulator is derived from the principles enunciated by media freedom activists, including the Media Institute of Southern Africa and the Media Foundation for West Africa, in the liberal-pluralist media tradition which sees media as operating as autonomously as possible from state, commercial and other interests and thus better allowing for the free flow of information and more accurately reflecting the diversity of society. The African Commission on Human and Peoples' Rights adopted in 2002 a Declaration of Principles on Freedom of Expression in Africa.

Media Studies: Volume 1

The declaration:
- encourages private broadcasting;
- urges the transformation of state broadcasters into genuine public broadcasters,
- stresses the need for independent broadcasting regulatory bodies.

This Declaration of Principles is itself a result of the African Charter on Broadcasting adopted in 2001 on the tenth anniversary of the Windhoek Declaration.

Extracts from the African Charter on Broadcasting

The African Charter on Broadcasting serves as a modern blueprint for policies and laws determining the future of broadcasting and information technology in Africa ...

We the participants of Windhoek + 10 declare that:

1. The legal framework for broadcasting should include a clear statement of the principles underpinning broadcast regulation, including promoting respect for freedom of expression, diversity, and the free flow of information and ideas, as well as a three-tier system for broadcasting: public service, commercial and community.
2. All formal powers in the areas of broadcast and telecommunications regulation should be exercised by public authorities which are protected against interference, particularly of a political or economic nature, by, among other things, an appointments process for members which is open, transparent, involves the participation of civil society, and is not controlled by any particular political party.
3. Decision-making processes about the overall allocation of the frequency spectrum should be open and participatory, and ensure that a fair proportion of the spectrum is allocated to broadcasting uses ...
4. Licensing processes for the allocation of specific frequencies to individual broadcasters should be fair and transparent, and based on clear criteria which include promoting media diversity in ownership and content.
5. Broadcasters should be required to promote and develop local content, which should be defined to include African content, including through the introduction of minimum quotas. States promote an economic environment that facilitates the development of independent production and diversity in broadcasting.
6. The development of appropriate technology for the reception of broadcasting signals should be promoted. (MISA 2004a)

Communitarianism and community radio

The international broadcasting policy campaign of the World Association for Community Radio Broadcasters (AMARC), headquartered in Montréal, Canada, legitimated community radio broadcasting as an alternative medium, one that is distinct from state and commercial broadcasting, in Africa. Community media channels multiplied along with private commercial channels (Bourgault 1995:224; Opoku-Mensah 1998). In Mali, Burkina Faso, Bénin, Guinea, Mauritania and Sénégal, the rise of community radio could be attributed to:

> Mali, Burkina Faso, Bénin, Guinea, Mauritania, Sénégal

- the overwhelming rural populations, with a strong oral tradition;
- little competition from television and newspapers;
- liberal economic policies;
- donor support to independent media and the promotion of human rights;
- international and local non-governmental organisations pressure for government to enact appropriate legislation, such as the West Africa-wide conference in 1993 which resulted in the adoption of the Bamako Declaration on Radio Pluralism (Myers 2000:91).

However, the emergence of both private commercial and community radio was not without its issues. As Bourgault observes, such services were concentrated in urban areas, excluding the majority of the rural poor. The programming is frequently more entertainment-based than developmental (Opuko-Mensah 1997; Bourgault 1995:103; Banda 2003). Community radio, in particular, was susceptible to many problems such as little funding, too few volunteers and a lack of training. After all, most such community radio initiatives were set up with the promise of donor funding in mind (Banda 2003).

An important point to note here is that while a large number of countries appropriated communitarian communication within their information and media policies, a number of countries, like Botswana and Zimbabwe, did not. For example, the Botswana Telecommunications Authority (BTA) refused to give World Vision Botswana a licence for a radio station aimed at empowering the *Basarwa* or "Bushmen," arguing "to some extent the needs of non-commercial applicants for radio broadcasting (namely community based radio broadcasting) are currently being met by similar programmes provided by Radio Botswana" (in Banda 2003:87).

In South Africa, the recognition and appropriation of the communitarian ethos is evident in the government-funded Media Development and

Diversity Agency, which is meant to:
- encourage ownership, control and access to media by historically disadvantaged communities;
- encourage training and capacity building within the media industry, especially amongst historically disadvantaged groups;
- encourage the channelling of resources to the community and commercial media sectors (Media Development and Diversity Agency 2000:2–3).

The South African legislation hopes to resolve some of the problems normally associated with community radio broadcasting, such as inadequate funding and lack of skills. In fact the Media Development and Diversity Agency has identified "the lack of resources to support the growth of community, non-profit and small commercial media" and "the legacy in media organisations of inadequate education, training and advancement of black South Africans" as being some of the major problems or challenges (Media Development and Diversity Agency 2000:27–28).

Some of the strategies envisaged by the Agency include providing funding, training and capacity building to promote diversity in ownership, control and staffing of media; stimulating debate and creating awareness about the importance of media diversity; striving to support the public broadcaster in carrying out its public service mandate; lobbying relevant self-regulatory bodies in the broadcasting, print and advertising industries to promote and develop their codes of conduct through open, public processes and to pay attention to advancing media diversity in the codes of conduct; and providing support to community and other non-profit media (Media Development and Diversity Agency 2000:35–36).

New information and communication technologies

Information and communication technologies (ICTs) have come to be perceived as a catalyst in engendering development in Africa. According to Dzidonu (2000:16), within the context of Africa, information and communication technology can be classified as traditional, conventional and modern. "Traditional" examples were rife in the pre-colonial period and the "conventional" in the colonial period. However, according to Dzidonu, both these have been supplemented – but by no means superseded – by the modern ICTs. Modern ICTs have come to dominate sub-Saharan African information policies. At the centre of the ICT policies in Africa has been the problem of access.

The Media in Africa

Nulens (1997) identifies three key sub-problems:
- operational;
- contextual;
- strategic.

Operational problems have to do with the lack of technical efficiency of power-plants, the low quality of the African electricity network and the inaccessibility of transmission channels, such as satellites. *Contextual* problems refer to the apprehension that the transfer of Western technology only leads to economic and cultural dependency. In other words, technology is not neutral, and ICT policies must thus take into account the potential socio-cultural problems in the appropriation of technology. *Strategy* problems are largely due to some telecommunications transnational companies whose business interests may go against the national-developmental aspirations of the governments of African countries. Such companies may influence international policy-making institutions, such as the World Bank, on ICT matters (Nulens 1997:6).

Despite these problems, Africa is at the centre of the debate about how modern ICT, especially the Internet, can enhance its development strategies in education, health, commerce, and other sectors. South Africa seems to have taken the lead, hosting in 1996 the Information Society and Development Conference of the G-7 or Group of Seven most industrialised countries (Fourie 2001:605). This policy trajectory resonates with policy developments elsewhere on the continent. Many countries have concerned themselves with the development of a national ICT infrastructure, including aspects of regulation, universal service provision, technological convergence (the coalescence of hitherto discrete media forms and processes through digital technologies), mechanisms to fund universal service rollout, the structure of markets and competition (James 2001:159).

To some extent, these debates have been carried on within the framework of the United Nations Economic Commission for Africa (UNECA). The Economic Commission for Africa launched the African Information Society Initiative (AISI) in 1996 to:
- bridge the digital divide between Africa and the rest of the world;
- create effective digital opportunities by Africans and their partners;
- speed the continent's entry into the information and knowledge global economy (UNECA 2006).

The AISI reflects a global move towards embracing computer-driven information and communication technology as the engine of economic growth in Africa, affording hitherto technologically backward societies an opportunity to leapfrog some stages of development and achieving an "information society" or "knowledge society".

2.5 CHALLENGES

There are some key challenges for the media in Africa. Firstly, although most postcolonial constitutions do recognise freedom of expression, there are still major limitations on that freedom. These limitations, some of them constitutional and others appearing in subsidiary legislation sometimes inherited from the colonial past, range from issues of national security, public safety and public morality to laws on defamation (Forbes 2005:93–115). Because of the often imprecise nature of such provisions, the media operate in a realm of uncertain constitutionality and legality.

Although there is an increasing recognition of freedom of the media as a universal right across sub-Saharan Africa, especially since the 1990s, there are generally no practical steps taken to entrench this freedom. This is particularly so in countries emerging out of conflict, such as Angola and the Democratic Republic of the Congo. The lack of effort to entrench the freedom of the media is also evident in most of the transitional democracies of Africa, in varying degrees. Associated with this is the unwillingness by most governments to enact laws that will promote access to public information (MISA 2006:13), sometimes taking advantage of the clampdown on information following the 9/11 terrorist attacks in the USA in 2001.

The policy and regulatory regime governing broadcasting generally does not promote the establishment of independent broadcasting regulators. This is a general trend, although there are some examples in which such regulators have been set up. But even then, there is a tendency by the state towards subtler forms of "re-regulation." Related to this is the unwillingness by most governments to transform their state broadcasting systems into proper public service broadcasting systems.

The lives and independence of journalists continue to be jeopardised, both from legal and extra-legal sources. What some media freedom activists refer to as "insult laws" – those statutes that make it a criminal offence to "insult" the honour or dignity of public officials – are seen as largely to blame for such insecurities suffered by journalists across

the continent (MISA 2004b). Media organisations have thus launched a campaign to get the African Union, under its African Peer Review Mechanism (APRM), to persuade its members to scrap such "insult laws" as a way of protecting the lives and independence of media practitioners. The APRM is a mechanism that the members of the AU are required to sign up to in order to demonstrate their commitment to good governance and democratisation. By 2005, only 23 countries out of the 54 African states belonging to the AU had signed up to the APRM (AfricaFocus 2005). But even where countries have signed up to the APRM, there is insufficient information placed in the public domain by the state to enable people to monitor their governments' adherence to democratic norms and principles.

Some media commentators have bemoaned the perceived lack of journalistic professionalism among African media and have pointed out that any disregard for media ethics can be used as an excuse for state intervention in media regulation (Nyamnjoh 2005). In Zambia, journalists are still struggling in their attempts to set up a more effective media council to regulate themselves. In Tanzania, however, such efforts have borne fruit with the creation of the Tanzania Media Council. In Malawi, like in Zambia, the media still appear to be disorganised, largely because of a lack of resources to step up their campaign to mobilise sufficient media support for the strengthening of the Malawi Media Council. In Swaziland, there is a move towards creating a Media Complaints Council (MISA 2006:109).

In trying to expand the communicative space, as a show of commitment to democratic values and principles, most countries in Africa are embracing community broadcasting. The main challenge here is the question of providing the people with universal access to channels of communication. Community media initiatives seem to be a viable option for reaching the hitherto un-reached rural populations with media services, despite the many problems that dog the sector, not least how to sustain the existing community radio stations while enhancing their community service.

Lastly, both media institutions and governments are increasingly under pressure to evolve regulatory and policy frameworks that take cognisance of the process of technological convergence. While there is political rhetoric on the issue, there appears to be little practical outcome in developing converged regulatory ICT policies. In part, this is attributable to the natural propensity by bureaucrats to hold on to their specific policy

Media Studies: Volume 1

domains – convergence might entail loss of sectoral sovereignty. To give one example: the Zambian ICT policy framework, partly to allay these fears, suggests a cautious approach towards the setting up of a converged regulatory authority for the ICT sector.

2.6 SUMMARY AND CONCLUSION

We began by noting the scarcity of media-historical research in Africa, noting that media histories can be presented as a variety of narratives from liberal to feminist, anthropological to radical. We then proceeded to carve African media history into three intertwining epochs, namely the colonial, post-colonial and globalisation historical periods.

Colonial-era media had specific functions: colonialist expansion, African nationalism, "palliative treatment" for the natives, settler federalism, capitalist expansion and missionary activity. In the postcolonial era, the media were seen as an instrument for further decolonisation but also as tools for suppressing political agitation. Postcolonial media were vehicles for national building, national unity, mass education and constructive criticism, but it fell almost entirely under the aegis of the state.

Globalisation was a departure from the state-centrism of the postcolonial media system. The global influences of liberalisation, deregulation, privatisation, commercialisation, communitarianism and technological convergence have reconfigured the media landscape in favour of freer and more democratic media systems. The role of the state, however, did not completely disappear, especially in the arena of regulation and public broadcasting.

The media in contemporary Africa continue to carry the imprint of colonialism, while at the same time reflecting new political, economic, social, cultural and technological realities. As the colonial legacy begins to fade, the new postcolonial experiences of African media, implicated in global geo-politics, are giving rise to a new media-historical trajectory of mixed fortunes of, among other things, greater communicative space through technology and communitarian communications, higher levels of media concentration and commercialisation, enhanced civil-society activism for media freedom, and over-politicisation of state media.

The Media in Africa

LEARNING ACTIVITIES

- Describe the key historic epochs characteristic of the media in Africa.
- Discuss some key events and issues within each of these historical epochs.
- Interpret their implications for the present status of the media in Africa.
- Analyse the impact of globalisation on the media in Africa.
- Discuss the impact of re-regulation in countries which have not deregulated their media systems.
- Analyse the impact of privatisation and commercialisation.
- Discuss what forms of community radio are available for people in your area. Discuss how the new forms of information and communication technology are helping or hindering access to information.
- Analyse the impact of South African satellite television on other African cultures.

FURTHER READING

Berwanger, D. 1987. *Television in the Third World: new technology and social change*. Bonn: Friedrich-Ebert-Stiftung.

Mbennah, E. Hooyberg, V. & Mersham, G. 1998. Mass media in Africa: from distant drums to satellite, in *Mass media – Towards the millennium*, edited by A.S. De Beer. Pretoria: J.L. van Schaik.

Price-Davies, E. & Tacchi, J. 2001. *Community radio in a global context: a comparative analysis in six countries*. Sheffield: Community Media Association.

Traber, M. 1989. African communication: problems and prospects, in *Africa Media Review*, 3(3).

Wanyeki, L.M. 2000. The development of community media in East and Southern Africa, in *Promoting community media in Africa*, edited by S.T.K. Boafo. Paris: UNESCO.

SELECTED MEDIA WEBSITES

The All Africa Editors' Forum (TAEF) http://www.sanef.org.za/african_editors
The Mail & Guardian (South Africa) http://www.mg.co.za
The Daily Nation (Kenya) http://www.nationmedia.com/dailynation
The Post (Zambia) http://www.postzambia.com
South African Broadcasting Corporation (SABC) http://www.sabc.co.za
Media Institute of Southern Africa (MISA) http://www.misa.org
Media Foundation for West Africa (MFWA) http://www.mfwaonline.org

Media Studies: Volume 1

Panos Southern Africa (PSAf) http://www.panos.org.zm
Pan-African News Agency (PANA) http://www.panapress.com
Southern African Broadcasting Association (SABA) http://www.saba.co.za
South African Editors' Forum (SAEF) http://www.sanef.org.za
Southern African Journalists' Association (SAJA) (No own website, but hosted by http://www.ifj.org)
Media Rights Agenda (Nigeria) http://www.internews.org/mra
Article 19 (Africa) http://www.article19.org

PART 2
Media and Society

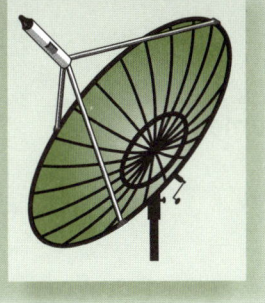

chapter three

Approaches to the Study of Mass Communication

Pieter J. Fourie

> **LEARNING OUTCOMES**
>
> At the end of this chapter you should be able to:
> - describe the characteristics of our present communication culture in comparison with earlier communication cultures;
> - define mass communication;
> - describe the value, goals and building blocks of a mass communication theory of your choice and the criteria that can be used to evaluate a theory;
> - describe and explain the underlying premises of the positivistic, critical, technological deterministic, meaning construction, information society, poststructuralist, post-modern, postcolonial, and Afro-centric approaches to the study and research of mass communication, as well as some of the criticism against these approaches.

Media Studies: Volume 1

THIS CHAPTER

This chapter is about:
- the development of mass communication culture;
- defining mass communication;
- answering the question "what is theory?".

The study of mass communication includes the following:
- the positivist approach;
- the critical approach, including mass society theory and cultural studies;
- meaning production theory;
- the technological approach (technological determinism);
- the information society;
- the poststructuralist/postmodern approach;
- the postcolonial and Afrocentric approaches;
- normative media theory.

The emphasis is on the general characteristics of the approaches and not on specific theories which are dealt with in subsequent chapters of this book and in volume 2, 3 and 4. In those chapters we deal with the effects of the media, the functions of the media in society, the media as a public sphere, theories related to the media's representation of reality, race, gender, sex, the environment, media audiences, and so on.

A brief overview of different mass communication cultures shows that contemporary mass communication is nothing new and has a long history. Although there may be differences in the ways people throughout history communicated matters of common interest, the issues and questions related to the state and value of mass communication have remained more or less the same. We distinguish between the oral, the written and printed, and the electronic and digital mass communication cultures.

This first part of chapter 3 is followed by a discussion about defining mass communication. Before the different theoretical approaches can be discussed in the last part of the chapter, some questions are necessary: Who is the communicator in mass communication? What do we mean by "medium"? What is the message? What do we mean by "audience"? What do we mean by "communication" in mass communication?

Finally, we ask the question: What is theory? We look at the value, goals, the building blocks of theory, how to evaluate theory, and mass media theory as sociological theory.

Approaches to the Study of Mass Communication

The chapter is divided into two sections: Section 1: Mass communication culture, defining mass communication and What is theory?, and Section 2: Theoretical approaches.

SECTION 1: MASS COMMUNICATION CULTURE/ DEFINING MASS COMMUNICATION/WHAT IS THEORY?

3.1 INTRODUCTION: MASS COMMUNICATION CULTURES

Throughout history people had their "media" to communicate about matters of public interest. As will be shown below, many of the questions, issues and topics about today's mass communication (newspapers, magazines, journals, radio, television, film, video, the popular music industry, and the Internet) are not new. Neither can we claim to be one of the first media societies or the first media generation.

In our discussion a distinction is made between the following mass communication cultures, each being dominant during a certain period of time:

- a dominant *oral* mass communication culture;
- a dominant *written and printed* mass communication culture;
- a dominant *electronic* public mass communication culture;
- lately, an increasingly *digital* culture.

three cultures

3.1.1 The oral communication culture

An oral public communication culture was dominant in the pre-industrial or pre-literate (before the advent of writing and reading) societies. In these early societies the spoken word (and verbal sounds) were the only available means of expressing ideas, attitudes and feelings – nothing was written (the ability to write did not exist or was extremely limited), there were no written reports, no newspapers, no television, no radio, no (or few) written records of anything. The spoken word was the main means of communication. Through the spoken word people had to refer to something and express their views about that something, be it politics, the state of their society, or matters of human interest.

Inglis (1990:6–7) lists the following characteristics of the oral public communication culture:

- the transmission of information, knowledge and opinion was face to face; the meaning of language was highly specific and local, and related to everyday practical and particular concerns; language was concrete

characteristics of oral culture

Media Studies: Volume 1

and symbols were solid. There was very little possibility of "reading" meanings "between the lines". Something meant what it was supposed to mean;

- the context of oral culture was/is memory. Memory is finite. People therefore expected their memories to store and keep accessible (in memory) only what was relevant;
- the pre-literate society placed a higher value on the present tense: myth, proverb, law, belief, may all be adjusted to suit the present.

In some illiterate societies where people cannot read and/or write, and where there are little or no "modern" mass media, oral public communication is still dominant. In these societies people rely on face-to-face contact and verbal communication about public matters with their leaders and opinion makers. Their histories are verbally told in the form of stories and myths through which their values and beliefs about what is wrong and right and about how one should behave in certain circumstances, are tested and communicated. Often these stories are closely related to human beings' experience of nature and the relationship between people and nature and to ancestry and ancestor worship. These beliefs and values are verbally passed on from generation to generation.

3.1.2 The written and printed communication culture

Visual recordings of history and messages started more or less 6 000 years ago with carvings and cave-paintings. Phonetic alphabets have been known for little more than 3 000 years, and writing as we know it today, dates back from about 800 BC (Before Christ). Writing therefore makes up a very small part of the more than a quarter of a million years of the history of *Homo sapiens* (Inglis 1990).

Some of the characteristics of the written and subsequently printed mass communication culture are the following:

writing

After people started to write, the spoken word came to be seen and experienced as more casual and "unofficial" than the written word, which the writer has presumably pondered and verified. As a result, the written word came to be experienced as more impersonal and objective than the spoken word. The written word is seen to be and experienced as permanent, as opposed to the fleeting, ephemeral nature of the spoken word. For all these reasons the written word was considered to be closer to the truth. Today we tend to believe that a written (or typed/printed) contract is more binding than an oral contract; that a published account

Approaches to the Study of Mass Communication

of something that happened is more reliable than a verbal account. If something happens, for example, a bus accident, people talk about it and there may be different accounts of what has happened. However, once it is recorded in print, for example as a newspaper story, we tend to believe that the written account is the official and correct version.

Writing makes the recording of events possible and is as such indispensable for the creation of a historical sensibility and for the existence of objective knowledge. For example, for science and rationality to be possible, we must have the principle of accurate and impartial written/printed recording. Writing makes debate about the comparative truthfulness of sources possible. Critical history is only possible with written records. A set of thought procedures like mathematics and logic is impossible without script (Inglis 1990:8–13).

Since the emergence of the Greek alphabet it took another 2 000 years before the invention of the printing press.

In the 1450s a German, Johann Gutenberg, invented the printing press and started to develop the art of printing. This invention can be seen as the beginning of the information revolution. More than anything else, publishing contributed to the advancement of literacy among billions of people. Suddenly documents, be they religious, legal, scientific or artistic writings were available to more people than to the previous few privileged people, the élite who could write and read. The increasing availability and accessibility of books and documents, the advancement of the print media as we know it today, and growing literacy over five hundred years since the invention of the printing press markedly changed the ways in which politics, science, education, religion, economics, art and mass communication were to be conducted.

printing press

Within three hundred years human beings adapted themselves and their institutions to the revolutionary changes brought about by the printing press, creating new institutions such as the school, new forms of government and an organised newspaper industry to shape and comprehend the new information environment. In short, by the end of the eighteenth century, the printing press had created an entirely new information and mass communication culture (cf. Postman 1992).

The period of adjustment to printing, and the consequent changes it brought about in the nature and quality of information and consequently knowledge, was not without its problems. The same kind of criticism

levelled at the media today about quality, objectivity, reliability and relevance was raised.

3.1.3 The electronic communication culture

Although written and oral public communication cultures still exist today (we still write and have newspapers and magazines and attend public speeches), in the realm of mass communication the electronic, photographic and digital media (radio, film, video, advertising, television and the Internet) dominate. Its dominance is expected to gain momentum as the electronic media and related technologies continue to develop. As the written and printed word undermined the authority of the spoken word, so the electronic media have undermined the authority of the written and printed word in the culture of mass communication. Today, it is no longer a matter of something being true or official because it was printed in a newspaper. Rather, it is true or official or important because it was on television and/or on the Internet. It can be argued, as Postman (1985; 1992) did, that this process of change in the culture of mass communication started with the invention of the telegraph in 1837.

<small>beginning of broadcasting</small>

The telegraph initiated a dramatic change in the form, volume and speed with which information could be produced and distributed. It was the beginning of the demolition of time and space as a restriction on the dissemination of information.

In the nineteenth century, photography and film brought about the so-called "graphic revolution" and the beginning of the so-called "image culture". It replaced the written and printed word as the dominant means of interpreting, comprehending and testing reality or an aspect of reality.

The discovery of the telegraph was the direct precursor of radio, and therefore of broadcasting.

After the invention of radio it was still to take about fifty to seventy years before the world felt the full influence of media technology on mass communication culture. Television has many qualities which characterise it as the dominant mass communication medium of our time. Yet perhaps the most outstanding is its ability to cross boundaries. The availability of television programmes on the international market, international news networks and satellite communication, and the influence of this on the dissemination of information, expose viewers in all parts of the world to divergent cultures, ideological stances, opinions and meanings. In brief,

Approaches to the Study of Mass Communication

the advent of television (with all its advantages and disadvantages) was the beginning of Marshall McLuhan's 1964 concept of the "global village".

The process of bridging time and space initiated by the telegraph has continued with television and today has almost reached perfection with the Internet. As a result of television's ability to bridge time and space, boundaries have been broken down and a continual cross-pollination between various cultures and subcultures is taking place.

Despite all the benefits brought about by electronic and digital media, many questions similar to those asked about the earlier communication cultures can be raised about today's dominant mass communication culture. These include questions about the value, quality, reliability and relevance of information and media entertainment, the fragmented and contextless nature of today's media-disseminated information and the argument that in the media's quest to reach the largest (international) audience, it has become trivialised, commercialised and the marketer of material values to the detriment of cultural values. These and many other questions and arguments are the topics of mass communication theory. They are being asked, approached and researched from a number of perspectives. Such perspectives or approaches are introduced in this chapter (see section two). But first, we need to define mass communication (see 3.2) and get clarity about what theory is (see 3.3), before we get to these approaches.

3.2 DEFINING MASS COMMUNICATION

Defining mass communication is not that easy and has become increasingly difficult against the background of the latest developments in information and communication technology (ICT) which has increased the number and kinds of media involved in transmitting messages of various kinds and in various formats to bigger, increasingly heterogeneous and global audiences. All of this makes it difficult to "get a grip" on exactly what constitutes mass communication today.

For this very reason mass communication can and is defined from various perspectives, each with its own emphasis. McQuail (2000:7), for example, distinguishes four theoretical perspectives:

different perspectives

The media-culturalist perspective

In definitions of this kind the emphasis is on the content, reception and context of the communication. For example, such definitions will

emphasise the nature of media content (information, entertainment, propaganda, and so on) and how the content is received and interpreted by different audiences in different circumstances, for instance in rural versus urban circumstances.

The media-materialist perspective

In this case the emphasis is on the technical aspects and how the technology of a medium impacts on the nature of media messages and audiences. For example, it is possible to differentiate between radio and television as media of mass communication because each medium involves different technologies, encodes their messages differently, and can reach different audiences who relate differently to the different media.

The social-culturalist perspective

In this perspective the influence of social factors on media production and reception and the functions of the media in social life is emphasised.

The social-materialist perspective

The media and their content are mainly seen as a reflection of a society. For example, media and media audiences in developed countries may differ from that in developing and in poor countries. Such differences will affect definitions and perceptions of what mass communication is, and can be. Given Africa's development needs we may define mass communication differently from definitions (and perceptions) attributed to it in Europe.

Whatever the perspective and emphasis may be, certain focal points are always present in definitions of mass communication (cf. Berger 1995:4). The focal points are the communicator, the medium, the message, the recipient or audience, the public nature of mass communication and the diverse content of mass communication. Around these focal points it is possible to at least formulate a working definition such as the following:

> **working definition**
>
> Mass communication involves the production of a large variety of messages (usually) by an institutional group or a collective communicator. The messages are distributed and transmitted (usually) by means of technological media (channels) to reach large, heterogeneous and widely dispersed audiences who may interpret the messages in a variety of ways.

Approaches to the Study of Mass Communication

The content of mass communication is a mix of information, views, entertainment and advertisements. The purpose is to mediate meaning and understanding, either overtly and/or covertly. By achieving this, the media create a unique kind of public sphere, and are seen to be one of the primary producers of mass/popular culture and a culture in and for itself. An outstanding feature of mass communication is its publicness compared to the private nature of other forms or levels of communication.

This may sound like a simplistic definition, but it raises a number of issues. Some of these topics are dealt with by asking a number of questions in the following paragraphs. The topics and issues also come to the fore in section 3.4. Nevertheless, wherever they are dealt with, we do not pretend to cover every aspect or to pre-empt them. To the contrary, they may even simply be mentioned, in which case references are made to other chapters in this book where they are dealt with in more depth.

3.2.1 Questions related to a definition of mass communication

Who is the communicator?

In interpersonal and group communication it is not that difficult to identify the communicator. In mass communication, however, the communicator is usually a "collective body", a group of people responsible for the production of programmes, news bulletins, films, a newspaper, web sites on the Internet and so on. For example, although the names of individuals (the director, the designer, the camera operator, and so forth) responsible for a television programme are shown in the credits at the end of a programme, it remains difficult to pinpoint a single communicator. Apart from the people responsible for the production of a programme, one might well ask whether the communicator(s) is not the presenter(s) of a programme. Furthermore, we must also consider the managers and owners of the television station. Although they may not be overtly involved with the production and presentation of a programme, they are responsible for policy. In the case of newspapers, the journalist whose byline appears below the headline forms part of a group consisting of editors, managers, a board of directors and other journalists who are expected to support a newspaper's values, ideology and codes of conduct. (See chapter 7 on ideology and chapter 7 in volume 2 on news.)

The issue of identifying a single communicator in mass communication can have far reaching implications when questions of responsibility,

identifying a communicator

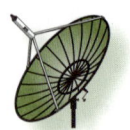

Media Studies: Volume 1

objectivity (particularly in the case of news and comment), liability and other related matters arise. Without pinpointing a single communicator, public service broadcasting (for example, the South African Broadcasting Corporation), is often blamed collectively for being the mouthpiece of a ruling government. All individual journalists and programme producers then risk being labelled as "government agents". (See chapter 4 on the functions of the media for a more in-depth discussion of public service broadcasting.)

From an artistic point of view it is also difficult to credit the real communicator in film, television and radio. In the so-called high art forms such as literature and music, it is easy to attribute the work of art to the intellect and skills of a single person. In film, television and radio this is more difficult and one of the reasons why these symbolic forms of expression are often not seen as art but rather as popular culture. (See chapter 6 on media culture.) For example, who is the artist (communicator) of a film: the director? the cinematographer? the sound engineer? the costume designer? the author of the screenplay? or the producer (manager/ financier)?

The difficulty of identifying a single communicator in the case of mass communication messages and products has complex consequences for the regulation of mass communication and its responsibilities, as will be pointed out in the chapters on media regulation and management in later volumes. As mass communication media converge, in which case radio, television and newspapers are available on the Internet, on television, on cellular telephones and vice versa, it becomes even more difficult to identify a single communicator (who can take responsibility for the communication), and its regulation becomes even more complex.

What do we mean by "medium"?

In mass communication, the *medium* (plural *media*) can be radio, television, film, newspapers, magazines, the Internet, videos, compact disks (CDs), sound cassettes and so on.

technology

The medium is usually of a technical nature and can involve complicated production and distribution technologies and techniques. It also requires that audiences or a member of a media audience must have the technological means to receive the transmitted messages, such as a transistor radio or a television set, as well as the financial means to buy a newspaper or a magazine, a computer, a video player, a digital video

Approaches to the Study of Mass Communication

disk (DVD), etc. In using the term "medium" we also mean the channel through which the media content is transmitted and distributed. In short, a single description of the medium in mass communication is much more complex than in the case of other forms of communication. In interpersonal communication the medium is the human body and all its communicative facilities. With the latest technological developments, multimedia are also increasingly utilised within a single medium. For example, the Afrikaans radio station belonging to the SABC, *Radiosondergrense* (Radio Without Borders) is, like many other, no longer just a radio station. It is also available on the Internet and satellite television, and is thus making use of the technologies of all these media.

In short, mass communication involves complex technologies, one of the reasons why mass communication in whatever form is usually expensive and requires technological knowledge and skills.

What is the message?

Message has both a concrete and an abstract meaning. It is concrete in the form of the content being produced: the newspaper story you can hold and read, the television programme you can see, the radio programme you can hear, and so on. Put in another way, the concrete content of the media is a whole range of stories in a newspaper varying from political commentary to sport, crime, economy, leisure, recipes, cartoons, disaster reports and the like; different television and radio programmes; different films on a whole range of topics, themes and genres; and the overwhelming content of the Internet. Thus, the concrete message is referred to as the *text* and/or *media content*. The message is abstract in terms of the meaning encoded in the content by the communicator and the meaning the reader, viewer, listener (in short, the recipient) attaches to and derives from the content through their own interpretation of the content. Message thus also refers to *signification* (see the chapter on media semiotics and the production of meaning in volume 2).

The point to emphasise is that in mass communication you should always be very specific when you use the concept "message". Do you refer to the concrete content or to the meaning(s) entrenched in the content which can be different to different people? Furthermore, and this is important for media analysis, the message can be analysed on four levels:
- Content: the subject or topic of the communication.
- Form: the way in which the content is dealt with; for example, the way in which something is linguistically or visually formulated.

levels of the message

- Substance: in the case of mass communication this involves the technology of presentation: radio, print, television, Internet, video, etc. And then, to give a few examples, in the case of radio: shortwave, medium wave, stereo; in the case of television, analogue or digital, the size of the screen, and so on; the different formats of the Internet; in the case of film, different sizes such as 16 or 35 mm, black and white or colour, and so on. The point is that the substance also contributes to the meaning of the message.
- Meaning: the literal meaning or the derivative meaning.

Together, these four elements constitute the message.

What do we mean by "audience"?

The *audience* (see the chapters on audience analysis in volume 3) are the listeners, viewers, and readers. Media audiences in mass communication are heterogeneous and usually unknown to the communicator. At the most, the communicator can target a specific group, for example, a language, region, income level or age; but it remains a broad group within which numerous differences as far as education, culture, taste, political views, needs, opinions and perceptions exist. With the latest developments in interactivity, however, all this is beginning to change. Interactivity raises the possibility of media users instantaneously reacting electronically to or with the communicator.

Media audiences usually receive and use media messages either as individuals (one person reading a newspaper, looking at a film, viewing a television programme, listening to a radio programme, surfing the Internet) or within a small or larger group (a family or group of friends watching a television programme, or an audience in a film theatre). With the development of computer technology, media audiences are increasingly global. For example, multinational corporations produce media content such as films, television programmes, magazine articles and comics, to be read and viewed by audiences from all over the world. Lately a newspaper from a specific country, for example, South Africa's weekly *Mail & Guardian,* can be read on the Internet in almost any place in the world. That is, media content can be read all over the world if it is not deliberately blocked by censorship laws such as, for instance, in China. And China is not alone. There have been efforts by the US government to establish forms of control over the Internet and other digital media, even efforts in South Africa to censor Internet content.

Approaches to the Study of Mass Communication

A prerequisite for being part of the media audience is, however, access. First of all one must be able to afford media. Secondly, in the care of the electronic media one must have electricity to be able to access media such as television, pay television, the Internet, etc. Access is still not wthin the financial means of the majority of the world population.

Given the development of both interactivity (which is one of the outstanding characteristics of the Internet and increasingly, a characteristic also of the older media as they converge with new technologies), and the increasing commercialisation of the media (with the effect that the media are increasingly seen as a commercial product) readers, listeners and viewers are increasingly referred to as *media users*. The connotation is that they *use* the media as consumers. This is a much debated point in media criticism (see chapter 8 on the media as public sphere, also referred to in 3.4 of this chapter).

interactivity

Nevertheless, the point to be made here is that whether we refer to readers, viewers, listeners, or media users, in mass communication the audience(s) remain heterogeneous and difficult to pinpoint. This makes any generalisation about media audiences almost impossible, which has important implications for media planning in the sense that the media business first and foremost relies on its publics (audiences) and their interests. Without an audience there is no media.

What do we mean by "communication" in mass communication?

Strictly speaking, *communication* means dialogue towards mutual understanding. It means a two-way exchange with mutual *feedback* between a communicator and a recipient in reciprocal roles. Against the background of such a definition, mass communication isn't communication. It is mainly one-way communication from a (collective) communicator to a recipient(s) unseen by the communicator; a recipient(s) in a different physical environment; different mental frame of mind; different contexts and circumstances; and not known to the communicator. "One-way communication" is understood to mean the dissemination and distribution of information and entertainment from a single source to multiple recipients. In mass communication, feedback existed only in the form of letters to newspapers, and in the form of telephone calls to radio and television stations.

information and communication technology

However, the above view of mass communication as one-way communication is changing rapidly with new technology, the introduction of new genres (or programme types), and a general change in the ethos of mass communication from a patriarchal top-down approach to participation with and between communicators and recipients. The development of information and communication technologies has introduced the possibilities of interactivity. The Internet has created platforms for continued feedback between communicators and recipients and communication among recipients. Via the Internet, recipients can enter into electronic newspaper debates on numerous topics, cast their votes on numerous topics related to matters of public interest, and come into contact with one another by joining Internet chat rooms. (Whether computer-mediated communication is "real" communication is a complex topic of scholarly debate and investigation.) Radio and television have introduced popular programme formats such as talk shows and phone-in programmes in which viewers and listeners can air their views on numerous topics. Furthermore, it seems as if there is a general trend in newspapers to provide more space for the publication of readers' letters and by so doing creating platforms for public debate. Lately some newspapers also publish the e-mail addresses of their journalists who can then be contacted by members of the public.

In short, against the background of the development of ICTs it is obvious that the concept of "feedback" will gain new meaning and that the lack of feedback will no longer be a distinct characteristic of mass communication.

The point to be made here is that mass communication is expected to provide a platform for public debate. The question is: what is the quality of the communication and debates taking place in or initiated by mass communication? (See chapter 8 on the media as public sphere.)

Other questions

Other questions related to the focal points in any definition of mass communication, are, for instance: What do we mean by the "mass" in mass communication? What do we mean by "public sphere", "publicness" and "democracy"? What do we mean by "meaning", "understanding" and "mediation"? What do we mean by "mass/popular culture"? These questions, as well as the topics referred to above, form the backbone of mass communication study. They have been and are approached from

Approaches to the Study of Mass Communication

a number of theoretical perspectives. Some of the main perspectives or approaches we deal with in section 3.4 but first we need to ask: What is theory?

3.3 WHAT IS THEORY?

3.3.1 The value of theory

In her book, *Communication theory in action* (2000), Julia Wood explains that apart from having a scientific value, theory has a practical value. The section below is based mainly on her explanation.

Theory's *scientific value* is that it teaches us how to *describe, interpret, understand, evaluate* and *predict* a phenomenon. It also provides us with an overview of the development of a discipline, its relation(s) with other disciplines and its possible future developments. For example, although it may not be the explicit purpose of media theory to provide a historical overview of the discipline, if we study media theory as it developed over time and as it focused on different issues in different historical periods, then it reveals much about the development of the discipline. A good example is the effect theories discussed in more detail in chapter 5. | scientific value

Effect theories started by focusing on the effect of the media on personal behaviour and then developed into a more holistic approach to the effects of the media on society and culture in general. It thus began with simplified assumptions about the power of the media and gradually developed into complex and multiple assumptions, saying a lot not only about the media but about society and humanity as such. The same applies to other branches of media theory. As far as the relation with other disciplines is concerned, effect theories started from a behaviourist perspective closely associated with the positivism and behaviourism of the social sciences in the first part of the 1900s and then moved on to the more critical approaches presently practised in the social sciences. Present theories related to the information society and globalisation include several predictions of how media theory may develop in the future, and for what we should be on the lookout.

If theory teaches us the skills of describing, interpreting and understanding, evaluating and predicting a phenomenon, such skills can become entrenched in the way(s) we have to deal with our everyday realities. Simple everyday problems such as tense relationships between colleagues or family members can be solved by carefully describing the problem and | practical value

the reasons responsible for the problem, interpreting them, evaluating the importance of the different reasons for the conflict and then predicting and deciding on solutions for the problem. Reading a newspaper story or watching a television programme can become a descriptive, interpretative, evaluative and predictive exercise, all leading to better understanding, enjoyment and critical awareness. Theory-building skills, once entrenched in one's ways of dealing with reality, can thus be applied to dealing with one's finances, interpersonal relations, group relations, and so forth. For the theoretician the task is thus to:

- describe something as accurately as possible;
- interpret it from different perspectives;
- evaluate different options;
- predict possible outcomes.

3.3.2 The goals of theory

Theory can be defined as a human account of what something is, how it works, what it produces or causes to happen, and how that something can be changed, if necessary (Wood 2000:33). Actually, all of us are theorising beings. When we tell someone how something happened, why it happened, what our reactions to it were, what we should have done, and how the issue or event could have been avoided or directed in another way, we are in fact theorising about that something.

theory is human account

From this definition it is clear that being a human account of something, theory cannot be objective, or necessarily true. At the most it provides us with different points of views about the same thing. In media studies, like in all other social and human studies, we therefore have different theories about the same thing: different theories about the power and effects of the media; different theories about how audiences use, interpret and understand media content; different theories about the nature of media content, and so forth. Each (new) theory may however, add and/or emphasise a different aspect of the phenomenon and as such contributes to our better understanding of the phenomenon.

The goals of theory are then to describe, explain, understand, predict and control, and reform.

- *Describe*: Before we can comment on how something works, we must first describe that something.
- *Explain*: Before we can understand, predict and/or change something we must first explain how something works.

Approaches to the Study of Mass Communication

- *Understand*: Description and explanation lead to understanding.
- *Predict and control*: On the basis of (an) understanding, certain predictions of how something works and how it can be controlled can be made.
- *Reform*: Description, explanation and understanding with the purpose of predicting and controlling can lead to changing something.

For example, say that the "something" is the media's portrayal of race. A theory about this will have to:
- describe how the media report race;
- explain why the media report race as they do;
- from this description and explanation come to an understanding of why the media portray race as they do and thus why such reporting can be predicted and controlled;
- on the basis of this understanding suggest ways of reforming the media's way of reporting race.

Many scholars believe that theory does not need to reform something. The act of describing, explaining and understanding something is in itself enough. However, critical scholars and critical theory (especially in the social sciences with its goal to improve society) emphasise the need to reform. In other words, a theory about the media's reporting of race and racial issues should lead to media practitioners changing their ways and habits of reporting race, even if it is only to be more sensitive about reporting race and racial issues.

Obviously description, explanation, prediction and reform can be done in different ways and by using different analytical methods and research techniques. This will depend on the theorist's (and researcher's) ontological and epistemological points of departure, which brings us to the building blocks of theory.

3.3.3 The building blocks of theory

The building blocks (cf. Wood 2000:54–68) of all theory related to human behaviour (of whatever kind) are:
- ontology;
- epistemology;
- purpose;
- focus.

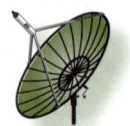

One may also say that a theory about something will depend on how you see something (ontology), how you investigate something (epistemology), your purpose and your focus.

Ontology

1st building block: ontology

How does one formulate a theory? A theory begins with a question or questions about a specific phenomenon in the mind of the theorist (or group of theorists). For example, can the media frame a person, a group, an event or a topic in a certain way so as to influence public opinion about a person, group, event or topic in a specific direction? Underlying an answer to this question, as to all questions dealing with humanity (its behaviour, products, thinking, and so on), will be the theorist's view of human nature (keeping in mind that media content is a product of human activity). Thus we say that all theory in the human and social sciences begins with a view of human nature.

In the philosophy of science this view of human nature is called ontology. As far as ontology is concerned we distinguish between two broad views of humanity: a deterministic view or *determinism* and a liberal view or *humanism.*

The point of departure in determinism is that human behaviour is governed by forces beyond individual control. A deterministic point of departure to the question about media framing will thus be: yes, the media *will* frame people and events and *will* influence public opinion about people and events in a certain direction, because that is part and parcel of the nature of the media and mass communication over which people (editors and journalist) have little control.

The point of departure in humanism is the belief that people have a free will and that they make choices about how to act. A humanist answer to the question about media framing will thus be much more cautious about an outright yes, and would rather be: yes, the media *may* frame people and events under certain circumstances and given certain conditions including the various conditions of the media audience(s), and *may* influence public opinion in a certain way, because people (editorial staff and audiences) can think for themselves and in a responsible way.

Approaches to the Study of Mass Communication

Table 3.1: Ontology

ONTOLOGY		
Do the media frame people and events to influence public opinion in a specific direction?		
Ontological point of departure	Determinism	Yes
Ontological point of departure	Humanism	Not an unqualified yes; it will depend on circumstances, conditions and the free will of people

Epistemology

The second building block that underlies theory is *epistemology*. Epistemology is about *how* we know *what* we know, or in philosophical terms, the science of knowledge. Broadly, we can distinguish between two schools of thought about this: those who believe in objective truth and those who believe in subjective experience, interpretation, perception and understanding. Put in another way, the "objectivist's" view will be: I know what I know because the phenomenon I'm investigating and/or theorising about exists objectively, *independent* from my understanding, interpretation, perception and experience. The subjectivist view would rather be: I know what I know because I (myself) can experience, think, interpret, perceive and understand.

2nd building block: epistemology

The first believes that reality is something outside to the human mind, independent of feelings, and the same for everyone (Wood 2000:60). Theorising can therefore also be objective, uninfluenced by values, biases, personal feelings, and other subjective factors when perceiving material reality. I can investigate and theorise about the media's framing of something in an objective way without allowing my personal knowledge, understanding and own interpretation of the media's ways of framing something, to interfere.

The second school does not believe in objective truth. They assume there are multiple views of reality, no one of which is intrinsically more valid than any other (Wood 2000:61). Theorising about the media's framing of something cannot be separated from our knowledge of the media, its history, its institutions, its ways of production, its people (workers) and so on. Such knowledge influences our interpretation and understanding.

The first school is often referred to as empiricism and the so-called Scientific Method, and the second as being critical, interpretative, hermeneutical and phenomenological.

To summarise: In the case of the media framing a person or whatever, the first school will believe that there are objective ways of investigating this that will lead to objective conclusions. The second school will believe that there are different ways of looking at this issue leading to different opinions; none of them being either true or untrue.

Table 3.2: Epistemology

EPISTEMOLOGY		
Do the media frame people and events to influence public opinion in a specific direction?		
Epistemological point of departure	Objective investigation	Yes or no
Epistemological point of departure	Subjective investigation	Not an unqualified yes or an unqualified no. It will depend on circumstances, conditions and the free will of people

Purpose

3rd building block: purpose

The third building block of theory according to Wood (*op.cit*) concerns the *purpose* of theory. What is the purpose of my theory about the media framing people and events? Is it to discover and formulate universal laws about the nature of the media, in other words to be able to say that the media always function in this or that way, or is the purpose to discover patterns of media behaviour that may prevail under certain conditions and in certain circumstances? Again we can distinguish two schools: *universalists* and *situationalists*. The first believe that the purpose of theory is to generate universal laws of human behaviour. The second believe that it is not possible and that theory can only articulate *rules* that describe patterns in human behaviour, rather than *laws*.

Approaches to the Study of Mass Communication

Table 3.3: Purpose of theory

PURPOSE OF A THEORY		
Do the media frame people and events to influence public opinion in a specific direction?		
To discover universal laws	Universalism	Laws about how and when the media frames people and events can be described and are universal
To discover patterns of behaviour	Situationalism	Given certain conditions and circumstances the media may frame people and events in different ways

Focus

Finally, as the fourth building block of theory, the *focus* of a theory has to be considered. Again it is possible to distinguish between two broad schools. As in the case of ontology, epistemology and purpose, it is important to keep in mind that the schools are not necessarily exclusive of each other. Theorists belonging to a certain school or point of departure may share some of the beliefs and points of departure of the other school. It is often a matter of degree.

> 4th building block

As far as focus is concerned, the two broad schools are *behaviourism* and *humanism*. Simply defined, behaviourism focuses on observable behaviour. Behaviourists believe that only concrete behaviour, such as the things people actually do and say, are relevant. Behaviour as such is the determinant and therefore the proper focus of theory. Contrary to this, humanists believe that the *meaning* of behaviour should be the focus of theory and that meaning may differ from circumstance to circumstance and from condition to condition. Humanism emphasises the fact that people have free wills, the ability to make choices and the capacity to create meanings. It is not so much a specific behaviour that is important, but rather the reasons why people behave in certain ways. External behaviour is only a sign of deeper psychological and physiological processes. What we perceive, think, and feel directly affects what we do and what we assume it means (Wood 2000:67).

Table 3.4: Focus of theory

FOCUS OF A THEORY		
Do the media frame people and events to influence public opinion in a specific direction?		
The media behave in a certain way.	Behaviourism	The media behave in a certain way therefore the media frame people and events
Why do the media behave in a certain way?	Humanism	For specific reasons the media may create certain meanings in its covering of people and events and may thus frame people and events in a certain way in the minds of certain people who are free to interpret the media's framing as they wish

To summarise this part: According to Wood (2000) theory and theory building always depends on:

- a basic point of departure about humanity and its activities (ontology) which can range from being deterministic to humanistic;
- a preferred way of looking at or investigating humanity and its activities (epistemology) which can range from being objective to subjective;
- the purpose of the theory which can range from being to discover universal rules to discover patterns;
- the focus of a theory which can range from being behaviourist to being humanist.

Table 3.5: Summary of building blocks

Ontology	Epistemology	Purpose	Focus
Determinism	Objectivity	Discover universal rules	Behaviourism
Humanism	Subjectivity	Discover patterns	Humanism

3.3.4 Evaluating theory

How do we evaluate a theory? Wood (2000:41–47) suggests five criteria:

- scope;
- testability;
- parsimony;

- utility;
- heurism.

scope of theory

In evaluating the *scope* of a theory we have to establish how much and how well a theory describes and explains. Some theories claim to describe and explain almost every aspect of mass communication including the communicator, the medium, the content and the recipient of media messages. They claim to offer a theory of mass communication in general. These are so-called grand theories, such as, for example, Marshall McLuhan's "the medium is the message" theory and George Gerbner's "cultivation" theory. Other theories offer a description and explanation of only one aspect of mass communication, for example feminist media theories. Although they can cover the whole domain of mass communication, the emphasis is on women

When deciding how well a theory describes something, we thus have to distinguish whether a theory describes all the essential aspects of a phenomenon or if it only provides a partial description. For example, does a theory focus on all the aspects of the mass communication process (communicator, medium, messages, recipient), or only on one or two of these. Both are acceptable.

As far as explanation is concerned, Wood distinguishes between two broad types of explanation, namely *law-based explanation* and *rules-based explanation*. The first argues that if this happens this will follow. If I send this kind of message this will be the audiences' reaction. In other words, the explanation is causal or correlational. Law-based explanation relates to determinist ontology, objectivist epistemology, universalist purpose and behaviourist focus.

Rules-based explanation identifies rules that explain why certain things happen. It aims to identify patterns rather than laws, to describe and explain what may happen under certain conditions. It relates to humanist ontology, subjectivist epistemology, situationalist purpose and humanist focus.

testability of theory

A second criterion for evaluating theories is *testability*. Can a theory be investigated to determine whether it is accurate or not? Or is it so farfetched that it does not even need to be tested? Again, the determinists (ontology), objectivists (epistemology), universalists (purpose) and behaviourists (focus) claim that the empirical scientific method allows for verification. The same topic can be theorised about and investigated

by different researchers and they will arrive at the same conclusions. However, other schools of thought believe that one should allow for differentiation, exceptionality, different views and different interpretations of the same topic based on different circumstance in order to arrive at a more nuanced understanding of something.

<small>simplicity of theory</small>

Thirdly there is *parsimony*. Parsimony refers to simplicity. A theory doesn't need to be complex. To the contrary, some of the best theories are simple and allow for clear description and explanation. A good example is Roman Jakobson's theory of communication functions: namely that we communicate to refer to something, express our feelings about something, explain something, to draw attention to something, and so on. This theory can and has been applied in numerous ways by numerous researchers to analyse components of mass communication, be it from an empirical or critical perspective.

<small>usability of theory</small>

The fourth criterion is *utility*. People tend to think of theory as being esoteric and academic. This need not be the case. Theories need to have a practical value in terms of our understanding, controlling and improving of the phenomenon. A theory helping us to understand how mass communication works might lead to media workers, media users and media researchers control of this phenomenon to the benefit of people and society.

Finally we evaluate a theory in terms of its *heuristic value*. Does the theory lead to new thinking? Does it contribute to our knowledge? Does it provide us with the potential for further investigation?

3.3.5 Goals of mass media theory

Mass communication theory, which originated from sociology, describes, explains, interprets (understands), predicts and tries to reform the media's social relationships, be it internal relations within the media or external relations with other social structures and the media's audiences. As put by Croteau and Hoynes (2003:13):

> "... media theory in general asks us to consider the role of the media in our individual lives (the micro level) and in the context of social forces such as the economy, politics, and technological development (the macro level). If we want to understand the media and their impact on our society, we must consider the social relationships (both micro and macro) between media and the social world."

Approaches to the Study of Mass Communication

In sociology a point of departure is that the individual is the product of certain structures and institutions in his/her society. These structures and institutions may be the educational system, the government, the judiciary, the church (or religion), the family, non-government organisations, the economy and so on. All these structures and institutions make up our living reality and are responsible for how we think and act in terms of values and norms defined, passed on and entrenched by these structures. These structures and institutions and their ways of operating are socialisation instruments. In other words, through these structures we are taught how to live and interact with each other and with the structures, and through these structures the individual's identity is constructed. Thus, sociology places a high value on understanding the relationships between people and these structures and institutions.

> structures in society

Today the media is one of the most important structures and institutions in society and as such one of the most important and invasive socialisation instruments. The media form our most important contact with the other structures and institutions. Through the media we learn about politics, our histories, how people behave, what is in and what is out, the big issues of society such as crime, poverty, HIV/AIDS, our place in society, global warming, disasters, products available on the market (advertisements), and so on. Also, we are taught by the media the values and norms of society as these are reflected in the numerous media entertainment products, ranging from films to soap operas, game shows, sport programmes, documentaries and articles on almost every possible topic, style magazines and so on.

Whereas sociology as an academic discipline studies social relationships in general, media studies are more specific. Therefore, the main goal of mass communication and media theory is to describe, and if necessary change, the social relations between the media and society (all the structures in society), the relationships between the media and its audiences (media users), and the relationships within the media.

Croteau and Honyes (2003:22) refer to three types of social relations as the object of media theory and research:
- the relationships between media institutions and other institutions in society (external relations), such as the media's relationships with and to the government, the judiciary, the economy, politics, etc;
- the relationships within media institutions (internal relations) such as the relationship between an editor and journalists or between the

> three types of social relations

Media Studies: Volume 1

editor and the board of the newspaper and/or newspaper group; the relationship(s) of individual journalists and/or radio and television programme makers with each other; and the relationships between different media in a society, for example the relationships with and between the public broadcaster and newspapers, advertisers, etc;

- the relationships between media institutions and their audiences and the audiences' relationships with the media.

What is meant by relationships is how the different structures and role players are involved with each other and influence and impact on each other. For example: what is the impact of the economy on the media? What is the influence of politics on the media? What is the influence a government's media policy or an opposition's media policy may have on the media? But also, what is the impact of the media on the economy or on politics? These are examples of external relationships.

As far as internal relationships are concerned, an example is the impact of internal or institutional policy and codes of conduct formulated by boards and managers on the practice of journalists, radio and television programme makers, film makers, Internet designers, and so on. All these relationships have an impact on what media users get to see, read and listen to and thus on the content of the media. Through its content the media establish specific relationships with their audiences and vice versa. Such relationships may impact on the ways in which audiences or individual members of audiences experience and understand their worlds.

In the description and analysis of these relationships two concepts are central: structure and agency.

structure and agency

Structure: How does the structure of a socialisation instrument (in our case the mass media) impact on our lives? Structure is meant to consider how a socialisation instrument is composed, how it works, how it is managed and what its values and norms are.

Agency: Agency is the way in which human actions impact on a structure. For example, the educational system in a country is structured in a certain way. The way in which it is structured impacts on the kind and quality of the education we get. How do we or can we (the people) influence these structures?

Similarly, we can argue that the way a country or a society's media is structured (see chapter 1 on the history of the South African media and the South African media map) impacts on the kind and quality of

Approaches to the Study of Mass Communication

information and entertainment we (media users) get and thus, impacts on our perceptions of reality as well as on our values and norms. How can we (the media users) and other structures in the society impact on the media structure in order to improve the media – and thus the quality of information and entertainment we receive through the media in such a way that may lead to an improved perspective on reality? Between structure and agency there is always tension.

To conclude: All media theory and research deal in one or another way with the relationships referred to above. The goal is to understand the structures involved and the human agency in influencing these structures. Our understanding(s) of the media and its structural relationships evolve from a number of theoretical perspectives or approaches. In the next section some of the main approaches are introduced.

SECTION 2: THEORETICAL APPROACHES

3.4 THEORETICAL APPROACHES TO THE STUDY AND RESEARCH OF MASS COMMUNICATION

3.4.1 Categorising theories

Describing and categorising different theoretical approaches is not an easy task and is, to a certain extent, impossible. Different authors may have different ways of categorising theories. It is, for instance, possible to categorise theories as those dealing with media institutions, those dealing with media content, those dealing with media relationships (such as explained in the sociological approach above) or theories dealing with media audiences.

Certain authors such as Littlejohn (1992: 341–374) distinguish between *macro* and *micro* theories: macro being those theories and approaches which investigate and explain the link between the media and other institutions; and micro being those theories and approaches concerned with the link between the media and audiences. The link itself may be the content of the media that is investigated and explained in numerous content theories and analyses.

> macro and micro theories

McQuail (2000:61–162), on the other hand, distinguishes between theories and approaches concerned with the relationships between media and society and between media and culture, and a third branch of new theories and approaches concerned with the relationship between new media and the information society. However, he emphasises that:

> media relationships

> "... there is no neat system for categorizing the available theories. These [typologies – PJF] are fragmentary and selective, sometimes overlapping or inconsistent, often guided by conflicting ideologies and assumptions." (McQuail 2000:68)

In other words, it is difficult to say that a theory and its research is only concerned with, for example, the relationship between the media and other institutions such as politics or the economy. The same theory and research will also have to concern itself with media content because media content reflects this relationship, and with audiences' responses to the content, because response determines the outcome of the relationship between media and other institutions.

Nevertheless, we can say that all media theory concerns itself in one or another way with the description, interpretation, explanation and evaluation of the power of the media to integrate people into society, and the media's role in changing society.

In doing this, the emphasis in media theory is thus on:
- the relationship between media and society, for example the media's political economy and the functions of the media (see chapters 4 and 7 on functions and ideology), media and culture (see chapter 6 on media culture and cultural studies), media and globalisation (see chapter 9 on globalisation), and feminist media theory (see chapter 10 in volume 2 on media and gender);
- media content: genre theory and analysis, narrative analysis, semiotics (see volume 3 where these topics are dealt with in more depth), and ideological theory (see chapter 7);
- media audiences: (see volume 3 of this book), for example reception theory and analysis, ethnography and psychoanalysis.

How we think about the power of the media, the media's effects on behaviour, the functions of the media in society and so on is usually done from a specific theoretical perspective and approach. For our purpose we distinguish between the following seven perspectives, often also called paradigms:
- the positivist perspective and approaches;
- the critical perspective and approaches;
- meaning production perspective and approaches;
- the technological deterministic perspective and approaches;
- the information society perspective and approaches;
- the posstructuralist postmodern perspective and approach.

Approaches to the Study of Mass Communication

And of specific relevance to us in South Africa:
- the post-colonial and Afro-centric perspective and approaches.

3.4.2 The positivistic approach

The emphasis in *positivism* is on scientific method, on knowledge derived from scientifically processed and analysed data about a phenomenon. The purpose is to arrive at a scientific description of the world and of individual phenomena (such as media).

In her 1989 book *Philosophy of mass communication research*, the late Professor Nerina Jansen of the University of South Africa's Department of Communication Science explained positivism as follows, here summarised:

Positivism originated from the need to place the study of society, its structures and social conditions on par with the *scientific method* of the natural and physical science of which the history, as we know it today, dates back to the seventeenth century. The scientific method of the natural sciences was seen by founding sociologists such as Auguste Comte (1798–1857) and Émile Durkheim (1858–1917) as an ideal for the study of social phenomena and human behaviour.

positivistic premises

The scientific method requires that all phenomena should be treated in the same way. In research the same rules and the same requirements had to be applied and met regardless of the nature of the phenomena under investigation. Some of the key assumptions in positivism (see Jansen 1989: 4–6) are that the proper object for scientific study is the observable world. The world is "out there", it is a given reality that exists independently from the human being and the human being's mind. The nature and characteristics of the observable world may be revealed by means of a special method of study, known as the scientific method. The application of this method involves processes of empirical research which will yield objective findings and will ensure that no subjective elements intervene to influence the validity of the finding. Factual evidence thus provides the researcher of the observable phenomenon with objective, reliable and valid knowledge about any aspect of the observable phenomenon and serves as a firm foundation for the prediction and control of the phenomenon, which is the ultimate aim of the positivist. This reasoning rests on the assumption that phenomena are governed by universal laws which may be revealed through the application of the scientific method.

The scientific method comprises certain fixed steps which must be followed by all researchers and requires the use of standardised procedures and techniques. Research that complies with these requirements not only yields objective results, but may be repeated by other researchers with largely the same results. The method is central. The researcher is important only in the sense that he or she must apply the method correctly.

In so far as the human being and his or her conduct complies with the requirement of observability he/she too is an object for scientific study to which the scientific method can be applied. In positivism it is believed that the human being, his/her nature, behaviours, social structures and social relationships can also be "measured" objectively. However, the human being as an individual (with his/her own peculiarities) is not important: they are merely part of the observable world. They and their behaviour(s), structures and social relations are all the same and governed by universal laws that can be described objectively.

methodologies

From a methodological point of view, positivistic research is usually empirical, behaviourist and functionalist. Typical research methods in these positivistic approaches are quantitative content analysis and survey research (see volume 3 for an in-depth discussion of these methods). Here, empiricism, behaviourism and functionalism are only briefly explained.

Empiricism

In *empiricism* it is believed that knowledge is derived from human experience and based on observation which needs to be tested and accepted or rejected in terms of measuring how the "knowledge" stands up against facts. Empiricism is closely related to the natural sciences and is also called the Scientific Method. From the perspective of the human sciences (the humanities – of which communication science is a part) this point of view is much debated. The humanities places a high priority on the human mind (rationality) understanding something that is not necessarily observable. In empiricism the concepts of "objectivity" and "measurement" are highly valued.

Behaviourism

Behaviourism concentrates on the experimental analysis of human behaviour – hence on the observable actions of a subject (person/group) as opposed to concealed cognitive processes underlying behaviour. In mass

Approaches to the Study of Mass Communication

communication theory and research, behaviourism is associated with the linear mass communication model of Shannon and Weaver (1949): a sender formulates and sends a message via a channel to a receiver. They developed this model in an attempt to construct a mathematical theory of information dissemination which would be applicable to a variety of situations in which information is transmitted, whether by human, mechanical or other systems. Within the framework of their model these authors identify three levels of problems in the analysis of information: level A (technical), level B (semantic, the meaning emanating from the transmitter's mode of address) and level C (effectiveness, measured in terms of the recipient's reception and understanding of the message). Their model was constructed mainly with a view to solving level A problems, the assumption apparently being that the resolution of technical problems through improved encoding of the message will *ipso facto* improve matters at levels B and C – in other words, improve the communication in terms of the desired effect the communicator (or sender) wishes to achieve with the message. Good examples of behaviouristic mass communication theories were the early theories about the effects of the media on human behaviour.

To a great degree this model still underlies the analysis of communication problems as executed within the framework of the positivistic approaches.

Functionalism

Functionalism, which to a great extent directed initial mass communication research, is closely associated with the sociology of Émile Durkheim (1858–1917) and Talcott Parsons (1902–1979). They viewed society as an integrated, harmonious, cohesive whole in which all parts (the school, the church, economic, political and cultural institutions) function to maintain equilibrium, consensus and social order. In other words, society can be viewed as a human body consisting of different organs all functioning together. Should one of the organs become sick or dysfunctional, it affects the whole body. In the case of mass communication, functionalism sees the media as one of the instruments in society that should contribute to the harmonious and cohesive functioning of society (see chapter 4 for a more in-depth discussion of functionalism and media functions). Being positivistic in nature, functionalism studies reality "out there", independent from the human being (see Jansen 1989:21). It concentrates on repetitive observable phenomena or observable indicators of phenomena. Objective

study is the goal; subjective interpretation falls outside the scientific ambit. Good examples of functionalist mass communication theories were the early normative theories about the role of the media in society.

Positivism and mass communication

origin

Positivism and its related traditions manifested itself in the previous century in the work of Robert E. Park, a member of the then-influential Chicago School of Sociology in the USA. Park followed in the footsteps of European sociologists such as Émile Durkheim and Talcott Parsons. Park's disciples included the founders of modern communication science, such as Paul F. Lazarsfeld, Kurt Lewin, Bernard Berelson and Ithiel de Sola Pool. A central assumption in their work was that the media help to shape public opinion and in this way may trigger and influence social change. Therefore, the mass media must be used to improve society.

We can argue that the purpose of all positivistic mass communication theory and research is usually to gain a better understanding of exactly how the media work. The purpose of such research is to contribute to better and more efficient media planning. Such planning may contribute to the achievement of certain goals which may be the economic growth of a media company, to influence people's minds about politics or other matters, to run effective campaigns, etc. In positivistic research the emphasis is thus mainly on the:

- efficient working and management of the media;
- efficient production of media content;
- functions of the media;
- media's effect on people and society.

functions and effects

In general, we could thus say that the empirical approaches see the media as instruments (in the hands of their owners, be they private or state) that can and should be applied to achieve a certain goal. Theory and research therefore need to focus on the functions and effects of the media.

The functions are seen to be the provision of information, entertainment and education. Insofar as effects are concerned, the argument is that the greater knowledge of the effects of the media will result in a more effective fulfilment of the functions of the media.

There are innumerable studies related to the effective political, cultural and economic functioning of the media; the ways in which the media are "used" by recipients (uses and gratification studies); quantitative analyses

Approaches to the Study of Mass Communication

of media content (how much and how often do the media reports cover something); and market research (who are the media users – how old are they, how much money do they earn?).

Typical research questions might be:
- What effect does political news have on the media user's voting behaviour?
- What does the portrayal of violence by the media have on the behaviour of people?
- What effect does television have on communication within families?
- What effect does the media have on children's learning?
- How many people watch a specific programme?
- Why do they watch it?
- What are the functions of the media in developmental projects?
- How best can the media contribute to education?
- What is the content of the various media?
- Does news coverage of acts of terrorism contribute to increased acts of terrorism?
- What is the public's opinion on a given matter?
- How is the public's opinion formed?
- How can the media best and effectively inform people about HIV/AIDS?

Research into these and related questions has lead to numerous theories such as the agenda setting theory, the accumulation theory, the diffusion of innovation theory, modelling theory and so on. (See chapter 5 for a discussion of these theories.)

The point of departure is usually a perception of the media as neutral tools, capable of serving a wide range of purposes. Research takes as given the purposes of media users, or would-be users, and then collects the information intended to promote the realisation of those purposes. This might include studies of people's media preferences.

In short, the positivistic approach is guided by the almost classic question of Harold Lasswell (1948): "*Who, says what, in which channel, to whom, with what effect?*"

Classic examples of positivistic mass communication research

Some of the classic examples of positivistic mass communication research and theories include Walter Lippmann's *Public Opinion* (1922), Bernard

| founding scholars |

Berelson, Paul Lazarsfeld and Hazel Gaudet's *The people's choice* (1948), Harold Lasswell's *The structure and function of communication in society* (1948), Robert K. Merton's *Social theory and social structure* (1949), Elihu Katz and Lazarsfeld's *Personal influence* (1955) and Joseph T. Klapper's *The effects of mass communication* (1960) (see Lowery and De Fleur's 1983 *Milestones in mass communication research* for an overview of the nature and influence of these works).

The US journalist and political philosopher Walter Lippmann, author of *Public Opinion* (1922), was one of the first to argue that information from the news media is refracted by pictures in our heads (stereotypes) and that the content of news is shaped by the characteristics of journalists and the press. Paul Lazarsfeld played a leading role in our initial understanding of the psychological and social processes that delay, inhibit, reinforce, activate and changes people's voting decisions. His main contribution was his demonstration of how the media permeate people's political, social and economic activities. The US political scientist Harold Lasswell laid the foundation of our understanding of the functions of the media to survey, correlate and transmit information and knowledge about society. He also played a leading role in the development of the technique of quantitative content analysis. Equally, the US sociologist, Robert K. Merton, did groundbreaking work in the field of the functional analysis of mass communication.

More contemporary examples of positivistic research can be found in the numerous quantitative content analyses of newspapers, television and radio programmes, the media in general, and surveys amongst media users. Good examples are the work of the Media Tenor Institute for Media Analysis. In a recent publication, based on empirical analyses, Media Tenor reported on, for example the media's role in covering (or covering up) corruption and AIDS, as well as considering international coverage of South Africa. (See http://www.mediatenor.co.za, accessed on 2007/01/17.)

Criticism of the positivistic approach

Max Weber

Criticism of the positivistic approach has its origin in the work of the German sociologist Max Weber (1864–1920). He drew on the work of Wilhelm Dilthey (1833–1911) who emphasised the difference between the natural and social sciences (see Jansen 1989:6–9). Dilthey maintained that a social researcher could only gain insight into the social world by not distancing himself or herself from it by claiming to be *objective*. Insight

Approaches to the Study of Mass Communication

came only by means of *identification* with the object of research, in short, the topic of research. For Weber this meant that the proper task of social investigation is the interpretative understanding of the meaning of social action.

Human action is not just an observable response to stimuli. It is based on interpretation and understanding. Such understanding is based on values. Interpretation, understanding and values are not necessarily observable. The positivistic claim that only that which is observable can be scientifically investigated and described is thus unacceptable. Furthermore, meanings and values can differ from individual to individual, from group to group, and from organisation to organisation. Therefore, in the case of social action, social meaning and social interpretation, it is always difficult if not impossible to *generalise* on the basis of only observable facts calculated in terms of statistics. Human action is also determined by *intention. And intention always relates to one's understanding of something and one's values. Similar to understanding and values, intention is not observable.*

To give a practical example: positivistic media research may claim that intercultural television soap operas teach people of different cultures to respect each other. Such a claim may be based on survey research amongst a population of a hundred people from different cultures watching the same soap opera on a regular basis. To generalise on the basis of this research that all intercultural soap operas (as a genre) will have as a consequence that people of different cultures will respect each other is, according to the above criticism, impossible. Although it may be true for *some* soap operas watched by *some* people, it does not mean that *all* multicultural soap operas will have the *same* effect for *all* people. To the contrary, different people may experience the same soap opera in different ways based on their different values, understandings and contexts, or may interpret and understand different multicultural soap operas in different ways. Their understandings will also be based on the intentions of the programme makers and their own intentions as viewers, which may differ from soap opera to soap opera. The same applies to the argument that violent films will lead to violent behaviour. Although such a claim may be valid in some cases, one cannot generalise that it will always be the case for all people.

Although positivistic research may claim that its findings are objective because of its use of scientific methods, human behaviour itself is

objectivity/
subjectivity

subjective and based on values, intentions, interpretations, understandings, meanings and contexts which may differ from person to person, group to group and circumstance to circumstance. For this reason we cannot generalise about human actions or behaviour. Social research need to consider numerous variables which makes generalisations on the basis of what has been observed in isolated and de-contextualised experiments impossible. The task of social research should rather be to understand a phenomenon contextually and to evaluate and consider various alternative understandings on the basis of which action could be considered.

Media – its institutions, workers, content production and its audiences – are the result of human action (behaviour) and thus the result of human intentions (to inform and entertain people, to influence people's thinking, to make money), values (political, economic, cultural, social and religious), and contexts (circumstances and needs), on the basis of which the media and its audiences interpret aspects of reality. The critique is that the positivistic approach (also called the dominant paradigm) with its emphasis on empiricism and quantification is too narrowly focused on discovering cause and effect relationships (see Griffin, 2003:366).

3.4.3 The critical approach

The development of critical thinking on mass communication has a long history. Since the earliest times there have been complaints about the abuse of the media for political purposes: in classical times in Mediterranean culture the complaints might have concerned the use of Greek theatre to propagate political ideals and in the Middle Ages in Europe the flysheet (a printed sheet or pamphlet) and the lyrics of the bard aroused controversy.

However for our purpose, modern critical thinking about mass communication started with what is called *mass society theory*.

Mass society theory

mass society theory

Mass society theories were formulated at the turn of the nineteenth century and continued through the middle of the twentieth century. They began as a reaction to technological innovation that in turn gave rise to industrialisation and urbanisation. Some of the underlying assumptions of mass society theory are that the media:
- have the power to influence the minds of average people (mass man);
- corrupt people's minds;

Approaches to the Study of Mass Communication

- initiate social chaos;
- trivialise culture and as such contribute to the decline of civilisation.

Originally critics (Kornhauser 1949) were concerned about the alienation and the depreciation of the individual in mass society, the destruction of traditional ties and relationships between people (the distinction between different classes of people), the destruction of political and other hierarchies, the decline of tradition, and the commercialisation of culture.

The foundation of mass society theory can be found in the work of the German sociologist, Ferdinand Tönnies (1855–1936). Tönnies drew a comparison between earlier societies, which he called *Gemeinschaft* (often translated as community) societies, and late nineteenth century European society, which he called *Gesellschaft* (civil society). In the first, the pillars of society were the family, tradition, strong community ties, clear-cut social roles and strong social institutions such as the church. In the *Gesellschaft* society these pillars began to crumble under the influence of industrialisation and urbanisation. It became a society characterised by formal regulations with strong and rigid laws, formalised and impersonal social relationships, and individual independence.

<aside>Ferdinand Tönnies</aside>

Social critics such as Matthew Arnold (1822–1888), José Ortega y Gasset (1883–1955), John Stuart Mill (1806–1873) and later Hannah Arendt (1906–1975) described the decline of the *Gemeinschaft* society. Their view of mass media is characterised by pessimism about industrialisation, urbanisation, the rise of the majority and the impact of this on democracy, the accessibility of education for all and the growth of the mass media.

<aside>the rise of the mass</aside>

The British philosopher John Stuart Mill (*On Liberty*, 1850) argued that democratic forms of government could lead to a new kind of despotism: the tyranny of the majority. He pointed to the danger that a self-assured and complacent middle class poses to the morality and intellectual authority of the high class. For the Spanish philosopher José Ortega y Gasset (*The Revolt of the Masses*, 1932), the development of democracy, media, and free and accessible education disturbed the natural balance between the élite and the mass. These developments erased the traditional distinction between social classes. The earlier clearly-defined subordinate state of the masses became obscured. The masses, although they may have access to information through the mass media and education, do not possess the ability to give and take the moral and intellectual lead

in society. Yet the masses claim the right to lead. The British cultural critic Matthew Arnold (*Culture and anarchy*, 1869) shared the concern that the disintegration of the traditional distinction between different classes could lead to moral and intellectual decline. In much the same vein, although later, the German political theorist Hannah Arendt (*The Human Condition*, 1958) argued that there is a relationship between the thinking and social conditions of the masses and the rise of totalitarian social and political movements. The rise of the Nazis in 1930s Germany, or Josef Stalin in Russia from the 1920s to the 1950s, and other totalitarian political trends can, according to her, be attributed in part to the entry of the masses in politics and an acceptance of mass man's thinking as the only acceptable norm. In all of the above the mass media were seen to play a central role.

Émile Durkheim

However, with the growth of modern society, the growth of economic and educational power, and the growth of democracy, the concept "mass" with its associated negative connotations has fallen in dispute. Perhaps this can be contributed to the thinking of people such as the French sociologist Émile Durkheim (1858–1917). Like Tönnies, Durkheim distinguished between two kinds of societies: folk communities (Tönnies' *Gemeinschaft* society) with social orders comparable to machines, and modern society (Tönnies' *Gesellschaft* society) with social orders comparable to a living organism. In the first, people were parts of a larger machine: well-ordered to perform traditional social roles and duties. In the second, people progress like a living organism, each with different cells and different purposes. Modern social orders undergo profound changes and the people in them progress and grow along with the changes. Durkheim thus favoured a more optimistic view of modern (mass) society. (See Baran & Davis 2003:58–59.)

As far as the media in modern society are concerned, research began to show that media users were not powerless victims as advocated by the mass society theorists, but active participants. As far as the relationship between the media and democracy is concerned, it was increasingly realised that the media are not detrimental to democracy, but rather a pillar of democracy in the sense that the media (can) provide people with a wide range of (critical) opinions on matters of public interest as well as expose corrupt politics and politicians. How the media do this is not above criticism, as was shown by the Frankfurt School, which can be seen as the next phase in the development of critical theory.

Approaches to the Study of Mass Communication

The Frankfurt School

The Frankfurt School or *Institut für Socialforschung* at Frankfurt am Main in Germany was established in 1923 to conduct sociological research. Eminent social scientists associated with this School included Theodor Adorno (1903–1969), Max Horkheimer (1895–1973), Walter Benjamin (1892–1940) and Herbert Marcuse (1898–1979). In 1933 the School was closed down by the Nazis. Its leading figures emigrated to the USA, where they continued their work at Columbia University.

> Frankfurt School

The ideas of the Frankfurt School are epitomised by Horkheimer's *critical theory*. His original aim was to demonstrate the presence of contradictions in existing theories of society (and in society itself). What is said to be democratic society is in fact not democratic.

With this as their primary concern, the 1950s saw members of the Frankfurt School such as Jürgen Habermas (1929–), Adorno, Marcuse, Erich Fromm (1900–1980) and Walter Benjamin (1858–1917) rebelling against modern society and the media as creators and bearers of contemporary culture and ideology.

Where mass society criticism was concerned with the influence of industrialisation, urbanisation and the mass media on the preservation of the organic society and culture, the Frankfurt School presented a vision of a new Utopian society, free from class and domination. The Frankfurt School's criticism of the mass media was that they hamper the road to a Utopian classless society and stand in the way of change. By *selectively* (re)presenting reality (or aspects of political, economic, social and cultural reality) the media confirm, support and circulate dominant capitalist ideology to the benefit of those with power and the detriment of the working class. The media's production of ideology thus became a central focus of critical theory (see chapter 7). Furthermore, the Frankfurt School focused attention on the media as a culture industry and the production of popular/mass culture in and through which capitalist ideology is spread and entrenched. This gave rise to the debate about high versus popular culture. In the next section this debate is briefly introduced, before we look at ideology as a main focus of critical theory.

> utopian society

Mass/popular culture criticism

The concepts "culture", "popular culture", "mass culture", "media culture" and so on, are explained in more depth in chapter 6 on media culture.

127

Briefly, the debate boils down to the following: the media (as an institution) is a culture of its own and for itself. It is a culture which can be explained as being a popular/mass culture with all the negative connotations associated with the concepts "mass" and "popular". In many ways this culture, the media as a popular/mass culture, characterises present-day society. Authors such as Gitlin (1981) and Hartley, Goulden & O'Sullivan (1985) describe this popular/mass culture in the following way.

> earlier popular culture

Popular culture, compared to other forms of culture, is seen as the product and direct result of technologisation, industrialisation, urbanisation and commercialisation. Compared with the popular culture of earlier societies, which was *spontaneously developed* and used by people, today's popular culture is known by the fact that it is *produced intentionally* and in bulk by a complex and multibillion-dollar media industry. Its main aim is to sell itself to the masses for mass consumption (Hartley *et al* 1985:7–12). Unlike earlier societies, popular culture in today's society is purposefully produced as a product with mass consumption envisaged.

Gitlin (1981) shows that throughout time, societies have had their forms of popular culture. People have always articulated meaning in some or other popular symbolic form which today are seen to be high art or culture. For example, in Neolithic society (the final period of the Stone Age), people in Europe, India, Africa and Australia spontaneously created cave art for functional, spiritual and artistic purposes. In Europe, in Greek and Roman times, throughout the Middle Ages and during the Renaissance, the theatre, street shows and gatherings, ballad singers, troubadours and so on expressed social and political issues of the day in form of popular art/culture which was seen to be a popular form of cultural expression. Today these forms of expression are regarded as art or *high* culture: William Shakespeare's dramas, the comedies of French playwright Molière, African oral tales and fables.

However, according to Gitlin (1981), early popular culture was characterised by meanings that were aesthetic and at the same time religious, political, or simply incarnations of everyday sentiment. Early popular culture exhorted, celebrated, cautioned, and denounced; it embodied morality and provided release from it; it gave pleasure and attached that pleasure to particular symbolic constructions. Because its artefacts were concrete, popular culture could make values stand forth to be recognised, appreciated, refined, and if need be, rejected. Social identity, whether of class, region, nation, community, religion, people, or

Approaches to the Study of Mass Communication

political ideal, could become publicly manifest when it was embedded in the stone and glass of cathedrals, in the rituals of dance and passion of play, in song and in story (Gitlin 1981:202).

Although the same qualities might apply to contemporary popular culture, it is distinguished from previous forms of popular culture at the following levels:

contemporary popular culture

- Popular culture is produced, usually by a central corporation which is often multinational in scope, for private consumption by members of the mass society. An example is Hollywood, known as the world's entertainment industry *par excellence*. Hollywood produces entertainment that is used by individual members throughout the world, without these members having any part in the production of the entertainment and/or the meaning of this entertainment itself. These products do not address or symbolically reflect individuals' personal, cultural values and issues, as was the case in earlier societies.
- Contemporary popular culture is accessible to all and even enters the private domain. For example, today television is accessible to almost everyone in the middle class and working class; it is easily available, relatively cheap and has practically become standard equipment and entertainment in private homes. The earlier forms of popular culture were, for example, limited to the town square, the regular carnival and/or the marketplace, traditional ceremonies and the church, and was only physically accessible to those who could attend, participate and afford it.
- Popular culture is known by rhythmic and cyclical mass production based on style and fads (*what's in and what's out*) for the sake of maximum and continued income for the producers. An appropriate example: pop stars' music and their influence on fashion fads.
- Popular culture is recognised by its secular nature. Unlike the popular culture of earlier societies that testified to spiritually and religiously symbolic meanings, popular culture today mainly aims at the secular and the here and now. The meaning of popular culture is mainly ideological by nature. However, the viewer is seldom conscious of these meanings, and neither is it expected of the viewer to be conscious of ideological and other meanings (see Hartley *et al* 1985:8–9).

To a certain extent the debate about high culture/popular culture, the media as popular culture, what this culture does to people and how it constitutes a consumerist culture and society, still continues. See for example the post-modern approach (see 3.4.7) (especially Baudillard's views) and the debate about the media as public sphere (see chapter 8), the nature and quality of media entertainment (see chapter 4 on the functions of the media and chapter 6 on media culture). From the perspective of critical theory, the bottom-line is that the minority who own the media have through their products of mass-produced information and entertainment created a de-contextualised and shallow cultural world in which consumerist (capitalist) values dictate the majority's everyday experience, understanding, and judgement of the world.

Critical theory today

With the above as foundation, critical theory today amounts to the following:

ideological instrument

The media are seen to be the most pervasive *ideological agent* in late twentieth and early twenty-first century society. There is hardly a person who does not come into contact with media of one or another kind and the ideas and values they convey, be it newspapers, radio, television, advertisements, popular music or the Internet. Small wonder then that the media are referred to as the *consciousness industry* – a description with far-reaching implications concerning the possible influence of the media on human beings, their thinking and existence.

Influenced by the ideas of Georg Wilhelm Friedrich Hegel (1770–1931), Karl Marx (1818–1883) and Sigmund Freud (1856–1939), critical theorists today are primarily concerned about the media's ideological manipulation of the masses and the capitalistic use and misuse of the media by owners to foster capitalist values.

The point of departure is that in order to understand how ideology and hegemony invades and pervades our common-sense, we have to describe as closely as possible the ideological instruments of society. These are instruments such as the church, the economy, the military, the state, educational institutions and the media. These instruments are responsible for the production, circulation and distribution of ideology. The concept "ideology" is therefore central in the critical approach.

What is ideology?

A straightforward definition is that ideology is the ideas and belief systems in terms of which individuals, society or group(s) in a society

Approaches to the Study of Mass Communication

understand and interpret their political, economic, social and cultural realities. For example, during the years of apartheid in South Africa (1948–1994), economy, culture and the society were interpreted by many white South Africans from the perspective of the ideology of apartheid. This ideology emphasised racial separatism, in effect, racial discrimination. Those in favour of apartheid believed that as an ideology it was the only way for white South Africans to survive on the African continent. They often based their arguments on the moral philosophy of Christian nationalism.

Inglis (1990) explains ideology as follows: Academic interest in ideology has a long history. As early as in the works of Italian political philosopher Niccolò Machiavelli (1469–1527) and English philosopher and scientist Francis Bacon (1561–1626) there was a clear relationship between "ideology" (as a concept) and the way people think (or the way they think about something). Officially the term "ideology" was first coined during the French Revolution by the Enlightenment aristocrat Antoine-Louis-Claude Destutt de Tracy (1754–1836) to describe the "science of ideas". At the end of the eighteenth century and the in the *Age of the Enlightenment*, "ideology" was known to mean the study of systems of ideas (the suffix -ology meaning "study of").

> history of the concept of ideology

The first negative use of the term "ideology" stems from the work of Karl Marx who used it to characterise the influence of idealism in German philosophy and to critique religion (see Hall 1982). Marx, as well as Friedrich Engels, argued that material processes and socioeconomic relations and ideas form the *base* of the *superstructure* of society. With this as the underlying premise, further key issues in Marx's arguments concerning ideology are:

- It is not the consciousness of people that determines their being, but their social being that determines consciousness.
- In bourgeois society, ideas are linked to class position and class interests.
- Political economy is the common-sense ideology of capitalism. Ideology therefore legitimates capitalist exploitation.
- Ruling classes maintain their position through their monopoly over cultural institutions that produce ruling ideology.
- Subordinate classes, whose ideas do not reflect their true class interests, have been deceived into false consciousness.

Media Studies: Volume 1

<small>class struggle</small>

For Inglis (1990:78) these standpoints gave rise to the theory of *class struggle* and the birth of ideology as a theory of partisan interests: that is, the view that the ruling class favours best those ideas which preserve its own property and power by persuading everybody else that things are just fine as they are, and that the ideas, values and frame of mind which suit them so well suit everybody else at the same time. Ideology is then nothing but a *false consciousness* created by the ruling bourgeoisie to keep the working proletariat in place.

Given the conditions of the Industrial Revolution and the economic issues of the nineteenth century, Marx regarded the class struggle as principally a struggle between the (capitalist) bourgeoisie and the workers (proletariat) of the time. For this reason Marx described "ideology" as the ideas of the ruling capitalist bourgeoisie and the attempts by the bourgeoisie to force their ideas, customs and values on others. Today, the concept of "ideology" is no longer only associated with Marxist criticism of capitalism but applies to all forms of power domination. Two modern thinkers who played an influential role in critical theory in media studies and in the shaping of critical thought concerning media and ideology are the Italian political theorist Antonio Gramsci (1891–1937) and the French Marxist philosopher Louis Althusser (1918–1990).

<small>Antonio Gramsci</small>

Gramsci (*Selections from Prison Notebooks*, 1971) is associated mainly with the concept *hegemony*, which he regarded as synonymous with ideology. Hegemony refers to the way in which we think and feel about things. According to Gramsci, this way (hegemony) is created and maintained by power structures in society. These are structures such as the school (education), the state (politics and politicians), the church (religion), the judiciary and the mass media. Through these structures we learn how to think about topics and even what to think about. A hegemonic culture is created by those who own, control and manage these structures – in other words, those with access to these structures who through such access possess the power to influence people. A hegemonic culture is a culture in which the values of those with power (the bourgeoisie) become the "common sense" values of all. The task of the working class (or proletariat) is to expose these values for what they are: to keep those with power in power, be it economic, political and/or intellectual power.

<small>Louis Althusser</small>

The French Marxist philosopher Louis Althusser described the above power structures as *Ideological State Apparatuses* (see chapter 7 on ideology). He argued that all these institutions are instruments

Approaches to the Study of Mass Communication

(apparatuses) through which certain beliefs and values are instilled in individuals and groups in order to align their thinking with those in power. These beliefs and values eventually determine how one sees oneself and your role and place in society. He described ideology as consisting of concepts, symbols and images representing the ideas and values of the dominant ruling class.

However, ideology is not merely something political affecting only the way we vote during an election. Ideology affects our whole way of being. It is how we experience life and others and how we think about our own culture and those of others. For example, apartheid was not only a political ideology, it also affected how people of different races or skin colours experienced each other, behaved toward each other, and how we looked at and thought about South African realities. This ideology was entrenched in the political, economic, educational, religious, cultural and media structures of the apartheid society. Another example of ideology is the ideology of consumerism which has spread almost worldwide. This ideology as characteristic of contemporary society has entrenched the value that "you are what you own".

Ideology is also not only something of or from *the other*, for example, the apartheid government, or another (not one's own) culture or ethnic group. For example, the present South African government, the African National Congress (ANC) also has an ideology entrenched in its political, economic, cultural and social policies. As the apartheid ideology affected all South Africans, this ideology also affects the lives and thinking of all South Africans. In short, ideologues will argue that we all are ideological beasts and the victims of our own ideologies (ways of thinking) and those of others.

Assumptions of contemporary critical theory

With the above as a brief introduction to ideology, we now look at some of the basic assumptions of critical media theory.

Critical theory assumes that the media (in all its variety), are *symbolic forms of expression*. Like other forms of symbolic expression (literature, theatre, paintings and other cultural texts), the media communicate values, beliefs and attitudes in a *structured* way. By so doing the media assign *specific* meanings to something, be this something a person, an event, a topic or whatever. For example, a newspaper story about the 80th birthday of the United Kingdom's Queen Elizabeth II is not only a "story".

| media as symbolic form

133

Media Studies: Volume 1

It is written (structured) in such a way that it would or could signify the specific newspaper's attitude towards the Queen and the British monarchy. Another example is SABC television's programme in 2006 to commemorate 30 years of television in South Africa. This programme was not only a (objective) programme about the history of television in South Africa, but it was produced (structured) in such way as to highlight the accomplishments of the SABC after apartheid.

media as text

Viewed thus, it is assumed that the media and its different forms and genres (news stories, editorial comments, articles, reports, commentary, soap operas, documentaries and so on) can be read as *texts* (as a novel is a text). The recipient (media user) understands and interprets the text in his/her own distinctive manner. The meaning that he/she attaches to it is the result of a confrontation between the recipient and the text (what the recipient sees on screen, hears over the radio or reads in the newspaper). In this confrontation, the text is interpreted and understood in terms of the recipient's own cultural, educational, political and economical background. However, as a major symbolic form of expression and ideological instrument in society, the media contribute in one or another way to the recipient's cultural, educational, political and social context and thus impact on his/her way of thinking.

media production

Critical media theory assumes that there is a relationship between production conventions (the ways in which the media produce content) and ideology. In other words, there is a relationship between the ideology of a media institution (such as a newspaper or a broadcast organisation) and the way in which that newspaper or broadcast organisation will produce a story or a programme about a person, group or organisation. A good example is the selection of news. News selection is done in terms of news values (what a media organisation will define as news or not). These news values are related to the news organisation's political, economic, cultural, social and even religious values. A political event will thus be reported (or ignored – which in itself is significant) against the background of the news organisation's own political beliefs. It will thus be "coloured" (structured) in such a way as to reflect the newspaper's own views and/or attitude about a political issue, a politician, a news event. (See chapter 7 in volume 2 of this book on news.)

political economy

One of the key assumptions in critical media theory is that there is a close relationship between the media, politics and the economy. In this regard the impact of ownership on media content and thus on how

Approaches to the Study of Mass Communication

media ownership contributes to the dissemination and entrenchment of (an) ideology is emphasised. This is called the political economy of the media.

Political economy

In critical theory it is argued that the media mainly support the interests (political, economical, social and cultural) of one group at the cost of another group. This criticism has led to the media being seen as:

> "not as an autonomous organizational system, but as a set of institutions closely linked to the dominant power structure through ownership, legal regulation, the values implicit in the professional ideologies in the media, and the structures and ideological consequences of prevailing modes of newsgathering." (Curran, Gurevitch & Woollacott 1982:16)

Political economy is an umbrella term for all those theories and analytical approaches which seek to understand how economic and political relationships, interests and affiliations determine the nature and functioning of social institutions (including the media), and the impact or lack of impact of these relationships on social transformation and development.

_{defining political economy}

Critical political economy developed out of Marxist-based social theory. In this theory it is believed that all means of production, including media production, determines the nature of a society. Economy is the base of all social structures including institutions and ideas. In a capitalist society the idea of making a profit drives production. Profit is closely related to the cost of labour. People are responsible for labour. Thus, it is argued in Marxist theory, the working-class is oppressed by those individuals and groups in a society who own the means of production and whose sole purpose is to make a profit. Only when the working class rises up against dominant groups, can the means of production be changed and the liberation of the worker be achieved (see Littlejohn 1992:245–246). In media studies an underlying political economy proposition is that the economic and political control of the media determines the content and thus the ideological power of the media.

Initially media studies emphasised the analysis of media content with the purpose of showing how information and entertainment reflect interests of the dominant classes in a society – their political, economic and

cultural ideas and values. Although such an analysis is valuable, founding scholars of political economy in media studies, such as Murdock and Golding (1977) argued that in order to understand the power of the media one should rather start with a concrete description and analysis of media ownership. From thereon we can consider how such ownership impacts on media content (see Murdock and Golding 1977:17; Curran, Gurevitch and Woollacott 1982:23–24).

Such an analysis, complex as it may be, will show that despite their claim of being objective messengers and the providers of "innocent entertainment", media owners are primarily interested in financial profits, or as put by Murdock and Golding (1977:37), in maximising audiences and revenues. Their primary interest is to uphold the principles of the capitalist mode of production in order to guarantee profit.

media and capitalism

Political economy argues that media markets are part of the capitalist economic system with close links to the political system in a country. The predominant character of what this cultural industry produces (information, entertainment and advertisements) can be accounted for by the value of different kinds of content, pressure to expand markets and by the underlying economic interest of media owners (and their shareholders and board of directors) and decision-makers (see Garnham 1979; McQuail 1994:82). As an industry the media adheres to the four standard features of the capitalist mode of production:
- mass production and the distribution of commodities;
- capital-intensive technology;
- managerial organisation of highly specialised divisions of labour;
- cost-efficiency as the criterion of success (see Inglis 1990:114).

To a great extent these interests determine what we read in newspapers, hear over the radio, see on television and in movies, and get on the Internet. The consequences of this mode of production may be:
- the reduction of independent media sources;
- a focus on the largest markets and their tastes;
- avoidance of risks;
- reduced investment in less profitable media tasks (such as investigative reporting and documentary film-making);
- neglect of smaller and poorer sectors of the potential audience (see McQuail 1994:82).

Approaches to the Study of Mass Communication

All this results in what Murdock and Golding (1977:37) describe as the consolidation of groups already established in the mainstream mass-media markets and the exclusion of those groups who lack the capital base required for successful entry:

> *"Thus the voices which survive will largely belong to those least likely to criticise the prevailing distribution of wealth and power. Conversely, those most likely to challenge these arrangements are unable to publicize their dissent or opposition because they cannot command resources needed for effective communication to a broad audience." (Ibid.)*

For example, in South Africa we only have a few major media institutions, be it in the field of print or broadcasting or Internet. These few institutions, with their newspapers, magazines, book publishing, radio stations, television channels, Internet and telecommunications interests, dominate the South African media market, leaving little room for the smaller independent newspapers, radio stations, and Internet service providers to enter or survive the media market. Even more importantly, from a communication perspective, the few major institutions have a monopoly on what South Africans get to read, hear and see, and eventually on how we think. This makes the few institutions powerful socialisation and ideological instruments. Internationally, only a few media institutions dominate global communication and thus may have the power to influence worldwide thinking about politics, the economy, the environment, social trends, cultures and so on (see chapter 9 on globalisation and the media).

It may be true that increased interactivity and new media such as the Internet with its numerous possibilities of forming interest groups and cyber communities, new genres such as blogs and YouTube, as well as the increased use of mobile telephones to contact and organise interest groups (and inexpensive, popular cellphone/Internet convergence with South African technology such as MixIt) may have weakened the power of the major media groups. Yet, for the time being, access to the new media remains to be restricted and are the privilege of those who can afford it. Also, in the end it should be kept in mind that the same groups who control television, radio and other "traditional" media are usually also the owners and distributors of the new media with its new communication platforms.

media ownership

For this reason, political economy's emphasis on "who owns the media?" is important. What are the owners' political, economic, social and cultural affiliations? Who are the journalists, editors, programme makers, etc., working for them? How are their affiliations streamlined with those of the owners? Who fund the media and why? How do affiliations and funding impact on the ideology of a media organisation and eventually on media content? As a main stream of critical media theory, these are the topics of investigation in critical political economy.

Some of the leading contemporary figures in the field of the political economy and the media are Americans such as Edward Herman and Noam Chomsky (see their 2002 book *Manufacturing consent: The political economy of the mass media*) and Robert Waterman McChesney and John Nichols (see their 2002 book *Our media, not theirs: The democratic struggle against corporate media*). Another important figure is Belgian-French academic Armand Mattelart (see his *Rethinking media theory: Signposts and new directions* (2002)). In South Africa, a recent example of political-economic research is Gabriël Botma's Masters dissertation, *Synergy as political economic strategy in balancing idealism and the market orientation at Die Burger (Wes-Kaap), 2004–2005* (here translated from Afrikaans). In this dissertation he shows how market considerations have infiltrated this traditionally Afrikaans newspaper's ideology. Herman and Chomsky show how, since the mass media are now controlled by large corporations they are under the same competitive pressures as all other capital-driven corporations and how this distorts news. They show how media corporations are increasingly dependent on major sources of news such as governments, who manipulate news in their favour, instead of independent news gathering, writing and distribution.

In critical political economy it thus argued that corporate ownership of media production and distribution affects society negatively. Journalistic practices and media policy (including ownership policy) can be seen as a deliberate and ideological misuse of economic and political power to create a false consciousness and awareness, thus deterring true democracy.

The underlying proposition in political economy is thus that the economic and political control of the media determines the content and thus the ideological power of the media. In order to understand such power, we should start with a concrete description and analysis of media ownership. From thereon we may be able to prove how such ownership

Approaches to the Study of Mass Communication

impacts on media content. It is argued that, despite their claim of being objective messengers and providers of "innocent entertainment", media owners are primarily interested in financial profits and debt avoidance. The emphasis is therefore on maximising audiences and revenues. Their primary interest is upholding the principles of the capitalist mode of production in order to guarantee profit.

Public sphere

From a more philosophical communication perspective, but in support of the criticism of the political economy paradigm, a final assumption and proposition of critical theory to be highlighted here, comes from the German philosopher Jürgen Habermas (1979) and a school of Habermasian theorists argue that the modern market-oriented media undermine the idea and ideal of the public sphere as a place for debate, where consensus can be reached on the basis of which rational decision and action can be taken. Mass communications in their present form, according to this view, disrupt instead of contribute constructively to democracy.

| public sphere

A rather gloomy picture unfolds as author after author questions the quality and value of the information and knowledge provided by the media, especially under the pressure of corporatisation, marketisation and eventually commercialisation. Despite technological advances (increased access and interactivity amongst others), the question remains whether mass media as a political force is independent enough not only of political but also of commercial pressure to achieve the journalistic ideals of political debate, namely representation, exposure and the mobilisation of citizens to participate in public life (McNair & Hibberd, 2003:272–283).

As far as the provision of entertainment and education are concerned, it is acknowledged that the supply of popular and popularised knowledge via a variety of popular print and broadcast genres is an important constituting and formative element of the public sphere (Fourie, 2001:277–288; Thomass, 2003:33). Yet it is questioned whether the mass media can achieve this when it has to sacrifice its integrity under the pressure of increased competition and commercialisation. (See chapter 8 for a more in-depth discussion of the public sphere.)

From the above description of some of the propositions of critical political economy it is clear that the concept of "power" is central in the critical perspective on mass communication.

Media Studies: Volume 1

Power

There are many definitions of power. Here we only look at Thompson's (1995:12–18) distinction between four kinds of power. They are: economic power, political power, coercive power and symbolic power.

Economic power, as described by Thompson, stems from human productive activity resulting in the production of goods that can be consumed or exchanged in a market. Productive activity involves the use of and creation of raw materials, tools of production (for example, land), consumable products and financial capital. These resources can be accumulated by individuals and organisations for the purposes of expanding their productive activity; in so doing, they are able to increase their economic power. (Ibid.)

For example, the media is an economic industry that produces goods: newspapers, books, videos, films, magazines, news, cd's and so on. The bigger a media company is and the more it is able to expand its productive activity to include, perhaps not only newspapers but also Internet services, computer software and programmes for television and radio studios, the bigger is its economic power. Small wonder that we constantly read about the expansion of media companies such as television channel M-Net into the field of film production, newspaper giant Naspers into the fields of book publishing, broadcasting, the Internet and educational industries, and radio owner Primedia into the fields of broadcasting, film distribution and advertising.

Political power involves the activity of coordinating individuals and regulating the patterns of their interaction. One may argue that all of us are in one or another way involved with political power. This may be within our circles of friends, family or work where there are certain patterns and rules of interaction. However, Thompson (ibid.) argues that certain institutions are primarily involved with political power. Such an institution is the state which in its various forms (ranging from the classical Greek city-state and various African tribal traditions of governance through chieftainship to the modern nation-state) has as its purpose and goal the governance of citizens. This is done with a complex system of rules and procedures which authorise certain individuals to act in certain ways. These rules and procedures are encoded in laws which are enacted by sovereign bodies and administered by a judicial system. Thompson also argues that for the state to command authority it is dependent on its capacity to exercise some influence over coercive and symbolic power.

Coercive power involves the use, or threatened use, of physical force. This form of power is usually associated with military (such as the army) and para-military (such as the police and related security forces) institutions. These institutions are used (or mis-used) for the purposes of external defence and conquest, and for the purposes of internal pacification and control or suppression.

Approaches to the Study of Mass Communication

> Symbolic power is the real and potential power vested in all cultural institutions such as the institutionalised practice of religion (be it Christian, Jewish, Moslem and so on) or educational institutions or the media. These institutions possess the power to influence people's thinking and behaviour. They guide people to understand and think about the world in certain ways.
>
> For example, religious doctrines entrench certain norms and values of what is right and wrong. Educational institutions, such as schools and universities, produce and transmit knowledge against the background of certain educational philosophies and points of departure such as Christian National education or liberal education.
>
> Fictional films, documentaries, news, radio programmes, newspaper and magazine articles, popular music, advertisements, political comment: all provide us with interpretations of the realities in which we find ourselves. This happens not only in or through the genres of political journalism. To the contrary, popular music says a lot about the human spirit of our times – its values, beliefs, joys and anxieties. A cartoon such as Madam and Eve in the weekly *Mail and Guardian* newspaper says, at least for English-speaking affluent middle-class citizens of South Africa, a lot about racial relations in South Africa. It comments in a humorous and often sharp way on the processes of transformation in South African society. Advertisements, with their various and most of the time unrealistic and glamorous messages, are central in creating and sustaining our present consumer culture.

The media thus have the power to form and guide our perceptions and interpretations of reality. It is therefore not strange that governments seek to control the media in one or another way. Apart from restrictions on the freedom of the media, in undemocratic countries often severe restrictions, this is usually done by means of the regulation of ownership. To conclude this section: The underlying propositions of political economy, and concerns about the media as a public sphere can be summarised as follows:

- media are controlled by economic considerations;
- media developments tend towards concentration;
- global integration is taking place in the media industry;
- media content and audiences are commodified;
- media diversity decreases;
- opposition and alternative voices are marginalised;
- public service media are declining (See McQuail 1994:83).

Some scholars claim that the need to investigate these propositions become even more important against the background of economic trends such as media concentration and media liberalisation.

Cultural and feminist studies as critical theory

Two fields of study closely associated with the critical approach are cultural studies and feminist media studies. Cultural studies has its origin in the 1960s in the work of Richard Hoggart and Stuart Hall of the Centre for Contemporary Cultural Studies at the University of Birmingham in England. Apart from Marxism, neo-Marxism and the Frankfurt School's influences, the intellectual foundation of cultural studies can also be found in the work of the influential and prolific Welsh cultural critic and novelist, Raymond Williams (1921–1988). His analysis of television's impact on contemporary culture and communication, how television has dramatised our consciousness of almost everything, how it has created a culture of distance (the distance between the viewer and reality) and a culture of commodification, and his analysis of television's numerous genres as cultural forms, still forms the theoretical basis for cultural studies' analysis of the media (See his *Television, technology and cultural form*, 1974; *Communications*, 1962).

> cultural studies

Cultural studies shares critical theory and critical media studies' views about power and the role of the media in the dissemination of dominant ideology to the detriment of the voiceless. However, it claims that mass communication and media studies tend to investigate the media from a narrow, media-centric and isolated perspective, separating media messages from the culture it inhabits. The media should be studied in the broader context of contemporary culture, of which it is a part. The media should be studied as part of the cultural discourse(s) which uphold dominant ideology in the struggle for power. Therefore, as Griffen (2003: 371) explains:

> "... cultural studies place the academic spotlight directly in the ways media representations of culture reproduce social inequalities. And keep the average person more or less powerless to do anything but operate within a corporatized, commodified world ... The ultimate issue for cultural studies is not what information is presented, but whose information it is".

The main criticism against cultural studies is that it usually and openly adopts a leftist ideological stance in its criticism of capitalist, commodified western society. In short, in its commitment to the values it wishes to propagate, cultural studies performs scholarship under an ideological banner (see Griffen, 2003:375). As such it is often seen to compromise the integrity of its own research.

Approaches to the Study of Mass Communication

Broadly speaking, feminist media studies are about the portrayal and position of women in the media. Initially the interest was on the one-sided and stereotyped portrayal of woman in and by the media. Numerous content analyses of magazines, newspapers, films, television programmes and advertisements showed how women were mainly portrayed as objects of sexual desire, housewives or mothers, and in subordinate positions to men. From a psychoanalytical perspective the interest moved to what is called the *male gaze*. The premise is that the portrayal of women in the media is the result of male perceptions of women. One of the reasons for this treatment of women by the media is deeply entrenched male patriarchy. In-depth study of patriarchy became part of feminist studies and showed how western society, its history, politics, economics and knowledge production has been dominated by men and how everything is thus seen and experienced through the eyes and minds of men, completely ignoring the female perspective. Feminist media studies made us aware of how almost all discourses in society are gender based or can be analysed from a gender perspective. How can the state of affairs be changed? In the case of the media, one solution might be to appoint more women as journalists, editors, film and programme makers. Many studies about the role of women in the media thus followed. Another focus of feminist media studies, especially in the field of reception studies, is the analysis of the differences between male and female use of media texts. Many of the truths exposed by feminist media studies laid the foundation for the analysis of discriminatory practices in the portrayal of black people in comparison with portrayals of white people, specific ethnic groups, gays and lesbians. Feminist media studies thus also very much focussed the attention on the media and stereotypes. (See chapter 5 for an in-depth discussion on stereotypes.)

`feminist studies`

Criticism of critical theory
From the positivistic side it is often argued that critical theory:
- does not acknowledge the libertarian, informative, educational and democratising role of the media;
- does not acknowledge the entertainment value of media for billions of people;
- makes too rigid a distinction between those with power and the masses who are presumed to be without power;
- is too often ignorant of media users' ability to judge and be critical.

As far as critical theory's Marxist foundation is concerned, it is argued by critics (see Karl Popper, 1999) that the 19th century society that Marx wrote about had radically changed by the 20th century.

pluralism

What needs to be acknowledged by critical theory is the concept of *"pluralism"*. This concept refers to the variety of available media in a democracy, especially to those with time and money. The underlying premise is that in view of the variety of media (various newspapers, various television stations, various radio stations, films, videos, publishers, advertising agencies) all ideally looking at reality from different perspectives, it is impossible to make one-sided and limited claims about the way the media function and about its possible impact. If one newspaper or television station adopts a particular ideological perspective, another newspaper or television station is perfectly free to propagate an opposing ideology or point of view. Furthermore, media users are free to be selective about their exposure to the media and the ideologies that may be propagated. Critical theory tends to ignore this variety or focuses its attention specifically on undemocratic societies. Variety is the only safeguard against the authoritarian misuse of the media.

The necessity of a free media, and the need for the media to be safeguarded from rigid forms of regulation and censorship, need to be emphasised. In order to guarantee a plurality of voices, the media should be allowed to operate in a free economy and according to the principles of a free (capitalistic) economy. Without such freedom, the media will not be in a position to provide a variety of views, opinions and options through a variety of media outlets.

The Marxist-inspired thesis that production is determined by the dominant class and that the output of mass media is ultimately controlled in the interest of that class is rejected by *liberal pluralists,* whom are often closely associated with the positivistic approach, which argues that such a view is too conspiratorial and tends to oversimplify economic and market realities.

From the pluralist perspective, the economically concentrated power of media ownership does not give media owners total control over output. To the contrary, the power of ownership is counter-balanced by the plurality of competing interests represented by diverse groups of shareholders and consumers, professional managers and producers,

Approaches to the Study of Mass Communication

advertisers and trade unions, all of whom are refereed by the state (See O'Sullivan *et al* 1994: 55). In a company such as *Media24*, there are (ideally) diverse shareholders. The company caters (ideally) for diverse tastes and cultures amongst their consumers; its various products ranging from newspapers to books, television, magazines and the Internet, are managed by professional managers and journalists who will resist interference from the owners as well as interference from advertisers, who in their turn will not be prescribed by media owners. Apart from this, a company such as *Media24* has to compete with others in the same markets, with different ideological perspectives. Finally, the public has freedom of choice between different media products from different media groups. This entails *pluralism*. Pluralism tries to create as many voices as possible for many and diverse audiences.

Critical theory's reply to this criticism is that although there may be a variety of media, they are all and collectively owned by a few people. For example, although a number of newspapers of widely differing ideological persuasions may be published in South Africa, and although there may be independent television and radio stations in addition to the public service broadcaster (SABC), the media, as in other countries, remain in the hands of a few and the majority of the voices of the populace are still silenced.

limited ownership

Summary

The positivistic approach and the critical approach are the two grand theories from which all mass communication research depart. The positivistic approach, with its emphasis on empiricism and its claim to be a "scientific method", aims to improve mass media, to achieve specific goals. The critical approach, with its emphasis on ideology, power and inequity, aims to expose the misuse of the media by a power élite with the purpose of spreading and entrenching the ideology(ies) of those in power.

The approaches introduced below are grounded in either the positivistic or the critical traditions. However, it is difficult to distinguish clearly between the theoretical approaches. They lend from each other. They build on each other. Therefore we talk of the fusion of paradigms. Little positivistic research is done today without critical interpretation and evaluation. Little critical research does not test its assumptions empirically or back it up with some empirical proof. It is a matter of emphasis and focus. For this reason, and because the following approaches in their many manifestations are dealt with in more detail in subsequent chapters of this book (and in volume 2, chapters 3 and 4), they are only briefly introduced. They are the meaning production, technological determinist, information society, post-modern, postcolonial, and the Afro-centric approaches. Keep in mind that in emphasis and focus, as well as in terms of aims and methods of analysis, the following approaches can be classified as being mainly positivistic (as technological determinist theories tend to be) or critical (as the majority of the approaches in the remainder of this chapter are). The focus is on these approaches because they are the most dominant of our time and in the case of the post-colonial and Afro-centric approaches, because of their particular relevance for South Africa.

3.4.4 Meaning production theory

Whereas positivistic theory has its foundation in empiricism, functionalism, and behaviourism, and critical theory in Marxism and neo-Marxism, meaning production theory has its foundation in *phenomenology* and *symbolic interactionism*.

The German philosopher Edmund Husserl (1859–1938) can be seen as the father of phenomenology. For Husserl, the basic question was: how is it possible to know what is real? (See Jansen 1989:49–51.) Husserl argued that there is only one way, namely through experience. Everything we see and know is filtered by our own experience and is thus a creation of one's own consciousness. But how does one penetrate the essence of consciousness? For Husserl it can be done by suspending one's natural attitudes and taken-for-granted beliefs about something and by starting to look at something anew. This requires a mental act of opening oneself up for new impressions and new understandings. To investigate something phenomenological thus requires one to rid oneself of any presuppositions.

Phenomenology

phenomenology

With this as point of departure, and, in the social sciences from the work of the Austrian philosopher Alfred Schutz (1899–1959), the following basic assumptions (Jansen 1989:51–60) of phenomenology arise:
- reality is not given, but it is a structure of meanings constituted by human beings;

Approaches to the Study of Mass Communication

- what we experience as "the world" or "reality" is constituted by common-sense knowledge and taken-for-granted interpretations about our daily lives which we share with other people;
- the shared world is a pre-structured world experienced inter-subjectively;
- we assume that our world and our experience thereof is the same for all people and that everybody acts accordingly to the same taken-for granted knowledge;
- social reality is a never-ending process of meaning construction;
- social reality is intersubjective – human beings subjectively experience events and subjectively interpret events, but in their interpretation of events they draw on a shared world of meaning, a common frame of reference which allows for the possibility of mutual understanding;
- in the process of the construction of reality the mass media play a significant part.

From a phenomenological perspective, the task of the researcher is thus to search for the general principles which underlie the taken-for-granted world. How are the shared assumptions about reality (about the social world) and thus our beliefs about something or someone brought about?

A good example of mass communication research departing from a phenomenological perspective is Gaye Tuchman's 1973 investigation of how taken-for-granted routines and practices in journalism establish a specific way of news production; how these taken-for-granted ways of news production (the entrenched ways of deciding what is news and what not, of gathering news, of writing news) affects the eventual construction of a (taken-for-granted) view about something or someone, and the consequences of all this for the newspaper reader's (or in more general terms, any media user's) construction of a view of reality (See Tuchman 1973).

Symbolic interactionism

Based on phenomenology (which is more a philosophy than a specific approach with its own methods of analysis), symbolic interactionism (see Jansen 1989:28–47) centres on the *processes* whereby meaning is socially constructed. From a symbolic interactionist perspective the mass media create and communicate meaning to large audiences, thereby

symbolic interactionism

allowing meaning and eventually the experience of something to become "shared".

Central figures in the symbolic interactionist paradigm are George Herbert Mead (1863–1931) and Herbert Blumler, who argue that the central assumptions of symbolic interactionism are:
- reality is not given but created by human beings by virtue of their capacity to give meaning to their experiences;
- reality is mediated, structured and organised for people by sets of meaning;
- meaning is embodied in symbols;
- the interpretation of meaning requires a self-conscious act and the ability to adopt and share another person's perspective;
- mass media play an active role in the construction of personal and social reality;
- mass media are not simply transmitters of objective information but active constructers of information and meaning – what is presented as news is an interpretation and a construction of meaning through the processes of emphasising some events and de-emphasising other events.

In both phenomenology (as a philosophy) and in symbolic interactionism (as a phenomenological approach) the emphasis is thus on meaning and how meaning is constructed. Various ways of investigating meaning and the construction of meaning exist. Various disciplines occupy themselves with questions related to meaning. Such disciplines include linguistics, anthropology, cognitive psychology and philosophy. In the field of mass communication the discipline of semiotics is of special importance.

Semiotics

semiotics

Semiotics is the study of signs and codes; how signs and codes convey meaning. The aim of media semiotics is to sharpen our critical awareness of the ways in which the media manipulate or use signs and codes to reflect, represent and imitate aspects of reality with the purpose of conveying a specific meaning – usually in support of an underlying ideology or point of view.

The point of departure in *media semiotics* is that media content is not reality itself but an imitation of reality. In these representations signs and codes are combined in a structured way to convey the specific meanings

Approaches to the Study of Mass Communication

the media wish to distribute about reality. Furthermore, the media are a very specific sign system in the sense that media accommodate numerous other sign systems. The media use a number of sign systems simultaneously to communicate: linguistic sign systems (language), nonverbal sign systems such as clothing (costumes), body language, visual sign systems such as moving and digital images (film, television, the Internet), photographs, graphics and verbal sign systems (voice, articulation, register).

Think about a television news bulletin. The images we see and the text we hear (or read on the screen) are captured in specific ways with specific kinds of shots – a close-up or a long shot, different angles, focussing on specific objects as well as different ways of writing a text. The image is edited in a specific way (preceded and followed by specific and selected shots) with a specific rhythm (tempo) in order to create a dramatic feeling of urgency. Whether this is done intentionally or unconsciously, the fact remains that through the ways of constructing a news item, a specific meaning about the something or someone is conveyed. The task of semiotic research is to decipher the ways in which specific meanings are created.

It is apparent that the assignment of meaning is a process. A process presupposes the transformation of the raw material of a product, a transformation that takes place through a specific kind of labour. In order to assign meaning to an event, such an event and the significance of the event is produced by means of the manipulation of *signs* and *codes*. In the process of *media labour* the actual meaning of an event thus undergoes a transformation.

All forms of communication use signs and codes. Even in our interpersonal communication we use signs (words and non-verbal signs such as gestures) which we combine according to certain rules (grammar) in order to express our views. The rules or grammar are the codes. Similarly, the media use signs (words and images) in certain ways (codes) to express a certain view. For example, it is argued that Western mainstream media, by portraying poverty, corruption and war in developing countries in a structured (codified) way, present a negative view of developing countries.

The basic building blocks of the semiotic approach are thus a focus on signs, signs systems, codes and meaning. The *sign*: What does a sign

sign

consist of? Which different types of signs are there? How are signs related to reality? How are signs related to the users? For example, how do linguistic signs (words) differ from pictorial or visual signs (such as a photograph)? *Sign systems*: this involves the study of how signs collectively form a sign system. Language is an example of a sign system, television (which consists mainly of audiovisual signs) is a sign system, nonverbal communication (gestures, facial expressions) is a sign system. Further variants are found within a particular sign system. For example, Zulu, Xhosa, Afrikaans, English and Sotho are variants of language as a sign system. The national costumes belonging to different cultures and peoples are variants of clothing as a nonverbal sign system; the different culinary styles of various peoples and cultures are variants of culinary practices as a sign system.

| code |

Codes: signs are related to one another by means of codes which are understood by the users; various sign systems are related to one another by means of various codes. How are spoken words (verbal signs) related to one another in a language by means of grammatical sentence constructions (codes) to form sentences? How are words (for example, the dialogue in a film) and the images in the film related to one another by the use of the camera and editing techniques (codes)? How do these codes develop? What is the role of culture and cultural conventions in the creation and comprehension of codes?

| meaning |

Meaning: what is meaning and are there different kinds of meaning? (See the chapter on media semiotics in volume 3 where these building blocks are discussed in more depth.)

The semiotic approach seeks to answer the following basic questions:
- How do the media create meaning?
- How does the meaning given by the media support a specific taken-for-granted view (ideology)?
- How does the media user understand and personalise media-created and disseminated meaning?
- How does it become part of his/her taken-for-granted understanding of social reality?

As said, the semiotic approach and its theories about meaning is only one of many approaches to meaning. The semiotic approach distinguishes itself from the other approaches in the sense that it zooms in on the

Approaches to the Study of Mass Communication

communicative tools (signs) and processes (codes) with which the media constructs meaning.

3.4.5 Technological determinism

In this approach the focus is on the technology of mass communication and on how such technology determines the nature of mass communication and its role in society and the lives of people.

In *determinism*, the basic claim is that a single cause determines all other aspects of life (cf. Wood 2000:244; O'Sullivan *et al* 1994:82–83). In *economic determinism* it is believed that the economy determines all social and cultural processes. In *biological determinism* it is believed that biological factors determine all behaviour. In *technological determinism* it is believed that technology and technological innovation drive social change, culture, economics and politics.

According to Littlejohn (1992:342–345) one of the best examples of technological determinism in media theory is Marshall McLuhan's theory "the medium is the message" and the ideas of his mentor Harold Adams Innis. Both these Canadian theorists saw the media as the essence of civilisation. Innis believed that the social,cultural, political and economic developments of each historical period can be related directly to the technology of the means of mass communication of that period.

> Marshall McLuhan

For example, Innis (cf. Littlejohn) argued that stone and clay (rock paintings), the technology of mass communication in pre-historic societies, were time-binding; paper and papyrus of early Egypt were space-binding and fostered empire building, large bureaucracies and military interests, as they have facilitated communication from one location to another. Speech as the major technology of public communication encourages temporal thinking, knowledge based on values and tradition and it supports community involvement. Here consider the high emphasis on rhetoric in early Greek societies and the many oral communication cultures of Africa. Writing as the dominant medium produced strong space-binding effects such as the growth of empires during the Middle Ages and early Renaissance in Europe. According to Innis, the invention of the printing press was the essence of early Western and modern culture. It did, however, contribute to spatial bias and the monopolisation of knowledge and development. In other words, it restricted knowledge to those countries that had and knew the technology of printing (cf. Littlejohn 1992:343).

Taking it from there, McLuhan argued that every technology is an extension of people's senses or some human faculty. For example: the wheel is an extension of the foot; the book is an extension of the eye; clothing is an extension of the skin; electric circuitry is an extension of the central nervous system. Littlejohn (1992) explains this tenet of McLuhan's theory as such:

Tribal people were primarily hearing-oriented: hearing was believing. The invention of the printing press changed this and sight started to dominate. This forced people into a linear, logical, and categorical kind of perception and reasoning. It encouraged the habit of perceiving things in visual and spatial terms. The electronic media (radio and television) changed this and the aural started to predominate again. Printing, being bounded by space, separated people and societies from each other. The electronic media, not being space-bounded, bring them together in a "global village".

According to McLuhan, the fact that we listen to radio and watch television programmes from all over the world affects our perception of reality and how we think about reality. S*pace* and *time* is more important than the *content* of these media. Therefore he argues that the medium as such is the message and not the content. The fact that electronic media, despite their content, are so all-pervasive and part of our everyday existence, make the medium as such more important than the content.

He then goes on to distinguish between "hot" and "cool" media in terms of how they involve people perceptually. "Hot" media, such as film, are those that give us everything and leave little to one's own imagination and participation. The image projected on the screen is complete in every detail and does not require the viewer to fill it in perceptually. Compared to this, television is a "cool" medium and requires the viewer to participate perceptually by filling in missing data. It provides the viewer only with a sketch through the illumination of tiny dots. It actually only provides a stimulus to which the viewer must respond (see Littlejohn 1992:345). Cool media such as television thus involve the viewer perceptually and on a sensory level, more so than hot media. Therefore, McLuhan argues, television is changing the very fabric of society in the sense that it changes our ways of seeing things.

From this distinction between "hot" and "cool" media it is clear that McLuhan was far more involved in the technology of the medium as

Approaches to the Study of Mass Communication

being determinant in the quality of the communication, than with the actual content conveyed by the medium.

The work of McLuhan, with an emphasis on how the technology of a medium determines the nature of mass communication and its impact on society and the human being, is continued by many. Notable here is McLuhan's student, later co-worker and presently the director of the McLuhan Programme in Culture and Technology in Canada, Derrick de Kerckhove. In one of his best known publications, *The Skin of Culture* (1996), de Kerckhove explores how media technology is an extension of our nervous system and consciousness; how violence on television impacts physically on the human body, how human emotion develops within the contexts of a dominant electronic modality, how virtual reality brought about by information and communication technology has bridged the gap between an "idea" and the consequences of an "idea", how the technology of the electronic media has changed language, literacy and the alphabet, and how media technology has developed a collective consciousness more powerful than individual consciousness.

Technological determinism also often underlies much of the hype about new communication technologies, such as the Internet and its information superhighway, mobile telephony (cell phones), the convergence between different media technologies, and how all this may contribute to economic, social and educational development. In this regard a clear distinction can be made between *technophile* and *technophobic* theorists. Technophiles see information and communication technology (ICT) as a magic wand while technophobics usually warn against the unforeseen consequences of the runaway development of ICT and its possible detrimental consequences for democracy, inequities between rich and poor nations, and the divide between the haves and have nots in a society. <!-- margin: new media -->

According to Wood (2000:249–251), the main criticism against technological determinism is that such theory often: <!-- margin: critique -->
- lacks empirical support, based mainly on experimental research;
- does not acknowledge other research;
- tends to be hyperbolic speculation;
- overestimates the power of the media;
- is overly deterministic in asserting that human consciousness is controlled and determined by the media;

- ignores the fact that only a small portion of the world's population has access to media and/or uses media to such an extent that it may have a powerful effect on their consciousness.

3.4.6 The information society approach

A fifth broad theoretical approach concerns the role of the new media and information and communication technology in society. In this approach, three broad areas of enquiry can be identified:
- the definition, characterisation and description of new media;
- the impact of ICTs on society;
- policy related to the new media and ICT.

Describing new media

In theories defining new media, the emphasis is usually on the capacity of ICTs to:
- increase the production and flow of information of all kinds;
- decrease distance and cross geographical borders;
- increase interactivity between senders and users;
- interconnect people, groups, nations and organisations;
- decrease the cost of the transmission of information and entertainment;
- provide speed and volume.

characteristics

Some of the characteristics dealt with in descriptive theories of new media are:
- increased interactivity of the new media: new media allow far more contact between the communicator and the user/recipient;
- sociability of the new media: new media allow far more contact between the user and other people (users);
- autonomy of the new media: new media allow the user far more control over the content;
- the playfulness of the new media: new media allow far more enjoyment in the sense of involvement;
- the privacy of the new media: new media are more personalised and unique. (See McQuail 2000:127–128.)

Descriptive theory usually departs from comparisons with earlier ICTs and their media. A good example is Fidler's 1997 work, *Mediamorphosis: understanding new media*. In this work he shows how the present "new"

Approaches to the Study of Mass Communication

media have developed out of preceding dominant media, taking over some of their outstanding characteristics.

Descriptive theories also emphasise the different uses of the new media: the use of the Internet for data creation, storage, collection and dissemination; for commerce (e-commerce), messaging (e-mail), entertainment, socialisation (chat rooms), advertising, canvassing, campaigning and research.

Descriptive theory and research are mainly driven by technophiles and therefore tend to emphasise the positive sides of ICT, the new media, and the information society. It is thus the theory and research most valued and preferred by the competitive ICT industries as it can be used to boost sales.

Theory dealing with the nature and impact of ICT on society and the nature of the information society

These theories are more critical than the descriptive theories. They focus on topics such as the following:

- the consequences of interconnectedness and information saturation on the quality and experience of life;
- the impact of Information and Communication Technology (ICT) on leisure-time spending;
- the nature and possible consequences of "virtual" or "cyber" communities;
- the nature and consequences of "cyber" or "virtual" identity or multiple identities;
- the changed nature of time and space on the Internet and/or in cyber space;
- the nature of participation in the cyber space;
- the consequences of ICT for democracy and the so-called "electronic commons", "virtual democracy" and the "electronic agora".

_{effects}

These topics are discussed in more depth in chapter 9 on globalisation and the information society. Leading scholars dealing with topics such as these are, for example, the Spanish sociologist Manuel Castells (see *The rise of the network society*, 1996), the American philosopher Hubert Dreyfus (*On the Internet*, 2001), the American historian Mark Poster (*What's the matter with the Internet?* 2001), the American communication scientist Howard Rheingold (*The virtual community: Homesteading on the electronic frontier*, 1993), and the British sociologist Frank Webster (*Theories of the information society*, 1995).

Policy research

policy topics

Thirdly, the information society approach has focused our attention anew on *communication policy*. Policy theory and research centre on topics such as:
- new and improved ways of access to ICT;
- the role of ICT in development;
- ICT's possibilities for economic growth;
- social issues such as the possibility of a growing gap between the haves and the have-nots;
- ICT and the growth and spread of democracy and its contributions to social change;
- privacy issues;
- regulation and control of the Internet;
- the impact of new ICTs on "old" media regulation and thus matters related to media convergence.

policy aims

The focus is on critical questions related to access to ICTs, the quality of ICTs, and democratic participation in the "world" of ICTs. The aim is to formulate policy that would:
- secure sound financial planning and financial management;
- prevent misallocation of scarce resources;
- guarantee cultural preservation versus social disruption;
- assure that real needs are accounted for and real uses are achieved in terms of capacity, regional versus global and grassroots needs and uses;
- ensure reasonable regulation and deregulation to, amongst other things, achieve a balance between public service obligations and free market interests;
- ensure sustainable development.

These topics are also discussed in more depth in chapter 9.

Approaches to the Study of Mass Communication

3.4.7 The poststructuralist/postmodern approach

In the present so-called era of postmodernism (postmodernity) characterised by new social, political, economic, technological, global and cultural dynamics, the validity of many of the old paradigms in almost every discipline of the humanities, including media studies, is being questioned if not overturned. It seems as if many of the old theories are no longer adequate to describe the media landscape brought about by new information and communication technologies and the new social, political, cultural and economic environments in which media producers and media users (the audiences) find themselves. This environment is often referred to as postmodern. To begin with, we need to address the question: What is postmodernism? In answering this question we distinguish between postmodern society and postmodern style.

Postmodern society

Some authors argue that postmodernism began in 1925 with the rise of Henry Ford's motor vehicle empire in the USA. Ford was amongst the first to introduce production-line industry practices with immense consequences for the ways in which all industries thereafter functioned. It can be argued that the new ways of labouring and thinking about labour, or the move from manual labour and production to industrial labour and production, changed the very fibre of society in the sense that it brought about changed labour, community and family relations. The year 1925 is thus seen by some as a watershed year in the move from modernity to early postmodernity. The British writer Aldous Huxley (1894–1963) was to speak in his novel *Brave New World* (1932) of Before Ford (BF) and After Ford (AF).

> nature of postmodern society

However, others argue that the sixties and the rise of multinational capitalism are directly related to the origin of postmodernism. (Also see Giddens' explanation of modernity and post-modernity as a consequence of globalisation in chapter 9.)

Table 3.6: Modern and Postmodern Society

Van Poecke (1994:1–25) provides the following brief schematic overview of what the changes between modernity and postmodernity involved on the political, economic and social levels:

MODERN SOCIETY	POSTMODERN SOCIETY
Politics	
Nation-states operating in the cultural, security and economic dimensions of society and supported by the pillars of literacy, bureaucracy and industry, institutionalised in the school, army and factory. These were engaged in mass education, mass conscription and mass production which gave rise to mass political parties, mass labour unions, mass professional associations and mass organisations.	A move to federalism and the creation of international organisations. Individual and universal liberalism rather than communal and national liberalism.
Economics	
Organised capitalism/socialism and national market.	Capitalism based on private enterprise and the global market.
Rigid labour division.	Flexibility. Industrial management engaged in multinational operations within a global market (high economy) but also mass of service workers engaged in low-skill tasks for a local market (low economy).
Goods economy. Labour ethos. Production.	Service economy. Hedonistic ethos. Consumption.
Society	
Collective identity.	Local/community identity but also the tendency to globalise.
Modern middle class in a production economy.	Postmodern middle class in a service economy.
Classification: a clear distinction between classes/race/gender/age.	Framing: the only classification is between those who control the socialisation processes (strong framing) and those who are socialised (weak framing).

Approaches to the Study of Mass Communication

MODERN SOCIETY	POSTMODERN SOCIETY
Technology	
Technology in service of man.	Man subordinate to technology.
Clear distinctions between technology and culture.	Technology is the culture.

From the above table it is clear that the transformation from modernism to postmodernism involved a move from the national to the global (both in politics and economics), from an emphasis on the mass to an emphasis on the individual, from rigid distinctions between class, race and gender to flexibility, and from an emphasis on technology as part of culture to technology as *the* culture.

Other distinctions between and descriptions of modern and postmodern society are possible. The French philosopher Jean-François Lyotard (see Dethier 1993:503) focuses on the difference between modern and postmodern *epistemology*. He argues that in postmodern thinking (about the arts, media, politics, the economy) there has been a move from:

postmodern epistemology

MODERNITY		POSTMODERNITY
necessity	to	randomness
universalism	to	relativism
continuity	to	discontinuity
history	to	genealogy
cohesive criticism	to	deconstruction
totality	to	metaphysical
politically ideological	to	anarchism
progressive	to	neoconservative thinking

Postmodern epistemological thinking is usually expressed and described with particular concepts such as "enlightenment", "fragmentation", "schizophrenia", "fantasy", "combination", "popularity", "consumption", "internationalism" and "postmodern style".

Enlightenment: Various authors regard postmodernism as the realisation of the ideals of the Enlightenment. The Enlightenment was an eighteenth century philosophical movement which emphasised reason and individualism rather than metaphysics (speculation, especially on the subject of the supernatural, and the meaning and nature of the human condition) and tradition. Postmodernism breaks with history and tradition and replaces them with an "eternal present". It deviates from tradition, puts the here and now first, redefines the traditional and emphasises the new and futuristic.

Fragmentation: Postmodernism ignores the whole and ignores time boundaries. The boundaries between the past, present and future disappear. Objects, entities, images and words are presented out of context.

Schizophrenia: There is alienation between a sign and its meaning (between the signifier and the signified). Things need no longer have their original meaning. We are free to ascribe to them any meaning we like.

Fantasy: The boundaries between the real and the imaginary disappear.

Combination: Various styles from various periods are mingled.

Popularity: The hierarchical distinction between high and popular culture and between art and kitsch disappears. The popular is generally acceptable.

Consumption: The consumer value of anything is of primary importance. Anything that does not have a consumer value is unimportant. Art, science, culture, religion, human emotion and in fact all conceivable activities are therefore commercialised.

Internationalism: Although physical borders between countries still exist, boundaries between countries (and cultures) no longer exist in the mind of postmodern man. It is only in terms of the international that national and indigenous culture acquires a value and meaning.

From the above it is evident that postmodernism is an encompassing *cultural shift*. In the words of Raymond Williams (1977:128) it is a general orientation, condition or a structure of feeling. This is characterised by multinational capitalism and its related consumer society. In this society capital has abolished particularity along with the coherent self in whom history, depth, and subjectivity unite.

Postmodern style

Postmodernism, especially in the case of the arts, literature, architecture and media content, is often also described as a specific *style*. This style is characterised by a mixture of styles and forms, *pastiche* (imitations), emptiness or superficiality and:

Approaches to the Study of Mass Communication

> *"a sense of exhaustion, a relish for copies and repetition, a knowingness that dissolves commitment into irony; acute self-consciousness about the formal, constructed nature of the work, a pleasure in the play of surfaces, and a rejection of history"* (Gitlin 1989:347).

As an example of postmodern style dealt with in media theory is best described with reference to television. An outstanding postmodern stylistic characteristic of television is its fragmented nature. This contributes to the decontextualisation of reality or a reality.

Fragmentation is caused by programme schedules, programme formats, the lack of a clear distinction between genres, the mixing of genres and the technique of *pastiche*. Television's daily offering is characterised by a succession of programmes that follow one another in sequence. This sequence is dictated by economics and popular taste (in the case of commercial television). The aim is to have the largest viewing public possible, which would be likely to bring in the largest advertising revenue at a given time of the day, in conjunction with the most suitable programme for this purpose, in the hope that both the broadcaster and the advertiser will benefit. Furthermore, the viewer can choose between different channels, usually with the aid of a remote, which certainly makes selection easier but does aggravate fragmentation. Technological advances which allow affluent viewers to manipulate live television with pause, rewind and store facilities, may increase such fragmentation.

<aside>fragmentation</aside>

But it is not only programme schedules that serve to promote fragmentation. In programmes such as police dramas, soap operas and situation comedies there is also a fragmentation of narrative structures – there are often five or more story lines that replace one another in a question of minutes or even seconds; the programmes are fragmented still further by advertising flashes, continuity announcements or even news flashes. Briefly, fragmentation is an obstacle to coherent meaning in the daily programme offering and in most programmes.

The gulf between image and reality and the creation of fragmented "reality" is aggravated by an increasing tendency to deny the difference between genres: the technique of *pastiche*. More and more frequently in fictional programmes characters are stepping out of the world of the story to refer to a reality outside the story, which may include politicians and burning social questions, the reality of the television production or themselves as actors.

Fragmentation is also a prominent feature of television news. There is fragmentation of images through montage, juxtaposition and the use of close-ups which are an inherent abstraction of reality and which, in addition to their visual qualities, heighten the effect of the irregular flow of the dialogue, giving television a rhythm of its own which is far removed from reality. The "adaptation" of a reality in news is aimed not at the meaning of the reality portrayed but rather at the simulation. While the existence of reality is never denied, reality and its meaning are made subordinate to the question: is it good television? Connor (1989) expresses this as follows:

> "... the TV network does not aim to represent the world, but enacts itself, its own forms and languages, in a pure performing present."

Terrorist violence is represented on a news programme by means of scenes of violence, interviews with victims, and opinions from politicians, the police and other interested persons. In this process the actual event, the terrorist crime, may simply disappear into the background. The violence as a referent becomes nebulous and ends up as a fragment of an image. A report of this kind is likely to undergo further fragmentation as a result of the alternation of various stories, the role of the presenters and the programme format, which usually starts with the most important events, followed by sport, the weather, a "human interest" story and so on.

To the postmodernist theoreticians in the long term the fragmentation created by television implies the fragmentation of experience. In time everything is seen as fragmented and there is little cohesion left in our experience of reality or a reality.

Key thinkers: post-structuralism, discourse theory and post-modernism

Insofar as media theory is concerned, post-modern thinking about the media has been influenced mainly by French literary critics and cultural theorists such as Roland Barthes (1915–1980), Michel Foucault (1926–1984), Jacques Derrida (1930–2004), Pierre Bourdieu (1930–2002) and Jean Baudrillard (1929–2007).

structuralism

To understand their work, the following brief introduction to structuralism is necessary. Structuralism had its origin in the linguistics of the Swiss linguist Ferdinand de Saussure (1857–1913) whose work *Course de linguistique générale* (1916) directed language studies for many decades. His basic tenet was that all languages can be analysed as formal systems of signs which derive their meanings based on the principle of binary opposition: a word's meaning is based on its difference from other words in the system. The system is the *langue* (grammar) whereas the individual use is the *parole*. This structuralist principle was adopted by the French cultural anthropologist Claude Lévi-Strauss (1908–) (*The structural study of myth and totemism*, 1964; *The savage mind*, 1966). He analysed the myths (social beliefs and habits) of so-called primitive tribes and came to the conclusion that in each society these beliefs and practices rest upon certain ground rules of which the members of a society are not aware. These rules are based on fundamental oppositions such as sacred versus the profane, nature versus culture, life versus death, healthiness versus illness, strong versus weak. This structure of binary oppositions is also present in developed societies. In a nutshell, all our thinking (for example about race, religion, ethnicity, identity, gender, sex) and our behaviour that follows from this thinking, is based on oppositions which we take for granted. We think, apply meaning to something or someone, and categorise in terms of oppositions. Structuralism sought to get to the bottom of and expose these structures of opposition with the purpose of questioning them as a basis for belief and behaviour.

As a paradigm (in other words, as a way of looking at, analysing and understanding something), structuralism in literature studies focused on texts and the grammatical structure of texts, concluding that the structure of a text determines its meaning and the readers' fixed interpretation thereof. If a text is structured in a certain way, a reader will attach a specific, fixed meaning to it. In sociology, structuralism investigated the structures of a society, of social behaviour, and of social development. It was argued that society and social behaviour are structured according to specific fixed rules (see Lévi-Strauss) to achieve specific goals and are thus predictable. The same applies to economics, anthropology and psychology. From a structuralist point of view these disciplines argued that all human behaviour and the products of human behaviour (art, economy, politics, language, individual and social habits and beliefs) could be analysed in terms of fixed structures with fixed outcomes or meanings. Media texts (newspaper stories, television programmes, films, songs and so on) were analysed as closed texts with specific structures and meanings. For example, numerous structuralist analyses focused on how the fixed structures of soap operas, situation comedies, films and newspaper reports produced fixed meanings that would be understood by *all* the readers or viewers in a specific way.

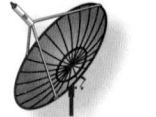

Structuralist analyses emphasised how the media tends to strengthen myths (and oppositions) instead of exposing and questioning them. For example, based on analyses, structuralists claimed that the media strengthen the differences between the non-scientific construct of race, between male and female, between normal and abnormal.

| post-structuralism | Post-structuralism rejected structuralism's emphasis on meaning as fixed.

Roland Barthes (1915–1980) and myth

| Barthes | Post-structuralist thinking can be traced back to French literary critic Roland Barthes' influential essay *The death of the author* (1969), in which he argued that meaning does not derive from an author's intention and structured representation but from the reader's interpretation which is open and can differ from reader to reader. The emphasis in post-structuralism thus moved from the author as creator of meaning to the recipient as creator of meaning. The author has no custody over a text once it is out of his/her hands. It moved from the structure of the text to the structure of interpretation which was seen to be an open structure. In his later writing Barthes expanded this idea to objects such as photography (*Camera Lucida: Reflections on photography*, 1980). In his *Mythologies* (1972) he analysed ordinary objects, gestures and practices in order to show how the meaning of things that surround us in our everyday lives are myths (beliefs and ways of thinking that masquerade as social truths). This work also contains a valuable exposition of what constitutes a social myth, the relationship between myth and ideology, and a method of how to analyse myths. Barthes shows that what we accept as being natural is in fact an illusory reality constructed in order to mask the real structures of power. Mass culture (its icons, stars, fads, objects), of which the media and its products are the flagship, constructs this illusory reality and encourages conformity to the values of the *petit bourgeoisie* who controls the media and who are part of a bigger power élite (see McNeil, 2006).

Michel Foucault (1926–1984) and discourse

| Foucault | As a post-structuralist the French philosopher Michel Foucault provided us with new insights about power, knowledge, and truth. As far as mass communication studies and research are concerned, he made us acutely aware of the concepts "discourse", "discursive practice" and

"critical discourse analysis". Discourse means dialogue, conversation, discussion, communication. Whereas linguistics in the structuralist tradition employed the perspective that the meaning of discourse is contained in a statement about something, Foucault showed how social rules precede the statement and draw the boundaries that dictate how a statement should be made or what is allowed in a discourse, dialogue or conversation about a topic. Meaning is not contained within a statement as such, (as the structuralist would have argued, but the meaning of a statement derives from all the myths, taboos, social rules, and knowledge about a topic at a specific time. For example, you may express your opinion about premarital sex in a statement about this topic. The meaning of your statement is not only contained in your statement as such, but in your thinking about the topic that precedes the statement and allows you to converse about the topic in a certain way. Such thinking is the product of your own background, culture, religion, politics and culture and is embossed on you by those with power, be it your parents, teachers, church leaders or political leaders.

Through psychiatric conditions (*Madness and civilization: A history of insanity in the age of reason,* 1965) and sexuality (*The history of sexuality,* 1976), Foucault showed how the boundaries of what allow us to formulate discourses about a topic changes over time. For example, through processes of socialisation and acquiring new knowledge about a subject, our discourses about premarital sex now often differ from what it used to be fifty years ago. Within a specific historical period there are underlying conditions of truth that determine how we experience, how we understand and how we attach meaning to something and which meanings are acceptable or not. (*Archaeology of knowledge,* 1969, and *The order of things: An archaeology of the human sciences,* 1966.)

Foucault thus argued that in order to understand the meaning of a statement about a topic one should go beyond the statement and rather focus on the conditions that made the statement possible in the first place; how such conditions at the particular time in history determines what is said, what may be said, and how we converse and think about a topic. What are the *conditions* for the existence of meaning?

These conditions are created through various *discursive practices*. For example, we can distinguish between judicial, medical, academic, political, church, and mediated discursive practices, each communicating about a topic in terms of its own discursive rules which together dictate how

we converse and impose on us the meaning and our understanding of a topic. These different discursive practices stand in power relations to each other; power and knowledge about a topic are intrinsically related. What we know about a topic is eventually the product of the discursive practices about a topic and their relationships to each other.

Take the case of homosexuality. In South Africa various discourses about this topic, each with its own discursive practices, were taking place at the time of writing. The judiciary debated the legalisation of gay and lesbian marriages according to the discursive rules of judicial interpretation and argumentation involving laws, legal philosophy and thinking about matrimony against the background of views about human rights. As such it focused on part of the "truth" about homosexuality and legal knowledge about the topic. The church and mosque debated gay matrimony against the background of theological discourses and discursive practices related to how to interpret religious documents and writings about the topic. Politicians debated it in terms of the discourses and the discursive practices of party-political rhetoric and thus what would please (or at least not alienate) their supporters and constituencies. The media debated in terms of the discursive practices related to the institutionalised production, presentation and representation of media content, frequently falling back on stereotypes about homosexuals. In the end, the individual and society's discourse about and knowledge of the topic was/is the result of all these discourses and their demarcated discursive practices allowing them to converse about the topic only in certain ways.

For media studies, the task is to decode the discursive practices of the media about a topic. In the case of the media, critical *discourse analysis* will begin with an analysis of the media's statements about a topic followed by an analysis of the rules which prescribe the ways of discussing, portraying, representing a topic and excluding other ways of representation (which are beyond the boundaries). It will involve an analysis of the subject itself as represented by the media; an analysis of how the media's representation of the topic acquires authority and is represented as the "truth" about the topic; an analysis of the discursive practices within the media institution; and finally, an analysis of the history of the discourse as dealt with by the media in order to establish how and if a new discourse has emerged. (For a more in-depth discussion of discourse and discourse analysis see the chapter on language in volume 3.)

Jacques Derrida (1930–2004) and deconstruction

Some scholars argue that Algerian-born French analyst Jacques Derrida's theory of *deconstruction* was the first major philosophical movement after phenomenology, existentialism and structuralism (see Reynolds, 2006). Much of Derrida's work involves a deconstruction of the "truths" about being, life, death, ethics, religion, thinking and believing as dealt with in Western philosophy. As part of post-structuralism, deconstruction seeks to expose and undermine the various binary oppositions upon which these philosophical or metaphysical "truths" are based. This Derrida did through a process of parodying the oppositions themselves by showing how within each component of an opposition, dualism and paradoxes can be found. For instance, in the dualism present/absent we should keep in mind that something can be present and absent at the same time. One of your parents may be dead and as such absent but he/she may nevertheless be present in your mind which makes it difficult to constitute the meaning of death as absence. Deconstruction thus seeks to *trouble* dualisms by revealing how they are always already *troubled*. The possibilities of mourning, giving, forgiving and hospitality are also the condition of their impossibility.

| Derrida |

One of the basic tenets of deconstruction is that in the contemplation of the metaphysical, Western philosophy has privileged presence rather than that which allows presence in the first place to be possible. Philosophers contemplate the meaning of life, which is a metaphysical act. Yet they do so from a perspective of not knowing what death is, a prerequisite for something being alive.

In pinpointing the meaning of something, we should be aware that meaning evades meaning, that in any text there are inevitable points of evasion and that undecidability betrays any stable meaning that an author might seek to impose upon his text. Therefore in one of his most influential books, *Of grammatology* (1976), Derrida disrupts one of the basic tenets of structuralism, namely the theory by Swiss linguist Ferdinand de Saussure (1857–1913) that there is a relationship between a sign (a word, an image, an object) and its meaning, between the *signifier* and the *signified*. Rather, the signifier is floating and open to numerous possibilities.

As a "method", deconstruction emphasises the sustained and rigorous analyses of the literal meaning of a particular text with the purpose of finding within that meaning alternative meanings. By doing this, the

reader/viewer will come across numerous dualisms or paradoxes which in themselves are troubled.

The bottom-line of deconstruction is that every word (sign) and eventually every text (be it a verbal, written or visual text) is made up of various signs and has layers of possible meanings. These layers, the possible meanings of something, are the result of cultural and historical processes. To really understand something we need to juxtapose possible meanings. Whereas post-structuralism had/has as its aim to expose oppositions, deconstruction goes further by trying to show how even these oppositions can and need to be juxtaposed, to expose the paradoxes within each component of the opposition.

Pierre Bourdieu (1930–2002) and structural limitations

Bourdieu

Contrary to Karl Marx's view that the deep structure of society rests upon the opposition between economic classes and their struggle for power, French sociologist Pierre Bourdieu, who worked in the disciplines of anthropology, education and cultural studies, argued that the analysis of power relationships should begin by focusing on how power is structured internally within different professions, such as in the field of journalism, and how these fields interrelate. He coined two concepts: *habitus* and *symbolic capital*. *Habitus* means that journalists may take certain practices and conditions as being natural, objective, as a social institution (the way "we" do things), a disposition. But are they? What are the alternatives? *Habitus* Bourdieu saw as being *structural limitations* that conceal truth. Those with power (such as journalists and media owners) may dictate and conceal *habitus* and own what Bourdieu calls *symbolic power*. In exercising their power they commit *symbolic violence*. The task of analysis should be to expose *habitus* and *symbolic power*.

In his book *On Television* (1998), Bourdieu argues that the structural limitations of the journalism profession include economic censorship brought about by the financial cost of covering a story and whether a story will be cost-effective in terms of the size of the audience it will draw (in short, journalism is a business and should be profitable). Furthermore, there are the limitations of time, space and format (in the shortest time or smallest space a story needs to be covered), work routines (deadlines, working against the clock), and conditions of labour (low salaries which do not necessarily draw the best and most responsible intellectual minds). Yet journalists may not always question these structural limitations as

Approaches to the Study of Mass Communication

responsible for them obscuring instead of exposing the truth. They may see it as part of the nature (*habitus*) of the job, the way in which things should be and are done and as the unquestioned rules of the profession.

These and other structural limitations of the profession may have lowered journalistic standards and quality, and may continue to do so unless a significant proportion of journalists themselves question the structures and practices of their profession. While journalists may pride themselves on isolating the truth that hides behind the rhetoric of governments and the business élite, in the end they may accomplish the opposite. Instead of exposing the way things work, journalism may mystify them further (Barnhurst, 2005). These structural limitations are contrary to moral and ethical conduct, given the fact that the symbolic capital of journalism lies in the fact that journalism is, after all, contemporary person's main lens on the social world. Through news (and the media in general), we understand our world(s) and rely on news to take crucial decisions (Szeman 2005a).

Neil Postman (1931–2003) and media as show business

On a more practical level, but nevertheless explaining the same concept of structural limitations and *habitus*, American researcher Neil Postman (1931–2003) argued that television turns everything into entertainment, even news. By so doing, television masks reality and the truth. In his book *Amusing ourselves to death! public discourse in the age of show business* (1985), he argued that news is guided by questions such as:

- Will the story (politics, human interest, crime, disaster, reality) "work" on television?
- Will it make for good television? Is it visually appealing? (1985:1992)

In order to make reality "good television", everything on screen acquires the character of show business. If the show is to go on, there is no time for searching discussion and inquiry, and this applies particularly to controversial public issues.

Postman suggests that thinking does not come across well on television, so there is little intellectual communication on television. The interviewee (who may be a politician, business person, academic, leader of society), like the presenter, is expected to be a showperson. He/she is there to show off an image: either that of the organisation or political party that he/she represents, or at any rate that of her/his own sagacity, which has to be captured in one or two punchy statements or sound-bites. It would fatally damage one's television image to say "I don't know" or "I'll check

up" on television. For this reason many people who are likely to appear on television are trained in the finer points of *acting* before the camera.

The effect of this on the eventual way in which people see, experience and react, especially to public affairs can be enormous. Do the television images of bloody wars and revolution really speak to people and touch us in an emotional and existential way, or do we experience them as just a part of the "show" on television?

It would be difficult to deny that entertainment is the dominant metaphor in and through which television discourse is conducted, argues Postman. Thus after every evening's ration of tragedy on the news, the presenters invite the viewer to join them again at the same time tomorrow night for another dose of the same. Things which should have kept the viewer awake all night are forgotten within seconds.

The format of news bulletins contributes to this effect: glamorous presenters, catchy introductory music, attractive graphic designs, advertising interludes, a concluding quip to give the news a cheerful ending. All this permits viewers to ignore the horrors they have just watched and accept the invitation to "join us again tomorrow night". Along with the presenters they become voyeurs, looking in on reality (or a fragment of it) from the outside. There is no real involvement. Rather there is a kind of sadism, in the sense that television provides an opportunity to take a highly sensational peek at the wretchedness and tragedy of other lives from the outside, just as one would watch a movie in a cinema or on television. (Postman, *op.cit.*)

What Postman thus argues is in line with Bourdieu's view that under the pressure of its own unquestioned ways of production, professional practices and styles (*habitus*), the media and journalism (in this case television) conceals a truth and reality, instead of exposing it.

Jean Baudrillard (1929–2007) and media as simulation

Baudrillard

The French social philosopher Jean Baudrillard's work on the media (again especially television) is perhaps the most outstanding example of postmodern media critique and analysis (*Simulacra and simulation*, 1981). Baudrillard argues that television creates a hyperreality without any history (see the earlier reference to postmodernism's break with history). The "reality" we experience through television is a simulated creation in which any distinction between real and unreal is difficult. Television creates a political and cultural *cul-de-sac*.

Approaches to the Study of Mass Communication

Barring Canadian researcher Marshall McLuhan (1911–1980) and Welsh academic Raymond Williams (1921–1988), there have been few thinkers on mass communication whose work has aroused as much intellectual interest as that of Baudrillard. This is probably because he was the first person to describe the media, especially the electronic media, as part of humanity's postmodern condition.

According to the Flemish philosopher Herbert Dethier (1993:512–520), Baudrillard's work can be summed up as a postmodern interpretation of late 20th century consumer society. In this society there is no longer any distinction between private and public or between intimacy and publicity.

> *"The reality we observe (and experience) in postmodern consumer society is a simulated reality – this simulation is chiefly the product of the media, which create a hyperreality without any material origin or reality. The foundation of truth is eradicated in the media culture and all that remains is a self-referent simulacrum of simulations or milky way of simulations which makes it impossible to distinguish between the real and the unreal. The media create a cultural and political cul-de-sac."* (Dethier 1993:512)

Like Friedrich Nietzsche (1844–1900), Baudrillard was primarily concerned with individual, cultural and social loss of reality. For Baudrillard the media play a cardinal role in bringing about this loss. Baudrillard's criticism of the media amounts to the following: Mass communication is non-communication. If we define communication as dialogue, then according to Baudrilllard we can do no other than to regard the "communication" of the mass media as non-communication.

Mass communication impedes the exchange of ideas and denies us the opportunity to reply. The talk shows and opinion and actuality programmes are mere simulations of dialogue. They are and remain a "show". A "show" is intrinsically a representation of something. When dialogue is simulated on television it is difficult to distinguish between television as the communicator, television as the transmitter (signalling device), television as the process of communication and television as the medium. Television has to be all these things simultaneously. In this sense television is an abstraction of communication. In addition to the intrinsic self-centredness and the egotistical, self-contained and self-reflecting nature of television, it should also be remembered that

television is a medium where ownership and control (in the case of private ownership) and power (especially in the case of state ownership) are internal. Television is a medium that exists in and for itself (see Dethier 1993:513).

To Marshall McLuhan's claim that the medium is the message, Jean Baudrillard replies that this is the very thing that means the end of the message, and of the medium, and therefore the end of mass communication. Like McLuhan, Baudrillard also uses the warm/cool metaphor in describing the media. McLuhan uses the warm/cool distinction to distinguish between the *technical* abilities of the various mass media.

A medium that is full of data and high definition, and which leaves little to the recipient's own interpretation and signification, is warm. Photographs, films and the radio are examples of warm media. In contrast, a medium containing relatively few data and low definition, which therefore invites the recipient to participate in completing the message, is cool. In comparison with a photograph which is full of data (warm), a cartoon strip contains little data and is therefore cool (see O'Sullivan *et al* 1983:134, explaining McLuhan).

For Baudrillard the warm/cool distinction doesn't refer to the technical capacity of the media but to what the media actually do. The media turn a warm event into a cool media event. "Warm" means that emotion, expectation, anticipation, *mise-en-scène* and spectacle are present, making the reality or actual event warm. With the aid of flash-backs, replays and close-ups, the media turn a warm event (reality) into a cold event. The media therefore have a *chilling* effect (see Dethier 1993:514; Kellner 1989:70; Baudrillard 1983a).

Mass communication leads to the disappearance of authentic communication (symbolic interchange) and the emergence of meaningless or empty signs. Instead of authentic communication (or symbolic interchange) in which we attempt to make signs meaningful, there is merely simulation (an imitation of signs). Signs in the media exist merely for the sake of simulation. What is more, the media effectively become a sign in themselves and for themselves without any real link with truth or reality. The media as a sign and a sign system, or as a symbolic form of expression, are merely a simulation.

Approaches to the Study of Mass Communication

The media user becomes so absorbed in the media world's use of signs (stars, products, objects, events), media spectacles, representation and simulations that he or she no longer has access to reality, or believes that the simulation of reality is the real thing. The media's simulation of reality therefore becomes the reality of human experience. People can no longer distinguish between reality and simulation and consider second-hand experience to be true experience (see Fourie 1993).

Baudrillard saw this media *reality* relegating us to a radical, relativistic, idealistic universe of the imagination. Individuals are enticed into a universe of *simulacra*, in which it is impossible to distinguish between spectacle and the real thing and in which spectacle dominates reality (see Dethier 1993:515). Baudrillard feared that this will eventually create people who have lost contact with reality.

Stuart Hall (1932-) and the active audience

Finally the work of the Jamaica-born British cultural theorist Stuart Hall needs to be mentioned here. Hall's work on media audiences illustrate a move in media studies from structuralism to post-structuralism in the sense that he emphasised the role of the receiver (reader/viewer, listener) in the interpretation of texts. Hall's model (see his influential article *Encoding and decoding in the television discourse,* 1973) serves the purpose of showing how media texts and discourses are not only the product of media producers but also of media users who may consume and understand media texts differently from the producer's intended way. In short he emphasised the active audience and differentiated between three ways in which media users may interpret a text: the so-called dominant-reading of a text, the negotiated reading, and the oppositional reading. Hall, like other poststructuralists, highlighted the importance of active interpretation and rejected textual determinism (see chapter 7 for a more in-depth discussion of Hall's theory).

| Stuart Hall |

Summary

We conclude by saying that structuralism (and in media studies, formalist semiotics) emphasised the relationship between a sign and its meaning (the fixedness of meaning), and the role of the producer or author of texts to encode a specific meaning into a text. Poststructuralism emphasises the role of the recipient (the reader/viewer/listener) in the production of meaning. Deconstruction emphasises the openness and almost

endless nature of meaning. Postmodernism adopts an almost nihilistic (indifferent, reckless, hopeless) stance in the sense that it emphasises the difficulty (if not the utter impossibility) of getting a grip on meaning; in any case, postmodernism points out the meaninglessness of the media and its detachment from reality. Later, in our discussion of normative theory, we will return to postmodernism with reference to the work of Australian academics Ien Ang (born in Java, educated in the Netherlands, working at the University of West Sydney) and Liz Jacka of the University of Technology Sydney, who show how it has become almost impossible to measure media performance in the post-modern media environment.

Structuralism came to be seen as being too rigid in its understanding of meaning and too ignorant of the impact of culture, history, and the recipient on the production of meaning and the understanding of something. Post-structuralism and later deconstruction and postmodernism emphasised that in order to arrive at a more balanced understanding, we need to interpret reality from different perspectives. What all these paradigms have in common are their involvement with meaning and how we attach meaning; the source of the meanings we give to something or someone; and how we should be critical of the taken-for-granted meanings we attach to concepts, objects and individuals. In media studies these approaches focused the attention on how media texts (of whatever kind) produce meanings and contribute to our understanding and interpretation of the world and how we should be critical of this.

3.4.8 Postcolonial theory and the Afrocentric approach

Postcolonial studies (see Shome and Hegde, 2002:249–270) seek to situate and understand phenomena within the context of the larger and unequal geopolitical histories of global and cultural power. A basic premise of postcolonial studies is that information and knowledge disseminated by the media are subjected to forces of colonialism. Whereas global theories of the media and international communication often emphasise the utopian and liberating effect of the media, these theories simultaneously obscure deep divisions and inequities brought about by slavery and colonialism (Shome and Hegde, 2002:261). What needs to be penetrated is the systemic and continuing structures of colonial power, the normativity of "Westerness" and the contradictions and tensions this causes in the realities of the everyday life of non-Westerners. This should be explored, not from the perspective of a "colonial gaze", but in terms of an indigenous epistemology.

Approaches to the Study of Mass Communication

The following are some of the main concerns of postcolonial studies and theory:

postcolonial concerns

- The historical structures of knowledge production and how we produce and circulate knowledge: the underlying premise is that indigenous knowledge is suppressed by Western knowledge or the knowledge of the coloniser. See in this regard, for example Edward Said's *Orientalism* (1978), India-born USA-based postcolonial theorist Gayatri Chakravorty Spivak's *In other worlds* (1988), and feminist and postcolonial theorist Lata Mani's *Contentious Traditions* (1999). These works are methodological and theoretical interrogations of the linkages between colonialism and knowledge production. The works seek to show how institutionalised knowledge is always subject to forces of colonialism, nation, geopolitics, and history (Shome & Hegde, 2002:251).
- The historical foundation of cultural power: issues of race, class, gender, sexuality, and nationality are situated in the context of larger (and unequal) histories and geographies of global power and culture (*op cit.*: 253).
- The contexts of colonialism and the impact of such contexts on power, culture and knowledge: it is now recognised that works such as Said's *Orientalism* is an understanding of colonialism at a time when the West-East, North-South divide was clear. Globalisation brought about a new context with complex forms of de-territoralisations and re-territoralisations in the power structures of nations and in the lifestyles and everyday practices of the inhabitants in many countries. Changing contexts necessitate the rethinking of issues such as third space, diaspora and nomadism (*op cit.*: 257). Another example of new contexts is the role of new ICTs in bringing about pockets of so-called tech cities within a nation and populations (usually middle and upper middle class professionals in their early thirties) that are not the result of any form of colonialism or colonial migration.
- Neo-colonialism: postcolonial studies are not only concerned with the historical impact of colonialism on knowledge production, power, issues of race, gender, and so on, but also investigate the continued power of colonisers and how independent nation-states are still dominated by European and American economic, cultural and even military powers.

postcolonial research

For Stefan Sonderling (2006) the major research issues in postcolonial studies centre round questions such as:
- how did the experience of colonisation affect those who were colonised while also influencing the colonisers?
- how were colonial powers able to gain control over so large a portion of the non-Western world?
- what traces have been left by colonial education, science and technology in postcolonial societies?
- how do these traces affect decisions about development and modernisation in postcolonies?
- what were the forms of resistance against colonial control?
- how did colonial education and language influence the culture and identity of the colonised?
- how did Western science, technology, and medicine change existing knowledge systems?
- what are the emergent forms of postcolonial identity after the departure of the colonisers?
- to what extent has decolonisation (a reconstruction free from colonial influence) been possible?
- should decolonisation proceed through an aggressive return to the pre-colonial past?
- how do gender, race, and class function in colonial and postcolonial discourse?
- are new forms of imperialism replacing colonisation and how?

Francis Kasoma

Postcolonial studies have focussed attention on how dominant media theories are a product of Western epistemology and thus emphasise a Western way of thinking about the role of the media in society. In this regard, the late Zambian scholar Francis Peter Kasoma produced groundbreaking work in the fields of an African perspective on media ethics, media training, and freedom of expression (*Journalism ethics in Africa*, 1994). Kasoma's work, as well as those from some other African scholars, suggest that an African epistemology would rather seek to understand the media and its role from the perspective of communal beliefs and values. *Ubuntu* (a Zulu word widely understood across Southern Africa which defines people's humanity in terms of their responsibilities in helping others) is then seen to be a possible African alternative to Western media theory (Kasoma, 1994, 1996; Blankenberg, 1999; Kamwangamalu, 1999).

Approaches to the Study of Mass Communication

Postcolonial media theory also readdress the unequal production and distribution of information and entertainment between the North and the South and focus the attention anew on unequal access to media and information and communication technology. See John Downing's *Internationalising Media Theory* (1996) and James Curran and Myung-Jin Park's *De-Westernising Media Studies* (2000).

Closely associated with postcolonial studies is the Afrocentric paradigm. This paradigm has it origin in the African-American experience. It came into prominence with the publication of Molefi Kete Ashante's book *Afrocentricity* (1980) followed by *The Afrocentric Idea* (1987). Ashante says Afrocentricity establishes:

> *"a frame of reference wherein phenomena are viewed from the African perspective ... it centers on placing people of African origin in control of their lives and attitudes about the world ... As an intellectual theory, Afrocentricity is the study of the ideas and events from the standpoint of Africans as key players rather than victims ... it is Africa asserting itself intellectually and psychologically, breaking the bonds of Western domination in the mind ..." (in Mazama 2003:5).*

	Afrocentric paradigm

In other words, while Eurocentrism imposes itself as a universal framework, Afrocentricity demonstrates that it is only one way of viewing the world. According to Sonderling (2006) the Afrocentric paradigm is concerned with:

- developing a philosophy based on African values and ideas;
- rediscovering African history and the contribution of Africans to the development of Western civilisation;
- developing African literature, culture and aesthetics;
- developing consciousness of African nationalism;
- developing African scientific methods and practice;
- encouraging African education.

Sonderling (2006) furthermore shows how, for the study of communication, the Afrocentric paradigm encourages awareness of the particular ways that African communication, such as oratory and rhetoric, differ from the Western modes of communication, and how issues of the representation of Africans in the mass media and African aesthetics are emphasised.

3.4.9 Normative theory

To conclude this overview of theoretical approaches, we end with normative theory. In a way it can be argued that all the approaches referred to above are in one or another way concerned with the role of the media in society. Simply put, the positivist approach is concerned with how the media could or should work in order to play a role in society and to achieve specific goals. The critical approach is concerned with how the media and its potential role in society are misused in power and ideological struggles. The meaning production approach is concerned with the role of the media in our perception and experience of reality; the technological approach with the technologic capacity of the media to provide access to information and entertainment; the information society approach with the role of the media as contemporary society's primary vehicle of information (and entertainment); and the postcolonial approaches with how the role of the media in society has been dictated by the colonisers.

role of media in society

Although the role of the media is implicit in all the previously described approaches, the branch of theory that explicitly deals with the role of the media is called normative media theory. Normative media theory (McQuail 1992; 2000) concerns the perceived and ideal role(s) the media are to play in a society or ought to operate if certain social values are to be observed or attained. The overall purpose of normative theory is to develop a yardstick against which media performance, accountability and quality can be measured and possibly controlled. Much of a country's media policy is thus based on normative theory. Such policy aims to ensure that the media are empowered to fulfil its functions in a controlled and responsible way. (See volume 2 where the topic of media policy and management are dealt with.)

freedom of expression

Thinking about the role of the media has a long history that stretches over three centuries, including books written by British-born American revolutionary Thomas Paine (1737–1809), French historian Alexis de Tocqueville (1805–1859) and British liberal political economist and member of parliament John Stuart Mill (1806–1873). It started with political-philosophical and legal questions about freedom of expression. How free should the media be? What is freedom of expression? What are the media's social responsibilities? Since the concept of the media as "fourth estate" was reputedly coined by Irish statesman and conservative Edmund Burke (1729–1797) (see McQuail, 2005:169) these questions

Approaches to the Study of Mass Communication

have been continuously debated. The concept "fourth estate" was coined once it was realised that the media (originally the press) possess equivalent power to that of the other three "estates", namely, the state (government), the church, and the school (education). In England it originally was the Lords (the ruling class), the Church and the Commons (government). Today industry and the economy of a society perhaps have overtaken the power of the Church.

Since the processes of political, social and economic transformation started in the early 1990s, questions about the role of the South African media foments debate. Although freedom of expression is entrenched in the country's Constitution, different perceptions exist about what freedom of expression is and how this should be realised in codes of conduct and practice. In this regard it is often argued that the South African media still function in terms of Western values and codes of media conduct, and that these codes should be replaced with codes based on African values. (See chapter 4 on the functions of the media for a further discussion of this issue.)

Much of traditional normative theory derives from the positivistic approach. The underlying assumption is that the media should play a role of some kind in society, be it to sustain democracy, to contribute to society's development, to educate and entertain people, to act as a watchdog over politicians, academia and financial institutions, among others. From this assumption, specific normative theories – libertarian, authoritarian, social responsibility and development theory – originated. The assumptions on which these theories are based are supported by empirical research (the observable, well-defined and described functions of the media) about the actual performance of the media in society, for example, how a specific newspaper reports a specific issue and through its reporting fulfils a specific function, with answers based on empirical measurement of the specific newspaper's performance. Yet, when it comes to asking questions about the intrinsic nature and value of the media's role in society (in other words, value- and norm-based questions) normative theory relies heavily on critical, interpretative and hermeneutical theory and research.

<small>normative theories</small>

The following questions (see Brants, 1998:169–179; Baran and Davis, 2003:93) are at the core of normative theory:

<small>normative questions</small>

- How do the media cover different perspectives in a society?

179

- What is perceived to be in the public's interest, and why?
- How is public interest defined?
- What are the social responsibilities of the media?
- How should the media be organised legally and financially in order to realise any potential as a carrier of public values?
- Should the media identify and solve social problems?
- Should the media provide essential public services without profit?
- What moral and ethical standards should guide media professionals?
- When may the media invade someone's privacy?
- What is the truth?
- What is objectivity?

Traditionally, these questions were raised mainly in the context of news and other information and focused on the values and roles of journalists, the quality of news performance and the accessibility of the news media (Brants 1998:169–179). Answers to them were rather straightforward. However, as the media grew to what it is today – a major information and entertainment industry – and as the media increasingly became commercialised, answers aren't that easy. The diverse roles and values of the media in contemporary society are heavily debated. Questions are also asked about the value of traditional normative theory (such as the libertarian and authoritarian theories), in a changed and new media environment and in an increasingly globalised world.

Central in today's critical questioning of normative theory are again questions about democracy and the changed nature of democracy, about the media as a "public sphere" and about the nature of "the public" in today's globalised societies. These topics and concepts are dealt with in more depth in chapters 4, 8 and 9.

3.5 SUMMARY

The purpose of this chapter was to provide you with an overview of different approaches to the study of mass communication and its media. We started by situating today's mass media in the context of preceding public communication cultures and showed how the questions being asked today about the quality and meaning of today's more electronic and digital mass communication were also raised in preceding oral, written and printed communication cultures. We defined mass communication by asking a number of central questions related to the nature of the communicator in mass communication and technological convergences combination of print (text), audio and visual codes. Such codes are combined to form a range of messages in different genres for an increasingly interactive media audience.

Before we started with the overview of theoretical approaches, it was thought necessary to get some clarity about what theory is. In this regard, we looked at the value of theory, the goals of theory, its building blocks and how to evaluate a theory. Most importantly we concluded that mass communication theory is a form of sociological enquiry. Its main goal is to contribute to our understanding of the structures and practices of the mass media and how these structures and practices impact on society and social relationships within society, both on the macro and micro levels.

In our overview of theoretical approaches we looked at positivism, often also referred to as the administrative or managerial paradigm. In this paradigm the key goal is to understand the working and impact of the media, its functions and effects with the purpose of improving the working of the media to gain specific effects. Contrasting the positivistic approach is the critical approach in which the ideological nature of mass media and its ownership are questioned. The focus is on the political economy of the media; the way in which the media represent people, groups and organisations; the need for freedom of expression as a pillar of democracy; inequities in the media industry; and inequities in society as exposed or not by the media.

These two approaches were followed by brief introductions to how the media plays a central role in our conceptualisation and perceptions of the world and its realities (and fictions). In this regard, we specifically mentioned phenomenology, symbolic interactionism and semiotics as approaches primarily concerned with how the media constructs meaning. We then briefly looked at the technological, information society, post-structuralist and postmodern perspectives and concluded with some observations about the rising postcolonial and Afrocentric paradigms.

LEARNING ACTIVITIES

Compose a portfolio consisting of the following:
- Write a one- to two-page essay in which you express your own ideas about the nature and value of our present-day public communication culture with specific reference to commodification and commercialisation.
- Identify the communicator in:
  - a newspaper story;
  - a television newscast;
  - a radio documentary;
  - an Internet website;
  - a television soap opera;
  - a film you have recently seen.
- Illustrate the similarities and differences in the concepts "message", "text" and "media content" with examples from media.
- Describe the characteristics of media audiences and how the nature of media audiences is changing against the background of the impact of ICTs on traditional mass media.
- Design/develop your own theory of mass communication. Describe the value, goals and building blocks of your theory and the criteria that can be used to evaluate the theory.
- You are invited by a special interest group to lecture on the state of art in mass communication theory and research. Prepare a lecture (10 pages) in which you explain (summarise) the underlying assumptions and point of departures in positivistic, critical, technological deterministic, meaning construction, information society, poststructuralist, post-modern, post-colonial, and Afro-centric theories.

FURTHER READING

Baran, S.J. & Davis, D.K. 2003. *Mass communication theory. Foundations, ferment, and future.* 3rd edition. London: Thomson/Wadsworth.

Burton, G. 2005. *Media and society. Critical perspectives.* Berkshire, U.K.: Open University.

Berger, A. 1995. *Essentials of mass communication theory.* Thousand Oaks, CA: Sage.

Croteau, D. & Hoynes, W. 2003. *Media society. Industries, images, and audiences.* 3rd edition. Thousand Oaks: Pine Forge Press.

Curran, J. & Gurevitch, M. 1996. *Mass media and society*. 2nd edition. London: Arnold.

Grossberg, L., Wartella, E., & Whitney D. 1998. *Media Making. Mass media in a popular culture*. London: Sage.

Inglis, F. 1990. *Media theory: an introduction*. London: Blackwell.

McQuail, D. 2005. *McQuail's mass communication theory*. 5th edition. London: Sage.

Thompson, J.B. 1995. *The media and modernity. A social theory of the media*. Cambridge: Polity.

Wood, J.T. 2000. *Communication theories in action: an introduction*. 2nd edition. Belmont, CA: Wadsworth.

c h a p t e r f o u r

The Role and Functions of the Media in Society

Pieter J. Fourie

LEARNING OUTCOMES

At the end of this chapter you should be able to:
- define how media functions are researched and debated;
- explain media pluralism (variety);
- define normative theory;
- explain the five main normative media theories;
- explain why it has become difficult to measure media performance;
- explain the postcolonial view about the Westerness of normative media theory and why it should change;
- formulate and substantiate your own opinion about the value of a moral philosophy such as ubuntu or Christian nationalism as a framework for normative media theory;
- explain the entertainment phenomenon from different perspectives.

The Role and Functions of the Media in Society

THIS CHAPTER

WE ALL KNOW how the media are often blamed for almost everything that can go wrong. Politicians frequently accuse the media of misinterpreting them, of framing them, of lying, of wrongfully criticising them, and of not doing what they wish the media to do or achieve. Similarly, celebrities and even ordinary people once faced with the media are often disillusioned that "the story didn't turn out to be what they wanted it to be". Organisations often complain that the media only focus on the negative about them. They then go on to criticise the media. In this chapter we are concerned with this criticism.

The chapter is divided into two sections: news and information, and entertainment.

We begin by locating media within the theoretical framework of functionalism, then focus on the informative role of the media and the issue of freedom of expression. Our point of departure will be the "traditional" four theories of the press. For many decades these normative theories, added and altered, formed the yardstick in terms of which media performance is measured and in terms of which freedom of expression in a society is described. They concern the information, surveillance and political functions of the media in society. However, against the background of globalisation, the rapid development of communication and information technologies and the emergence of postcolonial and postmodern approaches, these theories are increasingly criticised as inadequate to describe, interpret and evaluate the role of the media in the changed world. We briefly look at the criticism and suggestions for a new framework.

Given that more than two-thirds of media content is entertainment-oriented, this is the focus in the second part of the chapter. We pose this question: what is entertainment? We look at some general characteristics of entertainment and how we get to be entertained.

SECTION 1: NEWS AND INFORMATION

4.1 THE FUNCTIONS OF THE MEDIA

4.1.1 Functionalism

Since the beginning of the academic study of mass communication and mass media, scholars have concerned themselves with exactly what the functions of the mass media are or ideally should be. This was done under the influence of key sociologists such as France's Émile Durkheim (1858–1917) and America's Talcott Parsons (1902–1979). Their research was done predominantly within the context of functionalism (sometimes known as structural functionalism) which dominated sociology at the end of the nineteenth century and the first part of the twentieth century.

functionalism

The bottom line of functionalism is a view of society as integrated, harmonious and a cohesive whole. All parts of society, be it government, non-governmental organisations, privately-owned corporations, educational establishments, the military and economic structures and cultural institutions function to maintain equilibrium, consensus and social order. The goal of sociology is to describe and analyse these different social systems (O'Sullivan, Hartley, Saunders, Montgomery & Fiske 1994: 124). The same applies to the media systems in a society. As powerful socialisation instruments, media contribute towards integration, harmony and cohesion through information, entertainment and education.

latent and manifest functions

Some of the first communication scholars to provide functionalist analyses of media were a trio of American sociologists, Paul Felix Lazarsfeld (1901–1976), Harold Lasswell (1902–1978), and Robert Merton (1910–2003). Merton was one of the first to distinguish between latent and manifest functions and the fact that what might be functional to one group may be dysfunctional to another. More recently, American sociologist Charles Wright (1975) designed an almost classic model for the study of media functions, proposing the following inventory of questions (O'Sullivan *et al* 1994:125).

Table 4.1 Wright's model of functions

MODEL OF FUNCTIONS
What are:
(1) the manifest
(2) latent
(3) functions and
(4) dysfunctions of mass communicated
(5) surveillance (news)
(6) correlation (selection)
(7) cultural transmission
(8) entertainment for the
(9) society
(10) individual
(11) subgroups
(12) cultural systems?

The Role and Functions of the Media in Society

In this model Wright argues that the main functions of the media are to inform and entertain people and that through such information and entertainment the media contribute either manifestly or latently to cultural growth for both individuals and society. However this is, as with many other functionalist models, a rather simplistic model, especially when it comes to the political functions of the media.

Some objections to functionalism (O'Sullivan *et al* 1994:95–96) are that functionalism often:

- Tends to overlook the fact that the media do not necessarily function identically for the people or groups. It takes consensus as granted and disregards conflict in social relations. In other words, functionalism takes it for granted that the media will have the same functions for all the people in a society. This is not necessarily the case. What might function as information for some might be disinformation to others. What some people might experience as entertainment might offend others.
- Fails to account adequately for social change and transformation. Media functions in well-established democratic societies might be dysfunctional in societies in a process of change, development and transformation. In such societies the emphasis on the media's perceived role may be more on its role in development and less on surveillance, for example.
- Neglects to provide for feedback and the fact that feedback modifies both the message and the context. Put another way, functionalism often tends not to acknowledge the importance of context social, political and cultural as an influence on all stages of the communication processes (Watson & Hill 1984:149).

Nevertheless, as Denis McQuail (2000:79–80) argues, functionalist models provide us with basic ideas about the role of the media in society. As such, they provide a structured framework for reviewing the significant tasks of media as key socialisation and ideological instruments. For this introduction, McQuail's summary of media functions (here slightly adapted) suffices (also see McQuail 2005):

Table 4.2 McQuail's typology of functions

FUNCTIONS/TASKS OF THE MEDIA

Information: the media (can)
- provide information about events and conditions in society and the world;
- indicate relations of power;
- facilitate innovation, adaptation and progress.

Correlation: the media (can)
- explain, interpret and comment on the meaning of events and information;
- provide support for established authority and norms;
- socialise;
- co-ordinate separate activities;
- contribute to consensus building;
- set orders of priority and by so doing signal the status of a topic.

Continuity: the media (can)
- express the dominant culture and recognise subcultures and new cultural developments;
- forge and maintain commonality of values.

Entertainment: the media (can)
- provide amusement, diversion and the means of relaxation;
- reduce social tension.

Mobilisation: the media (can)
- campaign for social objectives in the sphere of politics, war, economic development, work and sometimes religion.

(McQuail 2000:79–80)

4.1.2 The political functions of the media: The case for pluralism

Dutch researchers Jan van Cuilenburg, Otto Scholten and G.W. Noomen (1992:317) argue that in a democracy the media has the following political functions:
- to inform about political developments;
- to guide public opinion about political decisions;
- to express different views about political developments and decisions;
- to criticise political developments and decisions.

In order to empower the media to perform the above functions:
- media policy should ensure media pluralism;
- media content should reflect social plurality.

The Role and Functions of the Media in Society

By social plurality we mean the acknowledgement of political, social, cultural and economic differences between people and groups in a society.

social pluralism

By media pluralism we mean:
- the acknowledgement of social plurality;
- the reflection thereof in a diversity of media content;
- the existence of different media: various newspapers, radio stations, television stations, magazines, films and so on, catering for different groups within a society.

media pluralism

Van Cuilenburg, Scholten and Noomen (1992:327) distinguish between internal and external plurality. Internal plurality refers to the differences within the information and entertainment content of a newspaper, radio station or television station, within which there should be a balance between information, entertainment and the like; different opinions must be offered, and so forth. External plurality concerns the difference between different newspapers, radio stations and television stations.

The authors also distinguish between three levels of plurality: *macro-*, *meso-*, and *micro-plurality*.

Micro-plurality concerns each medium on its own and is thus internal. An example would be the South African Broadcasting Corporation and its content, which includes both satellite and terrestrial television broadcasts, more than 15 radio stations in all of the country's 11 official languages as well as some radio stations that only broadcast outside South Africa in French and vernacular languages meant for the rest of Africa, as well as the sabcnews.com website. Micro-plurality would examine a weekly English-language newspaper such as the *Mail & Guardian*, with its website and related publications such as *The Teacher* and *The Media* and regular supplements on business, education and the environment, or within the Johannesburg daily newspaper *The Sowetan*.

Meso-plurality concerns media categories; does the country have different newspapers available? Different television stations, radio stations, different film companies, different magazines and so on? For example, how many radio stations are there in a country and what is the nature of diversity in their content and languages?

Macro-plurality concerns all the media, regardless of category, available in a society. In other words, one may have only newspapers and radio stations, but no television stations and no film companies.

To recap:
- Micro-plurality: the variety of perspectives and voices within a single outlet, such as a daily Gauteng newspaper such as *The Citizen*.
- Meso-plurality: the variety of choices available within the same category, so there are choices between between *The Citizen*, *The Star*, *The Mail & Guardian*, *The Sun*, *Ilanga*, *UmAfrika*, *Isolezwe*, *The Financial Mail*, *Business Day*, *Sunday Times*, *Sunday Independent*, *Pretoria News*, *Rapport*, *Beeld* and *Die Son*.
- Macro-plurality: the variety of choices between reading newspapers, whether daily or weekly, English, Afrikaans or isiZulu, and other media such as television, radio, film, DVDs, CDs, videos, etc.

In a democracy, media functions are closely related to the principle of pluralism. A single newspaper with its own ideology and political stance might perform a valuable informative function for a certain group; at the same time, it might not inform other groups or individuals. For this reason the question of pluralism is emphasised in democratic societies. The ideal is that there should be as many radio and television stations, newspapers, magazines and films as possible, for as many people and groups in a society as possible. Only through acknowledging the plurality of political views and tastes can the media be in a position to fulfill the needs, views and tastes of as many people and groups as possible in a society. Only then can it play a democratic role.

With plurality as an overall prerequisite for the media to function free and democratically we now look specifically at theories about the role of the media in a society, the so-called normative theories which started as the four theories of the press formulated in the 1950s in the USA by Fredrick Siebert, Theodore Peterson and Wilbur Schramm (1956).

4.1.3 Normative theory

By normative theory we mean views (from different perspectives and within different conditions) about the ideal role of the media in society. In short it means "the media should or could do this or that". J.J. Roelofse (1996:48–60) argues that since governments often have the power to restrict or limit newspaper, television and radio criticism of government, and since the press usually assumes a surveillance role on behalf of civil society, tensions and conflicts between these two institutions are natural and to be expected. The power that governments claim for themselves usually conflicts with the democratic right of freedom of speech, a right

The Role and Functions of the Media in Society

which is important to the media as it enables them to perform their functions properly.

Normative theories are thus mainly concerned with restrictions on (and freedom of) the media in various situations and how this impacts on the functioning in society. This was the premise of a 1950s study of the different press systems in the world (Siebert, Peterson & Schramm 1956). They developed the following four theories initially in relation to the press (newspapers), later adopted and adapted as a yardstick for the measurement of the freedom of expression in any country (from authoritarian to libertarian) of all media:

- the authoritarian theory;
- the libertarian theory;
- the social responsibility theory;
- the Soviet communist theory.

The first and second theories are regarded as the main or basic press theories, while the third and fourth are variations on these theories. A fifth, the development theory, was formulated to accommodate conditions in developing countries. A sixth, the democratic-participant theory, is a description of a new kind of media–government–public relationship which has in recent years developed in reaction to deficiencies such as corruption and abuse of power in traditional democratic, free-market societies. The following overview of these theories is based mainly on the interpretations of J.J. Roelofse (1996) and Denis McQuail (1987; 2005).

4.1.3.1 The authoritarian theory

The *authoritarian theory* prevails in dictatorial societies. It can also surface in less authoritarian societies when the freedom of the press may be presented as conflicting with the interests of the state or society, when there is a danger of terrorism or in times of war, for example. Authoritarianism can also be exercised with regard to one medium in contrast with other media – in some countries television is subjected to greater control than the newspaper industry. The authoritarian theory is not merely of historical or descriptive importance or simply an extraordinary deviation from established democratic norms. It continues to justify government suppression of the media (Roelofse 1996:50).

> authoritarian theory

McQuail (1987:111–112) identifies the following basic assumptions of the authoritarian press theory:

- the press should do nothing to undermine vested power and interests;

- the press should be subordinate to vested power and authority;
- the press should avoid acting in contravention of prevailing moral and political values;
- censorship is justified in the application of these principles;
- editorial attacks on vested power and authority would be seen as criminal offences and the violation of moral codes would be considered criminal offences.

Under authoritarianism the main function of the media is to publicise and to propagandise the government's ideology and actions. In other words the press is an instrument and mouthpiece of government.

Roelofse (1996:51) draws our attention to the fact that some of the most significant communication and political events in the past century took place in authoritarian societies. The fascism (the philosophy and practice of the absolute power of the state and the subservice of the individual) found in Europe in the 1900s in Adolf Hitler's Germany, Bennito Mussolini's Italy, General Francisco Franco's Spain, in communist regimes in Eastern Europe and elsewhere, in South Africa's apartheid regime from 1948 to 1994 and in many post-independence African countries, was and in many cases still is rooted in authoritarianism or totalitarianism, which gave much freedom to the rulers, little or no freedom to the ruled, and which defined freedom of expression as a right vested in the state.

4.1.3.2 The libertarian theory

Roelofse (1996:51–53) shows how the rise of democracy, religious freedom, expanded economic freedom and the general philosophical climate of the Enlightenment undermined authoritarianism and led to a new view of the role of the media in the west and increasingly also in Asia, Africa and Latin America. The emphasis on personal freedom and democracy that emerged in the late seventeenth century and flourished in the nineteenth century, gave rise to the libertarian theory in reaction to the authoritarian theory.

libertarian theory

According to *libertarian theory*, people are rational beings capable of distinguishing between truth and falsehood, and between good and evil. The search for truth is regarded as an inalienable natural right. In terms of these beliefs the media is seen as a source of information and a platform for the expression of divergent opinions, informing people about government affairs and other issues and enabling them to monitor their

The Role and Functions of the Media in Society

government and form their own ideas about policy. The media should be free from government control and government influence, and there must be a free market for ideas and information (Roelofse 1996:52). The USA, Canada and Britain have had this type of media for approximately 200 years, closely followed by mainland European countries such as the Netherlands and France. The media has been encouraged to act as a *fourth estate* along with the legislative, executive and judicial authorities in the governing process (Siebert *et al* 1963:3–4).

However, the application of the idea of a free media is not simple. McQuail (1987:114) comments:

> *"The question of whether a free media is an end in itself, a means to an end, or an absolute right has never been settled. Once freedom is abused, it is no longer freedom and should be restricted. Absolute freedom is in fact anarchy. Libertarian societies therefore all more or less agree with Mill's contention that the freedom of the individual is defined – and thus constrained – by the freedom of other individuals."*

Most societies that recognise freedom of the media sought the solution to this dilemma of determining the boundaries of freedom without infringing the rights of the individual in:
- the abolition of censorship on the one hand;
- the introduction of media laws designed to protect individual rights.

The protection of reputation, privacy, the moral development of individuals or groups and the security and even the dignity of the state were recognised in common law and enshrined in statutory laws. These rights often rode over the right to media freedom (McQuail 1987:114).

McQuail (1987: 115) identifies the following basic assumptions of the libertarian press theory:
- the media should be free from any external censorship;
- publication and distribution should be accessible to any individual or group without a permit or licence;
- editorial attacks on governments or political parties should not be punishable;
- there should be no coercion to publish anything;
- no restrictions should be placed on the acquisition of information through legal channels;
- there should be no restriction on the export and import of information across national borders.

4.1.3.3 The social responsibility theory

Exponents of this theory attempt to reconcile the ideas of freedom and independence with responsibility towards society (Roelofse 1996:53–54). The *social responsibility theory* is based on the following premises (McQuail 1987:116–118):

social responsibility theory

- the media should support democratic political principles;
- the media are under an obligation to create a forum for different viewpoints;
- the independence of the media should be emphasised in relation to their responsibility towards society;
- the media should meet certain standards.

The theory offers two solutions to the problem of reconciling freedom with social responsibility. These are:

- regulatory bodies, independent of government, for the organisation and partial control of the media through internal media regulations (often negotiated with the media themselves), such as the Independent Communications Authority of South Africa (ICASA) for the control of broadcasting and telecommunications, the Press Ombudsman for newspapers, the Broadcasting Complaints Commission of South Africa for electronic media, and so on.
- professional bodies such as the South African National Editors Forum (SANEF) which should advance and nurture balanced and impartial news presentation. (See volume 2 in which internal and external media regulation are dealt with in detail.)

McQuail (*ibid.*) identifies the following basic principles of the social responsibility theory:

- The media should accept certain responsibilities towards society.
- The media should fulfil their responsibilities mainly by setting professional standards with regard to the supply of information and the truth, accuracy, objectivity and balance of their reporting.
- The media should self-regulate within the framework of the law and established institutions.
- The media should avoid publicising information that can lead to crime, violence or social disruption, as well as information that can offend ethnic or religious minorities.
- The media collectively should represent all social groups and reflect the diversity of society by giving people access to a variety of viewpoints and the right to react to these viewpoints.

The Role and Functions of the Media in Society

- Society is entitled to expect high professional standards and intervention is justifiable if the media fail to meet these standards.

 ## Case Study 4.1: Public Service Broadcasting in South Africa

A good case study of social responsibility in practice is public service broadcasting. In South Africa, the South African Broadcasting Corporation (SABC) is the public broadcaster. In terms of The Broadcasting Act No. 4 of 1999, the SABC is expected to provide a number of cultural, linguistic, information and education services which are not prescribed for private or commercial broadcasters. (See chapter 1 for a discussion of the South African broadcasting system.)

It is generally accepted that British broadcasting served as a model for the establishment and functioning of public service broadcasting in much of the world, including South Africa. After becoming aware of the power of broadcasting in moulding public opinion and thus its power as a political instrument, and after lengthy investigations into the role of broadcasting in a society in the 1920s, Sir John Reith was appointed as the first director general of the newly established British Broadcasting Corporation (BBC) in 1927. Reith, who also played a leading role in the formation of the South African Broadcasting Corporation in the 1930s (Rosenthal 1974:150–159), formulated a manifesto for public service broadcasting which is historically seen as the philosophy underlying the nature of public service broadcasting. This manifesto says public service broadcasting should:

- foster the provision of an impartial space for free expression and open debate;
- provide audiences with information that will allow them to participate fully in their societies;
- be a cultural, moral and educational instrument for spreading knowledge, raising standards and improving behavior;
- offer programming for all interest groups;
- offer programming for minorities;
- provide competition in good programming rather than to get involved in competition for the largest audience numbers;
- liberate rather than restrict programme makers and by so-doing set an aesthetic standard;
- be a universal service and as such accessible to all;
- tap the best of a nation's cultural resources in literature, art, drama, music, science, history;
- express national and regional cultural identity;
- be free of commercial pressures (advertising) and therefore address audiences first and foremost as citizens and not as potential consumers.

Media Studies: Volume 1

A public broadcaster should strive towards:
- high programme standards;
- use of broadcasting to elevate public taste;
- bringing into the greatest possible number of homes all that was best in every department of human knowledge, endeavor, and achievement;
- preserving a high moral tone and avoid the vulgar;
- leading public taste rather than pandering to it.

The service was to be universal, meaning available to all the citizens in a country, at the lowest price possible. To be free of commercial pressure (advertising) it had to be funded by license fees and government subsidisation (Scannell 1990:13). In the educational, social and political fields, Reith saw broadcasting as a powerful tool for the creation of social unity, consensus and enlightened and reasonable public opinion. In short, Reith and his followers thus saw public service broadcasting as a cultural, moral and educational instrument for spreading knowledge, raising standards and improving behavior; as a kind of social cement to keep society together and build a nation; the role and function of broadcasting formed part of the government's task to uplift the working class morally, politically and culturally. In order to realise this, Reith was an advocate of a monopolistic and non-commercial broadcasting service under the control of the government (Scannell 1990:15–29).

Yet, in most parts of the world, public service broadcasting is undergoing radical changes. In general there is a shift to private or commercial broadcasting. These changes can be attributed to a number of factors but mainly to economic trends related to increased liberalisation, privatisation and internationalisation brought about by globalisation and the development of new information and communication technologies. (See Fourie (2004; 2005) for more detailed discussions on how influences such as satellite television are altering public service broadcasting.)

Despite criticism that public service broadcasting has often been misused for state propaganda, as in South Africa, few can deny the high standards and quality programming that can prevail in public service broadcasting. Critics such as Tracey (1998:50–60; 259–278) argue that commercialisation, privatisation and internationalisation have contributed to the decline of public service broadcasting bringing mediocrity, market centeredness and predictability. Public service broadcasting is now in growing competition with private and commercial broadcasters. It is now often ruled by a business philosophy instead of a social responsibility philosophy. In a market-oriented philosophy the emphasis is on:
- competition and beating the competitor;
- cuts in production costs, to produce programme content at the lowest cost;
- exploitation of new markets for what is bound to be an increasingly fragmented market;
- co-productions and facility sharing.

The Role and Functions of the Media in Society

All this has resulted in a lowering of standards. As far as the future is concerned, Tracey (ibid) argues that because of globalisation, public service broadcasting should and can play an even bigger role in helping societies to define their particular characters. A prerequisite for being able to do this is a coherent and stable belief system in the value and future of public service broadcasting among electronic media practitioners themselves and among policymakers. Only against the background of such a belief system will public service broadcasters and policymakers be able to define their missions and confront organisational and structural change, new policy environments, new proposals for funding and new programme philosophies. Only against the background of a sound belief system in the value of public service broadcasting will broadcasters be able to face the threats of downsizing and competition (Tracey 1998).

Tracey also warns that broadcasting policy should not take trends in politics and economics as its point of departure, but should be based on a clear understanding of what kind of society it is supposed to serve. "If a society has not decided its own preferred character in a broad sense, it will find it exceedingly difficult to determine its character in the particular sense of its broadcasting" (ibid: 278). This is where the impact of globalisation becomes relevant, as it alters the potential of societies to define themselves and their institutions, and to formulate coherent policies based on what a society wants to be (see chapter 9 on globalisation and Fourie 2003, 2004, 2005 for a further discussion of public service broadcasting and its future).

4.1.3.4 The Soviet communist theory

Until the fall of communism and the disintegration of the former Soviet Union there was probably no media system in the world as strictly controlled as the communist system. Western notions of freedom of the media were rejected as being fundamentally "unfree" because the Western media are controlled by capitalist economic interests that prevent them from publishing the Marxist *truth* (Siebert *et al* 1956:5, 125). The communist media, on the other hand, had no profit motive. McQuail (1987:118–119) and Roelofse (1996:55–56) identify the following basic assumptions of the *Soviet communist theory*:

- the media should act in the interests of, and be controlled by, the working class;
- the media should not be privately owned;
- the media should perform positive functions for society such as socialisation (to make people conform to desirable norms), educating, informing, motivating and mobilising the masses.
- the media should respond to the desires and needs of their recipients.
- society has the right to use censorship and other legal measures to prevent and punish anti-social publication.

Soviet communist theory

- the media should reflect an objective view of the world and of society in terms of Marxist-Leninist principles, and
- the media should support progressive (communist) movements.

Much has changed since the fall of communism. However, there are still many countries in the former Soviet Bloc, in Africa, Latin America and Asia that are battling to obtain media freedom.

4.1.3.5 The development theory

development theory

Some developing countries advocate the use of the national media to promote government-set national goals and promote particular forms of cultural identity. The most important principle of the *development theory* of the media is the emphasis on economic development. Media liberties should be made subordinate to the achievement of these ideals, in this view. At the same time, common objectives, as stated by government, are given priority over individual freedom (Roelofse 1996:56–58). For example, in South Africa, the media are often blamed by elected politicians, including the current president, for not doing enough to publicise government achievements in housing, telecommunications, education and health. The South African media is accused by government sources of focusing on the negative to the detriment of economic progress. McQuail (1987:119–121) identifies the following basic assumptions of the development theory:

- the media should make a positive contribution to the national development process;
- the state should restrict the media if economic interests and the development needs of the society are at stake;
- the media should give preference to information about national, cultural and language issue;
- the media should also give preference to information about other developing countries that are geographically, culturally and politically akin to one another;
- journalists have both responsibilities and liberties in obtaining and distributing information;
- in the name of protecting development objectives, the state has the right to intervene by restricting and censoring the media. State subsidies and direct control are therefore justifiable.

With regard to the role of the media in development it is important to take note of work of the Media Development and Diversity Agency (MDDA) in South Africa.

The Role and Functions of the Media in Society

 Case Study 4.2: Encouraging Diversity in South African Media

The Media Development and Diversity Agency

The Media Development and Diversity Agency was set up by an Act of Parliament in 2002 to try to enable "historically disadvantaged communities and persons not adequately served by the media" to gain access to the media. Based in Johannesburg and funded by a state body, the Government Communication and Information Service (GCIS) with additional funding from private print and broadcasting bodies, its beneficiaries are meant to be community (not-for-profit) media and small commercial media.

To achieve its objective, the Media Development and Diversity Agency claims on its website that its goals are to:
- encourage ownership and control of media by historically disadvantaged communities, historically diminished indigenous language speakers and cultural groups;
- channel resources to community and small commercial media;
- build capacity in the media industry, especially amongst historically disadvantaged groups;
- encourage research regarding media development and diversity.

Community Radio: The Media Development and Diversity Agency supports community radio stations in the rural areas, for example: Forte Community Radio (based in Bisho, Eastern Cape); Kgalagadi Community Radio (based in the Northern Cape); and seeks funding support for newly licensed community radio services.

Community Print: Amazwi Writers (a writing skills development project based in Hluhluwe in KwaZulu-Natal); Agenda Feminist Media (this Durban-based feminist media project produces a range of media and provides training for women writers across the country).

Community TV: The MDDA has been supporting research into the feasibility of community television stations in places like Soweto in Johannesburg.

Source: www.mdda.org.za

4.1.3.6 The democratic participant theory

This theory is primarily a reaction against commercialisation and monopolies in privately controlled mass media, and against centralisation and bureaucratisation in public broadcasting. The practical realisation of this theory is encountered primarily in developed societies (Roelofse 1996:58–60).

Media Studies: Volume 1

democratic participant theory

The *democratic participant theory* supports and emphasises the importance of the following:
- the multiplicity of media;
- the small-scale use of media; media's local nature;
- de-institutionalising the media;
- the reciprocal role of communicator and recipient;
- horizontal communication;
- interaction and involvement.

McQuail (1987:121–123) summarises the basic principles of the democratic-participant theory as follows:
- individuals and minority groups should be able to enforce their claim to:
  - the right of access to the media;
  - the right to have their needs served by the media.
- the organisation of the media and the content of messages should not be influenced by political or bureaucratic control;
- the existence of the media must be justified in terms of the needs and interests of recipients, and not exclusively in terms of those of the media organisations, professional media workers or advertisers;
- groups, organisations and communities should have their own media;
- small-scale, interactive and participatory forms of media are regarded as more beneficial than large-scale, unidirectional media which are used only by professional media workers;
- in general, social needs are neglected by established media;
- this theory regards communication as too important to be left to professionals.

 Case Study 4.3: Civic journalism

civic journalism

To illustrate the underlying thinking of the democratic participant theory we look at civic journalism. Civic journalism is thought to provide people with the news and information they need to allow them to function as citizens, to make the decisions they are called on to make in a democratic society. Veteran American tv journalist Edward Fouhy (2001) explains the aims of civic journalism:
- It is an effort to reconnect with the real concerns of viewers, listeners and readers, not in a way that panders to them and not primarily as consumers to whom goods and services are sold but as responsible citizens.
- It takes the traditional five w's of journalism – who, what, when, where, why – and adds a sixth w: "why is this story important to me and to the community in which I live?"

The Role and Functions of the Media in Society

- Civic journalists are trying to plug back into their communities, to cross the gap that has opened and widened between the news media and their constituents: the readers, listeners and viewers.
- Plugging into the community is hard. It's much harder journalism than dealing with the same old sources, the experts, the media-savvy advocates of the same old tired points of view, the self-serving talking heads always available for the interview, always ready with conventional wisdom or a cynical one-liner.

Civic journalists broaden their agenda from the usual overwhelming focus on political and governmental news to aggressively ferret out issues of interest to citizens who are not members of the élite: the education of their children, the security of their families and their economic future. That means covering an agenda that is set more by citizens, by the people, and less by those who would manipulate them. That means thinking about the news not only from the standpoint of conventional journalistic practice but taking it a step further and thinking about a subject from the standpoint of the public and public interest.

Source: "Civic Journalism: Rebuilding the foundations of democracy" by Edward M. Fouhy (2001), executive director and founder of the Pew Centre for Civic Journalism, USA Website: www.pewcentre.org

4.1.4 Rethinking normative theory

The above normative theories (or perceptions about the functions) of the press were revised by Finnish researcher Kaarle Nordenstreng with his American colleagues Clifford Christians, Theodore Glasser and Denis McQuail in 1997.

The four researchers argued that theories of the functions and roles of the media fall into two types of theory: those prescribing openly normative tasks for the media in society (such as the theories summarised above) and those describing the real role of the media in society. The latter approaches the issue from the "objective" angle of media sociology, while the former deals with the "subjective" conceptions held by various players (including public opinion leaders, government officials, cabinet ministers, and so on) about the mission of the media. In other words, we should distinguish between ideal theories and real theories, or normative and sociological theories.

> prescriptive and descriptive theory

In the researchers' revision, a nation's media system is not placed in any one category (or theory). Instead, Nordenstreng, Christians, Glasser and McQuail suggest that each national media system and individual medium, even each individual journalist, can combine roles. Instead of formalising specific theories to classify the role of a media system, they argue, we should rather classify the kind of arguments about media roles (functions) within the framework of a specific paradigm.

Nordenstreng, Christians, Glasser and Mcquail distinguish between five such possible paradigms:

five paradigms

- *Liberal-individualist paradigm*: arguments about the role of the media in which the emphasis is on individual liberty as the cornerstone of democracy and on the public's interest. The media's overall role is to contribute to and uphold democracy. Therefore the state should have a minimal role in media affairs.
- *Social responsibility paradigm*: arguments about the role of the media in which the emphasis is on active citizenship instead of abundant information. The media should contribute to the upliftment of society and its citizens.
- *Critical paradigm*: arguments about the role of the media in which the emphasis is on the potential of the media to emancipate the masses. The media should question prevailing and oppressive ideologies.
- *Administrative paradigm*: arguments about the role of the media in which the emphasis is on the objectivity of information and the efficient transmission of reliable information to as many people as possible. The emphasis is on professionalism and technocratic excellence.
- *Cultural negotiation paradigm*: arguments about the role of the media in which the emphasis is on the rights of subcultures with their particular values.

multiple roles

From the perspective of these paradigms Nordenstreng *et al* then argue that the media can play one or more of the following roles:

- *Collaborative*: A role the media plays when a nation state is young and insecure to collaborate towards development ideals, nation building and national interest. This is usually the role governments want the media to play and is the role the current South African government wants the South African media to play.
- *Surveillance*: The media plays an adversarial role, as a watchdog and agenda-setter. The media exposes violations of the moral and social order. The media informs by bringing important issues to the attention of the community. This is usually the role played by the media in established democracies and often the reason for its unpopularity with governments.

The Role and Functions of the Media in Society

- *Facilitative*: The media seeks to create and sustain public debate. This is the essence of the public or civic journalism movement.
- *Critical/dialectical*: Journalists examine in a truly radical way the assumptions and premises of a community. The media's role is to constitute public debate about, not within, the prevailing political order.

It is clear that the emphasis in the press theories is on the role the media can or should play in the dissemination of information and the formation of public opinion. There are no clear answers. From an academic point of view we can only try to group the different arguments in terms of their underlying assumptions and to identify them within the framework of a specific paradigm. If we accept that the media is, can and should be a pillar of democracy, then the only solution to the problem of defining the media's role is to acknowledge the importance of pluralism.

4.1.5 New thinking about normative theory

Normative media theory is in a flux (Brants, Hermes & van Zoonen 1998). It is questioned from mainly two perspectives, namely the postmodern and postcolonial perspectives (see chapter 3 for an introduction to these two perspectives or approaches).

4.1.5.1 The postmodern perspective: new society, new media environment

Amongst postmodern scholars (Ang 1998; Jacka 2003) there is almost general agreement that normative media theory needs to be re-visited against the background of the changed and changing nature of society, the changing nature of the media itself, and what is called the "crisis of democracy".

Postmodern capitalist societies are characterised by a new kind of public, which in turn is characterised by hybridisation, fragmentation and the rise of minorities and minority rights. It is a society in which the traditional clear-cut distinction between public and private is blurred. It is difficult to recognise a coherent population with shared values. A single idealised Habermasian public sphere with a common normative dimension no longer exists, or is difficult to recognise. Several public spheres claim legitimacy in the processes of democratic dialogue and debate.

postmodern society

These characteristics have profound consequences for the way in which communication scholars today have to deal with the concept of "public interest." And this new kind of public has profound consequences for normative theory, which monitor's media accountability in the name of the public (Jacka 2003; Ang 1998, Brants, Hermes & Van Zoonen 1998.)

new media environment

In this new society, new channels of public communication exist, brought about by new technologies, convergence, liberalisation, deregulation, and globalisation. Public communication is now characterised by new distribution platforms, a multi-media approach, interactivity, the blurring of the distinction between public and private (commercial) media, niche markets, diversity, choice and abundance.

In terms of content, a market orientation and commercialisation rules. New genres such as infotainment, talk shows and reality television are being produced, all of them blurring the traditional distinction between information and entertainment. It is argued that in this new media environment, journalism has become market-driven and guided by what is interesting rather than what is important; by an audience orientation rather than an ethical orientation and an institutional logic. The more or less taken-for-granted social responsibility of journalism has been undermined and a pressing question is whether market logic allows for an ethical journalistic practice.

Non-journalistic popular genres have gained importance, constituting the politics of popular culture. Mediated popular culture, ranging from popular novels, films and cartoons to soap operas, pop festivals and sport, have became important if not dominant expressions of social movements. They deeply affect the way people experience their immediate environment, realities and meaning (Jacka 2003; Ang 1998).

In postmodern society, new views are emerging as to who is responsible for social responsibility. It is increasingly argued that social responsibility is no longer the exclusive asset or responsibility of public organisations, such as public broadcasters, alone. In the light of liberalisation, deregulation and self-regulation, social responsibility is shifting from the state and its institutions to social institutions and commercial enterprises (Bardoel & Brants 2003). In the case of public service broadcasting, it is argued that it no longer needs to be restricted to public service institutions alone (Steemers 2003) and that public service broadcasting can take on a diversity of forms at different sites (Jacka 2003).

The Role and Functions of the Media in Society

Most of all, in postmodern society *democracy* itself is believed to be in a crisis. The ideal of republican democracy, be it representative, participatory or communitarian, is questioned. Democracy, it is argued, can no longer be viewed as a fixed ideal type but only as fluid and evolving. The changing nature of citizenship in a pluralised society needs to be acknowledged. The earlier clear distinction (Marshall & Bottomore 1992) between civil (involving rights and freedoms), political (involving representation), social (involving welfare) and cultural citizenship (involving identity politics) is disappearing , all being combined in what Hartley (1999) calls a "do-it-yourself (DIY) citizenship". In this kind of citizenship, arguably characteristic of advanced capitalist societies, identity is based on a choice people can make from available alternatives (choices), patterns and opportunities, rather than an identity based on a social contract between state and subject, heritage, or as prescribed by a given community.

> democracy

A new view of democracy is thus evolving as being pluralised, marked by new kinds of communities of identity, a system in which the traditional public-private divide does not apply, in which there are no universal visions of the "common good" but rather pragmatic and negotiated exchanges about ethical behavior and ethically inspired courses of action (Jacka 2003).

Against the above-sketched environment, the continued value of normative media theory in its present form is questioned. It is argued (Ang 1998 and Jacka 2003) that revisiting normative theory should use the following criticism as points of departure:

> questioning normative theory

- The complexity of normative theory lies in the inherent dichotomy between freedom of expression and measures to control it.
- Finding answers to how the media is supposed to behave in a specific society are rooted in world views, each with their own ideologies and ethics.
- The very concept of quality and performance can and should be problematised; measuring media performance and quality in public communication is a political act of power perpetrated in the name of the the public interest; cultural-pedagogic paternalism should end; there should be a radical break with implicit "hypodermic needle" thinking which legitimised much media regulation and normative theory; modernist thinking about social responsibility and quality has frozen arguments in indisputable and closed discourses by emphasising the dichotomies in regulated versus open markets, cultural versus economic

primacy, people-centeredness versus market-centeredness, quality versus quantity, public versus private, rationality versus subjectivity and emotion; fact versus fiction, seriousness versus pleasure, knowledge versus popular culture, citizens versus consumers.

- Normative research, despite efforts to blur, combine or bridge the gap between positivistic-critical research, is still guided by outmoded models of mass communication based on out-of-date assumptions of limited supply, homogenous content and passive mass audiences. These assumptions are deeply rooted in the social science tradition of communication research for which the linearity of the transmission model has been paradigmatic but are clearly no longer adequate to describe the postmodern media environment.
- In advanced capitalist societies, media production is more often than not a matter of how business driven not by the intention of meaningful communication but by spectacle and display; communication rights should include the right to cultural difference. There is pleasure in popular culture.
- The public is actively information and fun-seeking, and not simply political animals eager to join a discursive exchange in the public sphere.

For the postmodernists, both society and the media have become so complex, diverse and abundant with choices, so overloaded with media genres, outlets, products, meanings and messages, that normative media theory has lost its grip:

> *"The problem has become, first of all, one of scale and complexity; secondly one of assigning relative significance to the multiplicity of media supply. There are too many possible channels and sources to analyse and their relative salience is too variable and hard to assess"* (McQuail 1992:312).

diversity and pluralism

How should we continue to measure media performance? What should the ethical standards be? How should we describe and, if need be, prescribe the role of the media in a society? How should we think about freedom of expression and the existence (or lack) thereof in a society? For the postmodernists, the answer lies in the acknowledgment of diversity, the acceptance of pluralism, heterogeneity, ambivalence, and hybridity. As Liz Jacka (2003:183) puts it:

> *"... if we accept society and democracy as pluralized, as marked by new kinds of communities of identity, as a system in which the*

The Role and Functions of the Media in Society

traditional public-private divide does not apply, and as a system in which there are no universal visions of the 'common good', but, rather, pragmatic and negotiated exchanges about ethical behaviour and ethically inspired courses of action, then we will be able to face a plurality of communication media in which a diverse set of changes continuously occur. We will be open to the notion that ethical discourse can be present in many different kinds of genres of media texts and in many different forms of media organisations; we will no longer privilege 'high modern journalism', but nor will we mindlessly worship populist media; we will have a much more nuanced account of the connection between various forms of citizenship and the media."

This kind of thinking could accommodate different cultures, linguistic groups and media publics. It could provide room for all the media, be it private, public, commercial, community, regional or local media, to accept and play different roles: to act as a watchdog, to comment and to criticise, to inform and to entertain, but at the same time to actively contribute to development, education and nation building, all of which are part of the media's social responsibility.

4.1.5.2 The postcolonial perspective

The need to revise normative media theory is also emphasised in *postcolonial media studies* and from the perspective of *comparative communication theory*.

As part of critical theory, post-colonial studies (Shome & Hegde, 2002: 249–270) seek to situate and understand phenomena within the context of larger (and unequal) geopolitical histories of global and cultural power. Its basic premise is that institutionalised knowledge about issues such as race, class, gender, sexuality and the media are and were subject to forces of colonialism. For example, whereas global theories of the media often emphasise a utopian and liberating effect, post-colonial studies would argue that "behind the veneer of a seamless globe are the realities of deep divisions and inequities of exchange" brought about by slavery and colonialism (Shome & Hegde 2002: 261). What needs to be penetrated is the systemic and continuing structures of colonial power, the normativity of "Westerness" and the contradictions and tensions these structures cause in the realities of the everyday life of non-Westerners. This should be explored not from the perspective of a "colonial gaze" but in terms

> postcolonial theory

of an indigenous epistemology. From the perspective of post-colonial studies, normative media theory can be seen as product of Western epistemology.

comparative theory

It is from such a perspective that authors such as Shelton Gunaratne (2005) criticises Fred Siebert, Theodore Peterson and Wilbur Schramm's (1956) *Four theories of the press* as being western-centric and biased. Gunaratne argues that Siebert, Peterson and Schramm's theories were not conceptualised and thought through against the background of a horizontal integrative macro-history of human philosophies about freedom across space and time, leaving us with normative theory about the media that is not dynamic and universally applicable. These theories limit the scope and history of freedom of expression to the post-Gutenberg print press and imparts a Eurocentric bias. They are anchored on Western philosophical and political theory and therefore trace the authoritarian theory to the thinking of Plato, Niccolò Machiavelli, Thomas Hobbes and Georg Wilhelm Friedrich Hegel; the libertarian theory to the thinking of John Milton, John Locke, Adam Smith, Thomas Paine, Thomas Jefferson and John Stuart Mill; social responsibility to the United States Commission on Freedom of the Press (1947); the Soviet communist theory to Karl Marx and Josef Stalin. The four theories Siebert, Patterson and Schramm developed to categorise the press (media systems) of the world greatly informing and influencing our ways of thinking about freedom of expression lack the input of any non-Western philosophy.

Gunaratne (2002:4) further argues that although Siebert, Peterson and Schramm claimed that their book was about the philosophical and political rationales or theories behind the different kinds of press we have in the world today, their examination of those rationales or theories was vertical and separatist:

> "They drew their concepts only from Western philosophers and theorists, and yet tried to give the impression of universality to the theories they created as evident from their attempt to examine the degrees of press freedom in various non-Western countries" (ibid.).

Gunaratne then proceeds to develop a *humanocentric* theory taking into account Eastern (religious) philosophies such as Buddhism, Hinduism, Confucianism, Daoism and legalism. He sees this theory as an attempt to explore the elements needed to formulate a universally applicable dynamic theory of communication outlets and free expression at the levels of the

The Role and Functions of the Media in Society

world system, the nation state and the individual. He concludes that his *humanocentric* theory, in which cognisance is taken of non-western philosophies, could help us to see broad variations of "middle-path" systems of communication outlets and free expression situated between the extremes of libertarianism and authoritarianism.

Similarly, Winfield, Mizuno and Beaudoin criticise the four theories for looking at the world from a western perspective without examining the historical philosophies of other civilizations and point out that in the Far East the philosophical tenets concerning the group, the hierarchy and truth are indirectly linked with mass media and freedom of expression (2000:329). Also, Braman (2002:401) refers to the four theories as a Cold War-era typology and emphasises the need to:

> "come up with an alternative typology of media systems that is comprehensive and complex enough to be able to cope with the great variety of media systems currently in existence and emerging."

From the above, and in the context of the need for comparative media theory it is clear that the idea of "de-westernising" media theory and especially normative media theory is not new (Krippendorf, 1993; Tehranian, 1991; Dervin, 1991; Braman, 2002; Downing, 1996; Curran and Park, 2000). It emphasises the need to develop comparative theories that consciously avoid ethnocentric bias; to focus on elements that appear to be universal in most societies (Tehranian, 1991:49); to give due consideration to all human histories, experiences, philosophies, cultural traditions and values relevant to theory formulation (Wang & Shen, 2000:29); to show that paradigms are not just harmless models of explanation that guide intellectual work but also expressions of social ideologies and power (Dirlik, 2002:126); and to acknowledge that Eurocentric power and ideology associated with the dominant typologies or paradigms have prevailed over alternative explanations (Gunaratne, 2002:8).

4.1.5.3 Revisiting normative media theory in South Africa

In South Africa, the postmodern argument is eagerly adopted by the market. It provides South African media researchers with theoretical support to advocate pluralism and diversity as a cornerstone of media policy and regulation, and as a safeguard for freedom of expression. Diversity and pluralism may work in advanced capitalist societies with

strong democratic traditions and liberal pluralist arrangements. But arguments in favour of diversity and pluralism seldom consider that these may not necessarily be the *only* answer in South Africa with its diverse cultures and different worldviews interpreting freedom of expression and the media's social responsibility.

Thus post-colonialism and comparative theory, rather than the postmodern argument, provides the foundation for the project of investigating the philosophy of *ubuntu* in South Africa as a framework for the revision of normative theory from an Afro-centric perspective. At this stage, it is difficult to describe the discourse about *ubuntu* as a normative framework for media performance. It remains an emerging comprehensive theory, a device for interpreting and criticising.

The case of ubuntu as a normative media theory

ubuntu

Explaining the essence of *ubuntu* as a unique African moral philosophy is a daunting task. It demands a sound knowledge of the ontology and epistemology of traditional African culture, philosophy and ethics. Without such a knowledge and understanding, any explanation of *ubuntu* runs the risk of being a reduced account of a rich system of values. Authors such as Louw (2004), Blankenberg (1999), Ramose (2002), Shutte (2001), Christians (2004), Hamminga (2005), and Nussbaum (2003) explain it in the following way:

> "Ubuntuism can be understood as a social philosophy, a collective African consciousness, a way of being, a code of ethics and behavior deeply embedded in African culture. It is the capacity in African culture to express compassion, reciprocity, dignity, harmony and humanity in the interest of building and maintaining a community with justice and mutual caring" (See Nussbaum, 2003:1).

The term *ubuntu* appears to be derived from the Zulu maxim *umuntu ngumuntu ngabantu*, meaning "a person is a person through other persons" or "I am because of others". This maxim is also interpreted by different African cultures and in different African countries and languages to mean "a person is defined with reference to the community", "that I am because we are, and since we are, therefore I am", that "it is through others that one attains selfhood" and that "a person is born for the other". In the words of the Sènègalese politician-poet-philosopher, Léopold Senghor, "I feel the other, I dance the other, and therefore I am" (*ibid.*:4).

With regard to the consequences of *ubuntu* for mass communication, an outstanding characteristic is its emphasis on community and collectivity. In ethics and political philosophy the term "community" refers to a form of connectedness among individuals that is qualitatively stronger and deeper than a mere association. For Buchanan (1998) the concept of a community includes at least two elements:
- individuals belonging to a community have ends that are in a robust sense common and which is acknowledged by members of the group as common ends;
- for the individuals involved, their awareness of themselves as belonging to the group is a significant constituent of their identity, their sense of who they are.

Ubuntu moves beyond an emphasis on the individual and individual rights, and places the emphasis on sharing and on individual participation in a collective life. Community is the context in which personhood is defined. It differs from the emphasis on the self in mainstream Eurocentric philosophies. The essence of being is participation with other humans. Whereas Western individualistic democracy insists on freedom of the self from intrusion by others, a person's freedom in *ubuntu* depends for its existence and fulfillment on personal relationships with others. A person is first and foremost a participatory being dependent on others for his/her development. *Ubuntu* therefore places a high premium on negotiation, inclusiveness, transparency and tolerance.

The emphasis on collectivism should however not been seen as a collectivism in the sense of communism or First World socialism in which the individual is only part of the community (Shutte, 2001:8–9). "Community" in *ubuntu* is not opposed to the individual nor does it simply swallow the individual up. Rather, it understands the individual as a *unique centre* of shared life (Blankenberg, 1999:43). Christians (2004:245), in interpreting Louw (2004), formulates it as follows:

> "Since the self cannot be conceived without necessarily conceiving of others, ubuntu adds a universal and compelling voice against the Enlightenment's atomistic individuals who exist prior to and independently of their social order. In the West, where 'individualism often translates into an impetuous competitiveness', the cooperation entailed by ubuntu's 'plurality of personalities' in a 'multiplicity of relationships' is an attractive, though overwhelming concept. The modernist concept of individuality now has to move from solitary to

| collectivism

solidarity, from independence to interdependence, from individuality vis-à-vis community to individuality à la community" (ibid.).

Formulated differently, *ubuntu* acknowledges individuality not in the service of the self, but in the service of others and the community. What are the possible implications of *ubuntu*'s emphasis on collectivism for an African normative media theory?

journalistic values

Authors such as Blankenberg (1999), Christians (2004), Okigbo (1996), Shutte (2001), and Wasserman and de Beer (2004) show how an *ubuntu*-based normative framework would require a media and journalism whose primary role would be to provide a space for the concerns, ideas and opinions of the community. The overall purpose of the media would be to play a developmental role in the sense of stimulating citizen participation, community participation and consensus based on widespread consultation with the community. In the context of the needs of developing countries, it would encourage action towards civic transformation and community renewal. In this process the media would need to ensure the well-being of the collective, rather than the protection of individual rights. The media would be seen as a catalyst for moral agency and as such contribute to moral literacy.

Freedom of expression would be interpreted firstly in terms of the *freedom of the community* to articulate its opinions, questions, concerns and needs. Only thereafter will it be interpreted to mean the *freedom of the individual* to express the concerns, opinions, questions and needs as reached through consensus by the community. Freedom of expression is thus measured and valued in terms of its relevancy to the well-being of the community. Put differently, media freedom is a positive freedom that should contribute to the well-being of the community and not only to the largest number of individuals (Wasserman & de Beer, 2004).

As far as the question of "public interest" is concerned, the same emphasis would be placed on the community. The public's right to know would be assessed in terms of the potential harm the information could do to a particular community. How the media should fulfill this role is not based on a prescribed set of professional codes but rather on a deep-seated general morality that requires the journalist to act in harmony with the morality of the community. As Christians (2004:250–251) sees it: *ubuntu* morality does not construct an apparatus of professional ethics. Rather, it works and provides an ethic of general morality. It does not develop

The Role and Functions of the Media in Society

rules for professionals but urges a sensitivity and preoccupation with the moral dimensions of everyday life. The moral domain is understood to be intrinsic to human beings, not as a system of rules, norms and ideals external to society and culture. Professionals occupy the same social and moral space as the citizens they report on. How the moral order works itself out in community formation is the issue, not primarily what media practitioners by their own standards consider virtuous. The ultimate standard for media professionals is not role-specific ethical principles, but a general morality. This presupposes media workers' knowledge and sharing of the community's general morality.

From this follows a kind of journalism that does not place a high value on objectivity, neutrality, and detachment. In *ubuntu journalism* objectivity is neither necessary nor desirable (Okigbo, 1996). The journalist is seen to be an involved member of the community and cannot remain a spectator. Through the journalist's work, a voice must be given to the community. Active involvement and dialogue with the community rather than detachment in the name of objectivity and neutrality is required (Blankenberg, 1999).

As far as the requirement of factuality is concerned, it is argued that the Western conception of truth hinges completely on facts and does little to embed these facts in a network of cultural and social meanings generated within the community itself (Wasserman & de Beer, 2004:92). In *ubuntu*, it is believed that values such as truth, freedom and justice are to be constructed interdependently by and within the community. In practice, Blankenberg (1999) says, this requires reporting that:
- stimulates interaction among citizens, between citizens and reporters, and between citizens and politicians;
- enables people to come to terms with their everyday experiences;
- acknowledges the complexity of a matter or an issue;
- is not the hurried conclusion of an observer;
- penetrates the moral dynamics underlying the issue;
- is interpreted against the background of the community's contexts, beliefs, values and needs.

Most of all, whatever goes into print should be assessed in terms of the potential impact of a story on the community. Therefore, subjects or the community of a story should have the last say on the media product before it is offered for mass reception (Blankenberg, 1999). The public interest of the media is thus primarily defined in terms of the value of information and knowledge for the/a community, rather than in terms of the need to be informed about a topic in order to be able to make responsible political, social and/or individual choices and decisions.

The question arises if and how *ubuntu* differs from the functions and social responsibility of the media in western normative theory? Western epistemological thought about the media proceeds from a focus on the media primarily in terms of:
- information, surveillance, entertainment and educational roles;
- the media freedom and right to protection in order to be able to fulfill its social responsibility;
- the individual right to information, surveillance, entertainment and education.

The emphasis in *ubuntu* would first and foremost be on the media's role in:
- bonding a community;
- dialogue towards reaching consensus based on the social values and morals in and of a community.

The emphasis thus moves from the media as informant, gatekeeper, entertainer and educator to the media as mediator; from the media as observer, to the media as participant and negotiator.

moral philosophy questioned

Although the above may sound ideal, Fourie (2007) cautions that in practice a moral philosophy such as *ubuntu* as a normative framework for media practice, performance and regulation may have vast negative consequences for freedom of expression, Consider:
- the history of apartheid, in which the government employed a moral philosophy such as Christian nationalism to mobilise a patriotic media in the service of volk (a specific sub-section of citizens) and vaderland (a concept of country which excluded the majority from rights), with severe media restrictions as a consequence;
- the distinctiveness of *ubuntu* as an African moral philosophy compared to Western communitarianism and its associated civic journalism;
- the changed nature of contemporary African culture and cultural values often far removed from traditional African culture and values;
- the political misuse of moral philosophy, leading to intolerance of any oppositional opinions or deeds, including an intolerance of media criticism and exposure; the danger of indigenising theory: Nain's (2000)

The Role and Functions of the Media in Society

description of how efforts to develop Asian theories of communication and the media have ended up "legitimizing repressive regimes, undemocratic practices and tightly controlled media systems whose raison d'être were to uphold and help perpetuate these authoritarian regimes" (*op. cit.* 149);
- the need to take cognisance of the nature of the media in a globalised world and the changed nature of the media landscape.

Therefore *ubuntu* as a framework may have vast consequences for:
- defining news and universal news values such as frequency, threshold, unambiguity, consonance, unexpectedness, continuity;
- censorship;
- freedom of reception;
- freedom to obtain information;
- the independence of the media;
- the freedom to formulate editorial policies;
- diversity in terms of content, choice, access;
- the media as a forum for different interests and point of views;
- defining objectivity, accuracy, honesty, reliability, and fairness;
- addressing matters related to inequity, minority groups, law and order, national security, racism, sex and violence.

Fourie (2007) argued that instead of contemplating a moral philosophy as a normative framework, South Africa should adopt the postmodern acknowledgement of *difference* and *diversity*. By accepting difference (different publics, different public spheres, different audiences, different media) discussion about the South African media would be on par with the realities of the South African society and its media. The challenge would be to search for those common human values that bind all human beings on the basis of which a normative media theory and ethics could begin to be developed in a non-prescriptive and non-pedantic way. Such an approach need not hinder the South African media in fulfilling its social responsibilities related to the development and nation building needs of the country and its people, nor to interpret South African realities against the background of a sound understanding of Africa and thus from an African perspective. Neither would it prohibit the media and South Africans from honouring *ubuntu*'s values of humanity, the public good, dialogue and consensus.

SECTION 2: ENTERTAINMENT

4.2 THE ENTERTAINMENT FUNCTION

Entertainment has become a major if not a dominant function and activity of the mass media. On a daily basis we are confronted with numerous entertainment genres such as popular and serious dramas of different kinds, sports, game shows, quiz programmes, stories about celebrities, programmes and articles about people and their hobbies, their animals, their lives, their products, advertisements (which usually seek to amuse us), etc. Although this kind of media content has the purpose of entertaining us, they also inform and educate us, on a manifest or latent level about life and our societies.

What is entertainment? We provide a preliminary answer from three perspectives: rhetorical, behavioural and sociological. We specifically look at the phenomenological nature of film and television entertainment and focus more specifically on the fictional content of feature film and television such as soap operas and comedies (*Generations, Muvhango, Egoli, 7de Laan, Isidingo, Backstage, Going Up* and so on). However, keep in mind that news (information), documentaries, sport, content of a more serious kind such as in-depth articles in newspapers and magazines on various topics may also entertain us.

4.2.1 A rhetorical perspective

The rhetorical perspective argues that entertainment content has certain intrinsic *rhetorical motifs* that lead the media user to decide whether he/she is experiencing something as entertainment.

Rhetorical motifs

Rosenfield and Mader (1984:475–544) identify five rhetorical motifs as prerequisites for pleasurable or gratifying experience:

> rhetorical motifs

Communication pleases when it provides knowledge about *identity*: media content entertains when it offers the user latent or overt answers to the question: who am I? Rhetorically, this question is only answerable in terms of an analysis of the individual's relation with and to others, including his/her role, place and function in society, in a group, in a relationship. Entertainment content thus usually focuses on human relations. Communication pleases when it provides knowledge about:

The Role and Functions of the Media in Society

- *ability*: demonstrating possibilities to the user (how to solve a problem) and showing that he/she, or others, have the ability to achieve something;
- *survival*: making the viewer/listener/reader aware of eternal values (love, friendship, generosity and fellowship) and freeing the media user from anxiety about destruction and ultimately, death;
- *reality*: shedding new light on reality or an aspect thereof, leading the media user to a new understanding of his/her own realities;
- *knowledge*: the knowledge gleaned from the responses to questions about identity, ability, survival and reality is in itself liberating and is therefore experienced as pleasurable and gratifying.

Content analyses indicate that these motifs keep recurring in entertainment. Entertainment invariably contains some sort of information about values, attitudes, ideas, customs and behaviour towards which media users have to orient themselves in their daily lives. Entertainment content directly and indirectly conveys knowledge and understanding about identity, ability, survival and reality. Awareness of all these (albeit at a latent experiential level) affords the media user knowledge of him/herself as a person in relation with others and to society. Such knowledge is reassuring, at any rate to most viewers, and they therefore can experience these works as pleasurable and thus as entertainment.

 Case study 4.4: Rhetorical motifs in popular television genres

Soap operas, situation comedies, family series, hospital and police dramas, are sufficiently intimate to portray dramatic interaction yet generalised enough to reflect personal and social norms and values. Notwithstanding the portrayal of violence and themes of decadence and even amorality – usually on the part of the antagonists, particularly in police and action dramas – content analyses indicate that socially accepted norms, values and behaviour invariably triumph at the end of a programme and/or series.

Family series: In the numerous family series on television the family circle offers the communicator a symbolic background which can be constructed in any way he/she chooses in order to portray all sorts of characters and their moral values. To most viewers the family is one of the most familiar and readily comprehensible of worlds, thus permitting ready identification. These series present, in a very direct way, a number of ideals and (to viewers) desirable attitudes towards virtually every aspect of interpersonal behaviour and social responsibility. The stories and themes of family series usually present a diversity of problems, particularly the interpersonal kind that confronts every

one of us at one time or another, together with commendable and socially acceptable solutions to these.

Police and action dramas: Police and action dramas also portray ideal behavioural models. These programmes are usually explicitly concerned with the maintenance of law. Violent portrayals are in fact intended to dramatically emphasise the contrast between socially acceptable and socially unacceptable behaviour, favouring the former. Although these dramas are undeniably violent, one need merely call to mind written press reports of crimes to realise that they are not particularly unrealistic. In fact, crime reporting in the daily press presents far more violence than does television, which moreover offers it in fictional story form, and more acceptably in that justice always prevails.

Situation comedies: Situation comedies may be described as a form of institutionalised humour. When such comedies poke fun at individuals, groups and organisations, they do so in order to indicate what constitutes proper, acceptable behaviour. The power of comedy as a social corrector, with laughter as its main weapon, has been known since ancient times. As long ago as the fourth century it was known and accepted that comedy is a fable that teaches people how to behave. Comedy (and humour) is a socially sanctioned instrument to ridicule the sacred cows of society. It is used as a weapon against authority and serves as an outlet for frustration with authority. Grote (1983:31) puts it thus:

> *"There is no doubt that over the centuries, comedy and humour have been used as the bludgeon with which to assault the rigid, authoritarian and hypocritical aspects of society. Plautus attacked the core of all Roman society. The Commedia dell' arte took on all fathers, intellectuals, old men, soldiers and judges. Shakespeare ridiculed the money-mad Jew. Molière personified greed, religious hypocrisy, social and intellectual pretensions and doctors' ignorance and pomposities. The Restoration took on the social foibles and pretensions of the day. Shaw, of course, took on everything and everyone. And the most persistent method was exposure, peeling away the public face and holding up to public laughter the reality behind."*

(For a more in depth discussion of the rhetorical nature of entertainment, see Fourie's (1983) inaugural lecture *Van Jerusalem na Hollywood: parallelle tussen godsdiens en massavermaak (From Jerusalem to Hollywood: similarities between religion and mass entertainment)*.

It can be argued that media content, especially fictional film and television, may entertain us if it contains one or more of the rhetorical motifs referred to above. It provides us with answers to our own situations, problems and relationships. Through the characters of a soap opera we may see (and learn) how other people deal with certain situations and relationships. It can thus be argued that entertainment provides us with knowledge and educates us in certain ways.

The Role and Functions of the Media in Society

4.2.2 A behavioural perspective

Identification: projection and introjection

From a behavioural perspective an answer to the question "what is entertainment?" is associated with the human ability to identify with others, to project and introject feelings, but also to distance oneself from others. We are entertained when media content allow us to

- identify with something or someone;
- project our own feelings, values and views in the content or see it reflected in the content.

_{identification}

Identification and *projection* are two essential features of the social and emotional life of human beings. In order to stimulate such identification and projection, and to fascinate the media user, entertainment content must satisfy three requirements:

First, the *nature of the theme, content and action* should be of a kind that makes viewer identification easy and pleasurable. To this end, feature films follow a recipe which Lindgren (1963:47) summarised as:

> *"The function of fiction in general then and of the fiction film in particular, is to present an imaginary story of the thoughts and actions of individual human beings. We must, therefore, expect to find the unity of a work of fiction deriving, not from a subject or an idea or argument, but from the human activities which are its characteristic material; one should be able to summarise the essence of a work of fiction, in other words, in some statement about its action."*

The primary business of entertainment content, then, is to show events in a course of *action*.

The second requirement concerns the *identifiability* of *characters (cast/stars)*. They must be such that people can identify with them and with what they do. This applies especially to the character of the protagonist(s). Viewers must be able to identify with the character of British secret service agent James Bond and the actor who portrays James Bond, as well as with what James Bond stands (and fights) for.

Thirdly, entertainment content, with specific reference to the visual media, must make a *visual impact* on the viewer. Whereas all of the above concerns content (the story, topic and subject), the visual

impact concerns the form, style or way in which something is visually presented. To do so, entertainment content has to synthesise various communication sign systems, such as language (dialogue/text), acting, costuming, composition, music, camera and editing techniques, lighting and colour, and in the case of print, photography and layout. Failure at any one of these operative communication levels may mean failure as a whole. In effect it implies that without a good script, good photography, good cinematography, perceptive editing, good acting, imaginative lighting, mood-creating special effects and music, a film, game show, a sport broadcast, a soap opera, etc. may fail to have the desired emotional impact on viewers. Without imaginative layout and visual illustration an article in print may fail to grab and keep our attention.

In simplistic terms, identification is the human ability to empathise with others. Such feeling is based on shared values, a common background, education, culture and the like; in fact, everything that makes fellowship possible. Identification proceeds in two ways: *introjection* and *projection*.

Introjection means that the viewer assumes or adopts the feelings of the other party (such as fictional characters); projection means that the viewer projects his or her own feelings onto the other party (the characters). Research indicates that viewers usually also have some emotional predisposition towards a work which in itself may give rise to identification. This predisposition is referred to as *couche constituante* (French for constituent layer): the phenomenon of pre-existing emotions stimulating people's imaginations. It is reflected in the phenomenon of the viewer who watches a particular film or television programme with certain expectations. People expect to laugh when they watch a comedy. These expectations are raised partly by external factors such as the publicity preceding the film or programme or the actors (already known to viewers) appearing in it, and partly by personal taste which in turn depends on the viewer's cultural, educational, intellectual and social background. In other words, if publicity tells us that a specific actor, whom we like, plays the lead in a film, one is already inclined to identify with the film or television programme. If you know the work of a specific film director (such as American comedy director Woody Allen) and you like that person's earlier work, then you may already be inclined to identify with the film. Or if you know and like a specific genre, such as science fiction, then you may already want to see a new science fiction film, despite who the actors are or what the story is about.

The Role and Functions of the Media in Society

Distance and play

Although viewers may experience entertainment content as a pleasurable catharsis, and despite the fact that they identify with the characters and their imaginary world, they always maintain a personal *distance*. This is probably the real reason why they experience entertainment content as gratifying or entertaining. In the back of your mind you always know it is not the truth and although it may excite you, it can not harm you personally.

| play

It should be borne in mind that the emotions experienced by viewers are directed to a fictional object and can therefore not be regarded as genuine emotion. Even though viewers become emotionally involved, they realise that it is an ephemeral experience from which they could dissociate themselves if they so wished. They know that the experience of these emotions cannot do them permanent harm (like lasting sorrow) or afford abiding pleasure or joy. The crux of the experience is the distance that the viewer maintains despite possible emotional involvement with the events on screen. The viewer never becomes wholly part of them but preserves a safe distance, so to speak. This enables the viewer to experience even tragedy, violence and horror as entertaining. Entertainment content affords viewers the opportunity to see, experience and identify with themselves and other people. In this process, however, viewers are always outsiders rather than participants. We, the viewers, are actually "peeping toms" or "quasi voyeurs". To the voyeur, peeping is a pleasurable experience leading to gratification and sublimation.

The preservation of distance applies not only to the viewer but also to the producer, the director, and the actors. The same applies to all forms of photographic communication, be it documentary, film or fiction. In the case of news the editor, journalists, announcer/ television newsreader, the interposing of a camera between the communicator and reality (in the case of news) or an imaginary reality (in fictional film and television) at once creates a distance between the communicator and that (imaginary) reality. The result is a type of *uninvolved involvement*: reality is viewed from the security afforded by the camera lens. In the case of an imaginary reality (fiction), it is actually created by the camera (and other visual and sound codes). The end result is therefore a manipulated reality. In the case of entertainment content, the scriptwriter, the director, actors and other members of the production team have to step outside reality in order to create an imaginary world.

In view of all this, entertainment content and the experience of it as entertainment can be described as a *game* (Huizenga 1950). The characteristics of any game are that it always:
- is voluntary;
- is imaginary (not reality itself but a step-out-of-reality);
- has rules and one must understand the rules;
- has a specific duration and ends within a given length of time;
- has a social nature.

One can also argue that the act of viewing entertainment content, like any form of play, is always voluntary. The viewer knows that what he/she is watching is not reality but an imaginary world; the viewer understands the dramatic structure of the programme and the use of certain codes, together with their meanings (such as flashbacks). In other words, the viewer is familiar with the rules of film or a specific genre; indeed, the viewer is usually aware of the stereotyped structure of a comedy, a thriller, a drama, soap operas, family series, situation comedies and the like. In addition, the viewer knows that a film or programme will end within a given length of time. Watching a film or a soap opera constitutes a spatio-temporal interruption of the viewer's daily routine and the performance of his/her daily work, and is usually a social occasion.

Entertainment content professes, like play or a game, to be reality. It is, like play or a game, manufactured according to institutional rules and conventions, which often dictate the content and form as well. Consider in this regard the stereotyped content and production patterns and the fact that entertainment content has a certain length and that the content is enacted within specific spatio-temporal confines. True to the social nature of games and the fact that they are social occasions, entertainment content usually in some way reflects prevailing social values, norms and behaviour.

4.2.3 A sociological perspective

Being concerned with social cohesion, a sociological answer to the question "what is entertainment?" emphasises the media's ability to *orientate* and *integrate* people in their societies and to *educate* them. The media's ability to educate us and even to convince and persuade us to adopt a certain attitude is seen as an intrinsic quality in entertainment. The fact that it is usually presented in a non-pedantic and descriptive way makes it powerful.

The Role and Functions of the Media in Society

Orientation and integration functions

A fictional film may visualise the behavioural models of the society to which viewers have to conform. It provides information on social value systems and holds up ideals with which the viewer can identify. In an entertaining way, films (and other entertainment content) enable people to orient themselves towards prevailing behavioural models, norms and value systems. With this as underlying assumption, the following is argued:

- Media entertainment provides a frame of reference, enabling media users to understand other people and lifestyles within their own society and across societies and cultures.
- Media entertainment instils a certain degree of status aspiration. Sometimes media users may want to be like a character with whom they identify in a film, in a programme or in a magazine article. They want to have the same lifestyle, attitudes and behaviour. Put another way, media entertainment can promote anticipatory socialisation by putting lower socio-economic and educational groups in touch with other lifestyles. These people may then attempt to adopt the value systems and status symbols of a higher educational, economic and social class.
- The characters, stars and celebrities of media entertainment are often experienced by media users as personal friends and even as family. Media users may enter into so-called para-psychological and para-sociological relationships with them (see the chapter on reception theory in volume 3). Audiences learn from the characters, they want to be like the actors, they idealise the celebrities. Media entertainment therefore often serves the purpose of alleviating loneliness.
- Media entertainment can also contribute to the erosion and adoption of new moral and social values. This is one of the reasons for censorship. As far as the erosion of moral and social values is concerned, it is often argued that media entertainment has contributed to the adoption of new morals related to sex, violence, prostitution, matrimony, divorce and same-sex-relations. Arguments for censorship are usually based on these assumptions.
- Media entertainment may also contribute to the adoption of better lifestyles, new technologies, new fashions, new social values such as respect for other cultures, languages, multiracialism and so on. Socialisation is an ongoing process through which the individual learns how to interact with others. In this respect the media entertainment

orientation

Media Studies: Volume 1

may help a society to run smoothly by adding substantially to the things which people hold in common. Socialisation, on a large scale, helps people in a variety of different societies and cultures to know and understand each other better.

(See chapter 5 on the effects of the media for a further discussion of these possible effects of the media.)

4.2.4 Entertainment as a value judgement

We have only referred to a few of the possible perspectives on the topic of media entertainment. In the end it should be remembered that entertainment is a *subjective value-judgement* attached to media content by a media user. Each and every recipient may experience the same content in different ways. The media user decides for him/herself, independently of the communicator's intention. Attaching the value of "entertainment" to media depends on personal knowledge, education, culture, expectations, experience and taste. For this reason it is possible for different people to experience different things as entertainment, thus making it possible to experience news, sport, educational programmes, commentary, even tragedy as entertainment. Because entertainment is a *value* rather than an intrinsic quality, it is indefinable as a phenomenon or even as a specific genre. Yet the media has become a master in detecting the entertainment heartbeat of the public at a given time and how to capitalise on that.

4.3 SUMMARY AND CONCLUSION

We started this chapter by saying that we all have experienced how the media is often blamed for almost everything that can go wrong. This is because people subscribe certain ideal roles to the media. In this chapter we introduced you to some of the more formal and academic arguments about the role and functions of the media in society. They range from providing information to entertainment. We looked at the so-called normative theories of the press, followed by an overview of some of the arguments and theories related to the need for a revision of normative media theory, including post-modern, postcolonial and Afrocentric arguments. We concluded this part of the chapter with an analysis of the African moral philosophy of *ubuntu*. We completed the chapter with some observations about the nature of the media's function to entertain and specifically looked at film and television entertainment. What is

The Role and Functions of the Media in Society

entertainment? We argued that this question can be answered from a number of perspectives, but that in the end entertainment will always be a value judgement.

Questions concerning the roles and functions of the media will always be debatable, because they relate to people's expectations. As long as the media stand in the midst of democracy and the struggle for democracy this will remain the case.

LEARNING ACTIVITIES

- Write a one-page essay in which you define functionalism with reference to its limitations.
- Apply McQuail's typology of media functions to one South African mass communication medium: press, television or radio. Provide clear examples of the information, correlation, continuity, entertainment and mobilisation functions of the medium.
- Write a two-page essay in which you argue the state of pluralism in the South African media. Give examples to motivate your answer, such as the number of radio and television stations and the type and languages of radio programming available.
- Compare the basic assumptions of the six press theories. Explain on the basis of this comparison the present role of a specific South African medium. Is the medium functional in terms of South Africa's development and nation-building needs?
- Write down your own views about the role (functions) of the media in society. Thereafter, "classify" your view in terms of one or more of the paradigms identified by Nordenstreng *et al.*
- Interview five people about how film or television entertains them. How do they define entertainment? What entertains them? Why are they entertained by what they say entertains them? Why and how do they identify with programme content? What are their main leisure activities and how does film or television fit into their leisure programmes?
- Analyse an episode of a television situation comedy in terms of the presence or absence of rhetorical motifs in it.

FURTHER READING

Baran, S.J. & Davis, D.K. 2003. *Mass communication theory. Foundations, ferment, and future*. 3rd edition. London: Thomson/Wadsworth.

Branston, G. & Stafford, R. 1996. *The media student's book*. London: Routledge.

Brants, K., Hermes, J. & van Zoonen, L. (eds). 1998. *The media in question. Popular cultures and public interests*. London: Sage.

Burton, G. 2005. *Media and society. Critical perspectives*. Berkshire, UK.: Open University.

Croteau, D. & Hoynes, W. 2003. *Media society. Industries, images, and audiences*. 3rd edition. Thousand Oaks: Pine Forge Press.

Curran, J. and Park, M-J. 2000. *De-Westernizing Media-Studies*. London: Routledge.

Grossberg, L., Wartella, E. & Whitney, D. 1998. *Media making. Mass media in a popular culture*. London: Sage.

Huizenga, J. 1950. *Homo ludens: a study of the play element in culture*. London: Temple Smith.

McQuail, D. 1992. *Media performance: mass communication and the public interest*. London: Sage.

McQuail, D. 2005. *McQuail's mass communication theory*. 5th edition. London: Sage.

Mills, J.S. 1964. *On liberty*. Harmondsworth: Penguin.

Potter, W. 1998. *Media literacy*. London: Sage.

Thompson, J.B. 1995. The media and modernity. A social theory of the media. Cambridge: Polity.

Important websites

Independent Communication Association of South Africa (ICASA) http://www.icasa.org.za
Freedom of Expression Institute (FXI) http://www.fxi.org.za
Media Institute of Southern Africa (MISA) http://www.misa.org
South African National Editor's Forum (SANEF) http://www.sanef.org.za
UNESCO http://www.unesco.org/webworld
Global Campaign for Free Expression http://www.article19.org

chapter five

The Effects of Mass Communication

Pieter J. Fourie

LEARNING OUTCOMES

At the end of this unit you should be able to:
- differentiate between different kinds of media effects;
- describe different short-term and long-term effect theories;
- test the assumptions underlying effect theories against the background of your own experiences with media messages;
- consider criticism against media effect theory and research;
- understand and describe the working of stereotypes.

THIS CHAPTER

EFFECT STUDIES SEEK to discover, describe and explain the media's specific effects on our behaviour and thinking in a scientific way. It thus makes use of specific, mainly quantitative, research techniques such as quantitative content analysis, survey research (questionnaires) and experimental research. Effects studies are thus usually about the impact of pornography, violence and/or crime portrayed in and by the media on people's behaviour, the effects of political reporting and campaigns in and by the media on voting behaviour and outcomes, the effects of the media on consumer behaviour and so on. Compared to this, critical research, as far as effects are concerned, is more concerned with the power of the media on a macro level. That is, the power of the media to influence, sustain and change society and its citizens' ways of thinking through socialisation and by means of ideological manipulation.

Typologies of different kinds of affects are followed by an overview of short-term and long-term effect theories. Under short-term effects we take a brief look at the hypodermic needle, two-step-flow and uses and gratifications theories. Under long-term theories we briefly introduce accumulation, diffusion of innovation, modelling, social expectation, stereotyping, agenda-setting, framing and the spiral-of-silence theories. Given the prevalence of stereotyping, this topic is dealt with in more depth in a separate section. The chapter ends with a brief note about the complexity of effect research.

5.1 INTRODUCTION

When we consider how the media affects people's behaviour and thinking, immediate examples that spring to mind are the occasional public outcry about the possible effect of a violent film or television programme on children's behaviour, the effect of the media's portrayal of sex on people's and society's morals, or the effect of the media's portrayal of acts of terrorism on instigating further acts of terrorism. In South Africa we are also concerned about the media's contribution to racism through the use of racial stereotypes, the role of crime reporting in giving criminals new ideas, and whether AIDS reporting affects the spread of the disease.

Each and every one of us is affected on a daily basis by some media content. For example, we get information about the weather, what's on in the theatre and what's happening in sport. We are informed about the latest international and national political developments, the economy, and we are made aware of disasters all over the world. But we also listen to music, watch soap operas and dramas, go to the movies, and through

The Effects of Mass Communication

advertisements, learn about the latest products on the market. Surely, all this must have some kind of influence on our thinking and behaviour.

Potter (1998:259–260) compares the media with the weather. Although we may not be directly influenced by it or even aware of it, it is always there. Like the weather, the media is pervasive. Like the weather, the influence of the media is difficult to predict because many complex variables play a role. However, there is also a big difference between the weather and the media. In the case of the weather we can immediately recognise its influence. We may feel hot or cold, dry or wet, and we can see the devastation of a storm or a heat wave. Media effects are difficult to recognise. For many years, researchers, making use of various techniques, have investigated media effects. The results are still not clear-cut. At the most we can categorise different kinds of possible effects and postulate that after exposure to media content over a long period of time, the media may have certain cognitive effects on our thinking.

The purpose of this chapter is to create an awareness of the different kinds of possible media effects. As present and future communication researchers and media workers, a knowledge of past and continued effect research is strategic, scientific and ethically important.

Strategic importance: even although we cannot predict the effect of media content with precision, a knowledge that some kinds of message, structured in specific ways, may have a specific kind of response under certain circumstances, is strategically important in political, social awareness, marketing and advertising campaigns.

Scientific importance: the quest for knowledge about a pervasive phenomenon such as the media makes knowledge and continued research about media effects scientifically important. It can contribute to the increased beneficial use of the media for the improvement of people's circumstances and society in general.

Ethical importance: finally, it is an ethical responsibility of present and future communication workers to know about the possible consequences of their work on the lives of people and society.

5.2 CATEGORISING MEDIA EFFECTS

Grossberg, Wartella and Whitney (1998:278–284) suggest that we distinguish between the following different kinds of media effects:

Behavioural effects

Cognitive effects: media messages or a single message (story/article/programme) can affect our knowledge and thinking about something, for example, our thinking about racism.

Affective effects: media messages or a single message can affect our feelings about something, for example our feelings about child abuse, terrorism, violence. Conative effects: media messages or a single message can affect our behaviour towards something or someone, for example, it can contribute to political rising against a government, an organisation, a group and/or a specific person.

Manifest and latent effects: media effects can be overt or implicit. We may be aware that media messages have caused us to think or act in a certain way. Or we may not be aware that we have implicitly been influenced by media messages.

Intended and unintended effects: effects may be intended by the media or unintended. In other words, it may have been planned by the media to achieve a specific effect, or not. For example an HIV/AIDS awareness campaign in the media may be intended to warn people against the disease and to stop its spreading through unsafe sex. It may also have unintended effects in the sense that it may teach certain people how to spread the disease.

Time-scale effects: effects may occur on different time scales. Short-term message exposure: exposure to a single message. For example, exposure to a single television programme can have an effect on a person while the programme lasts or while a person reads a story in a newspaper. After that, the person forgets about it. For example, a person can be affected emotionally while watching a movie or reading an article. A media user may even decide to take a certain action based on what he/she is seeing in a movie or reading in an article, but in reality never takes an action. While reading an article on slimming or physical fitness, we may take the "serious" decision to go on a diet and/or to start exercising. However, shortly after reading the article or watching a programme we may completely forget about it.

Intermediate message exposure: exposure to a series of related messages such as a product campaign, a social awareness campaign, and so on, can influence our thinking about a matter and our behaviour. For example, after exposure to a number of articles and radio and television

The Effects of Mass Communication

programmes about the dangers of smoking, we are fully aware of the dangers of smoking or the risks of obesity and not exercising. Although media messages over a period of time may have changed our thinking about these matters we may nevertheless continue smoking, overeating, and not exercising.

Long-term media message exposure: Many cumulative exposures to related messages over time (media violence, pornography) or positive topics such as an awareness of environmental issues, can contribute to our response. Exposure over a long period of time to anti-smoking campaigns might eventually contribute to our decision to quit the habit.

McQuail (2000:424) suggests we distinguish between the following main kinds of media-induced effects:

- intended change;
- unintended change;
- minor change facilitated change (intended or not);
- reinforcing what already exists (no change);
- the media can prevent change.

McQuail's distinction

These changes may occur at the level of the individual, society, institution or culture. They can be located on two dimensions: time, namely short-term and long-term, and intentionality: planned effects and unplanned effects.

Planned and planned effects

Propaganda: a strategically planned and on-going campaign to influence peoples' minds by focusing on the negative aspects of an opponent (person, group, institution, topic); making use of various techniques including the withholding of positive or objective information.

planned effects

Media campaigns: an advertising campaign to promote a specific product or to inform people about AIDS; campaigns in the media on literacy and educational development; the distribution of knowledge by the media about a topic which many people initially knew little about such as global warming and its devastating effects should nothing or too little be done about it.

These effects can either be over a short or a long term.

Unplanned effects include the media's contribution to:
- cultural change;
- socialisation;

unplanned effects

231

- reality defining (the media's interpretations of the realities with which we are confronted daily and how we should understand them);
- institutional change;
- collective reaction;
- media violence (if a film or television programme causes violent behaviour in an individual or amongst a group).

These effects can also be over a long or short term.

5.3 AN OVERVIEW OF EFFECT THEORIES

The emphasis in this overview is on the historical development of effect research, primarily based on de Fleur & Dennis' (1994:533–606) comprehensive discussion of effect theories.

5.3.1 Short-term theories

There is almost general agreement that the media may have a direct effect on most people's behaviour only under extreme circumstances. Such circumstances may include war, when disaster of any kind strikes and social upheaval. Or in the case of media content such as advertisements which are intentionally designed to have a specific kind of effect, to get us to the closest shop to buy a specific product. These kind of effects are usually short-term effects. Under short-term effects we can list the following theories:

- the hypodermic needle theory, also referred to as the magic bullet theory;
- the two-step-flow theory, also referred to as the mediating factors theory;
- the uses and gratifications theory.

The hypodermic needle theory

hypodermic needle theory

In the 1930s and 1940s it was generally accepted that the media had a strong effect on the behaviour, thinking and attitudes of media users. Isolated research during this period (mainly on radio) largely supported this hypothesis. This research is today known as the hypodermic needle theory.

The theory equates the media with an intravenous injection: certain values, ideas and attitudes are *injected* into the individual media user, resulting in particular behaviour. The recipient is seen as a passive and helpless victim of media impact.

The Effects of Mass Communication

Among the best-known studies supporting the hypodermic needle theory is that of psychologist Hadley Cantril (1940) on the 1938 CBS (American radio station) radio broadcast of British author H.G. Wells's novel *The War of the Worlds*. The producer and actor Orson Welles' intention with this radio play about the invasion of planet Earth by warriors from Mars was to entertain. Listeners who tuned in and did not recognise it as a play panicked. The unintended effect of the broadcast was, as reported the following day in newspapers, that a tidal wave of panic and terror swept the USA.

Cantril's study underscored the power of radio to cause panic and incite individuals to instantaneous action. However, it is today accepted that research results that support the strong-effect hypothesis should be interpreted against the background of their time of origin: before, during and shortly after World War II. This was a period when people were often exclusively reliant on radio for information, when there were few rival media compared to today's media landscape, characterised by a diversity of media and mass communication outlets, and when the media (specifically radio) enjoyed remarkable credibility. It was a period when social scientists were critically scrutinising existing social structures and voicing grave concern about the influence of modernisation, technology and urbanisation on the intellectual and cultural development of human beings.

Strictly speaking the hypodermic needle theory is not applicable to television, the press, and film. Nevertheless, the sudden uprise of modern concern about the effects of these media – for example, when parents claim that a television series has negatively influenced their children – is reminiscent of the underlying assumptions of the hypodermic needle theory: namely, that the media has a strong influence on people and society.

During the sixties, when television emerged as the dominant public communication medium, concern about the influence of the radio made way for growing anxiety about the effect of violence and sex portrayed on television. Despite the fact that most of the time studies have shown that such concern is unfounded, and despite the fact that film and television differ from radio and other media, such concern still flares up periodically, especially amongst moralists and politicians who use moral issues for their own political strategies. Often concern is also blown out of proportion by the media themselves. As a rule none of these parties offer any scientific substantiation for their statements.

hypodermic needle theory

Moral concerns relate to the concept of *moral panic*. Watson and Hill's (1984:109) description of moral panic remains relevant: it is when individuals and/or groups perceive certain activities as seriously subverting the morals and interests of the dominant culture. Such reactions are disseminated by the mass media usually in a hysterical, stylised and stereotypical manner, thus engendering a sense of moral panic. In the social sciences the concept moral panic is usually associated with the concept of *anomie*. Anomie refers to a state to which a group or individual is prone when they feel that their accepted values, norms and culture are threatened. It usually manifests itself when societies are in the throes of change. With South African society in a state of transition since the early 1990s, we have had many examples of this with the changing of legislation on abortion, the death sentence, land distribution, gay marriages, censorship laws and so on. On all these changes the media reported and continues to report extensively. By so-doing, the media reflects the thinking of society about matters such as these and simultaneously infuses moral debates often to the point of mass hysteria.

How representative are debates presented by the media as a "public outcry"? Howitt and Cumberbatch already showed in 1977 that public concern about morals (and the effects of the media on morality) are public only inasmuch as they are expressed and initiated by the media themselves: the public, while condemning violence in principle, in fact may enjoy violent media content. This finding underscores the artificiality of surveys which seek to probe subjects' reactions to media content by means of questionnaires and experimental methods, and then present their findings as an honest reflection of people's experience of the media to substantiate the view that the public is concerned.

Two-step-flow theory

two-step-flow theory

During the 1950s it was realised that because of the large number of mediating factors, reliable measurement of media effects is extremely difficult. This gave rise to the *two-step-flow* theory. A prominent communication scientist, J.T. Klapper (1960), pointed out that studies of media effects should always take account of the following factors which co-determine human behaviour and attitudinal change:
- Media users are not at the mercy of the media but selectively expose themselves on the basis of their own knowledge, experience, background, education, culture, expectations and the like. In other

The Effects of Mass Communication

words, people expose themselves selectively to media content with which they agree, prefer, understand, and so on.
- The group (family, colleagues, friends) in which media users are situated can filter media users interpretation and experience of media messages and in a sense acts as a buffer against one-sided interpretations. For example, often you discuss what you have read in a newspaper or have seen on television with friends or family or colleagues who also air their opinions.
- Societies and people themselves have certain opinion leaders (parents, teachers, politicians, clergymen) to whom media users (children) defer when moulding their behaviour, developing their attitudes and ideas. These opinion leaders can represent a further filter and buffer in the interpretation and experience of media messages.
- In a commercial (capitalist) media system characterised by free market competition, the media themselves provide divergent and competing interpretations. A variety of newspapers, radio stations and television channels, and lately the Internet and cell phones, provide us with different interpretations of the same topic.

Klapper (*op. cit.*) came to the following conclusions about the nature of media effects:
- Media communication in itself is not a necessary or sufficient cause for behavioural change. At most it operates in conjunction with and via certain mediating factors and influences.
- Media can however contribute to behavioural change and reinforce existing behaviour.
- Where mass communication does change behaviour, there may be no mediating factors, or mediating factors themselves operate in the direction of change. This is found in authoritarian societies or in developing societies where the media are expected to play a leading role in transforming society.
- The effect exercised by the media is itself subject to situation, circumstances and context.

Klapper's and other corroborative research confirmed the "classic" statement of one of the founding fathers of modern communication studies, namely Bernard Berelson, about the nature of media effects:

> "Some kinds of communication on some kinds of issues, brought to the attention of some kinds of people under some kinds of conditions, have some kinds of effects." (Berelson 1949:500)

The two-step-flow theory thus acknowledges that mass media users are not passive, isolated individuals but members of a structured society, to which they belong. They form part of different groups, groups which themselves attach various interpretations to media messages.

The critical question of the hypodermic needle theory was: *what does the media do to people*? In the two-step-flow theory the question changed to: *what do people do with the media*? The latter question in turn formed the basis of the uses and gratifications theory.

The uses and gratifications theory

The *uses and gratification theory* proceeds from the needs of users and the probable gratifications that they derive from media use. Research is based on questions such as: What do people do with the media? What do they use the media for? What do they get from their media use? In general the following conclusions are drawn (see O'Sullivan *et al* 1994:326; McQuail 2000):

Diversion (distraction): People use media content to escape from their daily work and other routines, and from a wide variety of problems that confront and constrain them. The gratification is emotional release, albeit of a temporary nature.

Personal relations: Media provide content that gratifies the needs for companionship and sociability. People use media to keep them company and even experience media personalities and fictional characters (for example, the characters in television soap operas) as personal friends. Media use also provides a focus for interaction with others (people discuss with others what they have read, seen or listened to).

Personal identity: Media content is used to explore, challenge, adjust or confirm personal identity. People use media content to compare themselves and their situations and values with those of others.

Surveillance: The media gratifies the need for information about the immediate and distant world and circumstances. Media users need and get information about issues that can affect them directly or indirectly.

Although there are methodological critiques against uses and gratifications research, today it still forms the basis of continuing research about the ways in which and the reasons why people use media. (See volume 3 for a more in-depth discussion of uses and gratification. Lately much research

The Effects of Mass Communication

about the use of the Internet is also done against the background of the assumptions of uses and gratifications theories.)

One of the main methodological objections against uses and gratifications is the absence of a theoretical basis. Critics maintain that it is an a-theoretical approach arising from an underlying tautology, namely that use necessary leads to the gratification of needs. Being a-theoretical, it is argued that uses and gratifications do not really explain the complex cognitive processes involved in the experience and interpretation of media content.

Before empirical studies began, it was believed that the mass media produced direct, immediate and powerful influences on all individual members and audiences. The earliest research findings did little to challenge this prevailing belief, and in fact seemed to confirm it but the hypodermic needle theory no longer holds true. The selective and limited influence theories which replaced the hypodermic needle theories found that the factors causing people to expose themselves to the media were individualistic, part of social categories (age, education, gender) and part of social relationships (family, friends, colleagues). Uses and gratifications theories exposed the fact that media users are active and not passive in selecting media content for personal uses and gratifications. De Fleur and Dennis (1994:566–567) come to the conclusion that the numerous studies done within the context of the hypodermic needle theory, the two-step-flow theory and the uses and gratifications theory revealed only weak effects. Their conclusion:

> "... the preponderance of evidence about the effects of mass communication that emerged from these theories and decades of research, led to the general conclusion that the mass media are quite limited in their influences on people who select and attend to any particular message. In short, six decades of research revealed an overall picture of weak [short-term] effects."

5.3.2 Long-term theories

The underlying assumption of *long-term theories* is that the media do not have an immediate impact on behaviour and people's way of thinking, but can affect behaviour over a longer period of exposure to media content. Under long-term theories (as an umbrella term) we include the following:

long-term theories

- accumulation theory;
- diffusion of innovation theory;
- modelling theory;
- social expectation theory;
- meaning construction theory;
- stereotype theory;
- agenda setting theory;
- framing theory;
- spiral of silence theory.

All of them are closely related and can also be termed *cognitive theories*, meaning our faculty of knowing and understanding something in a specific way and how we base our behaviour and thinking on such knowledge. Research provides evidence that the media have a (strong) impact on our knowledge and understanding of the world and its people, and thus affects our behaviour.

Accumulation theory

accumulation theory

In *accumulation theory* it is believed that if the media focus repeatedly and in a relatively consistent way on an issue it can over a long period of time change people's attitudes and behaviour. If the various media corroborate each other by presenting the same interpretations, significant changes can take place in peoples' beliefs, attitudes and behaviour. De Fleur and Dennis (1994:579) list the following as the basic propositions of the accumulation theory:

- The mass media begin to focus their attention on and produce messages about a specific topic problem, situation or issue: for instance, race discrimination, the environment, social habits, crime.
- Over an extended period, the mass media continue to focus their attention in a relatively consistent and persistent way and their presentations corroborate each other.
- Individual members of the public increasingly become aware of these messages, and on a person-by-person basis, a growing comprehension develops of the interpretations of the topic presented by the media.
- Increasing comprehension of the messages regarding the topic supplied by the media begins to form (or modify) the meanings, beliefs, and attitudes that serve as guides to behaviour for members of the audience. Thus, minor individual-by-individual changes accumulate, and new beliefs and attitudes slowly emerge to provide significant changes in norms of appropriate behaviour related to the topic.

The Effects of Mass Communication

Arguably, accumulation theory provides an explanation for the role of the media in changing people's attitudes about topics such as divorce, sex, style and politics, over a period of time. If all the South African media, over a longer period of time, report in the same way about race relations in South Africa, either positive or negative, such reporting can have an impact on people's perceptions of race and race relations.

Diffusion of innovation theory

In modern and postmodern society there is a consistent flow of new products, ideas, solutions to problems, new interpretations and other kinds of innovations. As de Fleur and Dennis (1994:92–93) say, they can range from trivial, such as a new hairstyle, to the profound, such as a new political ideology. Whatever the innovation may be, sociologists have proven that every innovation is taken up by people in a particular society in a rather regular process that can be described by the *diffusion of innovation theory*.

> diffusion of innovations

This theory applies to mass communication in two ways: the innovation of news media products and the role of the media in spreading the innovation of new innovations, ideas, fashions, beliefs and fads.

First of all the media itself is an innovation. With each development in media technology new forms of media and communication are established. These new forms must be adopted by people. Recent good examples are the cellular phone and the Internet.

The printing press brought about a massive change in public communication culture and created a completely new information environment. The same happened after the invention of the telegraph, photography, radio, television and satellite. Today, we are adopting the changes brought about by the development of information and communication technology such as the fax machine, computer, Internet, e-mail, cellular telephones and so on. The theory of the diffusion of innovation can explain the ways in which people adopt these new media.

Secondly, the innovation theory is important to the study of mass communication, because the media, in modern society, are often largely responsible for bringing new items (products, ideas, interpretations, beliefs) to the attention of people who eventually adopt them.

De Fleur and Dennis (1994:93) summarise the basic propositions of this theory as follows:

- The adoption process begins with an awareness stage in which those who will ultimately adopt an innovation learn of its existence (often from the mass media), but lack detailed information about it.
- Awareness is followed by an interest stage. People interested in the innovation begin to seek additional information on it. The media often provides the additional information.
- This is followed by an assessment stage. People interested use the additional information obtained to evaluate the innovation in terms of their expected and future situations.
- The fourth stage is called the trial stage. A small number of the people interested acquire and apply the innovation on a small scale to determine its utility for their purposes (this, of course, can also be a political theory or an attitude towards a specific kind of behaviour, for instance, premarital sex).
- Finally, in an adoption stage, the innovation is acquired and used on a full scale by a few people. After that, increasing numbers adopt it and accumulation of users follows a characteristic S-shaped curve that has started slowly, but rises quickly and then levels down.

It is important to remember that not all adopters and innovations necessarily go through all the stages. Some innovations are adopted rapidly, some virtually overnight, by many people, while the adoption of others are spread over longer periods by a smaller proportion of the population. Some innovations are not adopted at all.

Modelling theory

modelling theory

The *modelling theory* is based on the social learning theory developed in psychology. In this theory it is argued that in some cases some media users can adopt the media's depictions of people's behaviour. In other words, in some cases some people can adopt media-portrayed behaviour as a model for their own behaviour. Because of their rich visual nature, showing and exposing actions in detail, film and television may have this kind of effect. The assumptions of the modelling theory (de Fleur & Dennis 1994:585) are:

- A media user encounters a form of action portrayed by a person (model) in a media presentation/representation. (A model can be a sport personality or a movie star but could also be a police officer, a politician, an ordinary person, and so on.)
- The individual media user identifies with the model and believes that he or she is like, or wants to be like, the model.

The Effects of Mass Communication

- The individual remembers and reproduces (imitates) the actions of the model in some later situation.
- Performing the reproduced activity results in some reward (positive reinforcement) for the individual.
- Thus, positive reinforcement increases the possibility that the media user will use the reproduced behaviour again as a means of responding to something or someone or in a situation.

Remember the outcry of parents after it was revealed in 2000 that the then South African cricket captain, Hansie Cronjé, was involved with game fixing. They claimed that many of their young boys' dreams were shattered because their model, Hansie, misled them. The same media which portrayed Hansie as a hero also had to portray his fall from grace. Many Afrikaners' political ideals, thinking and behaviour were modelled on the ideology and political styles of their leaders such as previous prime ministers Hendrik Verwoerd, B.J. Vorster and F.W. de Klerk. They were portrayed by the Afrikaans media as God-fearing, highly principled leaders. These images were shattered for many after the brutalities and inhumanity of apartheid became known and exposed by the media. Many black children and young people are now modelling their behaviour on that of South Africa's new political leaders, music stars, sport personalities and so on, who are now visible in the South African media.

Social expectation theory

The *social expectation theory*: by watching television, films, reading newspapers, listening to the radio and surfing the Internet, we can, over a period of time, learn the social norms adhered to by certain groups, people and organisations in society. We can learn from the media how medical doctors are supposed to behave, how newlywed couples behave, how elderly people in old age homes behave, and so on. We get an image of how police stations function from many police dramas, how court procedures are followed, how bills are debated in parliament. Often these images are idealised. Compared to the modelling theory, which is more concerned with personal behaviour, the emphasis in the social expectation theory is on social norms and roles. De Fleur and Dennis (1994:591) list the assumptions of this theory:

- Various kinds of content provided by the mass media often portray social activities and group life.

social expectation

Media Studies: Volume 1

- These portrayals, even if they are fictitious (soap-operas, comedies), are representations of reality that reflect, accurately or poorly, the nature of many kinds of groups in a society.
- Individuals, when exposed over a period of time to these representations, receive information, one can even say unintended lessons and education, about the norms and roles that prevail within the groups.
- The experience of exposure to portrayals of a particular kind of group results in incidental learning of behaviour patterns that are expected by others when acting within such a group. These learned expectations concerning appropriate behaviour for self and others serve as guides to action when individuals actually encounter or try to understand such groups in real life.

The social expectation theory can also be useful in explaining the role of the media in multicultural societies where one group is expected to understand the social norms and values of another group and to act accordingly when mingling or working with such a group. Think, for example, how we in South Africa can learn through media portrayals how different cultural and social norms and values are portrayed in soap operas such as *Isidingo, Egoli,* and *7de Laan*.

Meaning construction theory

meaning construction

In many theories it is argued that we act and understand something and that our behaviour is based on and defined in terms of:
- what we know (our knowledge of something/somebody); and/or
- what we believe.

In these theories the emphasis is on how the media condition us to attach certain meanings to objects, words, and concepts. These theories are known as *meaning construction theories*. They claim that often we obtain our knowledge, and what we believe something means, from how the media defines that something. In our present information society, much of what we base our beliefs on is derived from the media as a social source. This applies especially to new phenomena we have to confront. The media not only expose us to the known, but also to new developments, concepts and ideas to which the media apply certain meanings which we adopt. Think of concepts and their meanings such as "star wars", computer "bits", "chips", "software", "hardware", "globalisation", "unit trusts", "cultural transformation", "ozone layer" and "global warming". A few years ago we did not know or frequently use these terms. Today, many people

The Effects of Mass Communication

understand these concepts in terms of what they have learned about them from the media.

De Fleur and Dennis (1994:595) summarise the basic stages of the meaning construction theories as:
- The media describe objects, events, people or situations in ways that link labels (language symbols, such as words) to meanings.
- A member of the media audience is exposed to such a label and undergoes some change in his/her personal interpretation of the meaning(s) of the label or has a meaning already attached to it now stabilised.
- He/she now communicates with others using the label and its media-influenced meaning. By doing this, such media-derived meanings are further shaped and/or stabilised among other members of society.
- Eventually, through the communication of media-derived meanings, strengthened in and through the means of interpersonal communication, such meanings become social convention and are thus adopted as the real and/or only meaning of a concept, action or person.
- Individual behaviour toward objects, situations, or events is guided by the meanings people hold for them. In this way the media have played an indirect but significant long-term role in shaping people's thoughts and actions.

Take for example the label or concept "ozone layer". By far the majority of people attach the media's defined meaning(s) to this concept and not the far more complicated meaning scientists attach to it or which can be learned in geography texts. Often the meanings the media attach to concepts and phenomena are oversimplified and one-sided.

Stereotype theory

The role of the media in creating and sustaining stereotypes (stereotyping) of certain people, organisations and groups (for example, of women, white people, black people, Jews, Afrikaners, gays, financial institutions, political parties, politicians, professions, etc.), and how these stereotypes affect our perceptions of people, groups and institutions, are dealt with in depth in, for example, the chapters on representation in volume 2. Because stereotyping is one of the most commonly used examples of how the media affect our thinking and behaviour, it is also dealt with in-depth at the end of this chapter in section 5.5. Through stereotyped portrayals the media may reinforce existing patterns of attitudes and behaviour

stereotypes

toward specific individuals, groups, and institutions, especially minority groups. De Fleur and Dennis (1994:599) express the essential ideas of this theory in the following way:

- In entertainment content, and in other media messages, for instance in the way social and political journalism portray an issue and/or an event related to a specific group, the media can present us with negative portrayals of a specific group. See the mainly stereotypical portrayals of gay marches and ethnic rituals such as the annual reed dances.
- These portrayals tend to be consistently negative, showing such people as having undesirable attributes and fewer positive characteristics than members of the dominant group in which the media function.
- Such portrayals are similar among the various media, providing corroboration.
- These portrayals provide constructions of meaning for media users, particularly for those who have only limited contact with actual people of the stereotyped group.
- Viewers, readers and listeners incorporate these meanings into their memories as relatively inflexible schemata – stereotyped interpretations – that they use when thinking about or responding to any individual of a portrayed category, regardless of his/her actual personal characteristics.

Agenda-setting theory

agenda-setting

The basic assumption of the *agenda-setting theory* is that, consciously or unconsciously, the media create a particular image of reality. The media confront us on a daily basis with events which are, according to the media, important. Every day the media release a list of topics (issues on which the media focus) similar to the agenda of a meeting. The omission of certain events and issues, and the overemphasis of others, establishes a particular way for media users to think about reality. For example, at the time of writing, stories about crime, corruption and AIDS filled the columns of many South African newspapers, creating the image of society falling apart.

The attention given in news coverage influences the public awareness of the significance of an issue. (McQuail 2000:426.) Agenda-setting thus focuses on *what* topics the media present to an audience and secondly on *how* information on the selected topics are presented. It relates to the dynamics of news coverage: the spectrum of viewpoints, symbols and questions which are selected to construct the news and how they

The Effects of Mass Communication

are ranked or accorded legitimacy and priority. Finally agenda-setting is concerned with *how* the media's legitimisation of issues and events *affects* our perceptions of reality (O'Sullivan *et al* 1994:8).

Apart from applying the hypotheses of agenda-setting to everyday issues, the theory is of particular importance in analysing the effects of political reporting (especially during times of elections) on people's political views and voting behaviour. In other words, on which issues do the media focus during times of elections in order to prioritise certain topics compared to others?

Framing

Closely related to agenda-setting is *framing*. Whereas the emphasis in agenda-setting is on the media's *selection* of topics/issues/events, the emphasis in the framing theory is more on the media's *representation*, treatment and even production of issues. As a media effect, "framing" describes the influence on the public of the news angles used by journalists, the interpretative and ideological frameworks from which journalists report an issue and the contextualisation of news reports within a specific (ideological) framework. Such "ideologically coloured" reporting is known as *advocacy*. For example, the media may decide to report about a person, topic, group or institution in a certain way. They may only focus on the negative (or positive) attributes of a politician, a financial group, a gang or a proposed new law. The results are that the public, being only exposed to the negative (or positive) aspects perceive a person, a group, an institution or an issue mainly in a negative (or positive) way. We often hear about people, organisations, groups, and so on, complaining that the media, through its negative reporting, has *framed* them and as such has influenced, for example, a court ruling about them. Many recent examples of South African politicians complaining about being framed can be cited.

| framing

However, framing does not only include the ways in which the media advocates an issue, but also the investigation of those who have access to the media and who use such access to influence the media. In short, whenever you hear someone saying "I have many contacts in the media", be careful. How are such contacts used and for what purposes?

Lately, the increasing interactivity of traditional media (talk and phone-in programmes on radio, interactive television (where viewers can immediately respond with their comments by text messaging, for

245

example), interactive newspapers on the Internet, and the Internet with its blogs and chat rooms have created new research questions about framing. The main question is: to what extent do new forms of media interactivity prompt a broader range of actors (including public participants) contributing to the framing of topics as compared to the old mass media with its traditional top-down approach? For instance, in South Africa the media were blamed by some politicians during 2006 for framing former ANC deputy president Jacob Zuma during his rape trial. To what extent have the numerous participants to phone-in and talk programmes on radio and television and the participants in the debates on the Zuma issue on the Internet contributed to such framing?

Spiral of silence

spiral of silence

Finally, a note about the *spiral of silence theory*. Although evidence to support this theory is weak and inconsistent (see McQuail 2000:463) it nevertheless should be kept in mind, especially in studies about the formation of public opinion during political campaigns. The main assumptions of the theory are:
- Society threatens deviant individuals with isolation.
- Individuals experience fear of isolation continuously.
- This fear of isolation causes individuals to try to assess the climate of opinion at all times.
- The fear of isolation affects their behaviour in public, especially their willingness or lack thereof to express their opinions openly. (McQuail 2000:461–463)

Although the media pretends to represent the majority view, this may not be the case. Many people's opinions may differ from that expressed by the media. However, because of their fear of isolation, they remain silent. This silence gives the impression that they go along with opinions expressed by the media. Their silence has the spiralling effect suggesting that the opinion expressed by the media is the dominant public opinion. For example, the South African media may claim that the public opinion is against the unsubstantiated view that AIDS is caused by poverty (not a virus). Many people may believe this but are reluctant to air such a view. The result is that the media's opinion gains support as being the dominant public opinion. In the same way the media may present criticism against a political party as being the dominant criticism (public opinion) of the public. Although people may agree with the criticism, they nevertheless vote for the same political party, against whom the criticism is expressed,

The Effects of Mass Communication

out of fear of isolation within their group. Predictions about election results based on what the media presents as the public opinion is thus risky.

From the above it is clear that there is a correspondence between the different long-term or cognitive effect theories. They all support the view that over a longer period of time the media can affect our perceptions of reality and our understanding of things. However, each of the theories emphasises or focuses on a different aspect:
- *accumulation*: how corresponding or corroborative representations by different media affect our perceptions;
- *diffusion of innovation*: the process of bringing something specific under people's attention and how media users adopt such an innovation;
- *modelling*: how people model themselves and their behaviour on media representations;
- *social expectation*: how social values and morals are spread by the media;
- *meaning construction*: how we accept media interpretations as our own knowledge of something;
- *stereotypes*: how the media's negative representations affect our perceptions;
- *agenda-setting*: how the media's prioritising of events and topics affects our perceptions of reality;
- *framing*: how the media's deliberate framing of an issue, affects our perceptions;
- *spiral of silence*: how the media create a specific image of what the public opinion is and how media users accept that to be the public opinion.

5.4 STEREOTYPING

Stereotyping is probably the most frequently-used theory to describe the effect of the media on users' perceptions.

Why do we think about certain people and groups in certain ways? Why is our collective way of thinking about "other" people and groups often negative? Where do our ideas and perceptions of certain people and groups come from? Questions like these are investigated by many disciplines, including cognitive psychology, anthropology and language studies. In critical media studies we address these and related questions

| stereotyping

under one of the key topics and concepts in media studies, namely "representation".

When we talk about how the media represent specific people and groups, especially groups, we enter the terrain of stereotyping. The question of stereotyping is of special importance in South Africa – a society often known for its tension and conflict between different racial, ethnic and language groups. Many people believe that much of this tension is caused by the negative perceptions people of different racial, ethnic and language groups may have of each other. Should we wish to create one South African nation, these perceptions need to be changed. What is the role of the South African media in sustaining and often creating negative perceptions?

5.4.1 What is a stereotype?

A straightforward definition of stereotyping is:

> *"the social classification of particular groups and people as often highly simplified and generalised signs, which implicitly or explicitly represent a set of values, judgements and assumptions concerning their behaviour, characteristics or history" (O'Sullivan et al 1994: 299–300).*

For example:
- Afrikaners are essentially racists;
- Germans are essentially Nazis;
- black people are essentially inferior to the white race;
- Jews are essentially cunning;
- Zulus are essentially ferocious;
- women are essentially inferior to men;
- gays are essentially sexually promiscuous.

Why do people tend to think in these ways about groups? Why do they simplify and generalise to such an extent that these stereotypes become an unquestioned part of their way of thinking about groups and individuals? Why does stereotypical thinking form part of people's everyday discourse? Are stereotypes and stereotypical thinking institutionalised in media content?

There are many possible answers to these questions. It is easy to answer these questions in the affirmative. However, stereotypical thinking asks for a far more in-depth investigation beginning with questions about how

The Effects of Mass Communication

people ascribe meaning. From a social science perspective we want to draw your attention to two out of many possible answers:
- the social anthropologist Claude Lévi-Straus's view that the nature of human kind is to think, interpret and make sense of the world and others in terms of binary oppositions;
- the French structuralist, semiotician and social critic Roland Barthes' view that we think about and interpret our world and others according to socially constructed meanings and values.

Claude Lévi-Strauss (1908-) and the theory of binary oppositions

Claude Lévi-Strauss was born in Brussels in Belgium and studied law and philosophy in Paris, France. He then became a professor of sociology in Brazil, where he did research on the culture of the South American Indians. He was and still is regarded as one of the pioneers in the field of structural analysis in cultural anthropology. Lévi-Strauss drew our attention to the incidence and meaning of binary oppositions and the role of myth in human thinking

binary opposition

Binary oppositions suggest that the meaning of something depends on its opposite: "good" is dependent on "bad". Lévi-Strauss' point of departure was that a *collective* practice of laws, rules and values direct the individual's thinking and behaviour. Furthermore, society's collective existence shapes the individual and determines his or her individuality.

According to this line of thinking we could say "I am who I am on the basis of what society allows me to be". The individual abides by the norms and values of a collective existence. Anything that may threaten this collectiveness is experienced as negative and as an opposition. Anything that is other than the collective whole in terms of which the self is constituted becomes a threat.

From this we can deduct that it is human nature to feel threatened by anything that is other from the collective whole to which one belongs. Usually our reaction is to retreat from, combat or to humiliate the *other*.

According to Lévi-Strauss the purpose of structuralist analysis should be to uncover and describe the underlying structures which determine the individual's way of thinking. For Lévi-Strauss a possible way of uncovering these structures was:

249

- through the analysis of the laws of descent and the marital laws of indigenous tribes;
- the analysis of totemism and the role of totemism in a society;
- in the analysis of the myths of a society.

Lévi-Strauss concluded that each society can, in a unique way, give expression to binary oppositions (in ways of thinking, literature, theatre, behaviour) such as good/bad, rich/poor, belief/disbelief, order/chaos, hate/love, man/nature, intellect/emotion, capitalism/socialism, individual/group and fascism/democracy.

In other words, each society can understand oppositions and can express them differently in its thinking, behaviour and values. This thinking, this behaviour and these values are reflected in society's symbolic works, including its media.

In the analysis of racism in the South African media we can thus begin by investigating how the values of journalists as being part of a group (white or black, male or female) constitute their way of thinking; whether their own values as being part of a group inherently colour their interpretation of reality, defines their conceptualisation of what constitutes objectivity and hinder an openness to perceive reality from the *other's* perspective or not.

It can be argued that the role of collective values formed on the basis of oppositions is not only manifest and latent in the political content of the media, it permeates all content. Applying television genres such as soap operas, situation comedies and police dramas has shown how these genres constantly handle binary oppositions such as good/bad, right/wrong, hero/villain and the values which society attaches to these oppositions. A demonstration of oppositions such as these in symbolic forms of expression like the situation comedy, police drama and soap opera presents us with an image of the way a society deals with these values.

In structuralist media analyses, however, we are interested in more than the demonstration and description of binary oppositions in drama texts; our interest extends to the analysis of binary oppositions in propaganda (including news and documentary programmes). For example, how does a newspaper handle binary oppositions in its editorials? Without being explicitly "in opposition to" an issue, person or movement, an editorial

The Effects of Mass Communication

can be oppositional in perspective or in the style of writing. Without being explicit in terms of oppositions in crime reporting (us/them), crime stories can and usually are written from an implicit perspective based on us/them. The "us" are "we the victims" while the "them" indicates "they the criminals". The "us/them" divide could also be implicitly racial.

According to Lévi-Strauss, we define the world in terms of oppositions. This is done from the perspective of one's own values which are usually rooted in the values of the group one belongs to. If the emphasis is only on *oppositions* then the result is a stereotyped viewed of others and the world. If there is an unwillingness to openness and to focus on *similarities*, then the result is a closed and restricted view of others, reality and the world. We can thus, based on the theory of binary oppositions, say that stereotypes are the result of emphasising oppositions.

Myths

myth

A second point Lévi-Strauss made is that values derive from and are usually based on myths. Literally the word "myth" means narrative, fable or a story without foundation, handed down from one generation to another, such as the nursery tale *Red Riding Hood* in Western culture. Lévi-Strauss analysed the myths of various cultures in order to show that although the content may differ, the structure and intended meaning is the same from one generation to the next, namely to guide and reinforce the way society thinks about a certain question, such as acceptable behaviour and what is right and wrong. Although the story of *Red Riding Hood* might be adapted from one generation to the next, the underlying purpose is to warn children right from babyhood to beware of strangers. The older one becomes, the greater the number of guises the "stranger" can put on: the "stranger" can be a member of another race, sexual orientation, gender, language group, political group, and so on. What is important is that for society, a myth such as *Red Riding Hood* spells out an accepted behaviour pattern and way of thinking: beware of strangers/the unknown/whatever is different/the other. In Sotho culture this warning against strangers/the unknown finds expression in fables such as *Tselane le Ledimo*. This is the story of the little girl Tselane who was warned by her mother against the giant Kgokomodumo, but who disregarded the warning and was caught by Kgokomodumo.

Briefly put, Lévi-Strauss's analysis of myth and binary oppositions is intended to show that a universal logic lies at the root of our thinking.

It can be argued that today television is one of our biggest narrators of myths. If we accept Strauss' meaning of the word we might ask whether situation comedies, soap operas and police dramas – the very genres typical of television – do not fulfil exactly the same functions as the myths of earlier cultures. Are the stories of *Red Riding Hood* and *Tselane le Ledimo* not being repeated in one form or another in television scripts?

From this explanation of myth we can answer our question "What are stereotypes?" by deducing that stereotypes are mythical in nature. Although his work is in the same vein as that of Lévi-Strauss, Roland Barthes approached the concept "myth" differently.

Roland Barthes (1915–1980) and the theory of social myth

social myth

Barthes drew our attention particularly to the *mythical* character of culture, popular culture and the media. His work gave rise to media theories and analyses of the media as a myth, a narrator of myths and as a dynamic instrument for changing myths and creating new ones.

After his initial work, which was purely structuralist, Barthes reinterpreted linguist Ferdinand de Saussure's distinction between signifier and signified. In the spirit of poststructuralism he concluded that the meaning of a signifier (sign) is "open" for many possible meanings and interpretations but that whatever the meaning of a sign, it has a layered structure of *first*, *second* and *third order meaning*. The three orders are denotative, connotative/mythical and ideological meaning.

By mythical meaning Barthes meant *socially constructed values*. For him a myth is not so much a non-truth. Rather it is a socially constructed "truth" with an underlying ideological meaning, aimed at maintaining a *status quo*. Societies create and maintain myths for the sake of their own survival (and often at the cost of others).

To illustrate his view, Barthes used a series of photographs entitled *The family of man*, in which people of different nations, social backgrounds and ages are depicted. The communicator of this series of photographs wanted to convey the meaning that the everyday behaviour of people throughout the world, and despite their race and cultures, is much the same.

With this series of photographs, Barthes argued, the communicator (in this case the photographer or publisher of the magazine) is implying that birth, death, work, knowledge and play, irrespective of other differences,

are universal, and that in this respect all people are the same, almost like a large family. Barthes regards this so-called "universality of being" as a *myth*. The myth hides the real fate and state of man: namely extreme differences in power and wealth. The series of pictures therefore serves the myth, but:

> "... this myth masks the radically different social and economic conditions under which people are born, work and die." (Culler 1983:34)

According to Barthes, objects function in exactly the same mythical way, claiming:

> "Wine, for example, is not just one drink among others in France, but a totem-drink, corresponding to the milk of the Dutch or the tea ceremoniously taken by the British Royal Family. It is 'the foundation of a collective morality'. For the French, 'to believe in wine is a coercive act', and drinking wine a ritual of social integration. In generating mythical meaning, cultures seek to make their own norms seem facts of nature." (Culler 1983:34)

For the social scientist the concern is not with the quality of the wine, whether it is French or South African, but rather with the second-order or mythical meanings given to something such as wine in and by a specific culture, such as in France "... wine is objectively good, and *at the same time*, the goodness of wine is a myth" (Barthes 1977:158). We can analyse South African social practices such as *braaivleis* and everything that goes with it as a myth signifying many layers of meaning associated with a culture. When we see a group of people attending a *braaivleis*, or a photograph of a group of white people attending a braaivleis, it may embody meanings associated with Afrikaner culture, Afrikaner history, and Afrikaner values including political values. Based on Barthes' theory of myth it is argued that media analysts should always try to uncover that which is hidden in media messages; to see beyond the mythical meaning being conveyed. The social scientist should not be concerned with the qualities and effect of something such as wine, or *braaivleis* and pap (mealie meal porridge), but with the image or second-order meaning (mythical meaning) given to wine, *braaivleis* and pap by the social conventions of a particular culture.

In South African society, for example, we have myths about Africans, Afrikaners, the English, Muslims, Zulus, and so on. We also have myths about women, the status of the family in society and the role the church,

mosque or temple should play in society. These myths are expressed in various ways in our literature, theatrical performances, television advertisements, newspaper reports and films. For example, the myths about the relationship between middle-class Afrikaners and Englishmen were reinforced in the Sunday cartoon published by *Rapport* until 2006, namely *Ben, Babsie en Familie*. The cartoon strip *Madam and Eve*, originally published in the *Mail & Guardian* weekly newspaper, deals in similar vein with various myths about the social relationship between black and white South Africans.

At the political level the ideology of apartheid was founded on various racially based myths, such as the claim that black people were unable to govern a country in an orderly manner. Just as the state, education and the church, with their apartheid legislation, Christian-nationalist education and early justifications of apartheid on Biblical grounds, preached and reinforced apartheid, the media (as a symbolic form of expression) contributed during apartheid in various ways to the entrenchment of the apartheid myths. For example, for decades the mainstream South African newspapers were fairly negative in their reporting on Africans; there was a lot of emphasis on the *swart gevaar* (the black peril); Africans played negative roles in South African films; whites and blacks did not appear together in the same television advertisements. Because of the unfavourable publicity given to black people in the media, legislation, education, and the church, the myth that "blacks are unfit to rule the country" was reinforced.

Returning to what Barthes had to say about wine as a myth, we can analyse social practices such as *braaivleis* and everything that goes with it, as a myth signifying many layers of meaning associated with a culture. When we see a group of people attending a *braaivleis*, or a photograph of a group of white people attending a braaivleis it can embody meanings associated with Afrikaner culture, Afrikaner history, and Afrikaner values including political values.

Based on Barthes' theory of myth it is argued that media analysts should always try to uncover that which is hidden in media messages; to see beyond the mythical meaning being conveyed. The social scientist should not be concerned with the qualities and effect of something such as wine, or *braaivleis* or pap, but with the image or second-order meaning (mythical meaning) given to wine, *braaivleis* and pap by the social conventions of a particular culture.

The Effects of Mass Communication

In the same vein, the communication scientist should not be interested in a product advertised by the media but in the meanings associated through social convention with the product and with the meanings associated with its possession and consumption. For Barthes these meanings are usually determined by the bourgeoisie, who themselves are the victims of capitalist considerations (according to him). For instance, the possession of a certain car implies membership of a specific social class. This is why advertisements for motor cars are intended to reinforce the myths associated with a certain social class's ideas about what a fine car should be like. What are the myths to which motor car advertisements appeal? How? By means of what signs and codes is the appeal made?

What are the relationships between myths and stereotypes? How does the discussion of myth relate to our question: what are stereotypes?

The answer is that myths (social beliefs) are mainly communicated through *stereotypes*. Stereotypes are so much part of the culture of a particular group that members accept them unquestioningly as a kind of natural law. For example, during the apartheid years, negative myths about black people, that they are criminal, cannot rule a country, are unskilled, cannot be educated, and so on, prevailed amongst the supporters of apartheid who seldom questioned these myths or noticed how they benefited personally from these myths.

It can be argued that the media, with exceptions, played a role in strengthening these myths. In other words, in the apartheid years the media's mainly negative stereotyped way of portraying black people contributed to the ideology of apartheid. Newspapers might focus on stories portraying blacks associated with crime. Such focus supported the myth that black people are subordinate and inferior to white people and their so-called superior culture.

Under apartheid, South African movies tended to cast black people only in the roles of clowns, servants, labourers, thieves and murderers. Such movies fostered an image of black people as being impertinent or deceitful. Through stereotypes, media representations of black people implicitly and explicitly emphasised the differences (oppositions) between white and black. The exceptions in which the media questioned these myths and represented black people in a multi-faceted and contextualised way were few and far between.

Media Studies: Volume 1

Since the 1970s this began to change. Today, many examples can be sited of a more balanced media representation and even of a deliberate effort to question myths about race. This also accounts for the more nuanced portrayal of women and gays.

It is important to keep in mind that all groups tend to strengthen their myths about other groups by thinking and responding to them in terms of stereotypes. Black people also have myths and stereotypes of white people and the isiXhosa-speaking people, for instance, have been known to express stereotypes about the Zulus. In the South African English-language media many examples can be found of Afrikaners being portrayed as backward, Hitler-supporters, overweight, bombastic and conservative. This, however, is also beginning to change.

We have looked at two theories that can contribute to our understanding of the general nature of stereotypes. From these theories we can deduct that stereotypes are:
- the result of emphasising oppositions and differences between people and groups;
- have the purpose of strengthening myths about people and groups.

Let us now take a closer look at the characteristics and working of stereotypes.

5.4.2 The characteristics and working of stereotypes

characteristics of stereotypes

In critical media studies, a stereotype is considered to be a prejudice in terms of which people interpret people and groups and form particular conceptions about them. If we follow this approach, the outstanding characteristics of stereotypes are the following:
- Stereotypes depend on generalisation and simplification. Generalisation implies the denial of individuality; in other words a stereotype is considered valid for all the members of the group concerned: all Jews are scheming; all Afrikaners are racists; all black people are lazy; all gays are promiscuous; all women are inferior to men.
- Stereotypes may be negative or positive, depending on how the group or person is assessed. Up till now we have only concentrated on negative stereotypes. It is important to keep in mind that positive stereotypes, in other words refusing to acknowledge the negative aspects of a person or a group, can also blur one's perceptions about a person or a group.
- Notwithstanding their fictitious origin and lack of foundation, stereotypes have very real and mainly negative social consequences

The Effects of Mass Communication

for the group and the individual as part of the stereotyped group. For example, stereotypes in Western culture about women, Jews, gypsies, Turks, blacks, gays, lesbians, and so on can contribute to manoeuvring these groups into particular roles, including playing subordinate roles in society. Jews may tend to isolate themselves, gays may succumb to the stereotype of being promiscuous and become promiscuous, and so on. The result is a social reality that creates the impression that the stereotypes are accurate all along. In other words the self-image induced by stereotypes can persuade a person or a group to whom a stereotype is applied to see himself/herself or his/her group in a specific role and assume or learn this role as a form of anticipatory behaviour.

The rise of black, feminist and gay liberation movements and organisations is the direct consequence of the negative stereotypes regarding these groups and the role patterns, role expectations and image formation the stereotypes have created in society and forced on the groups in question.

With reference to the social consequences of stereotypes, a fourth characteristic is that people generally appeal to the stereotypes associated with a particular group in order to arrive at the verdict that a person or group "just is like that". Stereotypes create a vicious circle. To the critics of a particular group or person the stereotype seems normal and any resistance to it appears abnormal. Because stereotypes form part of the social and psychological make-up of a society, criticism of stereotypes is seen as an assault on security. From this point of view, stereotypes are only a problem for those who have been stereotyped, not for the users and communicators of stereotyped messages about a group, person or organisation.

- A fifth characteristic of stereotypes is that those who employ them consider them to be true. There stereotypes are not experienced as stereotypes but defended as to be a primordial and archetypical truth. A stereotype is then not seen as a prejudiced idea but as a true reflection of an essential characteristic of a person or a group on the basis of which the person or group should be typified or classified.

A weakness of this argument is that there is a distinction between a stereotype and an *archetype*. Although this is a complex distinction, we shall merely say that archetypes are primordial ideas/experiences/ opinions, which are inherited and may have a genetic basis in the unconscious mind, an inborn orientation which we bring into the world

archetype

with us. These are Jung's primordial images, the most famous of which are probably the primordial images of the opposite sex, the Anima and the Animus. In addition there are the archetypes concerning good and evil, light and shadow, witch and god, hero and villain, and so on.

The Jungian views on the collective unconsciousness imply that a child is not born with a spirit and mind as clean as a blank sheet of paper on which anything can be written. A child is predestined from birth to think and feel in the same way as his primordial ancestors did.

Whereas the archetype is an ancient primordial image, the stereotype has social and ideological conotations, it is socially produced, changeable and intelligible. In South Africa at present we are seeing how people are changing their stereotypes about those of different races or at least how attempts are being made, in the media as well as elsewhere, to get rid of stereotypes, especially negative ones.

A last remark regarding the truth of stereotypes: anyone who contends that stereotypes are true has not taken into account the fact that there are more differences between members of a single group than there are between different groups. The stereotype of Afrikaners as narrow-minded and bucolic loses sight of the fact that there are more differences and variations within the Afrikaner group than there are differences which serve to distinguish Afrikaners from Englishmen.

To sum up, a stereotype may be defined as a prejudiced, generalised, simplified conception of a person and/or group which could be either negative or positive, but which usually implies negative consequences. It emphasises the differences between people and groups. A stereotype is considered by those who employ it to be a true conception about what the individual or group is like; it is accepted as a "normal" typing and any deviation from the stereotype is seen as a threat to personal and social security. Unlike an archetype, a stereotype is the result of and is subject to changing social and ideological views. A stereotype is therefore not a constant, but a fluid and changeable concept.

5.4.3 The origin of stereotypes

origin of stereotypes

There are different theories about the origin of stereotypes. These vary from the complex theories of cognitive psychology, sociolinguistic theories of meaning, anthropological theories and sociological theories. Because race is such an issue in South Africa, we look at two popular theories on the origin of negative stereotypes about black people, one anthropological and the other theological. Note the Western origin of both.

One of the first written records of the negative stereotype(s) of people other than of Western origin as being "barbaric", "savage", "wild" and "primitive" can be found in Thomas Hobbes's book *Leviathan* (1651). In this work he describes South America Indians as a chaotic aggressive species, as *homo homini lupus*. He equates them with the medieval European myth of a werewolf. (Pieterse [*sine anno*] 32). This image of the "other" (meaning other than of European or British descent) was the topic of many debates and works by authors and philosophers such as John Locke (1632–1704) and Jean-Jacques Rousseau (1712–1778). In these first writings about other civilisations, Africans were generally described as wild and associated with animals and animal behaviour. These views were strengthened with visual images of naked black Africans, clothes and utility articles being Western signs and barometers of civilisation. The German philosopher Hegel (1770–1831), whose work later influenced Marx (1818–1863) and Engels (1820–1895), also contributed to the negative stereotypes about Africa. He wrote about Africa as "a continent without a history". This stereotype still surfaces today in the minds and thinking of many Western people.

The debates and writings gradually developed from portraying and emphasising the "other" as being barbaric, wild and savage (based on the werewolf myth, we can argue), to the origin of the concept *bon sauvage* (the noble savage), which in its turn gave moral support to the political idea and ideal of colonialism: to civilise the savage. (Pieterse [sa]:37) claims that the concept "noble savage" turned into *"noblesse oblige"* – the privilege and obligation of the "civilised" to civilise the "uncivilised". This in turn became the slogan of early socialist thinking.

In early Christian theological writings Africans were often stereotyped as the children of Ham, a character in the Old Testament of the Christian Bible who came to be associated with evil. As early as in the Church of Augustine (354 AC) this stereotype provided justification for slavery. Although slavery was at this stage "colourless", the association of Ham with slavery and with the Curse of Canaan then became a central theme in the Christian church's treatment of race in 16th and 17th centuries. From here, it was a short step to use this argument as theological justification for the use of Africans as slaves. The view of Africa as the continent of servants and to serve others can also be related to the Dutch theological

interpretations of the Book of Genesis in the 17th and 18th century, and to the interpretation that although all people are descendant from Adam and Eve and through their offspring via Noah and his wife, the continents are personified by Shem (Asia), Ham (Africa) and Japheth (Europe).

If the above paragraphs serve one purpose, it is to show how stereotypes are deeply rooted in
- people's thinking at a specific point in time;
- social, political and economic ideologies;
- theological interpretations and dogma.

For media practitioners and critics it is important to keep the above in mind, especially when they deal with matters of race, gender, sexual orientation and the interests of all minority groups, such as the physically handicapped, or lobby groups such as environmentalists. In dealing with these matters and groups they should critically reflect on their own possible prejudices and the origins of such prejudices.

5.4.4 The need to contextualise media representations

Similarly media critics and media users should take care not to pre-judge media representations as being stereotyped (Branston & Stafford 1999:130). Saying that a media text is "distorted" or "unrepresentative" may ignore:
- the unique character and nature of the medium;
- the specific genre of the text in which a so-called stereotyped representation may occur;
- the complex relationship between reality and representation;
- the motive of the communicator;
- the nature of perception and the eye of the beholder.

production demands

The *nature of a medium* places heavy demands in terms of time and space (codes of production) on journalists and programme makers. The nature of a medium often leads to the impossibility of contextualising a representation within the structural confines of a single story, programme, article or film. Rather than blaming the communicators, we must also take into account the intrinsic shortcomings of a medium. For example, a newspaper simply hasn't got the space to publish the complete speech of a politician, or to give a full account of all the different views on a topic. Of course, responsible journalism will try to do it in the most objective way possible. This may also be done in different articles in different editions

The Effects of Mass Communication

of a newspaper. Often media critics tend to ignore this and base their criticism on a single story in a single edition of a newspaper, or a single television/radio programme. The very nature of media communication, as symbolic forms of expression and as structured representations, must be kept in mind. They are intrinsically incapable of providing "the real thing" and we shouldn't expect them to do so.

Furthermore the *genre of a media text* is important. Comedy in particular lends itself to the depiction of stereotypes. Criticising a television situation comedy for containing stereotyped images of people and groups, is, to a certain extent, to criticise the nature of the genre. An Afrikaans-language television series such as *Orkney Snork Nie* on SABC between 1989 and 1992 was seen by some viewers as ridiculing Afrikaners. Although *Orkney Snork Nie* undoubtedly provides us with a stereotyped portrayal of the Afrikaner, criticism of it must be within the context of the genre. Degrading it because of its stereotypes will be ridiculous. The same applies to the popular cartoon strip *Madam & Eve* that communicates through the means of a stereotyped view of the relation between white people and black people in South Africa. One can also argue that editorials often tend towards stereotyping people, groups and issues. However, criticising an editorial comment as being stereotyped or not representative of reality is to ignore the fact that the editorial, as a genre, is ideological in nature.

| genre

Advertisements, as a genre, are often used in research about stereotypes. For example, in South Africa advertisements are used in research to illustrate race relations. In the apartheid years black people were hardly represented in advertisements of products aimed at a white market, or they were betrayed in the stereotypical roles of servants, filling in the background of an affluent white population (as if the whole of the white population was affluent). Since the demise of apartheid this began to change. Today black people are portrayed as being affluent and white people are sometimes portrayed in ridiculed roles, or in mixed-race scenarios which may not correspond with the experience of the majority of people in South Africa.

| advertisements

What is often overlooked in research is that advertisements are in their very nature abstractions of reality and thus unrealistic and idealised representations. Their communicative purpose is to create needs and desires, to act as aspirational role models and to sustain the capitalist ideology of consumption.

The phenomenological nature of media communication as symbolic communication (and advertising as often metaphorical communication) and the nature of genre emphasise the *complex relationship between representation and reality.*

communication intention

What can be unravelled and criticised in media representations is the *motive or intention of the communicator.* Is there, through the use of stereotypes, a deliberate motive to discredit a certain group, person, organisation or topic?

What, for example, is the motive of the author (and the publisher) in an article published in the *Mail & Guardian* newspaper (20–25 April 2001) in which the author generalised stereotypes about Afrikaners who attended the Klein Karoo arts festival in Oudtshoorn:

> *"They [festival attenders – PJF] fled with their children when I, with demonstrative verbosity, used the Cape lingua franca to the extreme by telling them that they were naaiers (fuckers), fokken dom konte (fucking stupid cunts), varkvretende (pig-eating) honkies and a bunch of deluded idiots for thinking that Brother Jesus even took the time to listen to meat-eating beasts who cared more for their pit bull terriers than they did for their fellow black humans...*
>
> *Thick-skinned, cellulite-ridden and varicose-veined tannies would routinely mutter their 'Sies! Sies!', only for me to berate them for not saying 'Sies' when they and their husbands perpetrated the apartheid wars against the nation. Icy glares from double-thighed, double-chinned and double-stomached males were met with sheer arrogance and a fearlessness that scared the carcasses in their overfed bellies as I would scream, for all to hear, that there they were again, the volk, the fokken volk, eating, drinking and talking kak (shit) as only they could".* (Zebulon Dread 2001:5.)

The author is falling back on stereotypes (amongst certain groups) of Afrikaners as being fat, dull and racist. He expresses himself in a mode that can be interpreted as hate speech and bad taste. In this case, one can argue that there is a deliberate motive to belittle and humiliate Afrikaners. Why did the *Mail & Guardian* decide to cover the Oudtshoorn national arts festival by means of what can be seen to be a derogatory article? What can one deduce from this about the *Mail & Guardian*'s attitude towards the group of people involved, the kind of cultural activity in which they engaged and whether they are of the opinion that such a report (review)

The Effects of Mass Communication

can contribute to better group relations and understanding in a multicultural society?

However, again, we should contextualise such criticism. It may be the perception of a member of the Afrikaans-speaking cultural group that the article is derogative whilst other people, even within the Afrikaans-speaking group, may not agree with such an argument. This brings is to the complex nature of *perception* itself. Art historian Ernest Gombrich (1977) made the argument that in perception:

- there is no such thing as an innocent eye (in other words, perception is seldom objective);
- the ways in which we perceive something involves intricate mechanisms of expectation, selection, and decoding (in other words, how we want and have been taught and conditioned to see things)
- we perceive things (people, reality, topics, groups) according to a definite, culturally structured mental set.

| perception

5.4.5 Changing stereotypes

From the above discussions it is clear that stereotypes and the acts of stereotyping are complex. One can even argue that it is part of human nature. The only way in which we can change our stereotyped views of groups and people is to be

- critical of our own views;
- sensitive towards the feelings of others;
- aware of the possible harm our views and perceptions can cause for others.

| sensitivity

When it comes to the media's representations of groups, organisations, people and topics, the same applies. The media and each journalist, programme maker, advertiser – in short, every media worker – should be

- critical of his/her own views and interpretations;
- sensitive towards the feelings of others;
- aware of the possible harm his/her views, perceptions and interpretations can cause for others.

On a more concrete level the following measures can be employed by media organisations:

Employment policy. A mix of staff can counterbalance stereotyped interpretations, representations and subjective and one-sided news and programme values, policies and practices.

| media measures

Policies and quotas can be introduced to reflect *planned balanced representations*: for example, policy could direct the inclusion of different races in television programming, or as is already the case in some countries, the inclusion of people (or characters) of different sexual orientation in television programming.

Both the employees of a media organisation as well as the public must have the *right of reply* and to object to what they perceive as stereotyped representations or as derogatory. Such objections must be investigated and the outcomes thereof published and/or broadcast.

Media organisations should be encouraged to formulate *codes of conduct* with the purpose of guiding their representations.

5.5 A CAUTIONARY NOTE ABOUT EFFECT THEORIES AND RESEARCH

From the above overview of theories it is clear that the media may have some influence on our thinking and in some instances on our behaviour. We end this chapter with a brief note about the complexity of effect research and criticism against the effects paradigm.

methodological questions

From a methodological point of view, effects research is difficult to undertake and must usually be done over a long period of time. Research is conducted mainly by means of surveys (questionnaires), interviews and experimental methods. However, it must be kept in mind that human beings (including their media experiences) – are not easily quantifiable or measurable by only quantitative and experimental methods. So far these methods have had difficulties conclusively establishing a direct causal relation between media and behaviour such as voting patterns.

contextualisation

Findings and conclusions must be contextualised. The effects the media may have in the USA are not necessarily the same in South Africa where different contexts, circumstances and patterns of media use and exposure prevail. In a developing country such as South Africa, the majority of people have far less exposure to media compared to people living in developed countries with higher levels of literacy, more media and greater spending power.

limited assumptions

Most effects studies are in fact based on certain limited assumptions such as: the media user is helplessly exposed to and at the mercy of the media. In other words, the media user is caught up in a stimulus-

The Effects of Mass Communication

response relationship with the media. Such an assumption is based on two behaviourist theories: catharsis and mimesis. *Catharsis theory* postulates that the portrayal of violence by the media, for example, can result in a release of aggression in the viewer, thus acting as a safety valve for such negative emotions. The key postulate of the *mimesis theory* is that the portrayal of violence, for example, causes media users to imitate violent behaviour in real life and to regard it as sanctioning their own aggressive conduct. The same applies to the imitation of other emotions, behavioural patterns or values and morals portrayed by the media. Despite extensive research, neither of these theories has been conclusively proved or refuted on scientific grounds. Finally, it must always be kept in mind that media users (including children with the necessary guidance) are not helpless victims of the media. Apart from their free choice to expose them to media as they wish, their personal values act as a buffer against media effects. Several variables are thus at play, which make it difficult to ascribe specific behaviour and thinking to the media.

It is therefore difficult to argue that a specific film or television programme can be responsible for a specific action, way of thinking or behaviour. It remains difficult even to argue that exposure to specific kinds of media content such as crime movies and television programmes over a longer period of time is responsible for a specific act or behaviour, violence, or a specific way of thinking and behaviour. In the same way it is difficult to argue that a specific newspaper's political reporting is responsible for a person's political thinking and (voting) behaviour.

Gauntlett's criticism in the late 1990s of the effects paradigm caused quite a stir. It is still often raised in debates about media effects research. Gauntlett (1998) lists ten points of criticism:

| Gauntlett's criticism

1. The effects model tackles social problems backwards: he argues that we shouldn't start with an analysis of the media's portrayal of social problems such as crime, violence and pornography, and then try to deduct from such analysis what the effects of the media's portrayal could be on people. Rather, one should start with an analysis of the social problem.
2. The effects model treats children as inadequate: he concludes that cognisance should also be taken of research which seeks to establish what children can and do understand about and from the mass media. Such research suggests that some children can talk intelligently and indeed cynically about mass media and that children as young

as seven can make thoughtful, critical and "media literate" video productions themselves (Buckingham 1996).

3   Assumptions within the effects model are characterised by barely concealed conservative ideology. For example, the condemnation of generalised screen "violence" by conservative critics can often be traced to (political/ideological) concerns such as "disrespect for authority" and "anti-patriotic sentiments".

4   The effects model inadequately defines its own objects of study. Definitions of concepts frequently used in effect studies, such as "anti-social", are often value judgements based on conservative ideology. Furthermore, how and who defines concepts and categories of analysis such as "verbal aggression" and "act of violence"?

5   The effects model is often based on artificial studies: research conducted in a laboratory test means viewers may be decontextualised from their natural media use, circumstances and environment.

6   The effects model is often based on studies with misapplied methodology. Wrong or inappropriate research techniques are used.

7   The effects model is selective in its criticisms of media depictions of violence: why just focus on violence as portrayed in fictitious programmes such as police dramas and not on violence as portrayed in news broadcasts? Why is the same kind of "anti-social" acts portrayed in news not seen in the same negative light as the acts in fictitious media content?

8   The effects model assumes superiority to the masses. Those who conduct the research almost never say that they (or their close relations) have been affected in the ways that they propose the media affects people. Are researchers superior to ordinary media users?

9   The effects model makes no attempt to understand meanings of the media. Effects research often assumes that the medium holds a singular message which will be carried unproblematically to audiences. It ignores the polysemic nature of media content and the findings of reception theory – how people "read" and interpret media messages in different ways.

10 The effects model is not grounded in theory: the effects model is substantiated with no theoretical reasoning beyond the bald assertions that particular kinds of effects *will* be produced by the media. The basic question of *why* the media should induce people to imitate its content has never been adequately tackled.

The Effects of Mass Communication

5.6 SUMMARY

In this chapter we discussed the different kinds of potential media effects and distinguished between behavioural, manifest and latent, intended and unintended and time-scale effects. Under short-term theories we distinguished between the hypodermic needle, the two-step-flow and the uses and gratifications theory. Under long-term theories we distinguished between accumulation, diffusion of innovation, modelling, social expectation, meaning construction, stereotyping, agenda setting, framing and the spiral of silence. We also discussed the possible origins of stereotyping in detail. We concluded with some warnings about the complexity of media effects and criticism of the effects model. We emphasised that users are not helpless victims of the media.

LEARNING ACTIVITIES

- Analyse a newspaper, radio news bulletin, television evening news show and an Internet news website on the basis of effect research.
- Distinguish between behavioural, manifest and latent, intended or unintended (planned or unplanned) and time-scale effects. Give your own examples of these different kinds of potential effects.
- Design two questionnaires for two short-term theories you have selected. Conduct interviews with five respondents (friends, colleagues, family) in which you try to test the assumptions of the two short-term theories. Compare their responses. For example, have any of your respondents confirmed that in their opinion, they acted on the basis of a media message (hypodermic needle theory) and if so, how and why? Or test whether your respondents discuss media content (a soap-opera or news) with others, and if so how such discussions contribute to their understanding of media content (two-step-flow theory). Or use your questionnaire based on the assumptions of the uses and gratification theory, for example, the respondents' use of the Internet: why and how do they use the Internet and which gratifications do they get from it?
- Use two long-term theories to design two questionnaires. Conduct interviews with five respondents (friends, colleagues, family) in which you test the assumptions of the two long-term effect theories. Compare their responses. For example, ask your respondents if they can remember how they became aware of the cellphone as a new technological phenomenon and how they adopted or rejected the cellphone as a means of communication

Media Studies: Volume 1

(diffusion of information theory). Or, interview your respondents on whether they can recall how they arrived at the meaning of a concept such as the "global warming" (meaning construction theory).
- Collect five examples of stereotyping in the media. Motivate the reasons for stereotyping against the background of the main arguments for the origins of stereotyping. How could this stereotyping be altered?
- Write an essay of two pages in which you formulate your own views about media effects.

FURTHER READING

De Fleur, M.L. & Dennis, E.E. 1994. 5th edition. *Understanding mass communication. A liberal arts perspective.* Boston, Massachusetts: Houghton Mifflin.

Grossberg, L., Wartella, E. & Whitney, D.C. 2006. *Mediamaking. Mass media in a popular culture.* 2nd edition. Thousand Oaks, California: Sage.

Hiebert, R.E. 1999. *Impact of mass media. Current issues.* 4th edition. New York: Longman.

McQuail, D. 2005. *McQuail's mass communication theory.* 5th edition. London: Sage.

Potter, W.J. 2001. *Media literacy.* 2nd edition. Thousand Oaks, CA: Sage.

Potter, W.J. 2004. *Theory of media literacy. A cognitive approach.* Thousand Oaks, CA: Sage.

Ruddock, A. 2000. *Understanding Audiences: Theory and method.* Thousand Oaks, CA: Sage.

Strassburger, V.C. & Wilson, B.J. 2002. *Children, adolescents & the media.* Thousand Oaks, CA: Sage.

chapter six

Media Culture

Magriet Pitout

> **LEARNING OUTCOMES**
>
> At the end of this chapter you should be able to explain the following:
> - the relationships between media and culture;
> - the history of academic study of popular culture;
> - cultural studies and its assumptions;
> - different definitions of culture, ideology, hegemony, reading positions, polysemy and intertextuality;
> - different forms of social and cultural expression as manifestation of culture.

MEDIA AND CULTURE

THIS CHAPTER DEALS with the omnipotent presence of the media, our dominant form of public communication and one of the most important vehicles of popular culture. We regard the media as symbolic forms of expression that are typical of late twentieth and early twenty-first century's popular culture. To investigate the relationship between media and culture, we distinguish between how we use media as part of our cultural practices and how media have their own culture consisting of words, images, uses and practices. In addition, we examine different forms of social and cultural expression such as sport, religion, architecture and the built-environment as manifestations of culture.

6.1 INTRODUCTION

In the previous chapters and in following chapters of the book, we discuss the media as our dominant forms of public communication, as symbolic forms of expression and as typifying of late twentieth and early twenty-first century's popular culture. With the emphasis on dominant forms of public communication, we tend to think of communication as taking place only through verbal, non-verbal and mass communication. Communication, though, takes on many forms of expression, from graffiti on the walls of railway stations and toilets to the grand façades of monuments and museums; from the noisy nature of popular music to the fickle nature of fads and fashions, and so on. We continuously use these symbolic forms of expression to express our culture – our beliefs, values, common experiences and our modes of existence. Put simply, this means that we live in and through communication. Communication is the medium through which our existence and our experiences (our daily lives), that is, our culture, finds its expression (Lemon 2001:355).

The relationship between media and culture can be interpreted in two ways:
- the media as culture;
- the media as a reflection and portrayal of culture.

In the first section of this chapter, we introduce you to the concept of media as culture which includes a discussion of high, mass, and popular culture. We then discuss the importance of the cultural studies approach for studying popular culture and the media. This is followed by a discussion of concepts without which cultural studies cannot be fully understood, namely ideology, hegemony, decoding and encoding, polysemy and intertextuality. These are the conceptual building blocks of

Media Culture

cultural studies. We use them to analyse and explain symbolic forms of popular culture. The second part of this chapter consists of a discussion of different forms of culture – religion, architecture and the built environment – as examples of the manifestation of culture.

When studying a form of popular culture, the critical question should always be: what does it communicate to us implicitly or explicitly? We discuss the indivisible link between culture and communication in the next section.

SECTION 1

6.2 CULTURE AND COMMUNICATION

One of the most important advances in human existence in the last two centuries has been the multiplying means and forms of communication such as film, television, computer technology, print media, the Internet and interactive video. These means and forms of communication have drastically altered our traditional frames of reference, values, experiences, belief structures and social relations. Today we live in a world in which constant circulation of social and cultural forms play a fundamental and increasingly important role in the definition and redefinition of our cultures. Each day we are bombarded with thousands of visual, written and verbal images (the culture of media). We receive and interpret these images as texts, which become part of our collective consciousness, our common experience, ultimately contributing to the evolution and development of our cultures (Lemon 2001; Thompson 1990).

The academic and scientific discipline of communication is directed at the study of all social behaviour as meaningful actions, concerned with all cultural forms of expression as sign systems of communication. The production of culture is organised into visual, verbal, nonverbal and/or sensory codes. These codes then find expression in the form of texts (discourses) such as television programmes, films, newspaper articles, poems, music lyrics and so on (Lemon 2001). We each interpret these texts or discourses differently because as individuals we are unique due to variables such as race, language, age, social class, gender, attitudes and values.

> cultural forms of expression

> texts as discourses

South Africa is a good example of a complex multicultural and multilingual society, isiZulu, isiXhosa, seSotho and Afrikaans speakers for example,

represent the four main language groups in the country; then there are the descendants of Indian indentured labourers and small shop-keepers, who can be further divided along linguistic, class and religious divides, so-called Coloureds, who may promote or reject the use of that term and who may be the descendants of Muslim Malaysian aristocracy or the offspring of so-called mixed-race marriages, English-speaking descendants of British settlers. Cultural groups have diverse forms of communication (or sign systems) to express their different cultures. This makes our cultural context particularly complex and provides fertile ground for the studying of our various forms of social and cultural expression: industrial theatre, township jive, boeremusiek and traditional folk songs, traditional art and crafts, flea markets, amongst others (Lemon 2001:356). These are all forms of social and cultural expression which reflect and affect our cultural practices.

In order to get a better understanding of the academic interest in popular culture, in the next section we briefly look at the historical development of theoretical perspectives regarding the debate between high, popular and mass culture.

6.3 HIGH, POPULAR AND MASS CULTURE: THEORETICAL PERSPECTIVES

organic folk culture

Since the inception of communication studies, popular culture has been under attack, especially from pessimistic and élitist academic circles. The pessimistic tradition defines popular culture in terms of new forms of mass entertainment (print media, radio, television, films and so on) generated by capitalist institutions. These new forms have been set against popular organic folk culture where the audience and artist work so closely together that we cannot clearly distinguish between them. That is, during the Middle Ages in Europe, meaning had been created democratically by the masses during folk festivals and theatre productions on the market square. According to the pessimistic culture tradition, this form of folk culture is more authentic than culture that has been mediated by the mass media.

aesthetic barren culture

This negative view of popular culture is also reflected in the cultural and civilisation tradition, which has been concerned with the development of popular culture at the expense of more organic folk cultures. The main cause for this decline was the spreading of industrialisation during the late 19th and 20th centuries. Turner (2000:39) refers to British poet

Media Culture

and cultural critic Matthew Arnold (1822–1888) who wrote *Culture and Anarchy*, published in 1869. Arnold warned against this "philistine culture" that threatened literacy and democracy. Industrialisation had blurred the division between the middle class (the *bourgeoisie*) and the working class: because the working class in organic societies never developed criteria for good taste and therefore did not know how to appreciate works of art. This, according to Arnold (Turner 2000:39), resulted in an aesthetically barren culture, a culture which failed to equip citizens for their social and political responsibilities.

The mass culture theory also echoes a negative view of mass/popular culture. According to this theory, "High Art" such as classical music is not aimed at mass consumption and commercial gain because it belongs in opera houses destined for the élite. However, since the introduction of mass media, the unique quality of classical music has become commonplace because the main aim of mass media is to reproduce as many as possible goods with the view of capital gain. And by bringing "Bach to the kitchen" the unique qualities of classical music, and by implication all high works of art, may have been destroyed. Furthermore, mass culture theory assumes that the reproduction of products of high culture are sold to passive audiences who cannot think for themselves and are therefore prone to manipulation by the mass media. The media, in this view, prevent audiences from acquiring the ability to distinguish between high and mass culture and to develop criteria for good taste (Kipnis 1986).

Apart from being unashamedly élitist, the mass culture theories do not clearly distinguish between mass, popular and high culture. How do we classify post-war jazz and popular avant-garde music? (Kipnis 1986:55). A rigid distinction between high, popular and mass culture does not make provision for changes taking place over time. What is regarded as popular (or mass culture) by one generation may be regarded as high culture by the next. For instance, to make ends meet, Wolfgang Amadeus Mozart (1756–1791) composed some of his classic works for "ordinary" people where they were played and enjoyed on market days and in gambling houses in Europe. Today these compositions are often regarded as high culture belonging in concert halls from Japan to Rio de Janeiro.

To conclude this section: according to Turner (2000:40–41), the mass culture theories were extremely patronising and remote. It was a discourse

of the cultured about those without culture (Bennett 1981:5). Kellner (a) agrees that the dichotomy between high culture and low culture is problematic and suggests that this dichotomy should be replaced with a more unified model that takes culture as a spectrum and applies similar critical methods to all cultural artefacts ranging from modernist literature to soap operas, from opera to popular music.

In the next section we see how the cultural studies tradition turned around élitist, negative mass cultural theories with their views that all products of popular culture are worthy objects of academic investigation. Furthermore, this tradition regards media users actively interpreting media messages against the background of their social and cultural circumstances.

6.4 CULTURAL STUDIES

Cultural studies is the title for an important set of theories and practices within the humanities and social sciences. Its international journal *Cultural Studies* clearly states that this field is dedicated to the study of cultural processes, especially that of popular culture (Turner 2001:1). The first studies regarding popular culture were undertaken by the Centre for Contemporary Cultural Studies in Birmingham in the United Kingdom and have since sometimes been called "British cultural studies". However, Turner (2001:3) points out that the "Brits do not own cultural studies" because this tradition has also been influenced to a great extent by European structuralists (Claude Lévi-Strauss, Ferdinand de Saussure, Jacques Lacan, Roland Barthes, Michel Foucault); European Marxism (Louis Althusser, Antonio Gramsci); the sociology of Pierre Bourdieu in France and the anthropological tradition as practised by James Carey and Clifford Geertz in the United States of America (USA).

It was, however, the work of pioneers such as Raymond Williams (one of Britain's greatest post-war cultural historians), Edward Palmer Thompson (a well-known English historian), Richard Hoggart (one of the founders of the Centre for Contemporary Cultural Studies) and his colleague, sociologist Stuart Hall, who established the academic and intellectual study of popular culture, from the mass media to dance crazes to sport. Cultural studies investigate how all kinds of cultural practices construct our everyday lives and how the media (as carriers of culture) mould their subjects. Cultural studies, in contrast with élitist assumptions, have set out to examine the everyday and the ordinary; those aspects of our lives that

Media Culture

so powerfully and unquestionably influence our existence and that are being taken for granted. Cultural processes that form us as individuals, as citizens, as members of a particular race construct, class or gender have become topics of central concern for cultural studies (Turner 2001:2, 3).

6.4.1 Theoretical assumptions of cultural studies

Cultural studies as a theoretical approach, is not based on a single, monolithic approach but is composed of several theories such as Marxism (ideology), semiotics, ethnography, feminism and psychoanalysis. It is therefore multi-theoretical and interdisciplinary.

This approach acknowledges the power of ideology and the hegemonic forces of the ruling class (the economic base). However, cultural studies also sees audiences as active participants in the communication process, with the ability to create their own meanings within, and often against, the dominant ideology of powerful ruling classes and institutions.

ideology hegemonic forces

Ideological critique is a central concern because this approach perceives culture as a mode of ideological reproduction and hegemony, in which cultural forms help to shape the modes of thought and behaviour that induce individuals to adapt to the social conditions of capitalist's societies (Kellner b).

hegemonic reproduction

Society does not consist of a homogeneous group of people that all share the same unifying ideology. On the contrary, cultural studies assumes a dynamic society consisting of different conflicting ideologies. For example, in South Africa there are different groups of people with different ideologies from right-wing politics of the all-white residents of remote Orania to official opposition parties to the ruling party, the African National Congress (ANC), to their partner, the South African Communist Party (SACP). The ideology of religion is also a case in point: in South Africa we find different religious ideologies such as Christianity, Judaism, Islam and the Forefather Spirits (sometimes known as ancestor worship).

conflicting ideologies

The studying of marginal discourses – products of popular culture such as music, sport, the built-environment and fashion – are central concerns of the cultural studies approach. Marginal discourses were traditionally not regarded as legitimate objects of academic and scientific studies. Cultural studies tries to explain how these discourses contribute to the integration and subordination of potentially deviant and oppositional

marginal discourses

elements in society. In other words, this approach studies the social construction (formation) of meaning by institutions and members of society and their distribution in industrial, heterogeneous societies. The distribution of cultural meaning takes place by means of the media and other artefacts.

social, historical, cultural and economic contexts

Cultural studies also assumes that the creation and construction of meaning is indivisibly linked to social structure (society, communities, institutions) and should therefore take into consideration the social, historical, cultural and economic contexts.

sexual divisions

racial structuring

Cultural studies assumes that cultural processes are intimately connected with the way social relations are formed within the framework of sexual divisions and racial structuring (racism, sexism and class divisions, for example). Cultural studies regards culture as inextricably related to the uses and abuses of power (hegemony) by those who control institutions such as media conglomerates, the state and schools (Fourie 2001:379).

Let us critically discuss different definitions of culture and central concepts associated with cultural studies: ideology, hegemony, decoding and encoding, polysemy and intertextuality. These concepts are the building blocks of the cultural studies approach and we may use them to analyse and explain symbolic forms of popular culture. These concepts contribute to the central issue of this chapter, namely the importance of studying media as culture and media culture.

6.5 CONCEPTUAL DEFINITIONS

6.5.1 What is culture?

There are many divergent definitions of culture. This is contested terrain. Popular definitions define culture broadly as everything that occurs in a society, that is, all the beliefs, norms, values, ideas and practices as well as material artefacts and instruments handed down from one generation to another (Lemon 2001). Thompson (1990:129) however, maintains that definitions like these are inadequate because they are merely descriptive, an attempt to quantify culture. Culture is too complex to be described as fixed, unchanging aspects of the complexity of human existence. Culture is not static or homogenous because it changes continuously as the history, economics, politics, social beliefs, values of groups and individuals change. Against this background, Geertz (1972:44) offers an appropriate definition:

Media Culture

"Culture is the pattern of meanings embodied in symbolic forms, including actions, utterances and meaningful objects of various kinds, by virtue of which individuals communicate with one another and share their experiences, conceptions and beliefs."

This definition clearly indicates a link between culture and communication. Williams (1981:13) says within this context, culture may be regarded as:

"a whole way of life ... and as a signifying system through which meaning is constructed."

We can further expand this definition by adding that culture is "historically transmitted patterns of meanings embodied in symbols" (Geertz 1973:44) and may be seen as texts, discourses, and artefacts which may be interpreted differently by different people (Thompson 1990:132). Within this context, culture and its manifestation in all forms of social and cultural expression (cultural products) are language systems (discourses) because they communicate something to us about our common culture.

When attempting to define culture, we should keep in mind that culture is never neutral and objective. We have indicated that all forms of social and cultural expression (architecture, sport, music, religion) are discourses. These discourses are produced in struggles between different people and different groups. For example, we find struggles between social classes, ethnic, racial and gender groups that emerge from conflicting ideological positions. Meanings are produced by individuals or groups who have access to sources and who are endowed with varying degrees of power and authority. Forms of social and cultural expression circulate among individual and group members who receive and interpret the different cultural forms against particular social, cultural, economical and political circumstances, using their frames of reference to make sense of (interpret) the phenomena concerned.

| cultural expression
| discourses

Fiske (1987:369) maintains that social and cultural forms deal with issues of power. Culture may therefore be defined as "a struggle for meanings ..." Against this background we discuss the notion of ideology, an important concept without which culture and cultural studies cannot be understood.

| struggle for meanings

6.5.2 Ideology

In this section we briefly discuss the ideological views of Karl Marx and Louis Althusser because of their importance for the cultural studies approach. (Study chapter 7 for a detailed discussion of the different theories of ideology.)

Karl Marx

ideology

false consciousness

We emphasise again that ideology is one of the most important concepts in cultural studies. In terms of classical Marxism conceptualisation of ideology, it means that a minority, the ruling class, maintains its position of power through their monopoly over capitalist and cultural institutions that produce ideology (Fourie 2001:245). These institutions refer to the state, churches or other religious bodies, educational institutions such as universities and above all the mass media are especially powerful tools to influence people and brainwash them to think in certain ways; that is, to create a false consciousness in duped masses who unwittingly participate in their own oppression (White 1987:137). Those who control the means of production – the mass media – essentially control culture, and therefore also the mindsets of media users.

false consciousness

In broad terms, ideology from the perspective of a Marxist theory can be negatively defined as an allusion or false consciousness. According to this theory, the media and other forms of expression serve as carriers of the dominant ideology. These media serve the interest of the ruling class, a minority grouping of intellectual élites. Passive mass audiences uncritically accept the dominant underlying ideological meanings of mass media. In other words they (the masses) do not have the ability to recognise that the belief and value systems being propagated do not serve their true interest, that these messages reflect the vested interest of the ruling class (Geus 1981:41; Lemon 2004:2369). According to this view, because the mass does not have the ability to think for themselves, they develop false consciousness as a result of the one-sided dominant ideological messages being forced unto cultural "dupes".

There are, however, at least two major problems with the ideological views of classical Marxism: firstly, the assumption of a false consciousness implies that true consciousness exists as an empirical, objective truth. False consciousness, furthermore, fails to explain how or why people readily adopt ideas different from their own. As Fiske (1987:256) points out, consciousness is never the product of reality but rather of

Media Culture

culture, society and history. Secondly, Marxist theory ignores the social and historical contexts within which social practices and institutions operate.

Louis Althusser

French philosopher Louis Althusser rejected the ideological assumption of Marx that ideology is always determined by economic and material conditions. Althusser identified important institutions that socialise and prepare people to accept society as it is. These institutions are the family, school, church, politics, language and the mass media, all of which Althusser called Ideological State Apparatuses (ISAs). These institutions constitute – by means of ideology – our sense of ourselves, our identity and our relationships with others in society. One of the most important ideological processes identified by Althusser is interpellation. In general terms interpellation means that ideology defines and determine our experiences, our identity and our place in society as a whole. When we accept the ideas, values and norms of powerful, dominant institutions, we are contributing towards the production of the dominant ideology and culture. For this chapter we emphasise the role of the media as cultural agents in distributing the dominant ideology. (Study the detailed discussion of Althusser's ideas in chapter 7.)

| Ideological State Apparatuses |

| interpellation |

Closely related to the Althusser's views of ideology is hegemony, a concept developed by Italian revolutionary Antonio Gramsci.

6.5.3 Hegemony

The Italian Antonio Gramsci (1891–1941) developed the concept of hegemony because he was concerned with the deterministic economic views of Marxism (Lemon 2001). Gramsci used hegemony to explain the power of a dominant, ruling group who continuously tries to persuade subordinate groups to accept its moral, political and cultural values (ideology). Hegemony, however, is readjusted and re-negotiated constantly and can never be taken for granted because people in a society do not always think the same way and may oppose the dominant ideology. Their resistance may take the form of active struggle, such as through riots or demonstrations, or it can be latent and symbolic, such as using a pattern of behaviour or a particular style of dressing (Stillo, Sa). In South Africa, for example, some of the people who support the fight against crime may wear black ribbons as symbolic tokens of their support, while

| hegemony |

followers of the Zionist church wear the church's distinctive coloured ribbon and medallion on their clothing and activists from the Treatment Action Campaign wear a curved red ribbon to signify their efforts to combat HIV/AIDS.

Strinati (1995: 168–169) says the following about popular culture and the media:

> "Pop culture and the mass media are subject to the production, reproduction and transformation of hegemony through the institution of civil society which cover the areas of cultural production and consumption. Hegemony operates culturally and ideologically through the institutions of civil society which characterises mature liberal-democratic, capitalist societies. These institutions include education, the family, the church, the mass media, popular culture, etc."

| battleground |
| negotiate |

For Gramsci, popular culture is the battleground upon which dominant views secure hegemony. However, the idea of hegemony is not achieved by dominating the world view of the mass. On the contrary, hegemony suggests that to achieve cultural leadership the dominant group has to negotiate with and persuade those groups who belong to different classes and have different value systems (Turner 2000:195). We emphasise again that the media are the instruments to express the dominant ideology as an integral part of the cultural environment. To summarise, the characteristics of hegemony are as follows:

- Hegemony is difficult to detect because on the surface it often appears as natural, normal and commonsense; that is, the way popular beliefs are produced and distributed.
- Hegemony keeps the dominant groups on their toes because there are always groups in society that question, negotiate, oppose or resist it, as we indicate in our discussion of music and Hall's theoretical model of preferred reading below.
- Hegemony is a dynamic process which changes constantly because it has to continuously be reworked, defined, and recreated (remember, hegemony is constantly under threat).
- Hegemony works through ideology and serves therefore also as a means of ideological domination and control.
- Hegemonic ideology as the total beliefs system of a society is produced and distributed through social institutions like the school, family, mass media and all forms of social and cultural expression.

Media Culture

- The media are an instrument to express dominant ideology as an integral part of the cultural environment (Lemon 2001; Kellner (b)).

We can see that hegemony plays a central role in cultural studies. Hegemony also served as an important source of inspiration for Hall's theoretical model of preferred reading, which tries to explain the conflict of interests and the positions that readers may occupy regarding the dominant ideology in messages. The development of this model was a great breakthrough from previous formalist views which regarded the message as the only source of meaning. With Hall's theoretical model, the audience's active involvement with media messages has been acknowledged and therefore audience research became an integral part of the research agenda of cultural studies. preferred reading

6.5.4 Hall's theoretical model of preferred reading

Hall (1980), one of the pioneers of the British cultural studies approach, developed a theoretical model of preferred reading to explain the different positions readers (viewers) take when using and interpreting media messages (such as television programmes). According to Hall's theory, the focus should be on the communication process as a whole, from the moment of producing a programme to the moment of audience exposure to that message and the interpretation thereof (Hall 1980). When we relate Hall's theory to culture, we see that he regards culture as a constant site of struggle between those with and those without power. Although major social practices and forms of cultural expression may offer a variety of meanings, their structure generally prefers a set of meanings that works to maintain the dominant ideology, for example, the portrayal of romantic relations between heterosexual partners in television programmes and films should result in marriage and the couple should live happily ever after. Such a dominant ideology ignores homosexual relationships or couples who prefer to live together outside the boundaries of a conventional marriage, the significant number of battered spouses or the statistic that roughly half of all South African marriages end in divorce. What is significant in Hall's theory is that these meanings – the dominant ideology – can be preferred but not imposed on media users.

preferred reading

reading positions

culture a site for struggle

Hall's theory consists of three possible positions which readers (audiences) can occupy in relation to the dominant ideology (the meaning) inscribed in the text: the dominant, the negotiated and the oppositional (Hall 1980; McQueen 1998).

dominant reading

A dominant reading or interpretation is produced when viewers accept the referential meaning (also known as the dominant ideology) produced by the text. Accordingly viewers whose social situation, particularly their class, aligns them comfortably with the dominant ideology, would accept its preferred meaning(s). Or as McQueen (1998) puts it, viewers accept the assumptions of the encoder, the person who composes the message. For example, conservative and fundamentalist Christians will reject views that question the death and resurrection of Jesus Christ in American movies such as *The Passion of the Christ* (Case study 6.1) or *The Da Vinci Code* (Case study 6.2).

negotiated reading

A negotiated reading is produced by viewers who agree to an extent with the dominant messages (ideology) but reserve the right to modify their views in accordance with the needs of their social situation. They can negotiate between accepting and rejecting the preferred meaning offered by the text. For example, from this position media users may accept the meanings offered by many advertisements about the respective roles of gender in general, but they intentionally adapt them to fit their personalities and values, adjusting or negotiating the preferred meanings of these messages.

oppositional reading

Oppositional viewers reject the dominant ideological meaning encoded in the text. Readers in this position defy or work against the dominant ideology. Although they understand both the literal and connotative meanings of the text, they intentionally decode or deconstruct it in a contrary or subversive manner. Because texts are polysemic, they are open to numerous interpretations and readings, and a correlation does not necessarily exist between the encoding and the decoding of the message (Hall 1980:130). For example, people from other religions, or atheists and agnostics, may interpret the religious views of Christianity completely different than many Christians do.

ideological closure

The most valuable contributions of Hall's theory are: it explains that a text is not a complete closed ideological discourse but that it allows for different interpretations; and it shifts the attention away from the text towards media users who now become the "site" for the struggle of meaning, where meanings are attributed or ascribed.

Media Culture

However, Hall's model is not without criticism. For instance Morley (1980) contends that Hall's three categories are too simplistic and that a wide range of readings resists simple categorisation. In reality, there are few purely dominant or purely oppositional readings (Fiske 1987:64). People engage in a continuous process of negotiation to take meaning from the text and its potential meanings. According to Morley (1980:163–173) the balance of power lies with the media user. Morley regards the text as a social discourse. As media users our experience is similarly made up of a number of discourses or texts (beliefs, ideas, attitudes or experiences) through which we make sense of our reality. Reading a text is defined as the moment when the discourses of the recipient meet the discourses of the text. Reading or interpretation become a constant process of negotiation between the meanings inscribed in the text and meanings ascribed to it by the recipients.

process of negotiation

Within this context, texts are open to many potential meanings (that is, they are polysemic) which will be read according to the discourses (knowledge, prejudices, experience, attitudes and/or political/religious views) of audience members.

potential meanings

6.5.5 Polysemy

According to John Fiske, the concept polysemy was coined in the early 1970s by British cultural studies researchers, starting with Richard Hoggart who postulates that audiences of popular culture have the capability to make subversive interpretations that were not intended by the producers of culture. Such thinking originated from French academic Roland Barthes' dramatic proclamation in 1967 of the "death of the author", by which he meant that readers of a text (viewers of film and television) create their own meanings regardless of the intentions of the author (or producer or communicator). Another French academic, Jacques Derrida, later drew attention to meanings being as much about what is absent as about what is depicted.

subversive interpretation

polysemy

The possibility of alternative interpretations has been termed polysemy. A good example is the youth, who most of the time question dominant ideologies and values. The youth are therefore not cultural "dupes" but actively engage with the media to give aberrant decodings of messages which are loaded with dominant ideologies. Research in Britain and the US has found that many people under 30 (and a significant minority of older people) deconstruct or question the intended ideological

alternative interpretations

messages we find in advertising, newspapers and television and radio news programmes, possibly because of the widespread cynicism this age group has for gatekeepers of news and, predictably enough, the political activities surrounding much of this news.

textual devices

Textual devices such as metaphor, humour, irony as rhetorical device, contradiction, exaggeration, myth, fantasy and parody help to create texts open to polysemic (multiple) meanings. These devices work against ideological closure of texts and allow for oppositional or subversive readings. For example, some newspaper cartoons during 2006 used parody to ridicule former deputy president Jacob Zuma after he confirmed that he had unprotected sex with an HIV positive young family friend who later unsuccessfully charged him with rape. Just imagine how his behaviour has been interpreted by different political groups in South Africa. Open texts thus allow for a multiplicity of voices and meanings (or discourses) often in conflict with one another. In this way texts are essentially intertextual as we explain in the next section.

6.5.6 Intertextuality

intertextuality

The idea of intertextually proposes that a text is read in relation to other, similar texts. Intertextuality suggests an interdependence between texts, the continual deferring of meaning through and between texts. Intertextuality occurs frequently in popular media such as television programmes, films, novels and interactive video games. In these cases, intertextuality provides depth to the portrayed fictional reality. For example, American comic book heroes such as Superman, Spiderman, and Batman share certain common genre characteristics, like the strong, macho protagonist or hero, with supernatural powers, who always beats the villain. These comic books have been recreated and used in other forms of mass communication such as a television programme (*Smallville*) and films (*Superman Returns*). Thus three different media (comic book, television, film) share the same generic codes of the super-hero action genre. These texts also have other intertextual tie-ins: magazine and newspaper articles, and television talk shows discussing the most recent Superman film. We may find more tie-ins in the form of Superman fan clubs, Internet websites and blogs (web logs, or Internet diaries). Other examples of intertexuality are American animated series distributed and translated around the world, like *Charlie Brown*, *The Simpsons*, and *Garfield*, which share humour as a generic convention.

Media Culture

However, each medium has its own unique signs and codes. For example, film and television use camera movement, camera viewpoint and editing techniques which cannot be used in print media.

In conclusion: the conceptualisation of culture, ideology, hegemony, preferred reading, polysemy and intertextuality help to understand the relationship between media and culture. In Section A our discussion centred mainly on the media as culture. In the next section we discuss social and cultural forms of expression as manifestations of culture.

SECTION 2

6.6 SOCIAL AND CULTURAL FORMS OF EXPRESSION

This section demonstrates that all cultural practices, objects and artefacts (that is, texts) have meaning. Everything cultural communicates, just as culture is created and maintained and perpetuated by means of communication. We illustrate this point with brief discussions of religion, sport, architecture and the built environment, all of which are frequently topics of media coverage.

6.6.1 Religion

Religion is an all pervasive cultural influence in many societies. When we talk about religion we do not talk about Christianity only because there are other faiths.

We first look at a general definition proposed by prolific French sociologist Émile Durkheim (1858–1917), who has been credited for making sociology a science. Durkheim defines religion as: | general definition

> "a unified system of beliefs and practices relative to sacred things, that is to say, things that are set apart and forbidden – beliefs and practices which unite into one single moral community called a Church, to all those who adhere to them" (in Lemon 2001:357).

Religion often finds expression by means of a belief system that consists of specific moral codes of conduct, values, rules and norms. Faith permeates and governs our public and private lives, what we believe about the world we live in, and determines the core of our existence, our being. Lemon (2001:357) reminds us that here we talk about how religious belief is institutionalised, thus acknowledging that there are many | belief system

| rituals

religions (Christianity, Islam, Hinduism, Judaism, traditional African ancestor worship). Any religion is characterised by rituals. Through the repetition of symbolic and religious rituals (like those associated with the arrival of babies, entry into adulthood, cleansing ceremonies, marriage and burials) worshippers are reminded of supernatural powers. They are unified in a common religious belief system which they share with others in the ceremony. Other signs and codes that may be studied especially in different religions are shrines, icons, proverbs, pilgrimages, testimonies, miracles and so on (Lemon 2001:357) and presumably the religious texts themselves, like the Bhagavad Gita, the Koran, the Torah and the Bible.

> **powerful institution**
>
> **socialisation, education, enculturisation**

Historically in much of Europe and during the colonial era, the church was a powerful institution forming the foundation of many societies. It exercised almost absolute control over the maintenance and creation of social and cultural life in many (not all) parts of the world. For most people in pre-industrial European societies, the Catholic church was the largest social institution of which they were a part (Hitchcock 1979:178). Information was controlled by the church who decided what should become public and what should remain private. The church may therefore be regarded as the first mass medium that had almost complete control over information and was therefore the primary agent for socialisation, education and enculturisation. The meaning of life was powerfully conveyed to community members by means of the signs and codes of rituals, moral injunctions, symbols and the customs and laws propagated by the church, who saturated social life (Lemon 2001:357).

> **printing press**

The invention of the printing press – one of the greatest technological inventions of the West – resulted in the emergence of Protestant faith and the concomitant splitting of the medieval church. The printing press produced relatively inexpensive books and other printed forms which destroyed the stronghold the Catholic Church had on the dissemination of information. Access to the Bible was no longer the privilege of the church. Mother tongue versions of the Bible were now within reach of people such as former priest Martin Luther, to invalidate and question the version of truth provided by the Catholic Church on the grounds of infidelity to other sources than the Bible. This dramatically altered the nature of the church and the practice of religion. In many contemporary societies in Europe (although not in the USA or in many countries in Africa) the church as an institution has little or no power and attendance

Media Culture

at traditional churches is declining. In other words, where the medieval church had the monopoly on the distribution of information and control over people's mindsets, in some contemporary societies, the church plays an increasingly less significant role, in part due to the mass media.

Important for our study of religion is also the emergence of the electronic church. Religion is now presented and packaged as an important source of mass mediated entertainment. Religion, as form of popular culture, reflects the emphasis of the mass media on consumerism. The electronic church offers viewers new forms of religious expression and experiences – from breezy Christian talk shows on television and radio to Gospel rock and other religious music genres, religious clubs and CD's offering advice on Christian lifestyle. Religion has become mass marketed, and takes different forms of social and cultural expressions such as T-shirts and car bumper stickers, portraying a whole range of values and beliefs that represents the morality of stable happy families, monogamy or healthy living, to name but a few attributes (Lemon 2001).

electronic church

mass marketed religion

Mass communication media (especially television and film) have begun to transform traditional religious practices, popularising religion as a form of mass entertainment. Perhaps it is not too far-fetched to say that a hegemonic relationship has developed between the mass media and some churches. For instance, religious ceremonies are being illustrated with examples of universal messages to be found in both television programmes and films, for example, *The Passion of the Christ*. This film was slammed by some critics for its brutality and violence. As Hammer and Kellner (ca) say:

mass entertainment

hegemonic relationship

> "The Passion presents a pornography of violence with savage beatings, brutality, and torture as extreme as any in S&M porn films. ... The fact that the violence is being inflicted on a major global religious figure adds to the horror and provides iconography of violence as extreme as any in cinema history... The film has been, somewhat surprisingly in view of its almost unbearable violence, a global success. Helped by all the advanced publicity, it appears that many evangelical and fundamentalist Christian churches organized their congregations to attend together, making the showing of the film a religious event. Many audiences allegedly wept loudly during Jesus' tormenting and found it a deeply moving and disturbing experience."

Media Studies: Volume 1

In spite of the violence, which is a big issue in media studies and in South Africa, many Christian church leaders have encouraged people to go and see Passion to strengthen their faith and to make them realise that Christ died a horrific death on their behalf.

However, films that are seen as a threat to the dogma of Christian faith are condemned in no uncertain terms. For an example, see the reaction to *The Da Vinci Code* (Case study 6.2). Briefly, evangelical Protestant clergy along with Roman Catholic groups have slammed Dan Brown's original mystery novel, published in 2003, and the subsequent movie (2006) because the divinity and resurrection of Jesus were questioned. Clergies were up in arms and warned Christians against pagan ideology, from secret sex orgies and idolatrous rituals to astrology and Tarot cards, from nature worship and symbols of Satan to goddess cultures and the "divine feminine". Therefore this book is filled with pagan indoctrination and propaganda. (Editors, 2006).

In reaction to *The Da Vinci Code*, Christian churches organised conferences, seminars and ceremonies where Brown's novel was discussed and analysed to illustrate its heresy. The reaction of the church and the uproar about *The Da Vinci Code* may be seen as having hegemonic function, an attempt to "claw" people back to the church.

To conclude this section: within the context of religion as a symbolic form of popular culture, we emphasise the study of signs, codes and the ideological-hegemonic functions of religious practice and ritual. Many of the things we do regularly are ritualistic. As far as the relationship goes between the media and religion, it is clear that the media (television, Internet, newspapers) has exposed us to many religious voices. For example, given South Africa's divided history, few Christians would have been aware of the many important rituals of Islam, the Muslim religion, such as the annual *Ramadaan* fast and the subsequent *Eid* feast if the media did not bring it into a shared public sphere. But it is a complex topic. According to Barnes (2006) research has found that the religious left's opposition to the American war with Iraq gets more attention than the religious right's support for the invasion. Barnes (2006) concludes that "the bad-news bias so prevalent in the media today also permeates the coverage of religion ... All the papers studied devote more coverage to religion in the context of bad deeds than they do to the good deeds religions do in their communities". The reason for this may be that most reporters, whether large papers,

Media Culture

television networks or magazines "are secular in the extreme and regard religion with disdain" (Barnes 2006).

6.6.2 Sport

In this section we attempt to understand the relationship between sport, culture and the media, and audience reception:

spectator-centred technology

> "The world of sports in the age of mass media has been transformed from nineteenth century amateur recreational participation in late twentieth (and early twenty-first) century spectator-centred technology and business" (Real 1998:14; Rowe 2004:12).

Sport as a manifestation of culture has become part of the everyday life of many people as a physical activity and as a popular form of entertainment. But is sport merely entertainment? What rituals, values and ideologies underlie our involvement with sport? Is it the stardom, the fanaticism of supporters or social dimension as part of our cultural practices? In this section we try to seek answers to these questions by approaching sport from the cultural studies perspective to investigate the dominant interests of business, governments, the economy, the mass media, the role of sport in education and in maintaining the social, political and cultural status quo, as well as audience participation in sport (Lemon 2001; Sage 1990).

Rowe (2004:35–36) provides an excellent discussion of how sport and the media developed as social institutions and how they intersected and penetrated industrialised societies, leading to large-scale consumption of sport. Couple this with the requirements for modern nation building, the circumstances have been created for a long-lasting intense union. Furthermore, because of the enormous investment of human labour, capital, social effort, political rhetoric, and cultural space, media sport has created the conditions for the playing out of many forms of power in order to:

- attract great proportions of the world's nations to watch sport on large scale; for example, an estimated 3.7 billion people in 220 countries watched the Sydney 2000 Olympics and the cumulative audience for the Korea/Japan 2002 soccer World Cup was about 28.8 billion people from 213 countries;
- determine the destiny of large companies and their employees, including giant media corporations like NBC in the USA, as well as manufacturers who sponsor sport attire, like Nike, and peddle soft drinks like Pepsi;

- influence the policies and spending pattern of government (South Africa's bid to present FIFA World Cup Soccer in 2010 was financially underwritten by the South African government as well as provincial and municipal governments while FIFA will benefit from many of the mandatory media arrangements);
- provide the ground for much social discourse ranging from the media and casual social conversations to serious academic investigations and scientific predictions.

<small>cultural phenomenon</small>

To study sport as a cultural phenomenon, it should be situated within its political, economic, cultural and historical contexts. Because we look at sport from a cultural studies perspective, we have to investigate the underlying ideology and myths as driving forces behind the presentation of sports events in the media. Kovecses (1990:139), Lemon (2002:362) and Leonard (1994:65–72) stress the symbolic values of sport, values that include discipline, loyalty, character building, competition and nation building amongst others.

<small>ritualised</small>

It is interesting to note that sport has many codes and signs in common with other social institutions such as the church and politics. It takes place within the confinement of a ritual time frame and space. For example, a soccer game lasts one hour with a 10 minute break in between and is generally played on a field (or in a stadium) specifically designed for soccer. And we know that when participants disobey the rules (for instance, committing a foul) they are punished, disadvantaging the team as a whole and letting their supporters down. Sport thus teaches us about value systems that include discipline, obedience, fairness and team spirit.

Sport is also a structured, ritualised experience that consists of a beginning, a middle, a climax and an ending, just like the circle of life and all stories. It is clear that rules govern a specific game and are used to regulate behaviour and construct the dynamics of the game. Novak (in Rowe 2004:72) agrees that sport can be a type of secular religion, taking over from the church as:

> "the primary place of collective and individual ritual, belief, ecstasy … When sports fans have their ashes spread on the 'hallowed turf' of their favourite sports stadium, the spiritual qualities of sport are very evident …"

A further similarity between secular religion and sport are that both have vested economic and capitalist interests. Both can be dedicated to the

Media Culture

worship of the god of obvious consumption of commodities, or as the pun goes: "religion is more concerned with profits than prophets" (Rowe 2004:73).

As far as the spectators (supporters and fans) are concerned, they know the rules of a game, the role of each player and the skills required to excel (Lemon 2001:362). Audiences thus have certain expectations when they watch their favourite sport and they become intensely involved while watching. During the course of a game they may experience a range of different emotions from elation to anger and disappointment.

Links exist between sport and the processes of hegemony and ideology. Hegemony refers to the way the dominant ideology of the powerful ruling class – businesses, government, the mass media – is maintained without reverting to force to subordinate the less powerful in society. Hegemony is subtle domination, where the subordinate classes are lulled into consent, particularly when showing visible signs of opposing the dominant ideology. For example, during apartheid in South Africa, one or two black rugby players (Errol Tobias in the 1980s, Chester Williams in the 1990s) were included in predominantly white Springbok teams – perhaps only to satisfy the less powerful groups' (the voteless black majority) outcries against racial discrimination, or perhaps as window-dressing to mollify international pressure groups outraged at sporting segregation. Since the coming to power of the ANC in 1994, sports quotas and affirmative action have been applied to make teams more demographically representative of the country. However, when there is opposition from the now less-powerful groups (the still economically-powerful white minority) the ruling party justified its action by claiming that rugby (and other sport teams) that are representative of the demographics of South Africa are in the interests of the country as a whole. However, negotiation between the parties is a continuous process because promises do not become a reality (promises are broken) and the whole process, typical of hegemony, is repeated time and time again.

| hegemony

In conclusion, politics is endemic in sports because sport is intimately related to the capitalist interests of the mass media, government, business and political leaders who are quick to see the potential for making profits, disseminating propaganda and eliciting national pride (Eitzen 1989:3; Lemon 2001:363). Many South Africans may still remember the unifying effect sport had in 1995 when the Springboks won the Rugby World Cup.

It was the day then-president Nelson Mandela appeared on the rugby field with a number 8 Springbok rugby jersey simulating the outfit worn by captain François Pienaar. Add to this wonderful example of nation building François Pienaar's televised victory speech, which emphasised that the win was not only for white South Africans but for all 43 million citizens.

6.6.3 Architecture and the built environment

cultural identity

The built environment includes structures designed by architects such as entertainment centres, houses, office blocks, parks, schools, shopping centres and museums as well as functional structures such as homemade shacks. All these structures provide shelter and a space to live in. Architecture is an important symbolic form of cultural expression because it is a physical manifestation of a nation's cultural identity and way of life. Inequalities are reflected in a built environment in which we find beautifully designed shopping centres, office blocks and five-star hotels which deny the poverty elsewhere.

Architecture and the built environment have from the time of the earliest civilisations been a physical manifestation of culture. An important relationship exists between human beings and their physical and contextual environment. Architecture and the built environment are important mediums of communication through which human beings express their needs, attitudes, values and social and cultural norms and are therefore important forms of social and cultural expression. Our physical and contextual environment is so pervasive in its influence that we tend to take it for granted. Human beings mould, alter and shape their physical environment to reflect their needs, values, and their social and cultural background (Lemon 2001).

Each cultural group's political, social and historical roots influenced the houses and buildings they designed to live in. All architecture, including less formally built structures, thus carry messages which will be read differently by different socially and culturally situated people.

We see the results of the Group Areas Act in South African architecture, the legislation that enforced residential racial segregation through forced removals. In Cape Town removals had been preceded by multiracial District Six being declared a slum. The former residents were moved to dormitory suburbs built on the Cape Flats. Similar removals happened

Media Culture

in Cato Manor in Durban, Sophiatown in Johannesburg, and, in fact, across the country. Apartheid gave architectural form to townships and suburbs such as Soweto, Mitchell's Plain, Mamelodi, KwaMashu, Umlazi, Khayelitsha, to name but a few. Vast tracts of open scrubland separated populations on racial grounds. Johannesburg, Durban, Cape Town and Pretoria spread out, consuming enormous areas of arable land to achieve this policy of separation. Apartheid created an environment in the so-called townships which destroyed any sense of identity in the displaced people. Rows of identical houses were placed on small pieces of land (van Graan & Winberg 2003:190–192).

These houses were the basic structures that represented architecture for most people. The need for work, coupled with the lack of opportunity in rural areas, drove many people to the cities in search of work opportunities. In common with the poor across the world, they created yet another form of architecture: the shack. Places such as Crossroads in Cape Town grew rapidly as informal settlements. Poor sanitation and a lack of infrastructure and basic services made conditions appalling. Although the new political dispensation has addressed the problem of housing since 1994, housing projects have not kept pace with population growth and the houses built in the townships are of a poor quality with no identifiable African characteristics. We therefore have yet to see a distinctive post-apartheid architecture in South Africa (van Graan & Winberg 2003:190–192).

To conclude: the language of architecture is mainly non-verbal communication. However, this does not mean that it lacks ideological meaning. We have indicated how the ideology of apartheid has been reflected in the housing and suburbs of less powerful groups during apartheid. The role of the media cannot be underestimated when it comes to setting the agenda for what is fashionable in architecture. The SABC television programme *Top Billing* for example, week after week, emphasises luxurious houses while the majority of South Africans barely have roofs over their heads.

6.6.4 Music

Unless born deaf, it would be hard to imagine a world without music. It pervades and permeates all areas of our daily lives, public as well as private. Music has the ability to transcend cultural boundaries and can therefore be regarded as a global language, representing a mediated reality that can

be experienced with others or alone (Lemon 2001:364). Music, according to Lull (1992:1) is a passionate sequencing of thoughts and feelings that expresses meaning in a way that has no other parallel in human life. It is a universally recognised synthesis of the style and substance of our existence, a blending of personal, cultural and social meaning that is confused with no other variety of communication. Music promotes extreme experiences for both its producers and listeners, turning the perilous emotional edges, triumphs, vulnerabilities, celebrations and antagonisms of life into reflective, hypnotic tempos, relaxation and elevation of mood.

There is a wide variety of musical forms or genres of expression each with its unique characteristics. Think for example of the range of classical music and opera to popular music such as rap, punk, kwela, rap, techno disco, folk, Christian rock, reggae, to name but a few. European classical music has frequently been regarded as high art while other music genres are merely popular art devoid of any aesthetic merit, shallow and culturally inferior. However, renditions of baroque Venetian composer Antonio Vivaldi's *Four Seasons* more than three centuries later by the British punk violinist Nigel Kennedy and chants by Gregorian monks have become international best-sellers because they have become popular with the general public (Lemon 2001:364).

Popular music has often been used as medium for social criticism which poses a threat to dominant ideologies. Music provides a voice to the voiceless, serves as a medium for the oppressed and the marginalised to create their own alternative cultural style and identity. In this section we discuss in detail the genre of rap, a form of popular music and part of the hip hop culture, that has emerged as one of the most controversial and distinctive genres of the past decade. According to Best and Kellner (1999:1), rap articulates the conditions and experiences of African-Americans living in marginalised situations ranging from racial stigmatising and stereotyping to striving for survival in violent ghettos. In this cultural context, rap has become a powerful vehicle for cultural and political expression and is sometimes called the "CNN of black people" (Best & Kellner 1999:1). In this section we discuss the popularity of rap in detail because of its ideological hegemonic role.

Some characteristics of hip hop culture are that it is energetic, expressive and dynamic. It has given rise to new forms of dance like break-dancing while movement and bodily rhythm is a central aspect of its cultural style as well as musical performance. Members of this cultural

Media Culture

group also have specific codes of dress and badges which serve as codes of cultural identity. As an organic expression of urban hip hop culture, rap quickly became the distinctive sound of African-American anger, cultural style, rebellion and contemporary experiences (Best & Kellner 1999:2–3).

Many rap music lyrics carry threats to white dominant power institutions, denouncing police violence and racial oppression. Rap celebrates a diverse realm of black cultural forms extending from Afro-centric nationalism to the gangster lifestyle. With its staccato beat, multilayered sound, aggressive lyrics, in-your-face messages and defiant style, rap provides a spectacle of revolt and insurrection in live performance, music videos and recorded forms. Some rap singers cultivate the outlaw or rebel image through their clothes, their lifestyle, and in some cases their crimes, serving as a warning of the rage and violence seething in underclass ghetto communities (Best & Kellner 1999:3–5).

Although rap involves the aesthetics, experience and cultural forms of African-Americans, Best and Kellner (1999) maintain that young suburban whites also identify with rap because they too feel deeply alienated and rebellious, and like to identify with the gangster image, such as "the wigger" subculture which appropriates the form of black culture for oppositional white identities, fleeing from a culture of:

> *"spiritual death where the dominant norms are careerism and consumerism, white youth finds creativity and passion in a far more vital black culture. From jazz to rock and roll to rap, many males have identified with black language, music, style and dress" (Best & Kellner 1999:8).*

Jackson-Opoku and West give a good overview of the influence of rap in South Africa. They point out that in South Africa, as in the US, rap music has emerged as both an urban folk form and a protest vehicle for black youth embracing an insurgent youth culture. A rap group like Prophets of the City, popular among the youth, is known for its entertainment and consciousness-raising value. The Prophets do not support any particular political faction but its lyrics exhort black people to exercise their recently won right to vote, a right enshrined in a new constitution after decades of armed struggle. The young rap artists have adopted African-American hip hop style: the dress, the dance and the intricate insignias clipped into their hair. Their message also has reverberations from across the ocean.

For example, one of The Prophets paraphrases was taken from the famous speech by American revolutionary Malcolm X:

"The only way we can get the movement we want is by the bullet or the ballot. Now we have a chance to use the ballot." (Jackson-Opoku & West, sa)

The group calls on black youth to use that ballot as a means of improving their socio-economic conditions and obtaining a better life:

The reason why we gotta vote
The government left us for broke
In each and every way
And now we have to say
Let us go for a better day.

Like so many South Africans before them, the members of Prophets of the City, who are drawn from the ranks of Cape Town's numerically dominant mixed-race and African communities, have appropriated an African American musical repertoire, re-creating it to suit the specific circumstances in which they live and work. As the name implies, the group interprets the harsh social reality of township life and holds out the vision of a new, more just society organised on radically different lines from apartheid South Africa (Jackson-Opoku & West).

Protest voices do not only belong to coloured and black South Africans. During the apartheid years white Afrikaans and English speaking artists – Johnny Clegg, Jennifer Ferguson, Johannes Kerkorrel, Koos Kombuis and David Kramer amongst others – also voiced their antagonism and dissatisfaction with the ideology of the then ruling National Party. David Kramer, a white South African writer and director, whose ground-breaking work in South African musical theatre has focused primarily on the coloured communities of the Cape. The thrust of the five musicals that he has written with Taliep Petersen, and one on his own, is in the retelling of a suppressed history of the so-called "coloured" people. One of the most heart-rending songs Kramer composed was *Skipskop*. This song has been written with great compassion for those who were forcefully removed from District 6 to the Cape Flats.

Many lyrics from the songs of the white rebels were thought to pose a threat to the ideology of apartheid and for a period in the 1980s their songs were banned from being broadcast on radio or television.

Media Culture

The above discussion serves as an example of the power of music and how it contributes to create social and political awareness. In other words, music could be used to express social reality and the struggle to change that reality. Music in the service of national liberation is consistent with a philosophy of culture espoused by many South African musicians and artists (Jackson-Opoku and West). This trend toward culture as an agent for social change continues into the present. From trade unions to professional organisations and political movements, from voter awareness to the treatment of childhood diseases and HIV/AIDS, songs exhorting social change are continually being composed and performed.

Despite controversies surrounding the messages of popular music, the recording industry has immense sales figures every year. In South Africa local artists are growing in popularity and festivals are organised each year as a forum for young and upcoming stars.

The link between the mass media and music is obvious: the success of pop and rap artists are to a great extent dependent on the media, especially radio and to a lesser extent television, although many relatively unknown artists have become famous after being part of story lines in South African television soap operas. The success of an artist is co-determined by the frequency that her/his music is played over the radio. Another synergy source is life style programmes: for example, Italian tenor Luciano Pavarotti's work was popularised by the media reporting on his personal life.

We conclude this section with the notion that a symbiotic relationship exists between mass media and different forms of cultural expression; the one can hardly survive without the other, a characteristic of the symbiotic relationship between the mass media and the different forms of popular culture.

6.7 RESEARCH

Research on popular culture is thriving because all artefacts of popular culture – film, television music, religion, sport, architecture, genre fiction, comics, to name a few – are worthy topics of scientific investigation. Research tells us which aspects of popular culture have the largest impact on the majority of the population; identity formation; what the relationships are between art, mass media, commerce and society and the impact of popular culture on other fields as varied as sociology, history, and anthropology (Curtis 2000).

As discussed above, cultural studies set out to examine the everyday and the ordinary, those aspects of our lives that so powerfully and unquestionably influence our existence and that are being taken for granted. Cultural processes that form us as individuals, as citizens, as members of a particular race, class or gender have become topics of central concern for cultural studies.

6.8 FUTURE DEVELOPMENTS

One of the major developments in popular culture is digital information and communication technologies (ICTs). The possible advantages and disadvantages of ICTs have become major topics on the research agenda because the Internet has changed the way we gather, send and store information. These consequences must be investigated to try to determine their influence on our cultural and political lives, our identity, our community life and interpersonal interaction. Furthermore, we should also consider the problems related to the divide between the "haves" and the "have nots" or the information-rich and information- poor sections of society. Will the gap widen or will it decrease? Cultural studies can contribute towards investigating the digital divide and find solutions to narrow the gap.

6.9 CASE STUDIES

 ### Case study 6.1: Critical Reflections on Mel Gibson's "The Passion of the Christ"

According to Hammer and Kellner, Australian-American actor and director Mel Gibson's *The Passion of the Christ*, released in 2004, is a major cultural event. It deals with the brutal and violent portrayal of the crucifixion of a major global religious figure, Jesus Christ. In their article, Hammer and Kellner investigate the movie's popularity and why it has caused such a huge controversy.

Jesus as Action Hero: *Passion* is to a great extent Mel Gibson's reinterpretation of Christianity. There is a clear-cut parallel with Mel Gibson's action hero films, like the stalwart in *Braveheart* (1995) where the main character, Scottish warrior William Wallace, is literally crucified at the end of the film. Other Gibson films that come to mind are *Ransom*, *Payback*, and *The Patriot*, where the hero is cruelly and violently beaten but ultimately redeemed and victorious. *Passion* is characterised by such violence, including the violent flagging and scourging of flesh, that it has been described as "a pornography of violence". It also contains elements of homoeroticism and fetishism of body parts.

Media Culture

Popularity: the violent movie has been a great success due to advance publicity and media hype. The popular press praised the film as a must-see cultural event. Evangelical, fundamentalist and mainstream Christian churches organised their congregations to attend together, making the showing of the film a religious event. Many audience members were deeply moved and allegedly wept during Jesus' tormenting because of the pain Christ suffered on their behalf.

Marketing: The intertextual nature of the film is reflected in the *Passion's* great merchandise marketing success: the selling of books, CDs and various religious items, such as nails emulating those that pierced Jesus. The book *The Passion: Photography From the Movie "The Passion of the Christ"* rose to number three on the *New York Times* newspaper's bestseller list in April 2004.

Thematic construction: A popular theme in *Passion* is the titanic struggle between good and evil, a staple of popular cinema. The story is one of a monumental clash between Good and Evil and the monstrousness and horror of the Crucifixion has never been presented in such excruciating detail.

Cinematography: Many critics praised Gibson's expert use of cinematography. For example, the use of natural lighting provided striking contrasts between night and day, and exterior and interior scenes, achieving a dramatic chiaroscuro quality reminiscent of religious art, while the outdoor scenes had a dusty and sun-drenched Mediterranean look. The soundtrack is extremely well produced, providing both exotic sounds that disorient audiences and induce a sense of the macabre.

Race: most of the main characters and cast are clearly white and Western, which is not an accurate portrayal of race and ethnicity of the biblical people of the period. Despite some attempts at authenticity in costumes, Gibson continues a long Western tradition of whitening Christian iconography and presenting images of Jesus and his followers as projections of the white, Western imagination.

Gender: The portrayal of women in *Passion* reflects Gibson's conservative patriarchal fantasy of how women are put on earth to serve and adore men. Two of the most important women in the film, Mary Magdalene and Jesus' mother Mary hold each other weeping silently, without any signs of resistance. Under these circumstances one would expect more emotions and feelings when eye-witnessing the brutality inflicting on a loved one. In Passion there are no strong female characters and women are to a great extent only part of a faceless crowd. Furthermore, Jesus' mother Mary and Mary Magdalene exhibit habits that reflect Gibson's idealised women – saintly, pure, quiet and obedient.

Anti-Semitism: The contemptuous look of the Jewish priests who buy Judas and the loud clink of the money thrown to him, dismiss Judas as a sell-out rather than probing Judas's motivations. Interestingly, the musical film *Jesus Christ Superstar* (1973) paints Judas as a resistance fighter. In contrast Gibson portrays Judas as evil, jealous and money-hungry. Crucially, *Passion* may promote hatred through its relentless caricatures

of evil Jews and Roman soldiers who condemn, torture, and brutally kill Jesus. It is too soon to evaluate the ultimate impact of *Passion* but apparently it has been highly popular in the Arab world where it could possibly intensify anti-Semitism.

Politics: *Passion* should also be read in the context of present-day politics, marked by a war of religious fundamentalisms, militarism, and accelerating societal violence and turbulence. With the election of George W. Bush as president of the USA, Christian fundamentalists have received high positions in government and at least part of Bush's invasion of Iraq was fuelled by a sense of crusade.

 Case study 6.2: "The Da Vinci Code"

The novel *The Da Vinci Code* by Dan Brown was an immediate success when it was released in 2003 – more that 40 million copies were sold (Hoover 2006), indicating its status as a bestseller. Why has this novel been so popular? Why has it at the same time caused public outcry and condemnation, especially from Christian churches?

The Da Vinci Code deals with an alleged centuries-old conspiracy of the Catholic Church, which tried to hide the marriage between Jesus and Mary Magdalena and their eventual off-spring, a daughter. According to the novel, their blood line (and identity as the Holy Grail) continues to this day (Hoover 2006 and Pacatte 2006).

A major problem is the premise that Jesus and Mary Magdalene were married, had a daughter and that their blood line continues to this day. However, this "problem" may also be the reason for *The Da Vinci Code's* success and the controversy. Pacatte (2006) points out that to accept this premise (that Jesus was an ordinary married man) Christian believers must first of all suspend their belief in the divinity of Jesus. Brown does so in his book by debunking Jesus' resurrection from the dead. The screenwriter of the film also ignores the resurrection of Jesus and repeats over and over that Jesus was only a man. Apart from questioning the nature of Jesus, *The Da Vinci Code* totally immerses its readers in pagan ideology, such as secret sex orgies, astrology, Tarot cards, nature worship, symbols of Satan, goddess cultures and the "divine feminine". Therefore this book is filled with pagan indoctrination and propaganda (Editor's Notes, 2006).

Clergymen and priests expressed their fear that:
- readers/viewers were unable to distinguish between fact and fiction in the storylines;
- the historical inaccuracies may lead to confusion (Hoover 2006);
- because most Christians are not informed readers, they don't approach a work of fiction with three questions in mind: Does it contain grains of truth? What half truths? What out-and-out lies? (Fant 2006). This means "that church leaders should teach their fellow believers to use their minds to engage in culture and to emphasise the truth of Christ and God's Word, even as we navigate cultural phenomena such as *The Da Vinci Code*" (Fant 2006).

Media Culture

Westheim (2005) contends that Brown creates a fictionalised world with easy answers to compensate for an increasingly complex reality, to fulfil the need for order and meaning. This need is deeply embedded in our collective subconscious, in the post 9/11 world, after the 2001 terrorism attacks on the World Trade Centre and the Pentagon in the USA, where the collective conscious of nations is paralysed by fear of terror attacks, wars and unsolvable social riddles. Brown's brave intellectual hero, Dr Robert Langdon, serves as an ordering principle that speaks to minds troubled by postmodern dilemmas.

The issue of racism has also become part of the media hype. According to Baker (2006) there is relative silence regarding the religious aesthetic and particularly racial inferences of Jesus and his descendants who are European and white, in the light of 500 years of white supremacy and normalisation, what Baker calls "the symbolic universe of ecclesial whiteness". He further notes that only one character in the story displays a concern for justice for women. However, she is dark-skinned and therefore marginalised and portrayed as a crack pot.

Most of the criticism and condemnation comes from the viewpoint of fundamental and conservative Christian ideology. However, Hammer and Kellner heralded Dan Brown for his courage to bring to the open hidden secrets of Christianity. Hammer and Kellner contend that while Gibson's version of Christianity is strongly masculine, there are attempts to stress the "feminine" side of Christianity with a series of studies stressing the importance of Mary Magdalene in early Christianity after lost Gnostic texts were discovered containing an alleged Gospel by her. Dan Brown (*The Code*) tells the tale of Mary Magdalene's important role in the live of Christ. Brown articulates alternative and resistant accounts of a far more egalitarian Christianity giving status to Mary Magdalene as the thirteenth – and most important – apostle of Christ's teachings. Part of the plot centres on the Catholic Church's attempts to suppress documentation regarding Mary Magdalene's active contributions to and importance in early Christianity, as well as the nature of her spiritual and physical relationship with Jesus (Hammer & Kellner).

Brown's novel is important for its investigation of the way the chapters of the Gospels in the New Testament are constructed, exposing the way the church selected some while rejecting others. Moreover, Brown accurately identifies the *Opus Dei*, a wealthy, élitist, fundamentalist and right-wing international sect of the Catholic Church. This identification provokes a recontextualisation of current dilemmas in contemporary institutionalised Christianity, especially concerning the corruption, secrecy and revelations of widespread sexual abuse related to the Catholic Church (Hammer & Kellner).

Case study 6.3: A brief history of South Africa's architecture and the built environment

Prinsloo, I. 1990. South African syntheses. (architecture)

From the time of European settlement, in typical colonial fashion, indigenous traditions (apart from colourful settlements of the Ndebele people in Limpopo (previous Northern) Province were largely neglected. Models from the countries of origin of the settlers were copied. South African architecture has been influenced by the following:

- The occupation of the Cape by the Dutch East India Company in 1652, resulting in a regional style of mainly domestic architecture known as Cape Dutch. This style was based on short span, often symmetrical, rectangular plan-forms. The country houses were single-storied, with thick lime-washed walls and relatively narrow, economically disposed door and window openings, thatched with reeds and adorned with local versions of the Baroque and then Rococo gables – for example, Groot Constantia wine farm in Cape Town. Urban houses were often double-storied with flat roofs.
- British imperialism with its concomitant colonial technology developed rapidly in the nineteenth century. In the 1870s, first diamonds and then gold were discovered in South Africa, ready-made architecture consisting of Victorian patterns, executed in Victorian corrugated and cast iron, proliferated throughout the country. The new prosperity attracted original talents such as Herbert Baker who had a great influence on South African architecture. Baker appreciated the Cape Dutch tradition and sought, in his early work in Cape Town (for example, Groote Schuur, 1890) to incorporate its elements into his already eclectic but sensitive and skillful architecture such as the Rhodes Memorial in Cape Town (1908), the Pretoria Railway Station (1908), the Supreme Court Building, Johannesburg (1911), and the Union Building, Pretoria (1913).
- By the 1950s a fairly widespread contemporary vernacular had emerged albeit with regional differences. For example, there were buildings in Pretoria designed under the influence of contemporary Brazilian architecture, for example, the Meat Board parastatal headquarters.
- Ethnic awareness has always been part of South African life. Racial segregation was practised from the time of the first European settlers. With the wider exploitation of the country by the British from the late nineteenth century, these patterns were systematically built into the policies and institutions of modernising South Africa. Economic opportunism found common ground with the ethnic prejudices of Afrikaners and others.
- From 1948 onwards, these tendencies were openly developed and systematically applied as the policy of apartheid. From that time, the principal cities were

Media Culture

- increasingly closed as places of residence to Africans, Indians and other "people of colour". Numerous formless housing settlements were developed away from the cities, devoid of all but the most rudimentary architectural considerations.
- There is little to learn about architecture from apartheid's "townships" (except possibly about the conditions for the absence of architecture), but there is much that can be learnt about politics, professionalism and associated roles of the architect as participant. Many architects refused to accept state work and either left the profession or emigrated.
- From the 1970s onwards, South Africa's increasing international isolation was experienced more tangibly, and architectural work became increasingly dissociated from any synthesising, life-supporting vision of collective life. Extravagant building complexes were built in nominally-independent African "homelands" established under the apartheid policy of decentralisation and resettlement – for example the Mmabatho government buildings, Bophuthatswana.
- Because of the attrition of public life and public buildings, exacerbated in South African cities by apartheid policy, domestic architecture acquired a particular importance and provides an expression of contemporary argument, ideologies and aesthetics. This can be seen from the canonical House at Greenside in Johannesburg which became a paradigm for much work and exemplified the Modern Movement in Africa.
- The Transvaal houses of Mike Sutton, Donald Turgell, Andre Hendrikz and others responded directly to local materials, climate and conditions, and Norman Eaton achieved a distinctive African quality in the houses such as Greenwood House and Village, Pretoria (1951). There are the houses of the Thornton-White school in the Cape, where Modernism is restrained by a harsh climate and a commitment to proper functionality. There are further examples: House Fagan (Die Es), which embodies the sensual qualities of the Cape in a modern idiom, and House Rich in Johannesburg, by Peter Rich, which exploits lessons learnt from intense study of African settlements. Since post-apartheid the opportunities have been favourable to start a recovery towards relevant, inclusive, life-enhancing and timeless architecture, serving the new South Africa; at once popular and profound.

6.10 SUMMARY

In this chapter we distinguished between media as culture and media as a reflection and portrayal of culture. We introduced you to different theories of high, mass, and popular culture. We then looked at cultural studies, and the importance of this approach for studying popular culture and the media. This was followed by a discussion of concepts without which cultural studies cannot be fully understood, namely ideology,

Media Studies: Volume 1

hegemony, decoding and encoding, polysemy and intertextuality. These concepts are the conceptual building blocks of cultural studies and we used them to analyse and explain symbolic forms of popular culture such as religion, architecture and the built environment.

LEARNING ACTIVITIES

- In one paragraph explain what you understand by the relationship between the media and culture. Distinguish between (a) media as culture and (b) media content as a reflection and portrayal of culture.
- Explain in one page *why* and *how* the cultural studies tradition turned élitist and negative mass cultural theories abound with their views that all products of popular culture are worthy objects of academic investigation.
- Make a list of the basic assumptions of the cultural studies approach. Find your own examples from media content to illustrate these assumptions.
- Write two paragraphs in which you explain the meaning of culture and then formulate your own definition of culture. Illustrate your explanation with examples from your own cultural practices.
- Summarise the concepts hegemony, polysemy, intertextuality and decoding and encoding. Illustrate your discussion with examples taken from the cases studies provided in this chapter.
- Explain the different forms of cultural expression (religion, sport, music, architecture and the built environment). Illustrate each of them with your own examples, preferably with visual material or the words of songs.
- Give an example of a cultural form of expression where the hegemonic status quo is challenged (with reference to sport, music, religion, or architecture and the built environment).

FURTHER READING

Barker, C. 2000. *Cultural studies: theory and practice*. London: Sage. Cultural Studies (international journal)

The Journal of Popular Culture. www.tandf.co.uk/journals/routledge/09502386.html

Kellner, D. 1995. *Media culture: cultural studies, identity and politics between the modern and postmodern*. London: Routledge.

Kellner, D. (a) [sa]. Communications vs. Cultural Studies: Overcoming the divide. [Online]. Available: http://www.gseis.ucla.edu/faculty/kellner/kellner.html

Kellner, D. (b) [Sa]. Cultural Marxism and Cultural Studies. [0]. Available: http://www.gseis.ucla.edu/faculty/kellner/

Strinati, D. 1995. *An introduction to theories of culture*. Routledge: London.

Turner, G. 2000. *British Cultural Studies. An introduction*. 2nd edition. New York, NY Routledge.

chapter seven

The Ideological Power of the Media

Stefan Sonderling

LEARNING OUTCOMES

At the end of this chapter you should be able to:
- identify various ideologies;
- explain the difference between neutral and critical theories of ideology;
- explain how ideology may be produced by language and the mass media;
- recognise how ideology creates meaning and experiences of reality;
- identify and describe the ways people accept, evaluate or reject ideology;
- analyse media texts to identify ideology;
- evaluate your own experience of ideology.

The Ideological Power of the Media

THIS CHAPTER

THIS CHAPTER IS to provide you with an understanding of the relationship between ideology and the mass media and explain how ideology may be produced by powerful groups in society through the manipulation of the mass media in order to serve their interests.

7.1 INTRODUCTION

The ideas people have in their heads or the beliefs they say they support are not simply a matter of abstractions. "Ideas", as Thompson (1990:2) puts it, "do not drift through the social world like clouds in a summer sky, occasionally divulge their contents with a clap of thunder and a flash of light; ideas circulate in the social world as utterances, as expressions, as words which are spoken or inscribed".

This points to the fact that the *ideas* are very real and powerful when they are communicated well and motivate people to take action. For example, ideas about equality and freedom motivated the African National Congress (ANC) to revolt against domination by the white minority in South Africa.

> ideas

Ideology has a close connection to the mass media, the main means for the communication and quite possibly, manipulation, in society. In the most general way we can say that ideology is concerned with the study of ideas and how people and societies think. However, there are many definitions of ideology:

- a general system of beliefs held by members of a particular social or cultural group, such as the beliefs of a Christian or Muslim religious group. More narrowly, it may describe the political ideals held by members of a political party;

> belief systems

- a system of false ideas; for example, the ideas of people who believe that the HIV/AIDS disease is not caused by a virus and who refuse to get tested until they are "ready";
- the production of meanings to support social domination of one group over another; for example, such a process includes the ideas about the existence of a white race, and its superiority, produced by the former apartheid regime and promoted by the mass media, legislation and social institutions.

In this chapter we will concern ourselves with explaining how ideas, attitudes, values, and belief systems held by a group of people are used

Media Studies: Volume 1

to guide their understanding of the world and enable them to function effectively. That is, ideology explains how a society is able to maintain itself by reproducing its institutions, social relations, and the things needed for the people to exist, such as the resources to produce food and material goods and the labour force needed for the economy to operate. Ideology also produces people with attitudes and beliefs that enable them to take their given social positions. An example might be how some poor people come to believe that they are unable to change or improve their situation. Such ideas help keep indigent people in their poverty and encourage them to depend on more affluent people in society. How a society comes to organise its people is not simply a peaceful matter performed by some neutral disinterested scientists, professional administrators or gods. The problem that faces every society is how to maintain social structures and relationships that may also be relations of power, inequality and domination.

One method to maintain social stability is the use of force or violence to compel people to conform to the demands of society. For example, if a government uses the police force and the army to intimidate its citizens they may well be afraid to express their dissatisfaction and will probably do what they are told to do by the government officials. However, the use of violence is not the best way to control people. A more effective method for to make them accept their position, respect their government and maintain the social order is to communicate to them ideas and images, or *ideology*, that present their society's structures and relations of inequality as the natural order of the world. For such a purpose, every government considers the mass media as important means for manipulating the ideas and opinions of the people. Governments, lobby groups and opposition parties often believe that through the communication of their respective ideologies by the mass media, people will be convinced and will do what they are told to do. Against such manipulation, the mass media responds by demanding to remain an independent voice within society and provide their own criticism of government and others.

7.2 A POPULAR VIEW OF IDEOLOGY

popular view of ideology

While the concept of ideology may be important for understanding society and the mass media, it is also one of the most hotly contested concepts in the social sciences and one of the most difficult concepts to define. When we use a concept such as ideology, whether in our everyday

The Ideological Power of the Media

discussions or in the social sciences, we encounter a concept that is elusive and has different uses and shades of meaning. The problem may be that in popular use, the term "ideology" has acquired a negative connotation and is used to denigrate and criticise ideas, attitudes, values, belief systems or worldviews that are held by another, particular, group of people – a group that the speaker does not like or does not agree with.

Thus, to characterise an idea or view as ideological is already to criticise and condemn it for being an illusion or untruth. For example, English-speaking Christians might refer to their religion as Christianity rather than Christianism and express their disguised criticism of other religions by naming these (in English at any rate) as Hinduism, Buddhism, or paganism and other forms of "misguided" "isms" such as Islamism and communism, where the use of -ism suggests a basis of prejudice or discrimination. Most people tend to think that their own views and ideas are not ideological; ideology is almost always the view of somebody else. For example, I can claim that my understanding of politics is a political theory and condemn your view as political ideology. Today no person would call himself or herself an "ideologist" but rather claim to be a conservative, a humanist, a capitalist or a socialist. For a scientific study of ideology and how it relates to society and the mass media we need a more systematic framework.

7.3 THEORIES OF IDEOLOGY

In the social sciences we can identify two main approaches: a neutral and critical theory.

7.3.1 Neutral theory of ideology

A neutral theory of ideology regards the concept as a system of thought, system of belief, ideas and values of a particular group of people or whole society. From this perspective, every group in society has its own ideology, a set of ideas that provides a selective interpretation of reality and serves as an action-oriented framework for the group to operate effectively in the world. The ideologies are ways of making sense of the world. In other words, each ideology can be considered as being a map of the social world and helps guide thinking and action in that world. Each such ideological map provides a competing interpretation of the world (Freeden 2003:2–3). For example, during the apartheid period people in South Africa were classified according to their skin colour and it was

neutral theory of ideology

believed by many white people (and even some black South Africans) that blacks were inferior.

All ideologies can be considered as equal and there is no attempt to criticise one ideology or promote another. It is also assumed that it is possible to study ideology from a neutral and non-ideological position such as offered by science. From this perspective, ideology refers to the way attitudes and beliefs are organised into a coherent pattern. For example, let us assume that we know a person who holds certain attitudes toward the risks posed by disaffected young people and who believes that young people should be conscripted by the army for national service because such an experience will give them strong character and solve social problems like high unemployment. From such knowledge we could also predict the sort of attitude that person will hold on other issues such as crime, death penalty, law and order, social class, race and gender. Such a person, one could assume, has authoritarian or right-wing ideology that provides a coherent framework to link his or her attitudes on the different issues.

However, such a neutral concept of ideology is not always very useful. If all ideologies are equal then how could we explain that a particular ideology, such as capitalism for example, is more successful in motivating many people in the world while communism has fallen from grace? How can we explain the fact that many people accept particular ideas about their inferior position in society even when these ideas may be against their best interest and maintain their own oppression?

7.3.2 Critical theories of ideology

critical theory

The term ideology is made of two Greek words: *idea* and *logy*, or science. The term ideology was first used shortly after the French revolution by the aristocrat and philosopher Antoine Destutt de Tracy (1754–1836) to describe a new science that would be concerned with the systematic study of how people think. But the term quickly acquired negative connotations when Napoléon Bonaparte, military ruler of the French republic, used it to accuse the philosophers of disseminating ideas that were undermining French society. In the 19th century German philosopher Karl Marx took the concept of ideology with its negative connotations and developed it to its present form. A more critical view of ideology that provides important understanding of the role of the mass media in society was developed from various Marxist theorists.

The Ideological Power of the Media

Marx's realist theory of ideology

Marx wanted to explain how ruling minorities or a small group of people were able to dominate large masses of people and hold on to power without using force and why the majority of subordinated people accept their subordination. Marx came to the conclusion that those in power were able to construct and communicate a dominant vision of society that justified their rule and the subordination of others and have such a vision accepted by those that were dominated. When such an image of society is accepted by the majority of the people as legitimate, the power of the ruling minority becomes secure and the use of force is unnecessary (Grossberg, Wartella & Whitney 1998:181). For example, most voters in South Africa believe that the ANC government, on the basis of its long liberation struggle, has the best ideas about running the country and accept these ideas and policies as true and legitimate. Such people may become annoyed when an opposition party criticises the ideas of the government.

power

Marx suggested that ideology in a particular society was always produced by a ruling minority or the élite. As he put it: in every society the dominant ideas are the ideas of the dominant class. Because the dominant class has power, owns the means for the production of material goods and controls the economy in a society and profits from it, such material or economic reality determines the consciousness of the people. Marx argued that the dominant ideology was *false consciousness*: the ruling class's explanations that the existing relations were the natural order of things were accepted by the dominated majority, preventing the dominated from seeing their own oppression. As such, ideology can prevent people from thinking about other ways of arranging society.

material base of society

false consciousness

In Marx's views, ideology can be considered a social cement that glues together different social classes and groups who assumed there were no other ways to think about reality. For Marx, ideology was always determined by economics and it always distorted reality. For example, apartheid ideology in South Africa justified the domination of the majority of the black people by a powerful white minority as a natural social order that was created by the Christian god. Many people, including those dominated, accepted such an explanation even when it was against their own interests. Another example is the ideology of patriarchy, also found in South Africa and elsewhere, which assumes that men are stronger and superior over women who are weak by nature. In some societies women

distortion of reality

Media Studies: Volume 1

are represented in traditional stories, legislation and the mass media as passive and subservient to men. In these societies, many women accept their position of domination as natural.

social position

Marx's view could be described as a realist theory of ideology because it assumes that a person's position within the economic and social relations directly determines his or her ideology. According to this theory, if we know a person's social class situation, then we have a much better chance of predicting that person's ideology. For example, a person belonging to the working class, such as a labourer, would hold views that are based on his experiences and relationships and we could predict that such a person might be a member of a trade union such as the Congress of South African Trade Unions (COSATU), might consider capitalism an oppressive system and might support labour reforms like the demands for minimum wages and the right to strike.

mass media

It is assumed that because the mass media are often owned by politically and economically powerful minority groups in a society, the mass media may purposefully communicate false information in order to support their owners. According to this theory the mass media function as important agencies of social control and reinforce domination by communicating the ideology of the dominant class, legitimising the social status quo, manipulating the thinking of the dominated groups and creating false consciousness. For example, it is assumed that a male-dominated mass media (with the help of dominated females suffering from false consciousness, presumably) would produce reports that propagate male domination, or that white South African journalists working for the then mainly white-owned mass media were racists who produced racially biased reports, as was the finding of the Media Monitoring Report of the South African Human Rights Commission in 1999.

shortcomings

Marx's views on ideology seem to provide a simplistic explanation. The shortcomings are the following: by defining ideology as false consciousness it is assumed that there is a true consciousness and that it is possible to understand reality from an utterly objective point of view. However, human consciousness is influenced by culture and meaning, "reality" and how we understand it depends on our language and meanings we acquire from our society. Marx's views are also simplistic as they assume that only economic and material interests directly influence a person's ideology and they neglect personal experience and how such experience influences views of the world. Marx's theory also fails to explain how

The Ideological Power of the Media

different and contradictory ideologies can coexist in a society. In order to overcome these limitations, neo-Marxist and cultural studies theories have attempted to provide a better understanding of ideology.

Neo-Marxist critical theories of ideology

The French philosopher Louis Althusser rejected Marx's assumption that ideology is always determined by economic conditions. Althusser suggested that there need not be such a direct and determining connection between the material conditions and the ideas and beliefs people have. He looked at the role of Ideological State Apparatuses (ISA), consisting of institutions such as the following:

- family;
- school;
- church;
- politics;
- language;
- mass media.

| Louis Althusser |

| Ideological State Apparatus |

These institutions help prepare people to accept their society as it is. For example, children at school may learn what types of jobs they could hope to have when they grow up.

Ideological State Apparatuses such as the family and school, economic conditions and Repressive State Apparatuses such as the military and police that use direct force, together promote the social norms that make people conform within their society.

| Repressive State Apparatus |

For Althusser, ideology is a system of representation. What Althusser meant by this is that it is not possible to have a direct understanding of any real relationships. Rather, people can only have meaningful interpretations and experience of their relationships. This means that people cannot have a direct and an objective view of a reality as there is no way to step out of ideology to some non-ideological position to measure how ideology distorts and misrepresents true reality. We live, experience and give meaning to our world by using a system of representations such as language, pictures and the mass media. For example, many people in South Africa have not been victims of crime but they may well believe that crime is a major problem because they hear about it on the radio, watch the aftermath of it on the television, read about it in newspapers and on the Internet and talk about it with their neighbours and friends. Ideology is a system of signs and meanings which explain and guide

| symbolic universe |

| system of representations |

313

people about how they should experience their world, and it is within such a meaningful world that people live.

As an example of the impossibility of understanding reality without meanings and interpretations, please read the following short story.

Case study: Short story analysis

One Monday morning I read the following report in the newspaper:

> "The city police report that they found a young man lying unconscious on a park bench in the city. The man's head was bleeding and it seems that in a state of drunkenness he fell to the ground and injured himself."

Later that day I met a friend who told me the following story: "I was walking with my husband in the park in the evening and as we passed next to a bench a young man looked at me, jumped up and grabbed my husband by the sleeve and asked if he had a light for a cigarette. Having been annoyed that the man looked at me, my husband pulled away and banged the man over the head with a walking stick and the man fell to the ground."

An hour later I met the husband and heard his story: "I was lucky last night and escaped being robbed. My wife and I were walking in the park when a man accosted me. I had a walking stick in my hand and hit the man on the head. Otherwise, we would have been robbed. It was obvious to me that we were threatened when a man accosts us in a dark spot, grabs hold of my arm and asks for a light."

That evening I met another friend whose head was bandaged. He explained that he was attacked by a lunatic last night, and told me his story: "Last night I was sitting on a park bench for a while, I wanted to light up a cigarette but realised that I had no matches or a lighter. Then I saw a man and a woman go by, and the man was smoking a cigarette. I got up, walked up to them, touched the man on the arm and politely asked him for a light. Suddenly and without reason this madman banged me on the head with a walking stick. I woke up in the hospital the next morning with my head aching and bandaged."

(Adapted from a short story by Arkady Averchenko in Charon 1979:1–2.)

> As the story suggests, there is no non-ideological position from which we can evaluate reality. The writer of the newspaper report accepts the story as told by the police because journalistic ideology dictates a reliance on official police reports, while each person involved in the incident believed that their story was the only true interpretation of the events.

The Ideological Power of the Media

There is no such non-ideological position because the very language of our community is one such system of meanings. Language as a system of representations defines much of how we experience the world as a meaningful place and so defines for us what is real, what is true and what should be accepted as the common sense or natural order of things.

Althusser suggests that we are unable to see our real situation in society and that we always produce an imaginary account of how we relate to the real world. For Althusser, ideology works by providing a place for each individual to identify himself or herself within the representations; for example, we identify with heroes in the movies. Such a process of identification he terms *interpellation*. Such interpellation provides each individual with the sense of identity. For example, language, film and television provide positions of identity for individuals. When I read text written in the first person I identify with the "I" in the text as if it is me; it is as if the text provides me with a position into which I can insert myself and experience the world as it was experienced by the original writer. In taking such a view I may well also accept the meanings and beliefs, interpretations and ideology presented to me. Althusser explains that interpellation is similar to the act of *"hailing"*. For example, you are walking down the street and you hear someone behind you saying "Hey, you!". On hearing these words you turn around because you recognise that possibly it is you that is being hailed or called. In a similar manner, film and television positions you as a viewer, the television announcer is speaking to you and you recognise yourself as the subject or individual. In viewing a film you are presented with a position that provides you with a particular fixed view on the action. When we accept such a position, we are in fact cooperating in the production of ideology.

| interpellation |
| hailing |

Hegemony

People's cooperation in production of the dominant ideology is termed *hegemony* by the Italian philosopher Antonio Gramsci. Hegemony helps the powerful ruling classes in society maintain domination without using force. The dominant class provides leadership within society and thus is engaged in manufacturing consent among the population (Freeden 2003: 20). The ruling class gains the approval or consent of the dominated classes. The dominated classes are co-opted into social institutions that support the power and authority of the ruling class. For example, working-class people are conscripted into the army or join the police force primarily to protect the powerful groups and help them maintain

| hegemony |

their wealth; however, the soldiers and policemen may believe they are protecting the whole country against enemies. Once again we can see that ideology seems like social cement.

British cultural studies

British cultural studies theorists proposed that society is not a unified collection of people. Society is more dynamic and characterised by many conflicting ideologies rather than a single ideology.

The production of meanings involve relations of unequal power. The production of meaning involves the power of a particular social group to represent its own views and images as the reflection of reality, to propagate its own meanings as the real experience. Such a process involves conflict and challenges from other groups who have constructed different ideologies. For example, the law on Capital Gains Tax that will make upper middle class and rich people pay more tax is presented by the South African government as a means to make taxation more evenly spread among the people. Many rich and upper middle class people on the other hand see the extra tax as an assault, while trade unions and the communist party have complained that the tax does not go far enough. Each group would like to promote their view as the real meaning of the tax.

From the cultural studies perspective a more comprehensive definition of ideology would be meaning in the service of power (Thompson 1992:1). This implies that ideology is always connected to systems of representations such as language and the mass media that communicate dominant meanings and serve the interests of power. For example, many newspapers and television programmes in the Western world reported on the war in Iraq as seen from the American ideology which describes Iraqi leader Saddam Hussein as a ruthless dictator and dangerous terrorist until the day he died, ignoring the fact that he had been bankrolled by the Americans for much of his dictatorship during the Cold War. But the dominant ideology is not uniformly shared by all mass media. Some journalists and commentators articulate an oppositional ideology in their reporting.

Thompson (1992:60–66) identifies five modes through which ideology is imposed on society by dominant groups:

The Ideological Power of the Media

Legitimation: relations of domination can be established and maintained if they are represented as legitimate and worthy of support. Domination is justified as *rational*; the interests of the ruling class are claimed as *universal* and representing the interests of everyone in society, and the mass media are encouraged to construct stories that present the existing social inequalities as timeless and unchanging. | legitimation

Dissimulation: domination is established and maintained by being concealed, denied or obscured. Dissimulation works by *displacing* attention from relations of domination and focusing attention on other issues; for example, media criticism of the excessive payments made to black members of a city council is described by a black trade union as attacks by white racists on deserving blacks. Another example is the criticism of current Zimbabwean president Robert Mugabe by the mass media, while such criticism is described by the ruling ZANU-PF government in Harare as a sign of disrespect for all African leaders. Dissimulation also works by the use of *euphemisation* that describes relations and institutions in different words or metaphors, for example the harsh South African prisons are described as "rehabilitation centres". | dissimulation

Unification: domination is maintained by constructing stories that unify individuals into collective identity regardless of their differences. | unification

Fragmentation: domination is maintained by fragmenting groups that may be able to challenge the dominant group. Such fragmentation is caused by promoting disunity in the political opposition and emphasising the differences between those groups that opposed power of the ruling group. | fragmentation

Reification: particular relations of domination are the product of changing history and are not permanent; through reification they are represented as natural, permanent and eternal and outside of history. Through such modes, the ideology of the powerful groups in society is communicated by the mass media and then accepted by the majority of the people in a society as the taken-for-granted, common-sense view of the world. The mass media excludes other alternative ideologies or ideas by not communicating them. As a result of such exclusion of alternative views the ideology of the dominant group becomes the dominant ideology and serves their interest and manufactures consent and consensus. | reification

317

7.4 IDEOLOGICAL STRUGGLES AND CONFLICTS OF INTERPRETATIONS

conflict of interpretations

While the dominant ideology manufactures consent and is taken as the common-sense view of the world, it is also challenged and resisted by other ideologies. There is a *conflict of interpretations* over meaning. Resistance and challenge arise because different groups compete to promote their own ideologies.

different interpretations

Ideologies are not entirely coherent systems of meanings. They are fragmentary and contain contradictions. Furthermore, individuals can interpret texts to create their own meanings and resist the dominant ideology. Such struggles over meaning occur in domains such as language, mass media and culture.

polysemy

Reports in newspapers or television programmes are *polysemic:* they have a multiplicity of meanings for different people.

7.4.1 Preferred reading

British cultural studies scholar Stuart Hall (Fiske 1987:260) suggests a theory of "preferred reading" to explain conflicting interpretations of texts. Hall identifies three positions that readers may take:

dominant reading

Dominant reading: a person who shares the views of the dominant ideology accepts the ideology and the interpretations of reality that are presented in the mass media texts. For example, a member of the South African Communist Party might accept the party's views on the economy and reject criticism as being "capitalist-inspired ideology".

negotiated reading

Negotiated reading: a person who does not entirely accept the dominant ideology attempts to negotiate or compare the meanings presented in media text to his or her own situation. Such a person may only accept some ideas of the dominant ideology.

oppositional reading

Oppositional reading: a person who is entirely opposed to the dominant ideology is likely to reject the meanings and interpretations presented by the mass media. For example, a person who considers abortion murder rejects as misguided a television programme that explains that abortion may be necessary to save a woman's life under certain conditions.

Hall's three reading positions are limited. Hall's theory nevertheless shows that ideological texts allow for a variety of interpretations. Dominant ideology cannot be entirely imposed on all the people in society.

The Ideological Power of the Media

7.4.2 Discursive practices

To account for the more complex ways people interpret text, extending beyond the preferred, negotiated and oppositional reading suggested by Hall, it may be that people interpret as members of different *discursive practices* in society. A *discursive practice* is any formal and institutionalised group of people, such as journalists, academics or lawyers, who have a specialised and rule-governed way, for using language and interpreting reality. The interpretation of media text then becomes a dynamic negotiation between ideology in the text and the various positions and dispositions a person may have as the result of being a member in a number of such discursive practices. For example, a priest may interpret a Biblical text on the value of capital punishment for crime first from a religious position demanded by his church and then explain how such an interpretation supports a particular political ideology or conflicts with the constitution.

discursive practice

Understanding ideology is important for our encounters with the mass media, a visible and important social and cultural institution. We conclude our discussion with two case studies. The first case study illustrates how journalists may promote their own *professional ideology*. The second case study illustrates how mass media journalists may propagate and support dominant ideas of a particular political or social group.

professional ideology

 ## Case study 7.1: The professional ideology of journalists

The *professional ideology of journalists* includes the practices by which journalists select news, the notions of what constitutes news values, the reliance on official and authoritative sources for news, and the belief in their ability to remain neutral observers and report objectively. Yet all these attempts at objectivity may still lead journalists to produce highly distorted representations of reality.

professional ideology of journalists

A pioneering study by Fishman (1978) shows how the news media reporting of crime creates media "crime waves" or heightened social awareness and excessive fear of crime that did not correspond to the real incidence of crime. Fishman observes that in a particular year the city of New York supposedly experienced a major crime wave. The city's newspapers and television stations reported on a surge of violent crime against elderly people. Once this theme began to appear in the city's media, it was taken up by national newspapers and television networks. The result was public outcry, criticism of the justice system, formation of a new police task force, new legislation and meetings between police and elderly citizens. Subsequent public opinion surveys indicated that

crime waves

Media Studies: Volume 1

the media reports increased public fear of crime and a perception that crime against the elderly was on the increase. Yet when the media reporting on the increase in violent crime against the elderly was compared with reality, there was no unusual surge in crime or violence against the elderly during this period. On the contrary, statistics showed a drop in murder and violent crimes involving elderly victims (Fishman 1978:532). Fishman's study shows how such a crime wave was constructed by the ideology and methods of news selection of the mass media.

news theme — Newspaper, Internet, radio and television news editors face the daily task of selecting a limited number of stories from a large number of raw facts and information supplied by various sources. From such a large number of sources, only a limited number of particular stories will be selected to be included in the newspaper or television news bulletin. The chances of the story being used increases if they can be organised into themes which may play out from day to day. For example, from all possible stories about crime an editor may select a report on the mugging of an elderly woman in one part of town, another story of police presenting a crime prevention seminar to the elderly and, follow-up report on a crime story involving an elderly person that a competing newspaper may have reported the previous day. Each story, seen independently, might not have merited attention, but grouped together all of them are made newsworthy by the perception of a common theme. It is as if the editor discovered the theme of crime against the elderly (Fishman 1978:536).

news-worthiness — According to Fishman (1978:536) the selection of news stories requires that an incident is stripped of its actual context. It may be relocated in a new symbolic context: the news theme. *Newsworthiness* is also dependent on the theme: the attention given to an event, such as a single mugging, may exceed its importance, relevance or timeliness and it becomes meaningful only as an instance of the theme.

For example, the mugging of an elderly person can be presented by the media as "the latest instance of the continuing trend in crimes against the elderly" (Fishman 1978:534). In other words, a serious crime trend is based on the media's news selection process rather than on any external reality (cf. Fishman 1978:536). Moreover, once it emerges in one media, the theme is often amplified by other media because journalists pick stories from their competitors. Others will pick up the theme and amplify it further (Fishman 1978:531).

news sources — There must be a sustained supply of crime incidents to fit within the theme. The sources that supply information to the media become important. For example, the police, politicians, government officials and agencies may supply the media with selected information to fit within the theme. Other officials begin to respond. The media then begins to report on the "doings and sayings" of the authorities such as official statements, new legislations, debates, formation of new police units, medical institutions' reactions, and community conferences on the social problem. (Fishman 1978:541).

The Ideological Power of the Media

Fishman (1978) concludes that many issues reported and presented by the mass media as *social problems* may be reporting "waves" constructed by the media. Indeed, sociologists now consider a social problem not as an objective problematic situation in a society but as a particular situation that is defined as a problem by certain dominant interest groups.

| social problem |

 Case study 7.2: How the mass media promote ideology

The way mass media legitimates a particular view by providing rationalisation and justification for a narrow perspective, while at the same time concealing other interpretations can be found in many newspaper editorials.

For example, an editorial opinion article in the *Mail & Guardian* (26 May 2000), begins with a headline: "A war that goes beyond reason" and declares that "The chances of quickly resolving the senseless, inexplicable, insupportable conflict between Ethiopia and Eritrea look slim." The editorial then continues: "The sheer, reckless imbecility of the war between Ethiopia and Eritrea is breathtaking. The fighting, which began in 1998 and flared again last week, seems totally pointless."

Having established that this war is unreasonable, the editorial writer thus presents himself or herself as a reasonable person and representing the voice of universal reason.

From such a perspective the writer then goes on in the next few paragraphs to uncover the causes of this unreasonable war, and writes that its "ostensible cause is a dispute over demarcation of the two countries' 1 000 km border. To the extent that there is a half comprehensible explanation for the conflict, it appears to be friction over trade and Eritrea's decision to have its own currency, valued independently of the Ethiopian birr." The editorial then briefly explains that Eritrea's decision to have its own currency increased Ethiopia's oil and transport costs considerably and that there also was a dispute over demarcation of the ill-defined border between the two countries, and that Ethiopia is landlocked and its only access to the sea is through Eritrean territory. These unreasonable causes and Ethiopian aggression lead to that "we now have a war, which has achieved a momentum and gravity wholly out of proportion to the original dispute".

What is important for us to note as readers of the article is that logically and reasonably there are good reasons and justifications for the war. All major nations have gone to war at one time or another for the same reasons. However, such facts are not presented by the writer who insists and emphasises the unreasonableness of the war. Such presentation distracts the reader from thinking differently; the editorial writer's own ideology prevents him or her from seeing that there are good reasons to justify the war.

The writer of the editorial article then goes on further and suggests that both Ethiopia and Eritrea have many things in common: a colonial past. Both were liberated by the

British who have "thrown out" the Italian occupiers of these countries. However, the fact that the British used military force and waged a war against the Italians during the Second World war is euphemised and evaded by the writer, who says that Italy was simply "thrown out" by the British" who had "non-altruistic reasons" to do so.

Then the editorial writer points out other similarities and some differences between Ethiopia and Eritrea:

> *"There are ethnic and religious differences, although Christianity and Islam predominate in both countries. But there are no great riches at stake, no oil wells or diamond fields. Indeed, both antagonists are pathetically poor. There is no great ideological or political gulf. So what exactly is the present-day casus belli?"*

The article then proceeds to make the point: "What then, can justify the recurring carnage which has claimed up to 10 000 lives in the past two years? What can possibly excuse the creation of yet more refugee armies in a region where millions are already suffering the cruel deprivation of drought and famine? Nothing excuses it. This war is reprehensible as it is futile ... It is beyond reason" (*Mail & Guardian*, 26 May 2000).

The editorial article suggests how ideology conceals facts and opposing interpretations and only presents facts that support the ideology or fixed ideas of the editorial writer. Of course, the same criticism could be levelled at any theoretical critique of the editorial as well.

The lesson that can be learnt from this case study is that readers and consumers of the media need to be aware of potential ideological manipulations by the media and by its critics. Even a report that claims to represent a commonsense view of the world is, in the final analysis, an ideological perspective.

7.5 SUMMARY

In this chapter we explained the difference between neutral and critical theories of ideology. We explained how people accept, evaluate or reject ideology. We applied our knowledge of ideology and its operation to the analysis of media texts and concluded that readers and consumers of the mass media should become critical interpreters as they become aware that ideology is to be found in all forms of representations, including this book.

The Ideological Power of the Media

LEARNING ACTIVITIES

Select a number of editorial opinion articles in different newspapers and do the following:
- Try to identify the ideology of the writer of the editorial article.
- Using Hall's theory of reading, explain what reading position the writer of the editorial article meant to communicate to the audiences.
- List other reading positions that you as the reader could adopt when reading the editorial opinion article.
- Explain whether you agree or disagree with the interpretation of the editorial article as given by the author of this chapter in case study 7.2 on page 321.

FURTHER READING

Fowler, R. 1991. *Language in the news: Discourse and ideology in the press.* London: Routledge.

Freeden, M. 2003. *Ideology: A very short introduction.* Oxford: Oxford University Press.

Grossberg, L., Wartella, E., & Whitney D. 1998. *Media Making: mass media in a popular culture.* London and Thousand Oaks, California: Sage.

Thompson, J.B. 1992. *Ideology and modern culture.* Cambridge: Polity.

Tolson, A. 1996. *Mediations: texts and discourse in media studies.* London: Arnold.

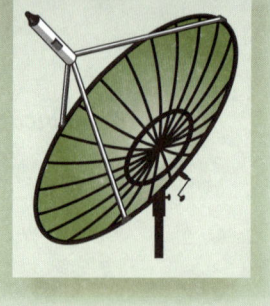

chapter eight

The Public Sphere in Contemporary Society

Pieter Duvenage

LEARNING OUTCOMES

By the end of this chapter, you should be able to:
- grasp the concept of the public sphere;
- understand related concepts such as public reason, communicative action, validity, practical reason, representivity and equality;
- comprehend Habermas's communicative-theoretical work;
- be able to apply Habermas's work on the public sphere in a context of your own choosing.

The Public Sphere in Contemporary Society

THIS CHAPTER

THE PUBLIC SPHERE is a major issue in communication and media studies. The aim with this chapter is to provide you with a good grasp of this concept, with close reference to one of the most important communication theorists, Jürgen Habermas. (Habermas is actually a philosopher and a social theorist, but he is also known for his work in communication theory.) Secondly, the challenge for you is to apply Habermas's theoretical insights in South Africa.

8.1 INTRODUCTION TO HABERMAS

In a lecture in 2004, German philosopher Jürgen Habermas said that *the public sphere as the space for reasoned communicative exchange* was the issue that most concerned him. The "conceptual triad of 'public space', 'discourse' and 'reason'", has dominated his work as a scholar and citizen (Habermas 2004). His work has biographical roots:

Habermas (1929-)

- As a young boy with a cleft palate, Habermas experienced the trauma of surgery. (He noted that the experience of illness or physical handicap is prominent in the biographies of many philosophers; of course, it is also true that not all people with childhood illnesses or physical disabilities go on to become philosophers.)
- When Habermas started school, his physical condition contributed to failures in communicating.
- In his adolescence, he was strongly affected by World War II and its aftermath, followed by the Cold War between the Soviet Union (now Russia) and the West, led by the USA.
- During his adult life, he struggled with the political experience of "a slow and repeatedly endangered liberalization of German post-war society and culture" (Habermas 2004).

The experience of World War II, and more specifically the Holocaust, made a lasting impact on his work. Habermas had to answer very painful questions: how was it possible that the intellectual accomplishments of an Immanuel Kant or a Karl Marx, in which the themes of critical rationality and practical realisation of freedom predominate, could have been such a fertile ground for the rise of a politician such as Adolf Hitler and the philosophy of totalitarianism? Why did this development not encounter greater resistance from the Germans? How was it possible for Nazism to develop within the logic of modernity? Habermas's response to these questions came down to

nothing less than a careful and comprehensive study of the trajectory of modern reason.

During the 1950s, Habermas became convinced that the spiritual fragmentation and alienation of the modern era is of a social-rational rather than a metaphysical nature. He became interested in post-war Germany's struggle to become a democratic state, but also the broader intellectual issue of the project of modern life from the viewpoint of the distorted or deformed realisation of reason (Habermas 1986:96). This concern with the modern paradox, the possible loss of freedom in the face of technical rational progress, brought Habermas into contact with the Frankfurt School.

critical theory

The critical theory of German-American sociologist Theodore Adorno (1903–1969) and others from the Frankfurt School, had four characteristics (Finlayson 2005:3–4):
- to study any theoretical problem from an interdisciplinary point of view;
- critical theory should be reflective or aware of the social context that gave rise to it.
- critical theory has a more dialectical (Hegelian) conception of knowledge; theories are part of an ongoing dynamic historical process;
- critical theory wants to diagnose the wrongs of contemporary society and identify progressive aspects to help remedy or transform society.

social rationality

Habermas moved away from his initial philosophical interests and became interested in Marxism, the psychology of Sigmund Freud, and the sociology of Alfred Weber, Émile Durkheim and Talcott Parsons. In the 1960s, he added hermeneutics (Hans-Georg Gadamer), pragmatism (Charles Sanders Pierce, George Herbert Mead and John Dewey) and language analytical theory (Ludwig Wittgenstein). Eventually Habermas started to develop his own version of the critical and normative foundations of social rationality.

The Public Sphere in Contemporary Society

WHO WERE THEY?

Immanuel Kant (1724–1804) was a German thinker, known for his enlightened thinking about the possibilities and the limits of human reason in modern life.

Georg Wilhelm Friedrich Hegel (1770–1831) was a German philosopher, who believed that our individual consciousness, and the groups and institutions in which we socialise, are all the result of the tension-filled movement of history (dialectic).

Karl Marx (1818–1883) is famous for his philosophy in which the material conditions of life determine human history and reason. The base (the material conditions of a society) determines the superstructure (law, symbolic order and religion). The German author is also famous for his distinction between the working class and the bourgeoisie (property-owning class).

Freudian psychology is the result of the work of Sigmund Freud (1859–1939). This Austrian-born psychologist introduced the position that our conscious life (our ego, which we normally equate with reasonableness) is influenced by our unconscious and by authority (the superego).

WHAT IS IT?

German idealism defends the position that ideas play a major part in shaping our world as human beings. Major figures in German idealism, in addition to Kant and Hegel, include Johan Gottlieb Fichte and Friedrich Schelling.

Hermeneutics refers to the basic human ability to interpret words, texts, cultures and life itself. Major figures in the hermeneutical tradition are Friedrich Schleiermacher, Wilhelm Dilthey, Martin Heidegger and Hans-Georg Gadamer.

Pragmatism is an American school of thought that puts emphasis on a fallible understanding about the working of things in the world and how we think about it. Major figures in this tradition are Charles Sanders Peirce, John Dewey and Richard Rorty.

Language analytical theory is an Anglo-American analytical philosophy which emphasises the meaning of words and the contexts in which they operate. Major figures in this tradition are Ludwig Wittgenstein, John Langshaw Austin, John Searle and Donald Davidson.

Enlightenment thinking is normally associated with the intellectual movement since the late 1600s in Europe that emphasises human reason rather than tradition and dogma.

> Modernity refers (like the Enlightenment) to an era where reasonable human beings take responsibility when it comes to structuring their material and symbolic lives. It is normally contrasted with pre-modern (feudal) societies.
>
> Feudal era refers to that era that precedes the Enlightenment or modernity.
>
> Bourgeoisie is, according to Karl Marx, the class of property holders in modern societies that prevent the working class from emancipating themselves. Accordingly, Marx suggested, the bourgeoisie must be destroyed in order to arrive at a classless society.
>
> Public sphere is the physical and symbolic space that opened up under modern conditions to allow free citizens to engage (communicate) with one another, in a reasonable manner, on all the major issues that constitute modern enlightened life.

8.2 TRANSFORMATION OF THE PUBLIC SPHERE

8.2.1 The historical argument

In his first major book, *The Structural Transformation of the Public Sphere* (1962), Habermas explored the evolution of the public sphere since the Enlightenment in Europe, especially from the late 1600s and early 1700s, in the context of a rapidly developing capitalist economy and the establishment of a bourgeois constitutional state. In his work Habermas follows three argumentative lines.

feudal society

Habermas describes feudal society as a historical phase in which art and culture are "represented" in public. It is a sphere in which the public and private spheres are not separated, making representation in a democratic sense impossible. Habermas (1989:7–8) writes:

> *"Representation in the sense in which the members of a national assembly represent a nation or a lawyer represents his clients had nothing to do with this publicity of representation inseparable from the lord's concrete existence, that, as an 'aura,' surrounded and endowed his authority ... As long as the prince and the estates of his realm 'were' the country and not just its representatives, he could represent it in a specific sense. They represented their lordship not for but 'before' the people".*

In other words, through art and culture, Habermas argued, the court and its allied classes established their higher authority to represent themselves in the public sphere on behalf of the nation.

The Public Sphere in Contemporary Society

8.2.2 Practices and institutions in the public sphere

Habermas's second line of argument is that the feudal public sphere was transformed into the modern bourgeois public sphere due to a change in power relations between the monarch and his/her subjects and the result of early capitalist commercial economy. This led to an idea of society separate from the ruler or state, and of a private realm separate from the public (Habermas 1989:18). The public sphere thus became a space of conflict between the interests of the bourgeois civil society and the interests of the state. The free citizens of the "bourgeois society" in the public sphere had the chance to debate this conflict about the rules of the exchange of social goods and ideas. It is important to notice that Habermas here emphasises the modern public sphere as an institutional location for practical reason and for the valid, if sometimes deceptive, claims of formal democracy.

| modern society

Habermas indicates that members of the bourgeois public sphere did not just defend their interests against the state but also institutionalised a range of practices. These practices allowed reasonable citizens to critically challenge the political norms of the state and its monopoly on interpretation and institutions. Habermas (1989:27) writes:

| rational-critical practices

> "The bourgeois public sphere may be conceived above all as the sphere of private people come together as a public; they soon claimed the public sphere regulated from above against the public authorities themselves, to engage them in a debate over the general rules governing relations in the basically privatized but publicly relevant sphere of commodity exchange and social labor. The medium of this political confrontation was peculiar and without historical precedent; people's public use of their reason ..."

For Habermas, the historical moment when validity trumps coercive claims in public discourse is also the moment when public discussion became the cornerstone and medium of debate through the press (later to become the media), political parties and an elected parliament. Only in a power-free discussion can the strongest argument be superior in the struggle of private opinions (Habermas 1989:53–54).

According to Habermas, at least three critical practices contributed to the institutionalisation of the concept of a rational public sphere:

| rational public sphere

Firstly, the family was constituted as an intimate sphere being represented by the father (the patriarchal head) in public.

Secondly, a literary public sphere emerged, contributing literary and art criticism. In this process the relationship between the public and the art critic (*Kunstrichter*) is one of communicative reciprocity. Habermas (1989: 259) writes:

> "In principle anyone was called upon and had the right to make a free judgement as long as he participated in public discussion, bought a book, acquired a seat in a concert or theatre, or visited an art exhibition. But in the conflict of judgements he has not to shut his ears to convincing arguments; instead, he had to rid himself of his 'prejudices'. With the removal of the barrier that representative publicity had erected between laymen and initiates, special qualifications ... became in principle irrelevant ... Hence, if the public acknowledged no one as privileged, it did recognize experts. They were permitted and supposed to educate the public, but only inasmuch as they convinced through arguments and could not themselves be corrected by better arguments."

It should be clear that although the critic's task is to expose dogmas and fashionable opinions in public, his or her expertise held only as far as it was not contradicted by a better argument. The importance of a rational-aesthetical debate in salons, journals, and newspapers and the educational role of the art critic all contributed to the institutionalisation of the literary public sphere as some kind of template (a *Vorform*) of the political public sphere. Novels of Samuel Richardson in England, Jean-Jacques Rousseau in Geneva and Johann Wolfgang von Goethe in Germany, reinforced this motive. Habermas (1989:50) writes:

> "The relation between author, work, and public changed. They became intimate mutual relations between privatised individuals who were psychologically interested in what was 'human,' in self-knowledge, and in empathy."

This form of rational-critical discourse about literary objects of common concern was carried over directly into political discussion, which paved the way for the political public sphere. In all of the above practices the normative ideal is that there is an essential humanness involved here that economic or other interests can not remove (Calhoun 1992:10–11).

<aside>institutions of public sphere</aside>

Habermas also refers to certain institutions or physical places such as coffee houses and salons where literary and political matters could be openly and publicly debated (Habermas 1989:49–50). In politics, the

The Public Sphere in Contemporary Society

obvious example of an open deliberative institution is parliament. Salons and coffee houses were and are physical places where people could meet one another in a city in order to discuss the pressing issues of the day. In an African context the example of the tribe or community meeting under the tree in an *indaba* (isiZulu) or *lekgotla* (seTswana) to discuss openly the important issues, could be a forerunner of this idea. The modern shebeen (informal unregistered drinking establishment) could be the equivalent of the European coffee house.

In this process, the normative ideal of the public sphere became institutionalised:

- Firstly, discussions in these institutions disregarded status. The idea was that one's official prestige, power and economic status are, in principle, absent in these institutions. In other words, the laws of the market and the state were suspended.
- Secondly, rational argument was the sole arbiter of any issue. Everything was open to criticism. In this way literary, political and philosophical works were no longer "represented" by the Church, court or authorities. Private citizens for whom cultural products become accessible were able to interpret aesthetical and philosophical issues independently.
- Thirdly, the public sphere was perceived as a universal auditorium. Anyone with access to cultural products – books, plays, and journals – had at least a potential claim on the attention of the culture-debating public. The public sphere did not become the forum of a power clique, but was seen as part of a more inclusive public comprising all private citizens who could participate in an independent way in a critical discussion as a result of being educated private owners (Habermas 1989:36–37). (Although participation was open to "all", we know that in practice it almost always applied solely to men.)

According to Habermas (1989: 46) these practices and institutions allowed the state to be in touch with the needs of society. This social evolution, though, could only take place based on a new economic order. This order was capitalism. Its crucial contribution to the public sphere was the institutionalisation of a new and stronger sense of privacy and free control of productive property. In Europe capitalism was also reflected in the codification of civil law, where basic private freedoms were guaranteed. A fundamental parity among persons was thus established, corresponding to that among owners of commodities in the market and educated individuals in the public sphere. Though not all people were full legal subjects, all legal subjects were joined in a more or less undifferentiated

needs of society

category of persons. The extension of these notions into the doctrines of *laissez-faire* (a French phrase meaning "let it be") and even free trade among nations brought the development of civil society as the private sphere emancipated from public authority to its fullest extent.

Habermas (1989:79), though, argues that this moment lasted only for a short moment "in the long history of capitalist development." He argues that the literary and political model of the bourgeois public sphere was undermined by historical and economical developments since the last part of the 1800s.

It is necessary to ask about the historical development of the public sphere in South Africa and how it follows (or deviates from) the line of thought in this section. We have to look at the pre-colonial, colonial and post-colonial conditions that contributed to the emergence of a public sphere. In other words careful historical work is needed to interpret the history of public spaces, including the press, radio, television and the Internet, in the South African context. In this process the issue of ownership, government influence and exclusion are important issues.

8.2.3 The decline of the public sphere

Habermas interprets the decline of the public sphere since the last part of the 19th century (his third argumentative line), as a shift to a public driven by consumption. This shift took place at the moment that the classic model of liberal competing capitalism was transforming into the monopolistic capitalism of cartels and protectionism. The classic function of public opinion, namely the free debate of general interests, was from then on undermined by the state's and other interest group's intervention. Even institutions such as parliaments could not prevent this erosion of a free public sphere (Habermas 1989:143–144; 205). Habermas (1989:164) writes:

> *"Discussions, now a 'business,' becomes formalized; the presentation of positions and counter positions is bound to certain prearranged rules of the game, consensus about the subject matter is made largely superfluous by that concerning form."*

The relationship between the private and public spheres and their relation with the state changed. State and society, once distinct, became interlocked, leading to the *refeudalisation* of the public sphere (Habermas 1989:142). The public sphere thus changed from a forum for critical and rational debate to an instrument for the manipulation of public discourse

The Public Sphere in Contemporary Society

where bureaucratic and economic interests use advertising, marketing and "public relations" to create a "social engineering" of voter behaviour and cultural consumption (Habermas 1989:202).

At this historical moment, then, the project of the Enlightenment and the cultural emancipation of the masses became endangered. The public sphere thus changed from a forum for critical and rational debate to an instrument in the manipulation of discourse by powerful bureaucratic and economical interests. Habermas describes the decline of the literary public sphere into a minority of art connoisseurs (high art) on the one hand and a large mass of art consumers (cultural industry) on the other. Art gradually distances itself from involvement while the cultural industry manipulates the critical discussion for political purposes (Keulartz 1986: 17). The arrival of new technologies, leading to lower book prices, may not have enhanced cultural life. Mass media such as the press, radio and eventually television quickly became the commercialised instruments of advertisers. These new forms of media speak directly to the consumer by ignoring the idea of a rational discourse between participants in a critical public sphere (Hohendahl 1979:90). Habermas (1989:170–171) writes:

| manipulation of discourse

> "With the arrival of the new media the form of communication as such has changed; they have had an impact, therefore, more penetrating ... than was even possible for the press ... They draw the eyes and ears of their public under their spell but at the same time, by taking away its distance, place it under 'tutelage,' which is to say they deprive it of the opportunity to say something and to disagree. The critical discussion of a reading public tends to give way to 'exchanges about tastes and preferences' between consumers ..."

Where works of literature and politics were previously appropriated through the critical discourse of literary publications, modern mass media and a new style of appropriation made it impossible. The world of the mass media is thus a public sphere in appearance only. With the expansion of access, the form of participation is significantly altered. Habermas (1989:166/200) writes:

| mass media

> "Serious involvement with culture produces facility, while the consumption of mass culture leaves no lasting trace; it affords a kind of experience which is not cumulative but regressive".

Habermas refers here to both the de-politicisation of the public sphere and its impoverishment by the removal of critical discourse. Nothing

333

remained of the cultural circumstances in which Samuel Richardson's novel *Pamela* (1740) was read by the entire public, that is, by everyone who could read and could afford (or knew someone who could afford) books. This structural change involves not only segmentation of audiences but also the transformation of the once-intimate relationship between cultural producers and consumers. It is precisely at this point that intellectuals begin to form a distinct stratum, those who produce culture and critique (Calhoun 1992:25–26). Habermas also cites the social and psychological effects of consumption on the members of the bourgeois family. This comes to the fore in a loss of individuality and moral autonomy in this important socialising institution. "To a greater extent individual family members are now socialized by extra familial authorities, by society directly" (Habermas 1989:156).

<small>manipulated culture</small>

These arguments on culture, identity and politics are clearly influenced by Max Horkheimer and Theodor Adorno's interpretation of contemporary society in the *Dialectic of Enlightenment*. This is reflected in the usage of concepts like "mass culture", "objectification" and "manipulated culture". Habermas, though, does not fully endorse their position on a fully instrumentalised public sphere. And he did not fully underwrite the pessimistic view of the public sphere sketched by Horkheimer and Adorno. One of Habermas's main objections was their reductive interpretation of history as well as pronounced negative views on the democratic potential of a rational public sphere. He prefers a more complex picture of the relation between emancipation and consumption. Habermas writes:

> "In the case of the structural transformation of the bourgeois public sphere, we can study the extent to which ... the latter's ability to assume its proper function determines whether the exercise of domination and power persists in a negative constant ... of history – or whether as a historical category itself, it is open to substantive change." (Habermas 1989:250)

Habermas's reading of the "dialectics of enlightenment" focuses on a theory of the public sphere, which holds up "the ideal of free rational discussion between equals as one that, though presently unfulfilled, is nonetheless worthy of pursuit" (Finlayson 2005:15).

8.3 CRITICISM OF THE EARLY HABERMAS

<small>critique</small>

Habermas's thought-provoking and wide-ranging argument concerning the formation and the disintegration of the public sphere was initially

The Public Sphere in Contemporary Society

well received in Germany and then became more widespread. Although *The Structural Transformation of the Public Sphere* has in many respects become dated, its central idea of a public community of individuals who are united by their participation in rational-critical debate remains a guiding thread.

However, liberal critics were sceptical about the historical comparison between the ideal-typical liberal public sphere and its decline in late capitalism (Hohendahl 1979:93–95). From a systems theory perspective, the communicative social function of public opinion was judged as unsuitable in contemporary societies characterised by specialised systems (Habermas & Luhmann 1971; Greven 1987). From a Marxist perspective, Habermas's sketch of the decline of the bourgeois public sphere was accepted, while his model of the public sphere found less favourable acceptance. In other words by focusing exclusively on the bourgeois public sphere, Habermas neglected salient "popular" forms of public discourse and activity, which were not subsumed by bourgeois sociability, and were sometimes ardently and militantly opposed to it (Hohendahl 1979:104–105; Negt & Kluge 1972). Habermas (1996) has acknowledged this deficiency.

More recently, though, due to the publication of a fine collection of critical essays (Calhoun 1992), Habermas's treatment of the public sphere became the focus for new critical perspectives, which include the following:

- Habermas has been criticised for following the pessimistic view of contemporary society, in which the media industries engendered a "false consciousness" and a "false consensus". This account of ideology presents an overly restrictive conception of ideology and its mode of operation in modern societies. According to Thompson (1990:117) "the phenomena of mass communication have become increasingly peripheral to his core concerns".
- Habermas argues that the commercialisation of media institutions and the use of quasi-commercial techniques in the presentation of political ideas has undermined the bourgeois public sphere and replaced it with a quasi-feudal arena. There is no doubt that "politics today has become a matter of staging, of cultivating images and controlling their diffusion" but as Thompson (1990:115) indicates, the "mediazation of modern culture and its impact on institutional politics" cannot be interpreted as a "refeudalization of the public sphere". Thompson proceeds:

"The development of mass communication has created new opportunities for the production and diffusion of images and messages, opportunities which exist on a scale and are executed in a manner that precludes any serious comparison with the theatrical practices of feudal courts".

- The problem here is that Habermas overstates the passivity of the "recipients of media products". Habermas, in his early work, treats:

"... the recipients of media messages as passive consumers who are enthralled by the spectacle, manipulated by clever techniques and numbed into acquiescent acceptance of the status quo. The active participation of citizens in rational-critical debate has been replaced by the passive consumption of images and messages." (Thompson 1990:116).

Elsewhere Thompson (1995:75) writes:

"we need to think again about what 'publicness' means today in a world permeated by new forms of communication and information diffusion, where individuals are able to interact with others and observe persons and events without ever encountering them in the same spatio-temporal locale."

To some, the very emphasis on rational-critical debate implies an incapacity to deal fairly with "identity politics" and concerns of difference. This is also implicit in the whole rethinking of the boundary between public and private broached by feminist discourse. Habermas's initial discussion of the literary public sphere shows how fiction serves to facilitate a discussion about selfhood and subjectivity and to reinforce a vesting of primary identity in a newly constructed intimate sphere. But his argument eventually imposes a neutralising logic on differential identity by establishing qualification for publicness as a matter of abstraction from private identity (Calhoun 1992:34–35). Thompson (1995:72–73) is thus correct in pointing out that:

"Habermas was not unaware of the marginalization of women in the bourgeois public sphere ... But it could be argued very plausibly that, at the time of writing Structural Transformation, he did not appreciate the full significance of this issue."

The point has been forcefully made that the public sphere was juxtaposed to the private sphere in a gender specific way. Habermas has since

The Public Sphere in Contemporary Society

accepted this criticism too, but perhaps without yet thinking through its ramification for his own position.

Given the previous points, it is quite pertinent to ask how we should use the concept of the public sphere today. Is it possible to reconstitute the public sphere in modern industrial societies? What about the public sphere under post-colonial conditions? Should we not make a difference between a singular public sphere and multiple public spheres? How do multiple publics interact? How do they connect with democracy? What kinds of political subjectivity do they suggest? How do multiple public spheres connect with notions of mass media and a mass subject? There is a widespread argument that professional specialists, using market and promotional campaigns, have come to dominate public communication. A *new public* is mentioned, subject to mass persuasion through relentless advertising, lobbying and other forms of media manipulation.

public sphere today

On the other hand Habermas's later work on communicative action addresses this challenge by devising means to facilitate and institutionalise the public use of reason. It is in this context that the concept of discursive or deliberative democracy becomes important (Scambler & Martin 2001:186).

8.4 PUBLIC REASON AND COMMUNICATIVE ACTION

In two decades (1960–1980), Habermas's work on the public sphere underwent important changes. The important thing here is that Habermas moved from a socio-historical sketch to a formal-rational grounding of the public sphere. Habermas hence sought a more formal-normative (transcendental) and less historical informed basis for the public sphere under democratic circumstances. Four stages of Habermas' work in these twenty years can be reconstructed:

8.4.1 Stage 1

In his critical engagement with Marxism, Habermas came to the conclusion that human relations cannot be reduced purely to work and labour. Human relations and interactions also take place between subject and subject, sometimes described as intersubjective. This gave Habermas a richer conception of human association than Marxist theories generally produce (Finlayson 2005:17). The implication of this position for communication studies is that human interaction has not only a material but also a linguistic base.

social and human association

337

8.4.2 Stage 2

science and technology

Secondly, Habermas developed a critique of technology and science, and of scientific and positivistic ways of thinking. The point he makes is that natural science's illusion of pure knowledge can hide its interests, thereby contributing to a one-sided form of knowledge. This may inhibit our understanding of the social dimension of knowledge. This critique led to Habermas' differentiated model of reason in *Knowledge and Human Interests* (1968) including:

- empirical-analytical;
- historical-hermeneutical;
- critical-social science.

Habermas then tied these three forms of reason to the interests of three distinct means of socialisation: work, language and power:

- natural or empirical science has a technical interest in the causal and controlled explanation of unconscious natural processes;
- the human sciences have a practical interest in understanding cultural or symbolic meanings (a process important for aesthetics);
- critical-social science has an emancipatory interest in analysing structural and social deformations with the hope to promote more equitable arrangements through self-realisation.

8.4.3 Stage 3

pragmatism and hermeneutics

Habermas also became interested in American pragmatism and Gadamer's hermeneutics, which shared the following assumption: philosophy must find its home in everyday life and preserve its links with everyday life. As Finlayson (2005:18) puts it:

> "Philosophical theories and concepts have to pay their way by making a difference to the lives and the experience of real people in the actual world."

It became more and more clear that Habermas was looking for an ideal of free interpersonal interaction as found in ordinary life. He sought specifically in linguistic communication, to see if it would serve as the key source of emancipatory impulses (Anderson 2000). Habermas (1968: 72) defended the normative self-understanding of communicatively socialised subjects against the social philosophical tendency to reduce all intersubjective-practical interests to technical-instrumental ones. One of Habermas's targets here was the reduction of all human socialisation

The Public Sphere in Contemporary Society

and interaction to instrumentalisation (McCarthy 1984:21–22). In his alternative, Habermas defends a collective solidarity which depends on both material reproduction and communicative agreement. His originality was in connecting labour and communicative interaction with different forms of rationality (Habermas 1968:71). From a social point of view, labour and political administration are socially organised in the subsystems of means-end-rationality, while the socially integrated norms of the life-world are produced by way of communicative reason (McCarthy 1984:23).

8.4.4 Stage 4

In the 1970s Habermas deepened his reconstruction of critical theory. His work, at this stage, was extensively empirical, by focusing on ego-identity, communicative competence, moral development, societal pathologies, processes of rationalisation, legal evolution etc. This was also the period in which he intensified his study of analytic philosophy of language as part of developing his universal pragmatics of communication (Anderson 2000). A theory of social evolution and systems-theoretical concepts were added to explain the logic of the development of social knowledge and concomitant forms of rationality (Habermas 1976a; 1976b). These different research projects eventually culminated in the defining work of the second movement of critical theory – *The Theory of Communicative Action* (1981).

critical theory

The theory of communicative action

In his theory of communicative action Habermas defends three aspects:
- argumentation (in which speech-act theory plays a central role);
- social rationalisation;
- an interpretation of modernity/postmodernity (Honneth 1989: 25).

> Speech-act theory is a kind of argumentation theory which deals with the meaning of language, the use of language and the presentation of validity claims between interlocutors (participants in dialogue).
>
> Social rationalisation refers to the differentiation between the life-world (symbolic structured world that is open for argumentation) and the systems world (the world of money and bureaucracy that is not always open to argumentation).

1. According to Habermas' speech-act theory, there are culture-invariable validity claims such as truth, normative correctness and sincerity.

speech-act theory

Each of these claims represented an aspect of rationality. The aim of understanding is to arrive at an agreement and mutual trust. If that resolution is impossible, the level of discourse may allow for resolving doubtful claims by way of the force of the better argument. This is the case in our everyday as well as our theoretical, practical, and aesthetical discourses. For example, it is possible to engage with one another as discourse partners in different contexts by appealing to argumentative rules.

<u>social rationalisation</u>

2. An important aspect of social rationalisation is the historical differentiation between *life-world* and *system*. Communicative understanding (in the life-world) is a fundamental reproduction mechanism of modern society, together with the historical development of norm-free action spheres that are accessible by way of system-theoretical analysis. According to Habermas, social reproduction takes place in both the communicative infrastructure of the life-world and the historically-developed norm-free systems (for example money and bureaucracy). In short: the interaction of communicative rationality and system theory is the framework in which a modern social theory conducts itself. In other words, contemporary society has spheres where we operate argumentatively in the life-world and certain systems where we operate according to the specific rules and functionality of that system.

<u>modernity</u>

3. It is possible to describe the invasion of systematic steering mechanisms in the sphere of communicative *praxis* as a particular pathology of *modernity* (Habermas 1981, II:293). Where Horkheimer and Adorno judged systematically organised complexes in the 1900s as the last step in the logic of instrumental reason, Habermas presents a distinctly different view. Here the social pathologies of contemporary societies are not the consequence of instrumental reason *per se* but rather the result of a one-sided invasion of the life-world by the market and administrative state, displacing modes of integration based on communicative reason. Habermas describes this, in a dramatic way, as the colonisation of the life-world. The primary task of a critical theory is to draw attention to this process of colonisation and indicate the ways in which various social movements are a response to it (Baynes 1998). Habermas, for example, believes that new social movement such as the feminist movement, the anti-nuclear movement and Greenpeace all have an important role to play by articulating and debating the encroachment of technical systems in the life-world of ordinary people.

The Public Sphere in Contemporary Society

The basic idea here is expressed in a principle of universalisability, intended to function as a rule of argumentation for testing the legitimacy of contested norms. Habermas's strong claim is that this principle can be derived from communication and argumentation. In other words, in making utterances, speakers at least implicitly raise different types of claims about truth, normative rightness, and sincerity or truthfulness. These validity-claims point to the notion of an ideal speech situation, freed from all external constraints, and in which nothing but the force of the better argument prevails. The principle of universalisability represents an attempt to formulate this counterfactual ideal as a fundamental rule of argument: norms or maxims of action are only morally legitimate if, when contested, they can be justified in a moral-practical discourse.

ethical theory

Habermas and politics

Habermas eventually guided his theory of communicative action and discourse ethics back to the political questions about democratic theory, practice and law. In *Between Facts and Norms* (1996), Habermas argued that the contrast between democracy (popular sovereignty) and constitutionalism (emphasising individual rights) should not be over-emphasised. Popular sovereignty and basic rights are co-original and both derive from an ideal implicit in the notion of communicative reason: the right not to be bound to norms other than those to which one could give un-coerced rational consent. Habermas offers a model of deliberative politics that steers between the alternatives of liberalism and republicanism. He accepts the republican criticism of a politics based on the competition and aggregation of private preferences. On the other hand (similar to liberals) he finds the republican vision of a united citizenry, actively motivated by a shared conception of the good life, rather unrealistic in modern, pluralist societies. In his alternative the emphasis is not on a collectively acting citizenry but on:

deliberative politics

> "the institutionalization of the corresponding procedures and conditions of communication, as well as on the interplay of institutionalized deliberative processes with informally constituted public opinions." (Habermas 1996:298).

Habermas thus argues for a *two-track* process in which there is a division of labour between *weak publics* (informally organised public spheres ranging from private associations to the mass media, all located in civil society) and *strong publics* (parliamentary bodies and other formally organised institutions of the political system). *Weak publics* assume a

strong publics, weak publics

central responsibility for identifying, interpreting and addressing social problems. Decision-making responsibility, however, as well as the further "filtering" of reasons via more formal parliamentary procedures, remains the task of a *strong public* such as the formally organised political system (Baynes 1998). On the issue of legal theory, Habermas resists the sharp contrast between positivism ("law as the will of the sovereign") and natural law theories. Legitimate law must in some meaningful sense be construed as the will of the people or *demos*, even as the democratic process itself requires legal regulation (Baynes 1998).

8.5 THE PUBLIC SPHERE: A RECENT STATEMENT

Habermas' renewed interest in the public sphere connects with the structure of mass communication and the formation of *considered* public opinions as well as the power structure of the public sphere and the dynamics of mass communication. Habermas also considers the specific pathologies of political communication in our time.

8.5.1 Democracy and the public sphere

modern democracies

For Habermas (2006:2) modern democracies have three elements, which he calls the "normative bedrock of liberal democracy":

- the private autonomy of citizens; each of whom pursues a life of his/her own;
- democratic citizenship; the inclusion of free and equal citizens in the political community;
- the independence of the public sphere, operating as an intermediary system between the interests of the state and civil society.

Against this background, Habermas distinguishes between three models of democracy (liberal, republican and deliberative). Each of these models, he says:

> "... gives a different weighting to equal liberties for everybody, democratic participation, and government by public opinion" (2006:3).

While the liberal model emphasises the liberties of private citizens, the republican and deliberative models more strongly favour the political participation of active citizens or the formation of *considered public opinion*. Habermas contends that these different models of democracy also impact differently on national political cultures, thereby creating different relations of theory and practice (2006:3). Of the three democratic models,

The Public Sphere in Contemporary Society

Habermas prefers the deliberative one. (Given his position on public reason and communicative action, this should not come as a surprise.) In the deliberative model the emphasis is on the function of discourse, rather than rational choice (liberal) or political ethos (republican). The deliberative model's main empirical point of reference is the democratic process. Important in this regard are three things (Habermas 2006:4):

- publicity for and transparency in the deliberative process;
- inclusion and equal opportunity for participation;
- a justified presumption for reasonable outcomes (mainly in view of the impact of arguments on rational changes in preference).

These three aspects constitute, according to Habermas, the heart of any democracy. The last point on the presumption of reasonable outcomes rests on the assumption that institutionalised discourses mobilises topics, promotes critical evaluation, and leads to a rational yes/no situation. Habermas refers to this as the *truth-tracking potential of political deliberation*. Deliberative politics grows out of our daily asking for and giving of reasons.

In order to strengthen his argument about the normative thrust of political deliberation Habermas (2006:6) links it with some empirical case studies. He says there is already an impressive body of small-group studies "which construe political communication as a mechanism for the enhancement of cooperative learning and collective problem-solving".

Habermas refers to Michael Neblo's studies on how experimental groups learn through deliberation on political issues such as gender or racial affirmative action or gays in the military (Habermas 2006:6). In these cases individuals were first asked for their opinions on the mentioned issues; some weeks later they were placed in groups and asked to debate the same issues and reach collective decisions; and some weeks after the deliberation they were each (individually) asked about the very issues again. It is here that Habermas uses his concept of *considered public opinion*. Considered public opinions come about when such a group undergoes a unidirectional change and no polarisation of opinions takes place. The point here is that the final decisions are different from the initial opinions. Impersonal arguments trump the interpersonal relationships in a process that Habermas (2006:7) calls procedural legitimacy.

Habermas also refers to James Fishkin's famous experiment with a group of Canadian voters who were randomly chosen to decide between three alternative proposals for a citizen's assembly.

Habermas finally refers to a case study where expert groups (from multinational corporations) and counter-experts (from non-governmental groups) deliberated about certain environmental issues under the auspices of a Berlin research centre (Habermas 2006:7–8).

The question, though, is what about the broader issue of mediated communication in the public sphere? When we move from the deliberation of small groups to the broader terrain of mediated communication we are faced with the following problems:
- a lack of face-to-face communication;
- the lack of a speaker and addressee;
- the media's selectivity and shaping of messages;
- the political and social power of agendas (Habermas 2006:8–9).

For Habermas the first two are not problems *per se*. The last two are problems, which takes us to the issue of political communication in a bottom-up and top-down multi-level system (Habermas 2006:10).

8.5.2 Mass-communication and considered public opinions

messages and opinions

For Habermas, the public sphere is an intermediary system between formal organised deliberation and informal face-to-face deliberations in arenas at both the centre and the periphery of the political system. The centre of the political system consists of the following: parliaments, courts, administrative agencies and government. Their outputs are the result of institutional deliberation and negotiation processes. On the periphery of the political system, the public sphere is:

> "... a network of wild flows of messages, for example: news, reports, commentaries, talks, scenes and images, shows and movies with a polemical, educational or entertaining content".

These messages and opinions come from a variety of actors in the civil society such as politicians, political parties, journalists, lobbyists, experts, moral entrepreneurs and intellectuals (Habermas 2006:10–11).

influencing the media

The important thing, though, is that there is a constant struggle by these actors to influence the media. According to Habermas, the stage of public opinion is entered from three points:
- politicians and political parties start from the centre of the political system;
- lobbyists and interest groups start from the vantage point of the functional systems and status groups;

The Public Sphere in Contemporary Society

- advocates, public interest groups, churches and other religious bodies, intellectuals, and moral entrepreneurs start from civil society.

These three groups of actors are joined by journalists to construct "public opinion". Public opinion thus takes place between government and various audiences. Public opinion is thus the result of both élites and diffuse audiences.

It is now necessary to look at how considered public opinions are created under circumstances of mass communication. According to Habermas's communication model, it is normal that the state faces demands from two sides:
- to provide rules and regulations;
- to "provide public goods and services for civil society, as well as subsidies and infrastructure for various functional systems, such as commerce or the labour market, health, social security, traffic, energy, research and development, education." (Habermas 2006:13).

The representatives of the functional system confront the state precisely on these demands. Habermas (2006:14) eventually argues that the political system must present an open flank to civil society if it wants to retain its legitimacy.

Given tension between the state and the civil society, both the government and voters can take a yes/no position on public opinion. The trademark of the public sphere is its reflexivity and openness to deliberation. Habermas (2006:12) sees deliberation as an essential element of the democratic process, which fulfil three functions:

| deliberation |

- to mobilise and pool relevant issues and required information and to specify interpretations;
- to process such contributions discursively by providing proper arguments pro and con;
- to generate rational yes/no attitudes.

While the political public sphere mainly fulfils the mobilisation requirement, Habermas's model of deliberative politics wants more than mobilisation in order to arrive at considered public opinions (Habermas 2006:13). In other words, it is not enough that media professionals report on issues. It is also necessary to provide space to rationally deliberate and argue about them in order to arrive at considered public opinions. Considered public opinion sets the framework for what citizens accept as legitimate decisions. Habermas (2006:16) puts it as follows:

> "It is the formal vote and the actual opinion and will-formation of individual voters that together connect the peripheral flows of political communication in civil society and the public sphere with the deliberative decision-making of political institutions at the center, thus filtering them into the wider circuitry of deliberative politics."

forms of power

Habermas's point is that the public sphere under mass communicative circumstances can generate considered public opinion. On the other hand he is also aware that the power structure of the public sphere may distort the mentioned dynamics of mass communication.

Habermas (2006:17–18) distinguishes between three forms of power:
- political power which by definition requires legitimation through the deliberative model of democracy;
- social power (which includes economic power and cultural capital);
- media power based on the technologies of mass communication and include the selection of news and agenda-setting.

The important thing about media power is that journalists operate within a functionally specific and *self-regulating* media system with its own code. This relative independence of the media system was only accomplished, according to Habermas, since the Second World War. From the inside, an informal hierarchy influences the agenda-setting. From the outside, politicians and political parties are the most important suppliers. Generally, though, the government has no control over how the media present and interpret government messages. Representatives of the functional systems and interest groups also have access to the media through corporate communication management methods. Compared to politicians and the lobbyists, other actors in civil society are in a weaker spot (Habermas 2006:18–19). It is at this point that the power structure of public opinion becomes clear and where it becomes important to play by the rules of the game. These rules include:
- the self-regulating media-system must maintain its independence in linking the civil society with the centre of the public sphere;
- an inclusive civil society must empower citizens to participate.

A big potential problem, though, is citizen apathy or public ignorance. Habermas relies on the results of a variety of empirical studies indicating that readers, listeners and viewers are reasonable and open for deliberation. People can be knowledgeable in their reasoning about political choices (Habermas 2006:20–21).

The Public Sphere in Contemporary Society

8.5.3 Pathologies of political communication

Habermas is the first to acknowledge that the requirements of deliberative politics are not easily satisfied in our everyday political communication and the so-called media society. He makes this point clear by indicating how the requirements for a deliberative public sphere are constantly under threat in contemporary societies. The two requirements under threat are:
- the independence of a self-regulated media system;
- the right kind of relationship between the media and civil society (Habermas 2006:21–22).

The incomplete differentiation of the media system from its environments as in Zimbabwe at present, is one problem. The second problem is interference with the independence of a media system that has already reached the level of self-regulation. A recent example in this regard, Habermas says, is:

> *"the manipulation of the American public by the White House's surprisingly successful communication management before and after the invasion of Iraq in 2003."*

media independence

The problem in the US-led invasion of Iraq was the total absence of any counter-framing (Habermas 2006:23). Another aspect that endangers the independence of the media system is the lack of distance between the media and specialised interest groups. This is especially the case when tycoons develop a special agenda in private media – the infamous example in this case is how the Italian media proprietor who became prime minister twice, Silvio Berlusconi, changed the whole complexion of that country's media (Habermas 2006:24).

The political public sphere needs active citizens who voice society's problems and respond to the issues articulated in élite discourse. There are, though, two reasons why this critical feed-back process does not always function:

media and civil society

- the social deprivation or cultural exclusion of citizens explain the selective access to, and uneven participation in, mediated communication. Habermas (2006:25–26) also refers to studies which suggest that people who use electronic media have lower trust in politics.
- the colonisation of the public sphere by market imperatives can lead to a peculiar paralysis of civil society.

More problems include the profit-motive of shareholders as well as the strong emphasis on entertainment in the media. Eventually the political discourse is also translated in entertainment terms, when the issues raised by political candidates easily become personalised. The market pressure of private media is in many cases an obstacle for proper deliberative politics (Habermas 2006:26–27).

8.6 UNCONCLUDING REMARKS

The aim of this chapter was to give an overview of Habermas's concept of the public sphere. It is clear that he moved from an historically informed concept of the public sphere to a more formal and normative one. In the latter case care was given to reconstruct Habermas's argument about public reason and communicative action and how it is applied to mass communication.

Although this is a forceful and influential position that Habermas develops, we should not lose our critical abilities in encountering it. One possible shortcoming of Habermas is that he is too optimistic about the rational aspects of our public life. On the other hand, we could counter that we cannot start developing the vision of a more emancipated public life without critically engaging with the present.

LEARNING ACTIVITIES

- Define in one paragraph the concept of the public sphere.
- Summarise in one page the historical development of the concept of the public sphere.
- Relate the concept of the public sphere to the concepts of:
  - public reason;
  - communicative action;
  - validity;
  - practical reason;
  - representivity;
  - equality;
  - public versus private.
- Summarise in one page Habermas's contribution to the critical study of mass communication in today's society.
- Apply in one page Habermas's work on the public sphere to the South African context and media environment.

The Public Sphere in Contemporary Society

FURTHER READING

Two of the best articles on Jürgen Habermas are:

Bernstein, R.J. 1985. "Introduction." In R.J. Bernstein (ed.): *Habermas and Modernity*. Cambridge: Polity Press.

Dews, P. 1986. "Introduction." In J. Habermas: *Autonomy and Solidarity. Interviews.* Edited by P. Dews. Norfolk: Thetford Press.

For important book-length studies on Jürgen Habermas, see:

Holub, R.C. 1991. *Jürgen Habermas: Critic in the Public Sphere*. London: Routledge.

Ingram, D. 1987. *Habermas and the Dialectic of Reason*. New Haven: Yale University Press.

Keulartz, J. 1992. *De Verkeerde Wereld van Jürgen Habermas*. Amsterdam: Boom.

Matustik, M. 2001. *Jürgen Habermas: A Philosophical-Political Profile*. Lanham, Md.: Rowman and Littlefield.

McCarthy, T. 1984. *The Critical Theory of Jürgen Habermas*. Cambridge, Mass.: MIT Press.

Outhwaite, W. 1994. *Habermas. A Critical Introduction*. Cambridge: Polity Press.

Rasmussen, D. 1990. *Reading Habermas*. Oxford: Basil Blackwell.

White, S. 1988. *The recent work of Jürgen Habermas*. Cambridge: University Press.

For the best compilations on Habermas's work, see:

Bernstein, R. (ed.). 1985. *Habermas and Modernity*. Cambridge: Polity Press.

Dews, P. (ed.). 1999. *Habermas. A Critical Reader*. London: Blackwell.

Hahn, L.E. (ed.). 2000. *Perspectives on Habermas*. Chicago: Open Court Publishers.

Honneth, A. et al. (eds.). 1989. *Zwischenbetrachtungen: Im Prozess der Aufklärung*. Frankfurt: Suhrkamp.

Rasmussen, D., and Swindal, J. (eds.). 2002. *Jürgen Habermas*. 4 vols. London: Sage.

Thompson, J. and Held, D. (eds.). 1982. *Habermas: Critical Debates*. Basingstoke: Macmillan.

White, S. (ed.). 1995. *The Cambridge Companion to Habermas*. Cambridge: University Press.

chapter nine

Globalisation, Information Communication Technology and the Media

Pieter J. Fourie

LEARNING OUTCOMES

At the end of this chapter you should be able to describe and explain the following:
- some characteristics of globalisation;
- the difference between modernism and postmodernism;
- some of the main economic trends of globalisation and their impact on the media industry;
- the basic premises of the New World Information and Communication Order;
- the goals of the Global Information Infrastructure and the World Summits on the Information Society;
- South African information infrastructure goals;
- information and communication technology policy in developing countries;
- research topics in the field of international communication with specific reference to the dependency and media imperialism theories;
- research issues and topics related to the Internet.

Globalisation, Information Communication Technology and the Media

THIS CHAPTER

IN THIS CHAPTER we situate the media in the context of globalisation using a number of perspectives leading to different kinds of questions, forcing us to think in new ways about media institutions, production, content and audiences. For example, multi-national corporations affect the way in which even small and local media companies now need to conduct their business. Information and communication technology, closely associated with the dynamics of globalisation, have changed the ways in which the media produce, distribute and disseminate content and have changed the relationships between media and audiences.

Our purpose with this chapter is to introduce you to a theory of globalisation, trying to answer the question: what is globalisation? We look at how globalisation has brought about new trends in media business, new media environments and new thinking about media regulation. We focus on the move from the New World Information and Communication Order to the Global Information Infrastructure Commission and the World Summits on the Information Society. We end the chapter with a closer look at research topics related to global communication and the Internet – probably the ordinary citizen's most immediate contact with and experience of globalisation – as a mass communication medium.

9.1 WHAT IS GLOBALISATION? A THEORY AND SOME CHARACTERISTICS

Many disciplines, such as sociology, psychology, political science and economics concern themselves with aspects of globalisation. Some theories and research emphasise the positive dimensions of globalisation and its contributions to economic development while others tend to emphasise its potentially negative impacts. In the fields of communication and information sciences, much of the emphasis is on telecommunications and computer technologies in globalisation. Many theorists such as Waters (1995), Castells (1996; 1998) and Giddens (1990; 1999), to name but a few, have contributed to our knowledge of the globalisation phenomenon. Here we look at Giddens.

9.1.1 Giddens' theory of globalisation

In his series of five BBC lectures, the renowned British sociologist Anthony Giddens (1999:1–5) pointed out that the global spread of the term "globalisation" is evidence of the developments to which it refers. As little as ten years ago the term was hardly used, either in academic literature or in everyday language. Now the term is almost everywhere and used by business people, academics, politicians and ordinary people alike. But what is globalisation?

From premodernity to modernity

disembedded organisations

For Giddens, globalisation is a social process involving people all over the world whose lives are affected on a daily basis by disembedded organisations, in other words, not local or national organisations. The disembedded organisations can range from international, financial, political, governmental, educational and cultural organisations to the media organisations that provide many of us with information and entertainment which, in turn, contributes to our understanding of the world.

modernisation

In his theory of globalisation, Giddens argues that the process of globalisation already started with modernisation. Modernisation (which followed pre-modernism, a stage characterised by traditionalism) was caused by and involved major changes in what Giddens calls four major institutional complexes and which affect the ways in which people governed and were governed; the ways goods were produced; the economic system; and the ways in which wars were conducted.

Administrative power: the development of the secular nation-state. Prior to modernisation people were governed in a feudal system by kings, queens, landlords, chiefs, religious bodies, and so forth. The nation state, on the other hand, is based upon rational and bureaucratic forms of administration, law and order formulated by states within the confines of national geographical borders.

Industrialisation: the development of technology displaced traditional forms of production and products and introduced a move from agriculture to factory and industrial production.

Capitalism: the move from agricultural to industrial production introduced capitalism and the concepts of "private ownership", "competition", "profit" and "profit-making".

Militarism: against the background of industrialisation, the manufacturing of warfare was mechanised and professional armies were introduced.

time-space distanciation

Giddens then explains that the changes that took place in these institutional complexes were the result of what he calls time-space distanciation. Time-space distanciation can be explained as follows. To begin with, we distinguish between pre-modern (or traditional) society and modern

Globalisation, Information Communication Technology and the Media

society. How did people relate to time and space in traditional society compared to in modern society? For Giddens the invention of the clock was one of the main historical moments that introduced the change from pre-modern to modern society (see Table 9.1).

Table 9.1 Pre-modern compared to modern society

	PRE-MODERN SOCIETY MODERN SOCIETY
TIME	Linked to seasons and seasonal change. No clock and no conceptualisation of national and international time.
	The invention of the clock changed people's conceptualisation of time. Time no longer seasonally linked or linked between day and night. The clock not based on seasonal time but on artificial social time. Time is linear and not cyclical. Time measured globally and not locally. This also introduced a sense of cultural distance (for example, at 8.30 p.m. in South Africa, in parts of Europe it is 9.30 p.m.).
SPACE	Space confined to the local: the farm, the village. Thus a narrow sense of space, both geographically and socially. People seldom moved beyond the borders of their particular communities. Ideas of space were fixed: people hardly knew about "other parts of the world". In other words, the majority of people (mainly peasants) were embedded in their local communities.
	The invention of the clock also started to change our sense of space as communities began to calibrate their sense of time with other communities. People increasingly began to move beyond the borders of their local communities.
STATUS	Social status was ascribed at birth, be it peasantry, landlord, royalty. There was little sense of what we today know as a career.
	The concept of "social mobility" is introduced.

In short, Giddens argues that modernisation and modernity are based upon a process whereby a fixed and narrow idea of "space" as "place" (prevalent in pre-modern times) is gradually eroded by an ever increasingly dominant concept of (universal) time. Giddens describes this conceptualisation of time as the key to processes of disembedment.

For Giddens, disembedment is one of the main characteristics of globalisation. He distinguishes between two types of disembedment (also known as delocalisation, deculturalisation, detraditionalisation):

- a change in symbolic tokens; and the universality of symbolic tokens;
- development of trust in and reliance on expert systems.

symbolic tokens

Money can be an example of a symbolic token. The economy of pre-modern societies was based on products being exchanged, or bartered, for the right to live on a landlord's property, to "pay" for goods, and so on. For example, labour was exchanged for food and a house; livestock, crops and other products were given in exchange for the right to live in the house and farm the landlord's property. The keyword was exchange of goods and products. Modernisation replaced these forms of payment with a symbolic token, money. Money, as a symbolic form of payment, made it possible for people to move between communities and countries, which in turn made the establishment of new social, cultural and economic relations possible.

In short, modernisation introduced the notion of a national currency, which wiped out local differences within national boundaries. Today, globalisation is beginning to wipe out differences between national currencies. For example, in Europe national currencies such as the French franc, Belgian franc or the Dutch guilder were replaced by the euro. Within the African Union the possibility of a single African currency is from time to time mentioned. Modernisation also introduced the credit card as a global form of payment, issued by a bank in one country but used all over the world. A South African bank account can be accessed by an ATM in London.

expert systems

By a reliance on expert systems Giddens means:
- a general increase in specialisation; standardised systems or models, for example, health care or education; reliance on science; trust in and reliance on technology, for example, the computerised regulation of air traffic.

To summarise: the processes of globalisation started with the move from pre-modern to modern societies. Modernism brought along changes in the ways in which people were governed (administrative power); the way they produced and manufactured goods (industrialisation); the way they sold goods – with profit-making as a primary goal (capitalism); and the way in which warfare was produced and armies constituted. Among many contributing factors, it was the invention of the clock which began to change people"s conceptualisation of time and space from the seasonal and local to an awareness of global time and other communities, locations

Globalisation, Information Communication Technology and the Media

and geographies. These changes also contributed to new symbolic tokens (of which we have only referred to money) and the introduction of expert systems.

From modernity to late modernity (globalisation)

Giddens further divided modernity into two phases: early modernity and late (or high) modernity. (Some authors and theorists also refer to late modernity as postmodernity or postmodernism.) The changes mentioned above formed part of early modernity. An outstanding feature of late modernity is globalisation. What we are experiencing now, namely globalisation, is thus only part of late modernity. Some authors and theorists also refer to late modernity as postmodernity or postmodernism, starting in the 1960s.

Outstanding features of globalisation

For media studies, some of the outstanding features of globalisation discussed by Giddens are the following:

The development of a world capitalist system dominated by transnational corporations operating independently of nation states (the World Bank, the International Monetary Fund, the United Nations). These transnational corporations can dictate (in the form of economic pressure and measures) to some nation states. It is against the impact of transnational corporations on national economies (especially those of developing countries) that some non-governmental organisations (NGOs) protest at IMF meetings and other events (even though some NGOs such as Greenpeace and Oxfam themselves share characteristics of transnational corporations). In general there can be a sense of loss of control over national economic affairs within elected governments. — world capitalist system

The growth of the so-called culture industry, including the growth of the media and international media corporations and all their products, has created the so-called information and knowledge society. The main characteristic of this society is that the volume, spread and availability of knowledge and information (sometimes redundant information) has increased to a level not known before in the history of humanity. This has far-reaching consequences. The accelerated availability of constantly changing information and knowledge, and with it a perceived dependence on information and knowledge for survival, may have created an existential dilemma. Whereas in pre-modernity and early — culture industry

modernity people relied more on religion, tradition and providence, they may now rely on knowledge and information. Some people (and possibly some small or poor nations) who do not have access to knowledge and information may well feel left out and threatened. In short, they can be overruled and experience a loss of status. Small wonder then that Giddens calls this new reliance on knowledge and information the main existential dilemma of globalisation. As far as tradition is concerned, Giddens argues that on the political level, globalisation has exhausted the old politics of "left" and "right". In early modernity it was possible to distinguish more clearly between the traditions of conservatism, liberalism and labourism. Lately, such distinctions are more blurred, as are some of the distinctions between class. On the cultural level there can be a feeling of loss of space and character.

localisation

A process running concurrently with globalisation is known as localisation. Although it may seem as if globalisation is all about interrelatedness on the economic, cultural, military and governance levels there is at the same time a rediscovery and re-appreciation of the local. Although some people, groups and nations may experience globalisation as a threat to their own cultures, beliefs and ideals, at the same time it creates new opportunities for the globalisation of their cultures, beliefs and ideals (although these may only became part of a new world culture). For example, through the media"s spread of information and knowledge many of us are today more than ever aware of the beliefs, practices and ideals of distant cultures, of the suffering of people and nations, of the crime and corruption of dictatorial regimes and even of the arguments of those opposing globalisation.

Giddens' theory of globalisation is not without criticism. Many authors claim that the processes now described as typical of globalisation have occurred throughout the history of humanity and that what we now call the processes of globalisation are nothing more than a continuation of processes started centuries ago as part of the evolutionary development of human control over nature. For example, what we term the "information revolution" can easily be explained as a process that started with the invention of the printing press in the fifteenth century – an invention with, at that time, the same far-reaching consequences as we are experiencing today with computer technology. The big difference is the speed with which the changes are taking place and increased geographical spread.

Globalisation, Information Communication Technology and the Media

Some characteristics of globalisation

When listing some characteristics (or trends) of globalisation, it is important to take into account that some of these characteristics are contradictory and that by the time of publication some of them may have changed or even moved in an opposite direction! This points to the fact that at this stage globalisation remains difficult to define, which may be so because globalisation is still an emerging phenomenon moving in the direction of the creation of a new kind of society – the so-called global society. We list the following characteristics:

Globalisation is an all-encompassing phenomenon involving economic, political, technological and cultural transformation. A new world economic order in which local economies are integrated into a global economy is developing. On the political level the ways in which nations are governed are becoming more globally transparent and nations are increasingly entering into interstate and regional agreements. All this is made possible by increased technological developments which in many ways form the foundation of globalisation and accelerate cultural diffusion creating what is called a global culture.

_{new world economic order}

Communication technology and systems play a central role in globalisation. According to Giddens (1999), new electronic ways of conveying news and information have altered the very texture of our lives. To explain this Giddens uses the example of South Africa's first democratic president, Nelson Mandela. He argues that when the image of Nelson Mandela is more familiar to people all over the world than the face of our neighbour, something has changed in the nature of our everyday experience. Nelson Mandela is a global celebrity, famous for having survived decades in prison, and celebrity itself is largely a product of new communications technology. The reach of media technologies is growing with each wave of innovation. It took, for example, forty years for radio in the United States to gain an audience of fifty million. The same number of people were using personal computers only fifteen years after the personal computer was introduced (although it is true that population expansion and increasing affluence would have also played a role in this dramatic increase). In the same way, it needed a mere four years, after it was made available, for fifty million Americans to be regularly using the Internet (Giddens 1999:3).

technology

357

personal lives

Globalisation does not only affect macro structures and institutions but also the personal aspects of our lives. Family structures as the basic building blocks of a society are always transforming but the changes seem to be particularly intense as the relationships between the sexes and between the so-called races, and among minority and pressure groups, are becoming more important. The global media may have opened up discussions about these changes and contributed to more liberal (or in some cases, a backlash against) thinking about them; the media appears to have questioned traditional views, and pointed to the restrictive and discriminatory in traditional views and values. Smaller families and family planning are the order of the day; women are becoming more equal to men and are playing leadership roles as never before in history; relationships between homosexual and lesbian couples are legalised in countries such as South Africa and Canada; racial discrimination issues are pushed to the fore; and the interests and issues of minority and pressure groups (even of those protesting globalisation and its impact on the economy and culture) are on the world agenda. Giddens (1999) pointed to the fact that as a reaction to this, fundamentalism may seem to be growing; this is only as a consequence of the irreversible impact of globalisation on the very nature of society.

local cultural identity

Globalisation leads (contradictorily) to the revival of local cultural identities. At the same time, and on the face of it contrary to the above, globalisation is also the reason for the revival of local cultural identities in different parts of the world. Many people think of globalisation simply as the disappearance of local communities into the global arena. This may be only partially true. Although nations and their governments may be more intertwined and linked than ever before (through numerous political, economic and military agreements and through their media institutions and media content), there is at the same time a move towards a rediscovery of own national and cultural identities and the recognition thereof by governments. In numerous parts of the world, groups are at work fighting for the acknowledgement of their freedom and recognition of their independence. One can argue that the acknowledgement of the right of the African National Congress to govern the majority of South Africa's people, following the first democratic election in 1994, and the recognition of the rights of the African majority in South Africa were, amongst other factors, a direct consequence of globalisation. In this regard the world media may have helped to open the world's eyes to the plight of people in South Africa which in its turn led world leaders (with

Globalisation, Information Communication Technology and the Media

notable exceptions such as Britain's Margaret Thatcher and the USA's Ronald Reagan) to increase pressure for apartheid's abandonment.

Globalisation is a product of human inspiration. Giddens (1999) emphasises that globalisation is not something forced upon us by nature. It is the making of human thinking. We tend to believe that economy and technology (as the two main driving forces of globalisation) are something above us. They are not. The collapse of Soviet Communism wasn't something that just happened to occur but was the making of human thinking inspired by the recognition of the fact that since the seventies the Soviet Union and the East European countries which the Soviets controlled were rapidly falling behind the West in economic growth. The ideological and cultural control upon which communist political authority was based similarly could not survive in an era of global media. Because of communication technology the Soviet and the East European regimes were unable to block the reception of Western radio and TV broadcasts. Television played a direct role in the 1989 revolutions in Eastern Europe, which have rightly been called the first "television revolutions". Street protests taking place in one country, Poland, were watched by audiences in other countries in which large numbers then took to the streets themselves (Giddens 1999). The same applies to the collapse of apartheid, although this is not to undermine the role played by decades of resistance movements, which ranged from quiet diplomacy to armed combat. Apart from economic sanctions against the apartheid government, the worldview against apartheid, through the globalising effects of the content of international communication and information, became so overpowering that the apartheid government could no longer hold out against negotiations with the African National Congress leaders.

_{product of humanity}

Globalisation widens inequalities. To many living outside Europe and North America, Giddens (1999) argues, globalisation looks like Westernisation or Americanisation. No one can doubt the status of the US as the sole superpower. The US has a dominant economic, cultural and military position in the global order, although this may have been somewhat undermined by their very public failure to enforce law and order after invading Iraq. Many of the most visible cultural expressions of globalisation are American, for example, Coca-Cola, McDonald's, big names in the fashion, industrial and financial world, the products of Hollywood, dominance in the provision of popular English-language television programming such as soap operas, and so on. Many of the

_{inequality}

359

giant multinational companies are based in the USA. Those that aren't, come from other rich countries. A pessimistic view of globalisation would consider it largely an affair of the industrial North, in which the developing societies of the South play little or no active part. In such a view, globalisation is seen as destroying local cultures, widening world inequalities and worsening the lot of the impoverished. Globalisation, some argue, creates a world of winners and losers; a few on the fast track to prosperity, the majority condemned to a life of misery and despair.

Many authors believe that although small improvements in some developing countries may have occurred, the divide is growing given the continued development and implementation of new and more advanced communication and information technologies. As far back as in 1999 Giddens provided the following statistics to illustrate the digital divide.

The share of the poorest fifth of the world's population in global income dropped from 2.3 percent to 1.4 percent within ten years, although some of this may be due to population expansion which may in turn derive from some of the benefits of globalisation. The proportion of global income taken by the richest fifth, on the other hand, has risen from 70 percent to 85 percent.

In Sub-Saharan Africa, twenty countries have lower incomes per head in real terms than they did two decades ago, although it is true that equally poor nations in Asia and Latin America have not suffered the same fate, so this may not be entirely due to globalisation

In many less developed countries, safety and environmental regulations are low or virtually non-existent, sometimes because of the lack of public pressure, sometimes because governments argue that job creation is more important than job regulation. Some transnational companies sell goods in less economically developed countries that are more controlled or banned in the industrial countries: poor quality medical drugs, destructive pesticides or high tar and nicotine content cigarettes.

_{reversed colonialism}

Globalisation involves a mix of nationalities (and their cultures) to such an extent that in some parts of the world one can even speak of "reversed colonialism". One has only to look at the population of big European and American cities such as London, Paris, New York, Los Angeles and Brussels where there is a mix of nationalities to such an extent that it is often difficult to recognise the "true" citizens of the country to which the city belongs. This is mainly due to the relaxation of immigration

laws, the relative ease with which work permits can be obtained and increased tourism as well as the infiltration of illegal workers and political asylum seekers. Eventually all this impacts on the culture and economy of the resident countries. Giddens (1999) specifically refers to the Latinising of Los Angeles, but the Africanisation of Johannesburg as skilled professionals from across Africa join the South African economy might be another example. Apart from "cultural de-colonialisation", there is an increase of smaller countries exporting their products to the major industrialised countries. Giddens (1999) refers to the emergence of a globally-oriented high-tech sector in India, the selling of Brazilian television programmes to Portugal, the export of African art and the export of Eastern furniture to the West.

Globalisation changes the nature of the nation state. One of the crucial topics addressed by Giddens (1999; 2000) is the influence of globalisation on the existence of the nation-state. Is a nation-state still in full control of its own policies and governance of the people? Are national political leaders still powerful, or are they becoming relatively irrelevant in comparison to the forces shaping the world? Giddens (1999) argues that nation-states are indeed still powerful and national political leaders still have a large role to play in the world. However, their emphasis is no longer in terms of facing real enemies, but rather in terms of facing and managing strategic, economic, technological and cultural risks: purchasing and implementing multi-billion-rand information and communication technological systems; arms agreements; of importing and exporting; of formulating immigrations laws; of entering into international environment protection agreements, and so on. This move from facing real enemies to facing and managing risks, is a massive shift in the very nature of the nation-state and the role of national political leaders.

_{nation-state}

Globalisation is the emergence of a global cosmopolitan society. Giddens (1999; 2000) concludes that we continue to talk of the nation, the family, work, tradition, culture, as if they are all the same as in the past. They are not. The outer shell remains but inside all is different. This is happening not only in the USA, Britain or France but almost everywhere. They are what Giddens (1999) calls "shell institutions" that have become inadequate to the tasks they are called upon to perform. As the changes to institutions gather weight, they are creating something that has never existed before; a global cosmopolitan society. He then points to the fact that:

cosmopolitan society

> "... we are the first generation to live in this society, whose contours we can as yet only dimly see. It is shaking up our existing ways of life, no matter where we happen to be. This is not – at least at the moment - a global order driven by collective human will. Instead, it is emerging in an anarchic, haphazard, fashion, carried along by a mixture of economic, technological and cultural imperatives. It is not settled or secure, but fraught with anxieties, as well as scarred by deep divisions. Many of us feel in the grip of forces over which we have no control. Can we re-impose our will upon them? I believe we can. The powerlessness we experience is not a sign of personal failings, but reflects the incapacities of our institutions. We need to reconstruct those we have or create new ones, in ways appropriate to the global age." (Giddens 1999:5).

In the following section we look at some of the implications of globalisation for the media. The focus is mainly on information and communication technology and economic trends.

9.2 THE IMPACT OF GLOBALISATION ON THE MEDIA

The rapid development of information and communication technology (ICT) may be the most important catalyst of globalisation. The impact of globalisation on the media thus goes hand in hand with the development of ICT. Globalisation and ICT has brought about the renewed and accelerated development of international media conglomerates, spreading their information and entertainment across the globe with speed and in volumes unknown before. Like never before the media and its new technologies, such as the Internet and mobile telephony (cell phones) distribute knowledge about different cultures, world events, values and beliefs across the globe. All this has brought about new ways of conducting media business and has urged governments to revise the ways in which the media are regulated.

To describe how globalisation affects media ownership, production, distribution and the changed relationships between the media, its audiences and governments, in a few pages, is impossible. Rather, we focus on some of the broad economic trends which has changed the face of the media landscape.

Globalisation, Information Communication Technology and the Media

9.2.1 Economic trends

The following economic trends in the media have intensified with globalisation and the development of ICT:
- concentration;
- convergence;
- liberalisation;
- privatisation;
- internationalisation;
- commercialisation.

Concentration

Concentration happens when the means of production in market sectors is owned by fewer and larger groups. One example of concentrated media ownership is the merger of computer company America Online (AOL) and magazine publishing and movie empire Time Warner in the USA in 2000. This merger created a $350 billion empire. The new company, called Time Warner, incorporated the ownership of some of the world's biggest film production studios, television stations such as CNN, TNT and the Cartoon Network, record and CD companies, numerous magazines including the weekly newsmagazine *Time*, book publishing companies, and cable television networks. It included online services such as Netscape, Compuserve, MovieFone, and Internet Messenger. For Time Warner the merger included possibilities such as the development of the emerging Internet movie business and the digital delivery of movies-on-demand, more interactive television, online radio stations, broadband outlets, and so on, although increasing movie piracy has affected profits. For AOL, although hurt by the so-called dot.com bust and a stagnating subscriber base, it meant access to Time Warner's cable customers and speedier Internet and television services (*Time* 2000:39–50).

> concentration

Immediately after the merger, *Time* magazine (part of the new company) reported extensively on the merger. In an essay "Is big really bad? Well, yes" Victor Navasky (2000:48) wrote that "fewer and fewer corporations would come to dominate the media environment, resulting in the free-enterprise equivalent of a Ministry of Culture. It has to do with mega-communications conglomerates that are bigger than the economies of countries whose monopolistic information policies we condemn as a violation of democratic values."

A good example of media integration in South Africa is, for instance, the company Naspers. Naspers consists of two groups: Media24 and the MIH Group. Media24 has interests in newspaper, magazine and book publishing as well as in private education. The company publishes five daily, two weekly, three Sunday, 11 community newspapers and 21 free sheets in different towns. It publishes 38 magazines and has an interest in seven book publishers and five retail and distribution companies, such as Leisure Books and Van Schaik Bookstores. It has interests in printing and distribution and in consumer related Internet businesses. As far as education is concerned, Media24's interests concern Educor, Damelin and ICG (an international college distance education group) education providers. Naspers' broadcasting interests are dealt with by the MIH Group with its interest in MultiChoice with 74 video, 65 audio and 8 data channels, M-Net with 15 entertainment channels, SuperSport with nine sport channels and M-Web as one of South Africa's major Internet service providers. Internationally, MIH is involved with MultiChoice Africa, Netmed in Greece and Cyprus, Tencent (Internet China), Sanook! (Internet Thailand), Mail.ru (Internet Russia), Irdeto (content protection solutions), Entriq (content protection and subscriber management services), Media Zone (broadband for small audiences), as well as printing interests in China. (See http:www.naspers.com for a full overview of the company.)

Convergence

convergence

Convergence means the coming together of information and communication technologies (ICTs), especially the merging of telecommunications and traditional media, creating new ways of producing, distributing and using knowledge, information and entertainment. Mansell and Wehn (1998:13) argued that convergence means that there are fewer clear boundaries between media and telecommunication technologies. The telecommunications network provides the electronic/digital platform for the development of new communication and information services including database access, the Internet, pay television, high definition television and multimedia. All this is made possible by the digitisation of the information and media content and the introduction of a new variety of interactive services (*ibid*:132).

For van Cuilenburg and McQuail (2003:197) technological convergence also means that the boundaries between information technologies and communication networks are technically blurring: computer and

telecommunications are converging to telematics; personal computers and television become more similar; and formerly separated networks become more and more interconnected to render the same kind of services. Multimedia integrates text, audio and video. Along with technological convergence there is also economic convergence: the merging of the branches of computing, communications and content (publishing).

A broader understanding of convergence focuses on hybridisation, intertextuality, intermediality and multimodality, an important extension that contributes to our broader understanding of media culture (Briggs & Burke, 2002.) Convergence affects much more than the mutual identities of different media: it is crucially about legitimating media's social and political roles (Hujanen & Lowe, 2003:9). Thomass (2003:37) stresses how convergence creates new combinations of different platforms for distribution and access, terminals, services and content. Different media will continue to exist side-by-side, but via convergence a new environment is created in which broadcasting, for example, becomes part of a diversified communication and information system offering services with overlapping sectors.

An example of convergence's impact on traditional mass media is the SABC's Afrikaans radio station RSG (radiosondergrense or Radio Without Borders). In 2000 it became one of the first radio stations in the world to go multi-media and thus available on radio, television (an audio channel on DStv), the Internet (http:www.rsg.co.za) and on WAP-enabled cellphone. Convergence allows listeners to become audience and producer with immediate interaction with the station (feedback). The Internet site enables listeners to tune into the frequency, search archives, advertise events, post comments, visit celebrities' home pages and interact with DJs in the studio. In short, RSG is no longer just a radio station.

> "but a purveyor of information; ... not a simple extension of existing media, but encourages each media platform to reflect audience interaction; its free-to-air channel on the Dstv satellite bouquet and Internet portal is revolutionising this medium and language, offering advertisers value for money" (Hunter 2001:16).

A further example of the impact of convergence on the traditional media is the fact that almost all the big South African newspapers are now also available on the Internet. A good example is the weekly English language

Media Studies: Volume 1

newspaper *Mail & Guardian*, now available daily on the Internet as the *Mail & Guardian Online*, with news updated daily and even hourly, including an African service providing news, opinion and features from Africa. Another example is DStv, South Africa's main satellite television provider. Apart from providing numerous specialised television channels to subscribers, DStv also provides free interactive services such as GameZone, allowing viewers to play games and test their skills.

Apart from the fact that convergence leads to new methods of media production, distribution and access, and demands new computer-related skills from media workers, convergence also has many implications in the field of media policy. South Africa adopted an Electronic Communications Act in 2005 to promote convergence in the broadcasting, signal distribution and telecommunications sectors and to provide the legal framework for the convergence of these sectors. The act also seeks to make new provision for the regulation of electronic communications services, network services and broadcasting services.

Liberalisation

liberalisation

Liberalisation is a process of state intervention to expand the number of participants in the market, typically by creating competing providers of communication services. Usually, this involves establishing a private competitor in a public or private monopoly market. Liberalisation aims specifically to increase market competition (Mosco & Rideout 1997:170). A good example of liberalisation in South Africa was the introduction of the country's first free-to-air television station e.tv. (Free-to-air means viewers do not have to pay additional money to receive the signal, whereas in the case of M-Net viewers have to pay a subscription fee and own a decoder, although the title is something of a misnomer as e.tv relies on the same network of terrestrial broadcasting towers which is funded and maintained by the SABC television licence.) Although it is subscription television, the introduction of M-Net in 1986, the first South African television broadcaster besides the SABC, can also be seen as a step in the direction of liberalisation. The same accounts for the separation of the SABC in terms of the new Broadcasting Act (4 of 1999) into two operational entities, public and public-commercial. Another example of liberalisation in the communications industry was legislation to introduce a second fixed-line telecommunications operator, besides the state parastatal Telkom. More recently (2006), the Independent

Globalisation, Information Communication Technology and the Media

Communications Authority of South Africa (ICASA) introduced the possibility of allowing more role players in the field of subscription television.

Privatisation

Mosco and Rideout (1997:173) define privatisation as a process of state intervention that literally sells off a state enterprise such as a public broadcaster or a state telephone company. They explain that privatisation takes many forms, depending on the percentage of shares to be sold off, the extent to which any foreign ownership is permitted, the length, if any, of a phase-in period, and the specific form of continuing state involvement, typically constituted in a regulatory body, in the aftermath of privatisation. According to Mosco and Rideout the main reasons for privatisation are:

- the rise of governments that are ideologically committed to private control over economic activity;
- the attraction, if only as a once-off event, of revenues for government coffers;
- the pressures of transnational businesses and governmental organisations such as the International Monetary Fund.

> privatisation

Some of the criticism against privatisation is the nation's loss of sovereignty in selling off to foreign firms, and the consequent possible loss of local control. An example of privatisation in the South African media was the SABC's sale of public radio stations to private owners. Another example is Telkom. In 1997, 30% of Telkom was sold to Thintana Communications, a consortium made up of US-based SBC Communications Inc. and Telekom Malaysia. Three percent was set aside for economic empowerment and awarded to Ucingo Investments, which in turn represents 20 empowerment groups nation-wide. The remaining shares in Telkom were listed on the Johannesburg Securities Exchange and New York Stock Exchange early in 2003.

Internationalisation

Internationalisation involves the processes of states creating their own wide range of teaming arrangements or strategic alliances that integrate them in different degrees of internationalisation. A first stage is usually regional alliances such as the Southern African Development Community (SADC). Other examples include institutional planning

> internationalisation

organisations (Group of Seven), and interstate agreements such as the General Agreement on Tariffs and Trade (GATT) from the World Trade Organisation. Internationalisation requires some degree of interstate coordination. It shifts communication responses from national policy applications to ones where bilateral, trilateral and multinational trade agreements require structural policy changes. Internationalisation can challenge national sovereignty and raise questions about national identity. All countries, but particularly those whose markets are too small to sustain substantial indigenous production for the local market, are faced with declining capacity for independent governance and cultural formation (Mosco & Rideout 1997:174–177).

Commercialisation

<aside>commercialisation</aside>

Mosco and Rideout (1997:168) define commercialisation as the process that takes place when the state replaces forms of regulation based on public interest and public service with market standards. In the communications industry this has meant greater emphasis on market position and profitability. In other words, the emphasis is no longer on providing a universal service to the public such as public service broadcasting. To the contrary, the emphasis is now on the marketability and thus popularity of media content. The result can be commercially-successful broadcasting with an overload of popular programme genres and content such as talk shows, popular music, games, sport and advertisements. Everything depends on audience size, advertising revenue, and producing programming/content that searches for the biggest audience and linkages to other revenue-generating media. One can argue that the commercialisation of South African broadcasting started in the '50s with the introduction of the now defunct English/Afrikaans commercial radio station, Springbok Radio, and in television with the introduction of M-Net in the '80s. The process of commercialisation continued with the adoption of the new South African Broadcasting Act no. 4 of 1999. This Act provides for the division of the SABC (public service broadcaster) into two sections: a public service section and a (public) commercial section. (See the case study on public service broadcasting in chapter 4.)

<aside>new media environment</aside>

To conclude: all these trends contributed to a new media environment in which the emphasis is on:
- a multi-media approach (technological convergence);
- diversity and choice (liberalisation, privatisation, increased competition and commercialisation);

Globalisation, Information Communication Technology and the Media

- new distribution platforms (technological convergence);
- the blurring of genres: infotainment (commercialisation);
- increased interactivity, for example, talk and game shows/programmes (made possible through increased technological convergence);
- the convergence of public and private media, for example, the previous clear distinction between three main types of national broadcasting systems, namely a core public service system, a core private system, or a core state system started to merge into a single system made up of a mix of public, private and other types of broadcasters in which public service broadcasting may still play a significant, but no longer dominant role;
- the rise of niche markets (increased liberalisation, privatisation, internationalisation).

All these trends have created what is called in post-Saussurian semiotics (see the chapter on media semiotics in volume 3) a media sphere as part of the semiosphere of meaning (Hartley 1999, 2004; Jacka 2004; Lotman 1990). Semiosphere refers to all the meanings and objects of meaning, including art, theatre, architecture, photographic images, the environment, objects, and texts of all sorts. These sources of meaning surround us and determine our sense-making of the world, people and their behaviour. However, given the omnipresence of the media and media culture (see chapter 6 on media culture) in today's world, our sense-making of the world is saturated with media representations, interpretations, and messages. The "media sphere" has come to occupy a central place within the semiosphere and refers to the whole universe of media, both factual and fictional, in all forms (print, electronic, digital and so on), all genres, all taste hierarchies, all languages, in all countries. It encloses and contains as a differentiated part of itself the Habermasian public sphere (see chapter 8), which in itself is contained by the much larger semiosphere (Lotman 1990). Against the background of globalisation and the internationalisation of the media, it can be asked: do different countries and language groups still have different media spheres?

9.2.2 A new regulatory paradigm

Globalisation and the development of ICT, including the convergence of media technologies, seems to have partially replaced a public service orientation with a stronger emphasis on market orientation in and by the media. This necessitates a new way of thinking about media regulation.

Van Cuilenburg and McQuail (2003:181–207) distinguish the following three paradigms in media regulation.

first paradigm

The first paradigm is called The Emerging Communications Industry Media Paradigm. Media policy before World War II was focused mainly on the emerging "new" communications industry brought about by the telegraph, telephony and wireless. The main reason for policy was to harmonise state interest and financial corporate interests. Policy was often created from *ad hoc* measures in response to new innovations. It focused on separate telecommunications technologies and on means of distribution. It was also characterised by international cooperation in the field of international agreements about telecommunications. In the USA a model of partly-government-regulated private monopoly with the emphasis on private ownership emerged. In Europe (and in Canada in North America, and in much of Asia, Africa and Latin America) the model of state/public monopoly emerged: media were seen to be a public utility and as such a branch of government. A state/public monopoly ideally was to serve the national (also seen to be the public's) interest as determined by the state rather than audience demand. Both the USA and Europe emphasised the strategic importance of the communications media. At the end of this first phase of communications policy, it became possible to distinguish a divergence of communication policies for the different media and the beginning of key issues that would dominate media policy in the years to come. For example:

- The print media: guarantees of freedom of publication and expression with an emphasis on self-regulation and private initiative. In general, the role of the government was limited. Policy was not so much concerned with the structure of the press (in other words with who owns and may own what) and with quality.
- Common carrier policy (telegraph and telephony): This was characterised by strong regulation of ownership and infrastructure (not of content), taking into account public rights of access and privacy and with an emphasis on efficiency, good administration, and a public service ethos.
- Broadcasting (first wireless or radio, and later television): This was characterised by strong regulation of content and access, restricted freedom of expression, some form of monopoly and oligopoly, a notion of public service and pressure towards universal provision.

The second paradigm, after World War II until roughly the 1990s, is called The Public Service Media Policy Paradigm (van Cuilenburg & McQuail 2003). During this phase, media policy can be described as normative policy derived from the needs of democratic politics rather than policy inspired by political and technological considerations. It stood in the sign of the lessons learned during the Second World War about misusing the media for propaganda. The emphasis was on democracy and the role of the media in democracy and on the role of the media in establishing national coherence and stability. Broadcasting, for example, was seen to function in the spirit of social reform encouraged by post-war reconstruction, whereas in print the emphasis was on the promotion of diversity of ownership and content, limiting monopolies and dealing with complaints against the press (van Cuilenburg & McQuail 2003). Policy was bound by the limits of national territory and focused on national interest. It legitimated government interventions in communication markets for social purposes and active and continuous policy-making and revisions were required. Especially in Europe, but also in Australasia, Canada and elsewhere, values related to freedom, equality and solidarity guided policy, and policy was expected to create institutional expression of these values. The end of this phase saw the beginning of privatisation and competition. The policy challenge was how to break monopolies under the banner of deregulation but at the same time to do so in the spirit of social responsible normative theory.

second paradigm

According to van Cuilenburg and McQuail (2003) we are presently experiencing the third phase of media policy, called The New Communications Policy Paradigm. The emphasis is on convergence, the breaking up of monopolies and deregulation. As far as convergence and new technologies are concerned, policy trends remind us of those in Phase 1 – dealing with new technologies such as the satellite television, pay television, Internet and mobile (cellphone) telephony. However, this has to be done in a completely new social, political, economic and cultural environment brought about by globalisation. The lever of change is technology leading to convergence of communications infrastructures and services. The new environment is characterised by a possible decline of ideology such as the fall of communism in the 1980s and the end of apartheid in the 1990s, although this may be counterbalanced by rising conservative religious ideologies. A respect for the market, pragmatism, populism and globalisation are all characteristics of the postmodern era.

third paradigm

In the third paradigm, policy is driven by an economic and technological logic. Although normative elements are still present, policy now seeks and needs to cover a wider range of values less focused on democracy and politics, encompassing economic and consumerist values. Despite rhetoric about equality and access to media, present policy's emphasis on equality may have more to do with commerce and control than with social equality and social welfare. Where policy is still open to the influences of public opinion, then it especially concerns matters of morality, taste, human rights and harm to young people. (In volume 2 of this book, van Cuilenburg & Bardoel expand on these paradigms.)

For authors such as van Cuilenburg and Bardoel, the challenges now facing media policy are to:
- develop policy against the background of a changing definition of public interest;
- find a balance between economic and non-economic goals;
- ensure participation of all groups of civil society;
- facilitate supervision by state regulators;
- maintain quality standards;
- ensure access to the media.

To conclude: globalisation, together with the development of ICT, has created a media environment in which the emphasis is on the media as a market – as a commercial product, compared to the previous emphasis on the media as a social product ostensibly in service of the public good. Secondly, from a technological perspective, globalisation has pushed convergence to the fore as probably the most characteristic feature of the new media environment.

From an economic perspective, the media are today big business, with profit-making being a main drive. It is characterised as being a hybrid business depending on fixed costs, creativity involving lots of uncertainties, and on the multiple and recycled use of its products. As a business it tends towards concentration and is difficult to enter. Most of all, it depends on the public's interest which may constantly change. (See volume 2 on media management for a further and more in-depth discussion of these characteristics and the strategies employed by the media to cope in the business world.) In the next section, we focus on technology and convergence as the second most prominent characteristic of the media in the era of globalisation.

Globalisation, Information Communication Technology and the Media

9.3 FROM THE NWICO TO THE GII AND THE WSIS

For O'Sullivan, Hartley, Saunders, Montgomery and Fiske (1994:130), one of the main issues of globalisation is that national culture and identity are replaced by a global–local dimension and that everyday experience of the local is now saturated with references to the global. Central to this process has been the emergence of information and communication technologies and its media networks which allow for faster, more extensive, interdependent forms of worldwide exchange, travel and interaction. In communication science these concerns have led to numerous debates about media imperialism, and the inequalities as far as access to and the use of the media are concerned. Today these debates rage in forums such as the World Summits on the Information Society, focusing on the digital divide insofar as lack of access to ICT is concerned. However, it can be argued that the New World Information and Communication Order (NWICO) and the debates that characterise the discourse about inequities in the traditional mass media laid the foundation for today's debates. For this reason we first focus on the NWICO.

9.3.1 The New World Information and Communication Order

The history of the New World Information and Communication Order

The emphasis on the role of communication in democracy and the acknowledgement of communication and information as a basic human right underlie the development of the New World Information and Communication Order's concerns about the inequalities in the state of international communication. How can we talk about a free and just world if, as Vincent (1997:378) mentioned, the following existed in 1997:

digital divide

- The developing world has only four percent of the world's computers.
- Thirty-four countries of the world have no television sets.
- Africa (in total) has less than three newspapers per country whereas the United States has 1 687 and Japan 125 dailies.
- There are more telephone lines in Tokyo than on the entire African continent (although this is also due to the reliance on mobile numbers in Africa).

(For updated figures see the list of websites at the end of the chapter. These websites monitor, amongst other issues, inequities related to media

access, media use, women in the media, community access and inequities between countries.)

Vincent's figures, although more than a decade old, emphasise huge communication inequities in the world, especially if we want to argue that communication is crucial for economic and social development. The New World Information and Communication Order tried to find answers to inequities such as these as well as to inequities in the production and distribution of media content. As such the New World Information and Communication Order can be described as a first attempt towards an international communication policy.

Basic premises of the New World Information and Communication Order

basic premises

For Brown-Syed (1999) the basic premises of the movement for a New World Information and Communication Order, were that:
- An imbalance existed in the direction, volume and types of information exchanged between developed countries and the so-called Third World. In the 1970s and 1980s the world situation was characterised by the dominance of information-producing nations (North or centre nations) over those (South or periphery nations) which were meant to consume cultural and information products. This is also called the centre-periphery situation in international communication (Galtung 1981:165–166).
- The ethical notion is that information should be viewed as a shared resource or as a social good rather than as a commodity. In other words, information should be seen as an essential and basic resource for people to develop and function well in a democracy, and not as a product that is primarily produced and distributed for the economic gain of the few who own media.

However, right from the beginning, the road towards the establishment of the New World Information and Communication Order was characterised by a struggle between First World and Third World countries. The First World stance was led by the USA and to a lesser extent Britain. Their governments' views about this issue are often called the "liberal school of thought". The view held mainly by members of Third world or developing governments is called the "structuralist school". The former is determined by economic considerations; the latter by development needs and ideological considerations. The labelling of the two schools as "liberal"

Globalisation, Information Communication Technology and the Media

and "structuralist" comes from Brown-Syed as used in his classic 1993 article "The New World Order and the Geopolitics of Information" in the journal *LIBRES: Library and Information Science Research*. This article is available on the Web and could, at the time of writing (September 2006), be accessed at http://www.valinor.ca/csyed_libres3.html. Much of the discussion that follows relies on this article.

Two schools, two ideologies

In the *structuralist school* (see Galtung 1981) it is argued that:

- Unprocessed information flows from developing countries to the developed countries of the West or North.
- Information users in the developed countries then interpret, process and act upon the information they receive from their own news organisations (including their own journalists) operating in the developing countries. They thus act upon biased information that forms their perceptions of less-developed countries, which in turn affects their responses to political, cultural and economic support.
- At the same time, the biased information is redistributed to less-developed countries that rely on dominant Western news organisations for their information. They are thus bombarded with negative perceptions of themselves.
- Concurrently, dominant news organisations from the West provide less-developed countries with more (positive) information about their own activities, cultures, and politics.
- Besides this, developing countries are dependent on developed countries for the raw materials of the communication industry: equipment, hardware, software, infrastructure, training and so on.

> structuralist school

Thus, the Third World nations come to be viewed through the eyes of the information interpreters of the developed nations, whose organisations control both the finances and infrastructures of the distribution system, while the developing nations never quite receive the latest information, nor the latitude of interpreting it to their own advantage. As well, in terms of pure volume of information produced and consumed, the developing nations lag far behind. (Brown-Syed 1999:3)

Galtung's major contribution to the structuralist model is his "centre-periphery" typology (also see Meyer 1988:10; Galtung 1979:165–166):

- nations at the centre dominate a feudal network of communication;
- the centre owns the major news agencies;

- the centre news takes up a much larger proportion of periphery news media than vice versa;
- users in the periphery come to see with centre's eyes.

Against the background of the above structuralist model, arguments about the range of problems that had to be addressed by the NWICO included cultural dominance, concentration of media ownership among *de facto* cartels, trans-border data flows controlled by multinational corporations, the effects of tourism and advertising, and the uneven global allocation of radio, satellite, and telecommunication technologies and infrastructures. The NWICO proposals held that all of these relationships ran counter to the interests of the developing world and threatened their self-determination, sovereignty and economic development. Although the notion of a revised world information structure would entail the establishment of a "free and balanced flow" of all sorts of cultural, scientific, technical and financial information, the debate over the NWICO proposals, however, tended to focus on perceived problems with the news media (Brown-Syed 1999:6).

> liberal school

In the liberal school, based on the economic and development theories of Daniel Lerner and Ithiel de Sola Pool, it is believed that the system of free enterprise in the field of information and entertainment provision is inherently liberating and would develop of its own accord. Problems related to the provision of information can be adapted to address the problems of developing countries through sufficient attention to education, technology transfer and the development of Third World infrastructures. The liberal school sees the structuralist school as Marxist and as an inherent attack on capitalism in which news, information and entertainment are increasingly seen as being economic commodities. Providing developing countries with news, information and entertainment programmes, as well as the raw material for the development of their own media infrastructures and the production of their own media content, even if this is in the form of co-ownership, can contribute to economic development and cultural and political liberation.

The main documents of the NWICO

> United Nations Educational Scientific and Cultural Organisation

The difference of opinion between the two schools led to serious conflict between mainly the USA and the non-aligned countries. It is also argued that the eventual adoption of the New World Information and Communication Order was one of the reasons why the USA

withdrew from the United Nations Educational, Scientific and Cultural Organisation (UNESCO). Nevertheless, using UNESCO as their main forum of discussion the non-aligned countries pushed ahead for the adoption of a NWICO. On 28 November 1978, in Paris, France, the twentieth general conference of UNESCO issued a proclamation calling for the establishment of a New World Information Order. The document on which it was based was the UNESCO Media Declaration of 1978. At the same conference, the International Commission for the Study of Communications Problems (also known as the MacBride Commission) established by UNESCO in 1976 presented its interim report. The final draft of the MacBride Report was published in 1980. UNESCO's policies toward the media are to be found in both sources, and in attendant documents such as the 1980 Statement on Journalistic Ethics, which was reaffirmed at the 1983 Mexico select committee meeting (Brown-Syed 1999: 7). To recap, the three crucial documents of the NWICO are thus:

- The UNESCO Media Declaration of 1978 (The full title is: Declaration on Fundamental Principles concerning the Contribution of the Mass Media to strengthening Peace and International Understanding, to the Promotion of Human Rights and to Countering Racialism, Apartheid and Incitement to War). (See http://www.casi.org.nz/statements/decmedia.htm (Accessed on 2006/09/29).)
- The UNESCO Statement on Journalistic Ethics (1980/1983). (See The Declaration of Sofia (1997) and numerous UNESCO documents and websites related to journalistic ethics.)
- The Report of the International Commission for the Study of Communications Problems (the MacBride Commission and the MacBride Report), 1978/1980.

Today these documents are classic texts in debates concerning international communication issues, the role of the media in development, and media ethics.

The final report of the MacBride Commission (chaired by the former Irish foreign minister Sean MacBride, winner of both the Nobel and Lenin prizes) was published under the title *Many Voices, One World*. Today the work of the Commission is continued by the MacBride Round Table created in 1989. (See http://www2.hawaii.edu/~rvincent/macbride.htm (Accessed on 2006/09/29).) This is a communications rights advocacy group. It accommodates scholars, activists, journalists and other communications experts devoted to the monitoring of world

| MacBride Commission |

communication, legal ramifications, and information imbalances. It disseminates its findings to community groups, United Nations agencies, non-governmental organisations and the news media. A spin-off of the MacBride Report was the establishment of UNESCO's International Program for the Development of Communication, charged with the promotion of freedom of expression and media pluralism, developing community media, and developing human resources in the communications sector. It concentrates its efforts on four areas, namely assistance, coordination, information and financing of international communication development and the promotion of self-reliance.

The NWICO today

In subsequent years the emphasis of UNESCO's communication programme shifted from the promotion of the NWICO theme to more operational activities, like media training and education. This agenda seems to have been designed to avoid politically sensitive issues (Galtung & Vincent 1992:99). UNESCO policy also moved closer to the position of the USA by reaffirming the organisation's commitment to:
- promoting the international free flow of information (not limiting or filtering information);
- addressing imbalances by improving the capacity of all countries to communicate (cf. Roach 1990:287–288).

changing emphasis

Subsequent research has also started questioning the dominance of news that is dispatched from the big industrialised news services to the developing world (Sussman 1990:341), as well as the effects of First World media programmes on the cultures of people in developing countries (Roach 1990:293–296). Although we can accept that these findings are not necessarily conclusive, they will probably again strengthen the arguments for promoting the free flow of information through the international arena. However, we can concur with Galtung and Vincent (1992), as well as Roach (1990) that the debate about the balance of information is far from over. Economic and political differences between countries and their different national and international interests will probably ensure that it continues.

The NWICO debate has also shown that it is often difficult to overcome these differences and to transform policy into a concrete plan. The NWICO, as one observer remarked, has therefore remained more of a slogan than a plan of action (Galtung & Vincent 1992:99). As

Picard (1991:81) indicates, the NWICO was not a unified, well-defined programme for change in communication but rather a philosophical approach to the role of communication that manifested itself in various international discussions and documents. Galtung and Vincent (1992:78–104), however, argue that a NWICO could again in future become a reality if the Third World is successful with the implementation of a New International Economic Order (NIEO). If these countries could, for example, agree on better terms of trade between Third World countries, obtain more control over their productive assets (nature, capital, labour, and technology – so that import and export substitution can occur), increase economic interaction among themselves, and obtain more control over world economic institutions, these authors predict that:

- better news ratios for the Third World will follow more news about the Third World in the First World and less about the First World in the Third;
- Third World control over communication assets will increase in terms of what First World reporters extract from the Third, and in terms of local control over local media;
- more news about other Third World countries in their own media and less about the First World will be published;
- Third World countries will start exerting control over the First World in terms of the events that should be processed into news, and Third World control over local media will also increase;
- there will be some Third World control over world communication institutions.

When the NWICO debate was at its height, Galtung and Vincent pointed out that this new order (described above) was already taking shape. They argued that Third World countries have already increased their news coverage of each other substantially over the last thirty years and that the media in former colonies have also decreased their coverage of the former colonial mother countries – a process that continues today (Galtung & Vincent 1992:104–105).

Lately the NWICO is overshadowed by a new buzz-word, namely the Information superhighway – a metaphorical concept that refers to all our contemporary means of communicating through a network of high-tech communication networks made possible by state-of-the art information and communication technology (ICT) which moves news across borders in something very close to real time. The "hype" about the economic

fortunes associated with ICT and the so-called possibilities of growth that ICT may create for developing countries somewhat obscures the NWICO's concerns about media content, the meanings signified by the media's content and the content's contributions to a global culture in which the emphasis is on dominant Western values and beliefs. In short, we can argue that the NWICO has almost been replaced by the Global Information Infrastructure Project and the World Summits on the Information Society.

9.3.2 The Global Information Infrastructure Project (GII)

The "information superhighway" was firmly placed on the map when the G7 countries (USA, Japan, United Kingdom, France, Germany, Italy and Canada) met in Belgium in 1995 for the Brussels Summit to discuss the Global Information Infrastructure project (the GII Project). In preparation for the Brussels Summit, the then vice-president of the USA, Al Gore, declared at the 1994 conference of the International Telecommunications Union in Buenos Aires, Argentina, that "... the development of the GII must be a democratic effort ... In a sense, the GII will be a metaphor for democracy itself ... I see a new Athenian Age of democracy forged in the *fora* the GII will create" (Gore, 1994). A few years on, we can ask if this remark wasn't a vast exaggeration.

Brussels Summit

The purpose of the Brussels Summit was to concentrate on a regulatory framework and competition policy in the field of telecommunications and related ICTs, the implementation of information infrastructure, their accessibility for the public, and the social and cultural aspects of the information society. The Group of Seven's (G7) final declaration stated, amongst others, that key prerequisites and objectives for a global information infrastructure to work are:

- dynamic competition;
- private investment;
- the promotion of universal service, meaning access to the information infrastructure for all;
- dialogue on worldwide cooperation such that industrialised countries will work towards the participation of developing countries in the global information society;
- democratic control of both the information infrastructure and information content provision;
- the acknowledgement of access to information as a basic right of every citizen;

Globalisation, Information Communication Technology and the Media

- the benefits of the information society should not be limited to business but should be available to society as a whole;
- the right of the public to be properly informed, which means the right to receive a full, impartial, accurate, and independent account of events;
- acknowledgement of the right of all people, including ordinary citizens, to participate and be involved with policy for and the use of information infrastructure.

Although these objectives are creditable, the question is: are they attainable? Critics argue that much of this master plan remains nothing but political rhetoric, that developing countries do not have the financial means to achieve the project's ideals, and that in the end only rich countries, rich people and the big international ICT and capitalist-driven ICT industries will gain from it. We will return to this criticism later on.

The Global Information Infrastructure and South Africa: objectives

In 1996 the South African government hosted the Information Society and Development Conference of the G-7 countries. At this conference a number of information infrastructure goals were proposed for South Africa, and within each a number of projects were identified and accepted. Some of the goals formulated were:

South African goals

- The setting up of integrated information systems to meet people's needs in the fields of epidemiological surveillance, telemedicine and interactive health networks; the interconnection of hospitals to improve access to international literature and distance diagnosis; natural resource management, regional environmental information systems and satellite communication to improve telecommunications services in rural and remote areas.
- Improved universal access: multi-purpose community telecentres, use of ICT in training and the empowerment of disabled people, the use of ICT in youth development projects.
- The development of appropriate applications and content, for instance centres of excellence.
- Human resource development: the development of courses in ICT policy and management, the improvement of distance education, school networking and linking schools globally.
- Support for business: the development of ICT trade points to the need to gather and disseminate trade-related information.

Media Studies: Volume 1

- Support for good governance: a one-stop information service providing access to a range of government information.
- Heritage: a culture and tourism network.
- Building the ICT infrastructure: satellite communications for remote areas providing a range of services.
- Reach-out services to countries with special circumstances, such as those regions that have faced civil strife and are prone to natural disasters.

To ascertain how much South Africa has achieved in this regard since 1996 is not the purpose of this chapter. This can be done through a study of the annual reports of the key role players in the sector, including the South African government's department of communications (DoC) and the Independent Communications Authority of South Africa (ICASA). For example, as far as Internet penetration in South Africa is concerned, the following statistics were available at the time of writing:

Year	Users	Population	% Penetration	Usage Sources
2000	2, 400, 000	43, 690, 000	5,5%	ITU
2001	2, 750, 000	44, 409, 700	6,2%	IWS
2002	3, 100, 000	45, 129, 400	6,8%	ITU
2003	3, 283, 000	45, 919, 200	7,1%	Wide World Worx
2004	3, 523, 000	47, 556, 900	7,4%	Wide World Worx
2005	4, 780, 000	48, 051, 581	9,9%	C+I+A

Figure 9.1: Internet Usage and Population Statistics South Africa
(Source: Epnet. available: http://www.epnetwork.co.za/Internet-usage-africa.asp Accessed: 2006/10/03)

9.3.3 The World Summit on the Information Society (WSIS)

Related to the GII, one can even see it as an outcome thereof, the World Summit on the Information Society (WSIS) was conceived in 1998 in Minneapolis in the USA at a meeting of the International Telecommunication Union (ITU). Resolution 73 of that meeting instructed the ITU secretary-general to place the question of the holding of a World Summit on the Information Society on the agenda of the body then known as the United Nations Administrative Committee on Coordination (ACC), now the United Nations System Chief Executive

Globalisation, Information Communication Technology and the Media

Board (CEB), and to report back to the ITU Council. The outcome was the Summit. The Summit is held under the patronage of the UN secretary-general, organised by the ITU. It took place from 10 to 12 December 2003 in Geneva, Switzerland, and in November 2005 in Tunis, Tunisia.

The WSIS aims to provide an opportunity for all key stakeholders in ICT to develop a better understanding of the "information revolution" taking place and its impact on the international community. It aims to bring together heads of state, executive heads of United Nations agencies, industry leaders, non-governmental organizations, media representatives, civil society and academics in a single high-level event. The overall aim of the summit is to develop and foster a clear statement of political will and a concrete plan of action for achieving the goals of the Information Society. Delegates to the 2005 Tunis Summit adopted a 40 point commitment plan followed by an action plan, the Tunis Agenda for the Information Society. Amongst others, bridging the digital divide, freedom of expression, cooperation between governments, the private sector, civil society, the United Nations and other international organisations in order to improve access to information and communication infrastructure and technologies, capacity building, security in the use of ICTs, the widening of ICT applications, respect for cultural diversity, the recognition of the role of the media in building the information society, and the ethical dimensions of the information society, were emphasised.

WSIS aims

9.3.4 Criticism of the Global Information Infrastructure Project and the World Summit on the Information Society

Although the aims and goals of the Global Information Infrastructure project (GII) and World Summits on the Information Society (WSIS) are commendable, and although there may be little doubt about the potential of Information and Communication Technology (ICT) for development, creating just societies and a global society in which human rights and equity are of paramount importance, scepticism warns that many of the ideals may remain empty rhetoric. In the case of South Africa, only a few citizens may have really gained from ICT, when basic needs such as housing with electricity and running water, the provision and maintenance of infrastructure, basic health care, basic telephone services and basic educational needs have not yet been fully met, particularly among the poorer communities. The academic task is therefore to monitor government and industry's performance insofar as access to and use of ICT are concerned.

_{Liberal and Luddite critique}

Academic critique falls into two groups, namely liberal and Luddite critique. In liberal critique the emphasis is on the anti-social potential of Information and Communication Technology (ICT). This form of critique nevertheless maintains that as long as people are alert to the dangers of ICT, development will be appropriate and socially beneficial. The main focus is that the information society should be the outcome of an informed democratic process. In Luddite critique the main point of departure is that although technology itself may be neutral, it is in the hands of and managed by people and groups whose primary interest is in making money and not necessarily in the possible social good. As an example of liberal criticism we focus on some of the arguments of Cees Hamelink (1997:415–424), one of the most prominent communication scholars in the field of ICT monitoring. Hamelink suggests that we ask critical questions about:

- control;
- access;
- quality;
- participation.

Using these four factors as criteria, Hamelink shows how the New World Information and Communication Order (NWICO) has achieved very little and how the Global Infrastructure and Information project (GII) is following suit.

Control

_{control of ICTs}

Hamelink argues that as far as democratic and participatory control of information is concerned, the success of the GII is debatable. To the contrary, there has rather been a consolidation of control over the provision of information since the 1990s. The major players are actively striving to gain control over the production of messages (ranging from digital libraries to TV entertainment), the operation of distribution systems (ranging from satellites to digital switches), and the manufacture of the equipment for the reception and processing of information. There is no indication that the major role players in the ICT sector are more willing to be held accountable than they were in the 1970s.

Globalisation, Information Communication Technology and the Media

Access

As far as access is concerned, Hamelink emphasises that there are different schools of thought (1997:421). One school restricts the notion of "universal service" to "availability". Availability means that all citizens should have access to basic communication services at affordable prices. Another school proposes that apart from availability, access also means that people should also be "able to use" communication services at profitable prices. In other words, the "ability" to use communication services, content and ICT also form part of access, and training towards such ability should be part of providing a universal service. A further question is which services should be labelled as universal. For example, only basic telephony services (a telephone line within reasonable distance)? Or a host of value-added services such as access to the Internet, e-mail, fax services, and so forth? In other words, where does one draw the line as far as universal service is concerned? (See the Universal Service Agency's discussion paper on *The Definition of Universal Service and Universal Access within South Africa, 1999.*) The problem of access intensifies if:

- governments, although they acknowledge their universal service obligations, want the private sector to pay for it;
- universal service provision is left to a market driven by commercial interests;
- Third World countries without the necessary ICT infrastructure "leapfrog" into the information society, as many of them may be pressured to do by trans-national ICT organisations and trans-national agreements. This has often led to the rapid development of digital capital cities that may become part of the global network, leaving the rural populations once again behind (Hamelink 1997:422).

> access to Information and Communication Technologies

Quality

Hamelink (1997:423) asks if the GII will be able to deliver quality information. Isn't it more likely that the information superhighway will mainly provide opportunities for teleshopping, video games, pornography, and so on? The closest the world gets to the projected global information superhighway is the Internet which is emerging as one of the most exciting places for doing business and perhaps very little else, especially if one thinks about development and development needs. According to Hamelink, the Internet has been guided by the rule of sharing information free and has now been discovered as a major vehicle for commercial advertising. One may ask whether this contributes to

> quality

the quality of development and adheres to development needs in, for example, education or whether other alternatives need to be considered?

Participation

participation

Hamelink (1997:423) argues that just like the New World Information and Communication Organisation, the Global Information Infrastructure project is steered by the interests and stakes of governments and corporations. It is the bilateral playing field of "princes" and "merchants", and ordinary people are addressed as consumers or occasionally citizens, but they play no essential role. The GIIP therefore needs to persuade people that the information society will bring them great improvements in lifestyle, comfort, and general well-being. This makes people important targets for marketing and propaganda; it does not make them serious partners in the project. In short, there is no serious involvement of "people's movements" in the making of the GIIP. There are no trilateral negotiations among governments, industrialists, and social movements to decide on a future that we all may want. The GIIP, argues Hamelink, is guided by "democratisation-from-above" and doomed to fail in making world communication more democratic (ibid:424).

WSIS

Hamelink's criticism above of the GII can also be found in critical discussions of the WSIS. See in this regard, for example, the complete edition of *Gazette – The International Journal for Communication Studies* (Volume 66, No 3–4, June/August 2004), of which Hamelink is the editor-in-chief. In the last article of this edition devoted to the Geneva Summit, Hamelink (2004:281–290) argues that despite the WSIS:

- the fundamental human right to free speech is universally violated through forms of political and commercial censorship;
- the Internet in particular has become the focus of censorship initiatives;
- the movements of citizens are at all times under surveillance from law enforcement agencies and intelligence bodies;
- the rights to corporate ownership of intellectual property are greatly extended;
- the access to information and knowledge is increasingly dependent upon the access to purchasing power;
- the consolidation of power in information and knowledge markets is consolidated in the hands of only a few conglomerates;

Globalisation, Information Communication Technology and the Media

- there is minimal public accountability from the corporate actors controlling most of the technologies and the contents of the information society;
- profitability more than human security drives ICT developments;
- the public sphere is increasingly limited. (Hamelink 2004:289).

This kind of criticism is also repeated in contemporary critical work on the Tunis Summit. The critical task thus remains to monitor developments in the fields of ICT.

From the above criticism, concerns and questions about ICT, it is clear that sound policy is necessary to manage the implementation and use of ICTs. In the next section, seven questions are suggested on the basis of which such policy could be monitored.

9.3.5 A yardstick for ICT policy monitoring

Although the literature referred to below is mainly from the 1990s, the arguments and warnings put forth by the authors remain relevant especially in and for developing countries.

Does policy provide for and is it based on sound financial planning?

Talero and Gaudette (1995) emphasise that that developing countries need to marshal substantial resources, often from abroad, to achieve ICT goals. Therefore they need to establish effective incentives and management schemes to facilitate adoption and the effective use of new systems. Apart from finding the financial resources and to manage these resources efficiently, a further important prerequisite for success is the training of qualified ICT workers, policy specialists, engineers and technical support staff to operate, maintain and produce hardware and software.

| financial management

Does policy prevent misallocation of scarce resources?

In the development of an ICT infrastructure there is always the possibility of waste and misallocation of scarce resources. In the absence of appropriate policy incentives, adequate quality standards, and competitive discipline, a country could allocate scarce development resources to information infrastructure investments that create waste or an increase in social inequality. Such is the case when ICT services are available only to the urban rich; when incentives favour use of technology

| misallocations

more for recreational than productive purposes; when an excessive share of investments is directed toward military purposes; and, when there is an inadequate definition of the expected benefits and inadequate measurement of the actual results. Again, note should be taken that many of the so-called benefits of ICT are likely to be uneven and unequal and may have resulted in increasing polarisation of rich and poor. The notion of "comparative advantage" became more of an ideological rationale for the status quo than a concern for equitable exchange relationships or commitment to social justice (see Talero & Gaudette 1995:220).

Does policy guarantee cultural preservation versus social disruption?

cultural preservation

ICT and the actual use of ICT go hand in hand with questions and issues related to cultural preservation versus social disruption. In this regard governments should inform themselves thoroughly of the prevailing debates about media and cultural imperialism and the need for a balance between cultural production and import. Burgelman (1994; 1995) provides numerous examples of how and where the introduction of ICT failed in which developers had not considered the cultures, needs and circumstances of societies and communities.

Does policy prevent employment inequities?

employment inequities

Many studies show that ICT development, like any new technology, can create jobs but it can also lead to the loss of jobs. People, particularly unskilled workers, can be replaced by ICT technologies and, in the face of competition, companies can be downsizing their human resources to become more cost-effective and streamlined. Policy, within capacity limits, should try to ensure that this consequence of evolving technology is limited, through, amongst other measures, the provision of education and lifelong learning in the fields of ICT.

Does policy ensure that real needs and real uses are achieved?

needs

Here we should distinguish between capacity, regional versus global needs, and grassroots needs and uses.

Capacity

Technologically advanced ICT systems may be of little or no use for specific needs, such as the needs of a small business or a small country

compared to the needs of a big business or a big country. Nevertheless such advanced systems are installed. This can be a waste of money and policy should ensure that this doesn't happen. Melody (1991:29) shows how the ICT systems in technologically advanced countries are being redesigned to meet the technically sophisticated digital data requirements of high-volume, multiple-purpose global users. For traditional, simpler communications requirements, such as a basic telephone service, the new upgraded systems may serve well at substantially increased costs to smaller users. The ICT options available to small, localised, and even regionalised businesses often do not reflect their unique needs. But what sometimes happens is that their range of choice is dictated by the national and global needs of the larger firms and government agencies. A more efficient ICT system for the needs of smaller users is being cannibalised in the creation of technologically advanced systems.

Regional versus global needs

If developing countries and regions are to implement ICT networks that will serve their interests in local and regional economic development, the new communication systems must promote local and regional communication and information networks within the context of the particular economic, social, political and cultural needs of the region. The new systems should try to increase the incentive to look first inside the region for economic activity, before going outside. Efficient domestic postal, telex, and basic voice telephone networks clearly would work in this direction. These issues require a more detailed examination of all significant dimensions of local and regional economic conditions, and the particular roles that communication and information networks do play and can play in promoting local and regional networks as a priority over international and global networks (see Melody 1991:39–40).

Grassroots needs and uses

Policy should ensure that the grassroots needs of people are met. What do we really know about the public's ICT needs? Are these needs thoroughly investigated, especially in developing countries? One rarely comes across research on the impact of or need for new communications technologies conceptualised from the point of view of the user, unless the user is an affluent consumer. In this regard the following is also important to keep in mind:

- Information technologies are mainly modelled and designed according to the sociocultural habitat of Western users. There may be unforeseen social consequences when applying a system engineered from Western logic into a non-Western context (see Lind 1990).
- Some research (see Metoyer-Duran 1991) indicates that the information-seeking and handling behaviour of different ethnic groups vary substantially precisely because of different cultural standards, values and practices.
- The success and acceptance of new ICTs in the professional sphere cannot be extrapolated to the public sphere (see Burgelman 1992:72; Carey & Moss 1985).
- The surplus value for the user of a new technology must be taken into account. To explain the success or failure of the introduction of a new communication technology in regions where they previously did not exist, one must look at the social or economic surplus value and/or relevance which can be realised by that new technology in terms of what the user defines to be his or her surplus value (see Dervin & Schields 1990).
- There is also something like an "acquisition substitution": the consumer seems to consider replacing a new technology only when it substitutes an older one with better quality and/or at a lower price. This too differs fundamentally whether the consumer wants to use it for professional or public/private purposes (see van den Brink 1987).

Does policy achieve a balance between public service obligations and free market interests?

regulation

In the ICT sector we distinguish between the free market model and the (monopolistic) public service model. The free market model is closely associated with transnational ICT corporations which, it is often feared, do not necessarily operate in national interests (in other words, in a specific country's interest), although it is often difficult to define the dividing lines between national interest, the ruling party's idea of what constitutes national interest and various competing public ideas of what is a priority in terms of the national interest. The public service model, or the so-called PTT monopoly administrations, were established in countries by governments to provide basic universal public services in post and telecommunications. This model is often criticised for not delivering. On a world scale PTTs are gradually being replaced by private companies through a process of deregulation and privatisation.

Globalisation, Information Communication Technology and the Media

Developing countries should be alerted not to privatise universal services under the pressures of globalisation and transnational corporations. Although it is commendable that services such as cellular, paging, data communications and long distance services should be deregulated and privatised, the privatisation of these money-making services, holds important social consequences. One such consequence may be that even less money will be available to develop a universal service in telephony. The question arises: if public services are privatised, where will the money come from to make the necessary huge investments to provide universal services?

For Burgelman (1994:66) the analogy that what is good for developed countries (namely deregulation and privatisation) is also good for developing countries does not necessarily hold. He argues that deregulation started in most Western countries only after universal service was realised and not before. The real challenge for developing countries is then not whether they should deregulate and privatise, but when to deregulate and privatise: after they have made their public services more efficient or before? One of the fears is that the movement to competitive, global conceptualised and market-orientated ICT services will benefit mainly the big professional users who can afford to pay. Although the idea is that this should finance universal service to the majority of the population, this might not be the case and there are few guarantees that this will happen.

Does ICT policy support sustainable development?

Mansell and Wehn (1998) suggest that the bottom-line goal of a national ICT strategy should be to serve the consumer and citizen. What is good for them is good for everyone including the producers of the ICT products and services. Instead of beginning with the most sophisticated users (as is often the case), the strategies of national ICT planners could be designed for the marginalised people in urban areas and rural villages. Furthermore, sustainable development means that:

- qualified and able people must be assigned to keep abreast of the latest developments in the ICT field;
- a clear vision should be formulated and clearly communicated to citizens;
- a high-powered, effective, flexible and authoritative unit should be created for the implementation of policy;
- pro-active decisions must be taken;

sustainable development

- most importantly, policy and planning for the sector should be closely integrated into broad economic, trade and social planning and effectively linked with other social policy initiatives such as education, welfare and a broader economic policy.

Despite the warnings, criticism and arguments, we should not forget and need to accept that the development of ICT and its concomitant information society has brought about numerous advantages:
- an increase in the spread of information and knowledge;
- a growth of and in market economies;
- an increase in global trade and investment;
- social transformation and democratisation;
- institutionalised accountability;
- awareness of environmental issues;
- awareness of human development, including the treatment of disease and the provision of education;
- world-wide distribution of cultural, intellectual and artistic products.

9.4 RESEARCHING GLOBALISATION, THE INFORMATION SOCIETY AND ICT

We conclude this chapter with a brief overview of some of the research topics and concerns related to the media and globalisation. We specifically focus on international communication research and research on the new media, especially the Internet.

9.4.1 International (global) communication research: media imperialism

International communication research (see the work of one of the most prominent scholars in this field, namely the late Herbert Schiller) focuses on the nature and impact of international media ownership, international production and distribution of media content and media culture and on the impact of international communication on local or national media content, media, use, economy, politics and culture. It investigates:
- the political economy of international media conglomerates;
- international media production companies' dominance of the music, film and popular entertainment industries;
- global news agencies;
- the international flow of news and information;
- the impact of international communication on public opinion;

Globalisation, Information Communication Technology and the Media

- the technology of international communication;
- international non-governmental media organisations;
- the nature and impact of global media on international and national media and communication policy.

The focus is therefore on the histories, markets, industry relations, growth, reach and consequences of multinational media conglomerates. Examples are North America's AOL/Time Warner, Viacom, Disney, Bertelsmann (Germany), Vivendi Universal (France), British Sky Broadcasting (UK), Canal Plus (France), Pathé (France), Pearson (UK), Mediaset (Italy), News Corporation (Australia), STAR TV (China), CanWest Global (Canada), etc. One can also begin to include South Africa's Naspers with its growing interests in Africa and Asia. News organisations such as BBC World, Deutsche Welle, CNN, El Jazeera, Channel News Asia (CNA), and global news agencies such as Reuters (UK), Associated Press (US), United Press International (US), Bloomberg (US), Agence France Presse (France) are under the spotlight. Furthermore the role of international organisations such as the United Nations' Educational, Scientific and Cultural Organisation (UNESCO), the International Telecommunications Union (ITU), the World Trade Organization (WTO) and the Organisation for Economic Cooperation and Development (OECD) are investigated. Obviously, as the major multimedia corporations become increasingly global, so their need for global advertising increases, and, as the global economy expands so does the need for global products, global brands and global services such as advertising (McPhail, 2002). International communication research therefore also includes the study of major multinational advertising agencies such as the UK's WPP Group, Omnicom (US), Havas Advertising (France) and Dentsu in Japan. What all these corporations have in common (McPhail, 2002) are:

- huge financial resources (individually often more than the annual budget of a developing country);
- focus on the homogenisation of tastes, values, culture and English as their main language;
- focus on export and not on import;
- aggressive competitive approaches.

Media studies' main concern with the role of international media communication relates to the concept of media imperialism. The topic of media imperialism closely relates to the concerns of the NWICO and WSIS. The main tenets of the media/cultural imperialism thesis are:

media imperialism

- Global media may promote relations of dependency rather than economic growth.
- The unequal relationship in the flow of news increases the relative global power of large and wealthy news and media producing countries and may hinder the growth of an appropriate national identity and self-image.
- Global media flows (information, news and entertainment) give rise to a state of cultural homogenisation or synchronisation leading to a dominant form of culture that has no specific connection with the real experience for most people (see McQuail 2000:222). The imbalance in the flow of mass media content therefore undermines cultural autonomy or holds back its development.

Crucial to the notion of media imperialism is the understanding of the relationship between economic, territorial, cultural and international factors. In the 19th century, or in the age of territorial, political and economic colonialism, the flow of information was a vital process for the spread and reinforcement of the colonists' economic and political power. Put in another way, apart from reinforcing their economic, political and military power in colonised countries, the colonisers also needed to establish their own political and cultural ideologies and values. This was done by means of enforcing their ideologies through education, including education through the provision of news, information and entertainment. Despite the fact that many developing countries or Third World countries have gained independence, there are in many countries still a dependence on transnational media corporations for news, information and entertainment.

dependency

Dependency is thus a priority issue in the study and research of international communication. Given that a few countries, with the United States at the top, dominate the media world, the purpose of research is to analyse who dominates whom on the levels of media production and distribution. In this regard Mowlana's (1997) model is often used: he distinguishes two dimensions as important determinants of the degree of dependency or autonomy. These are the technology axis (hardware and software) and the communication axis (production versus distribution). For example, although it may seem as if South Africa has a highly developed and independent media system, the question is: to what extent is South Africa dependent on the dominating countries for its media hardware and software? Dependence therefore not only

Globalisation, Information Communication Technology and the Media

concerns dependency on media content and its ideological and cultural implications but also dependency on technology – which, in any case, can never be seen as ideologically neutral because people always use it with specific outcomes in mind.

Apart from technology's impact on production and distribution, dependency also relates to sources of news and programming. Whereas in a typical national media situation communication occurs from easily identifiable spatial (geographical), organisational and cultural sources, with a sender (communicator) known to the public (or recipient), the communicator and recipient of international communication content are spatially, organisationally and culturally distanced. This spatial, organisational and cultural distance may have an impact on the quality of communication in the sense that it has no bearing on the real experience of the recipient. For example, one may look at and even enjoy a soap opera or situation comedy produced in Hollywood, but deep down the culture of the characters, their physical and psychological environments and the topics they address may be removed from one's own culture and experience. It is therefore argued that if foreign media content dominates the output (content) of national and/or local media, then it can contribute to the homogenisation of culture. This may happen to the detriment of one's own culture (own way of looking at and experiencing reality, life and its meanings). In short, the whole world can look at things in the American way, America being one of the dominant media producers of entertainment. It is therefore also argued that locally produced programmes and news about local happenings and events are always more relevant (if not always more popular) – because they speak to the culture, understanding and experience of the recipient. For the same reason there is often an increased emphasis on local content in national media policies, although this can be counter-balanced by pressure from advertisers for the largest possible audience. Other main aspects of the dependency theory are:

- The centre-periphery thesis (Galtung 1981). Nations can be classified as either central and dominant or peripheral and dependent, with the predominant media flow from the former to the latter.
- The dominance of mainly western professional standards and practices, including journalistic ethics and news values.

Apart from being dependent on the dominant nations for news, programming, hardware and software, dominant countries also "export" their news values, ethics, production practices (for example styles and genres of film and television production) to less-developed countries. In South Africa, for example, it is sometimes argued that the South African media has not yet escaped its colonial past, in the sense that many editors, journalists and media study academics still think in terms of Western ideas about news and programming.

foreign, bilateral, multilateral content

As far as analysing and monitoring international media communication is concerned, a distinction is made between national and foreign content: Foreign content (not locally produced) is distributed through the infrastructure of a national system. For example, in the case of television, the SABC, e.tv and M-Net distribute American-produced soap operas, situation comedies, talk shows films, etc., as well as outside news inserts such as BBC (British Broadcasting Corporation) of a news event in Zimbabwe (instead of the SABC's own coverage of the news event). Even imported programme concepts, such as the concept of the popular television programme *Big Brother* although filled in with local content, can be included in this category. Bilateral content originating in and intended for one country is received directly in a neighbouring country; for example, Namibians receive SABC programming. Multilateral content is produced and disseminated without a specific national audience in mind. For example, see the content of various niche channels such as the programmes of the National Geographic and Discovery channels, BBC Food, and so on.

9.4.2 New media research: The Internet access, its nature, uses and impact on culture and democracy

The topics and issues referred to above are in the field of international communication, usually researched from the perspective of the political economy of the traditional media (print and broadcasting). A second main branch of research related to the media, globalisation and the information society focuses on the nature and impact of the new media (like the Internet and mobile telephony). Typical topics are, for instance:
- the development and use of on-line newspapers;
- the dynamics of the new media and new economy;
- globalisation and the structure of new media industries;
- the information society and its relation to trade and industry policy;
- the economics of information and cultural exchange;
- the new economy: Internet, telecommunications and electronic commerce;

Globalisation, Information Communication Technology and the Media

- universal access to the new information infrastructure (Lievrouw & Livingstone 2002).

Here, we only focus on research about the Internet, specifically in relation to policy, the communicative nature of the Internet, the uses of the Internet, the impact of the Internet on culture and identity, and the Internet and democracy.

Policy research

Although key scholars such as Castells (2003), Poster (2001) and Rheingold (1994) acknowledge the long-term benefits of the Internet for economic growth, education and development, including the expansion of democracy, they also pose critical questions in the light of restricted access to the Internet. Despite great expectations, only 1.12 billion people out of a world population of six billion people had access to the Internet in 2004. Many were in the USA. In South Africa only 3.1 million people out of a population of more than 40 million had access in 2002. These figures illustrate the digital divide which may be growing instead of declining. Policy research from a social science perspective is thus mainly concerned with the necessity to ensure that an ICT such as the Internet instead of contributing to prosperity, enlightenment and empowerment may contribute to increased inequity between rich and poor countries and rich and poor people within countries. If the digital divide is not addressed satisfactorily, ICT may contribute to polarisation.

| digital divide

Even though one may have access to the new media, it may mean nothing if a person or a group doesn't know how to use it in order to gain from it. A computer and the Internet on a table in an office, study, telecentre or post office doesn't guarantee food on the table, and should not be presented as capable of doing so. Thus, policy research also emphasises the use of ICT and literacy related to ICT.

| ICT literacy

The communicative nature of ICTs (the Internet)

Apart from research seeking to monitor the growth of ICTs and their capacity to circulate ever-greater volumes of text, graphics and moving images (see Mackay, Maples & Reynolds, 2001:67), a growing body of media and social science research seeks to understand the communicative nature of the new media, especially the Internet. In the case of the Internet

| cyberspace

397

the emphasis is on how sound, text, image, in short, data of numerous kinds, are produced, distributed, received and stored in/on a worldwide network – the World-Wide-Web; on how this is possible and happens in a so-called cyberspace which is a virtual space and thus does not exist physically but only in terms of existing and changing software. The cyberspace is sometimes described as "a space to explore or discover but never to comprehend" (Dodge & Kitchen, 2000). We try to understand cyberspace by making use of metaphors such as "Internet rooms", "Internet places" and "Internet sites", to which we gain access through "browsers" and "portals" – metaphors which seek to chart cyberspace in terms of known and comprehensible spatial concepts.

interactivity

Research also investigates how movement in the cyberspace is made possible by means of hyperlinks responsible for interconnectivity. The moment an Internet user goes "online" he/she has access to an ever-increasing 40 million or so websites. Much attention is thus given to what is probably the most outstanding communicative quality of the Internet, namely interactivity, made possible through hyperlinks and hypertexts. Through such interactivity the previous boundaries between communicator and receiver are blurred with far-reaching consequences for the way(s) in which we have until now thought about and defined communication.

timeless-time

Another outstanding characteristic of ICT now being researched is that of timeless-time. For Manuel Castells (1996; 1998), probably the most well-known social scientist in the field of information society research, timeless-time is the most outstanding characteristic of what he calls the network society – a society characterised by the flow of information. With timeless-time, Castells means the use of ICTs in a relentless effort to compress years into seconds and seconds into split-seconds of time. Although most of us still live and work in terms of biological time and in terms of a mechanical and/or digital clock, it appears that industry, groups, and the economy function above time – a continuous stream of time in which it is difficult to distinguish between a beginning and an end. Although everyday life, the conduct of politics and social and cultural activities still take place in specific and concrete spaces, such spaces are overshadowed by visible or invisible flows of information in which financial institutions and industry depend for their existence and functioning. The question is: how does this affect the individual, culture and society?

Globalisation, Information Communication Technology and the Media

ICT usage

As was and still is the case with traditional media such as television, an important branch of ICT research concerns how and why we use the new communication technologies. Is it to communicate, to access and use information, to be entertained or to shop and trade? What is the quality of the different uses? In this regard, and as far as the Internet is concerned, we distinguish between different Internet uses and applications of virtual spaces such as a:

- virtual library and publisher: in which information and data such as scientific, technical, financial data, news, music, movies, pornography etc. are produced and/or stored and ready to be accessed;
- virtual post office: to send and receive messages, such as email;
- virtual community hall: to discuss and debate different matters: blogs, chat rooms, etc.;
- virtual market/shop: to trade and buy goods and do financial transactions;
- virtual sport stadium: to play games of all sorts;
- virtual battlefield: to protest and campaign;
- virtual spaces: to visit art galleries, museums, cathedrals, as well as churches and other religious institutions in which one can partake in religious services (e-religion).

Internet applications

In short, for what and how do people use the Internet and what are the personal effects of these as well as the effect on the structure and fibre of contemporary society and culture?

Whatever the use of the Internet may be, an outstanding characteristic is the user's choice to be either a passive visitor or an active participator. If the latter, he or she need not be predisposed to the visual point of view or movement of a producer/director/provider (as in the case of television and film) but he or she could be a co-producer of Internet content together with other users. In comparison with, for example, television, it is significant that we talk of an Internet user instead of a viewer. That is despite the similarities between television and the viewer: sitting in front of a screen confronted with visual images, texts, sounds and designs. In the case of the Internet the user is either a purposeful seeker of something (information/entertainment/products/transactions/games) or an incidental visitor "surfing" through the possibilities of the Internet who may acquire something useful. In the light of this move in

participation

emphasis from passive viewer to active user, the activity of the Internet user is emphasised in user research.

global participation

Another outstanding characteristic is that users are not confined to a single space (building, organisation, country). They could be from anywhere in the world where the user has access to a computer, a modem and the Internet. These characteristics of Internet use and the Internet user are researched from different perspectives. For instance, the visual and design arts are interested in how the user actively deals with the aesthetics of the interface (the screen) of websites; computer and engineering sciences in the technology of the Internet and how the user deals with it; information science in how data are collected, processed, stored, retrieved, distributed and received; and linguistic and cognitive sciences in the intellectual processes involved with the use and comprehension of Internet communication and information. On the other hand, the social sciences, like media studies, focus on the possible impacts of ICTs like the Internet on society, culture, political processes, and democracy. This interest is briefly introduced in the next paragraphs.

The impact of ICTs on culture, identity and democracy

Although social science's main interest is on the possible political and economic consequences of ICTs, its cultural impact is increasingly investigated. That is, cultural changes brought about by globalisation and ICTs not only on a macro level, but also on the personal level: how ICTs such as the Internet have changed daily routines, increased the types of experiences available to us and how information and images of numerous types have saturated our daily lives.

identity

From this stems media studies' interest in how the Internet may influence or could influence identity formation, or how we think about ourselves and act in terms of such thinking (see chapter 11 for a discussion of media and identity). The issue, as Maples (2001) describes it, is that whereas one's identity was traditionally culturally determined by nationality, gender and generation there are now, because of globalisation and through ICTs, a variety of identities from which we can choose more actively.

> "Culture and beliefs are no longer confined to geographical locality but are shared and dispersed across nations and continents. An individual identity is no longer seen as 'static' or 'fixed for all time'; instead, identities are re-articulated and reconstituted throughout

the lifecycle. ICTs are seen as instrumental in this regard, with some theorists suggesting our identities are increasingly intertwined with computers, to such an extent that we are becoming 'cyborgs'" (Maples, 2001:68).

In cyberspace new identities – so-called on-line identities or virtual identities – can be formed on the basis of which new relationships with new rules can be conducted. A key issue with far-reaching social and political consequences is that one can remain anonymous or fabricate a false identity. Whereas identity is usually linked to one's physical and psychological appearance and make-up, this need not be the case in cyberspace. The Internet user can change his/her identity with each visit to the Internet. Identity can be created through textual, graphic and photographic manipulation. The user can thus compose an identity far removed from relatively stable identity markers such as gender, skin colour, age, and other aspects of physical appearance and even alter the psychological dimensions by taking on a new personality. On the Internet, you can be what you write you are – a man, a woman; a transsexual, heterosexual, homosexual; Christian, Muslim, Jew, atheist and so on. Slater (2004:600) refers to this as the "disembodiment of on-line identity". Van Driel (2003) argues that this has changed the existential question of "Who am I?" to "What am I?" In short, the possibility of taking on an on-line identity may have many social, political and psychological consequences, leading to numerous research questions. (For a more in-depth discussion of this, see Fourie 2005).

> on-line identity

Unstable and changing identities on the Internet, as well as the possibility of remaining anonymous, appear to be irreconcilable with the formation of a stable political community, generally considered a prerequisite for political action. Given the possibility of false identities, Internet discussions and political debates cannot necessarily contribute to forming a consensus on a topic on the basis of which political action could follow. Such discussions rather contribute to a proliferation of opinions and little else. On the Internet there are few conditions and prerequisites which could contribute to compromise and consensus about a matter. Everyone can contribute an opinion. A prerequisite for political action is a community with a fixed structure composed of members with stable identities committed to a particular opinion. To the contrary, Internet communities are composed of individuals who contribute their opinions spontaneously and voluntarily. Although this may contribute to the

> politics and Internet identity

uninhibited expression of opinion, there is little obligation as far as commitment, loyalty and participation are concerned.

The question is: can a group of strangers without any geographical and cultural bond and without any necessary indication of ethnicity, gender, race, age or social status, without any obligation to make such identity known, be called a community? How authentic and valid can such a community be? (see Poster 1995) Questions like these lead contemporary social philosophers such Dreyfus (2001; 2004) to criticise the Internet as the philosopher Kierkegaard criticised the press of the 19th century. Whereas thinkers such as Mill, de Tocqueville and Ortega attributed the decline of 19th century society to the rise of the tyranny of the masses, Kierkegaard blamed the press for the decline. According to him, the press created a public sphere (see chapter 8) conducive to risk-free anonymity and idle curiosity. With that, he argued, the press undermined a responsible and committed public, destroyed qualitative distinctions between people, and contributed to a nihilistic "so-what" life and worldview. Similarly, Dreyfus argues that the Internet creates a platform or a space in which it is difficult to distinguish between relevancy and irrelevancy, and in which information is offered without context. It creates a space with access to each and every one who can stay anonymous and fabricate an identity, who can say anything without the necessary experience, knowledge or real expertise about a topic, and without taking responsibility for it. Such discussions cannot be called a democratic discourse.

Internet and democracy

Then again, for many, the Internet is the hope for democratic emancipation. The so-called cyber-democrats refer to the Internet as the "electronic commons", "virtual democracy" and the "electronic agora". (Underwood, 2005) Some of the arguments are the following: because the Internet is not restricted to a specific geographical region it broadens the right to freedom of expression to those living in countries where freedom of expression is restricted or non-existent. Cyber-democrats (Lovink, 2005; Underwood, 2005) believe that the Internet provides a platform and opportunity to every member of the public to participate on an equal base in discourses of public interest in view of the establishment of an informed and rational public opinion that may lead to solidarity. They see the Internet as the realisation of Habermas' ideal public sphere and as an answer to his criticism against the traditional media as a profit-driven, sensationalist and commercialised public sphere.

Globalisation, Information Communication Technology and the Media

To scholars such as Dreyfus and Poster, cyber-democrats such as Lovink and Underwood respond that "conservative" views about Internet democracy are caught up in the critical thinking of Adorno, Horkheimer and Habermas (see critical theory in chapter 3) conceptualised in a time of monopolistic media systems in Europe. ICTs have changed the media landscape drastically. It is no longer possible to speak of the media (or a single medium) as a single public sphere. The media, of which the Internet is part, consist of several public spheres. The Internet, more than any other public communication medium, provides several and diversified platforms for interactive discussions, debate and mobilisation. Despite the shortcomings of the Internet, such as anonymity and false identities, it broadens the possibilities and advantages of freedom of expression, a prerequisite for democracy, and gives new meaning to the concept of "participatory democracy".

Furthermore, critics are obsessed with interactive chat rooms and blogs as if these Internet applications are definitive of the nature of Internet democracy. Focusing on chat rooms is the same as describing talk and phone-in programmes on television as definitive of television's contribution to democracy. In the process, the value of the availability of information on the Internet of and about non-government organisations, political parties, Internet newspapers for democratic decision-making and action is forgotten. For Lovink (2005), the matter of anonymity is in any case a myth. Apart from the fact that anonymity is only one of the choices an Internet user may execute, very little of what appears on the Internet is really anonymous. He, in any case, foresees that Internet users will in the future probably have to identify themselves with their "Microsoft passports".

Many authors and researchers warn that like television, the Internet may lose its value for democracy should it primarily become an economic instrument. This may happen when, according to critical political economists, the Internet becomes primarily a platform for commerce controlled by a few financial and industrial moguls. They further warn that talks to regulate the Internet centrally are not necessarily in the interest of protecting freedom of expression, the autonomy and protection of the nation state, and the protection of cultural goods (such as resisting the domination of English). Such talks are rather motivated by the greed of world powers, world organisations and governments to monopolise the Internet to their own political and

Internet regulation

economic advantages. There are still no clear answers as to how and why the Internet should be regulated. Should regulation be inevitable (for instance, for security reasons), it looks as if the solution would be a regulating model between the telecommunications regulating model and the broadcasting model. In the first the emphasis is on ownership, cost, and access. In the second model the emphasis is on ownership, frequency, and content. However, not one of these models would probably succeed in inhibiting political and economic control. The challenge to find a regulatory model for the Internet without inhibiting it as a democratic forum thus remains.

digital divide

Finally, as far as the Internet and democracy is concerned, we should take cognisance of Castells' warning (1997:351). Despite all the hype about the Internet, the agreements, summits, research and promises, access to the Internet remains limited and the digital divide between rich and poor nations and people is a threatening reality. Castells thus warns that:

> "... while a relatively small, educated and affluent elite in a few countries and cities would have access to an extraordinary tool of information and political participation, actually enhancing citizenship, the uneducated, switched-off masses of the world, and of a country, would remain excluded from the new democratic core, as were slaves and barbarians at the onset of democracy in classical Greece."

We conclude this section on new media research by saying that as it was the case with television and the then "new" media before television, ICT and Internet research often tends to be paranoid about the possible effects of ICT on human behaviour and society. This is usually the case when researchers are confronted with new media. For example, early research about television were for many decades dominated by the so-called hypodermic needle paradigm (see chapter 5 on the effects of the media). Television and the nature of television as a mass communication medium were seen to have mainly negative effects on values and attitudes; the viewer seen as a passive victim. Gradually research moved in the direction of uses and gratification and reception theory (see chapter 5, and the chapters on reception theory and uses and gratification in the next volumes), emphasising the media user as an active and interpretative reader/viewer. In the same way, seminal research about the Internet as the most common application of new ICTs (Turkle, 1995; Miller & Slater, 2000) indicate that the initial paranoia about the Internet is beginning to

make way for more balanced views about and approaches to the possible impact of the Internet on humanity and society. As the newness of the Internet declines and it becomes more integrated and assimilated in society as a communication medium, the strangeness and difference of being on-line (and all this involves) disappears. It becomes just another alternative medium for information and communication. The otherness and strangeness of the Internet as a different space is becoming no longer a strange and different kind of experience. Today, we seldom think of television or telephones as being strange, different, unique experiences creating and taking place in strange spaces.

Thus, Slater (2004:611) wonders if, in the case of the Internet:

> "... the distinction between online/offline will not be regarded as rather quaint and not quite comprehensible inside ten years. Users and researchers are already well advanced in the process of disaggregating 'the Internet' into its diversity of technologies and uses, generating a media landscape in which virtuality is clearly not a feature of the media but one social practice of media use amongst many others."

As in the case of television, the emphasis is thus moving away from what ICT is doing to people to what people are doing with ICTs.

9.5 SUMMARY

The purpose of this chapter was to introduce some of the main issues and topics related to the impact of globalisation on the media. After a brief introduction which focused on Anthony Giddens' explanation of globalisation, we elicited some of globalisation's characteristics. We introduced some of the economic trends which have created a new media environment and media regulatory paradigm. Information and Communication Technology (ICT) is one of the catalysts of globalisation and so we focused on how this has lead to technological convergence in the media industry, with far-reaching consequences for the ways in which media content is now produced, distributed and received. We showed how the concerns and ideals of the New World Information and Communication Order (NWICO) about inequities in the field of mass communication were taken over by the (GII) and the World Summits on the Information Society (WSIS). Some of the criticism and warnings related to these projects was discussed, as well as the concerns about ICT policy in developing countries. Finally, we briefly introduced

research in the field of international communication and the new media, emphasising the notion of media imperialism. Given that the Internet is probably many people's chief experience of globalisation through media, we looked at some of the topics being addressed in related research: access to the Internet, the communicative nature of the Internet, Internet usage, and the impact of the Internet on culture and democracy.

LEARNING ACTIVITIES

- Briefly explain your understanding of Anthony Giddens' theory of globalisation.
- Explain the difference between modernism (early-modernity) and postmodernism (late-modernity).
- List five characteristics of globalisation.
- Give five examples of how globalisation affects your own life.
- Briefly explain, with your own examples, each of the economic trends brought about by globalisation and how these trends affects the media industry today.
- Give five examples of what, according to you, are remaining inequities between developed and less-developed countries as far as the flow of information and media ownership and production are concerned.
- What are, according to you, the ten most important goals of the GII and WSIS. Explain how you think these goals could be achieved.
- List at least ten South African information infrastructure goals and evaluate to what extent these goals have been achieved or are and how they are in a process of being achieved.
- Evaluate the South African goals in terms of control, access, quality and participation against the background of your own experience of the availability and your use of ICT.
- What, according to you, are the most important issues for ICT policy in developing countries?
- From an ICT website, obtain the latest statistics on the availability of Internet usage and services in South Africa, Africa and a developed country.
- Write a one-page essay in which you motivate why the sustainable development model should or should not form the basis of ICT planning.
- Explain dependency related to media content and production with five of your own examples of what you experience as media imperialism.

Globalisation, Information Communication Technology and the Media

- List five social science/media studies research issues and topics related to the Internet. Motivate why you think these topics are important for a better understanding of the Internet.
- List five of your own research topics related to the Internet and explain why you think the topics you have identified are important for your own community.

FURTHER READING

Castells, M. 1996. *The information age: economy, society and culture*. Oxford: Blackwell. Vol 1: *The rise of the network society* (1996); Vol 2: *The power of identity* (1997); Vol 3: *End of millennium* (1998).

Castells, M. 2003. *The Internet galaxy. Reflections on the Internet, business, and society*. New York: Oxford University Press.

Dodge, M. & Kitchen, R. 2000. *Mapping cyberspace*. London: Routledge.

Dreyfus, H.L. 2001. *On the Internet*. London: Routledge.

Fidler, R.F. 1997. *Mediamorphosis: Understanding new media*. Thousand Oaks, California: Pine Forge.

Flichy, P. 1995. *Dynamics of modern communication. The shaping and impact of new communication technologies*. London: Sage.

Gazette – The International Journal for Communication Studies. Volume 66 (3–4) June/August 2004.

Giddens, A. 1990.*The consequences of modernity*. Cambridge: Polity Press.

Golding, P. & Harris, P. (eds). 1997. *Beyond cultural imperialism. Globalization, communication and the new international order*. London: Sage.

Hamelink, C. 1994. *The politics of world communication*. London: Sage.

Mackay, H., Maples, W. & Reynolds, P. 2001. *Investigating the information society*. London: Routledge.

Mansell, R. & Wehn, U. 1998. *Knowledge societies: information technology for sustainable development*. Oxford: Oxford University Press.

Poster, M. 2001. *What's the matter with the Internet?* Minnesota: University of Minnesota Press.

Rheingold, H. 1994. *The virtual community: Homesteading on the electronic frontier*. New York, N.Y.: Harper Perennial.

Schiller, H. 1996. *Information inequality: making information haves and have nots*. London: Routledge.

Servaes, J. & Lie, R. (eds). 1997. *Media & politics in transition. Cultural identity in the age of globalization.* Leuven: Acco.

Slater, D. 2004. Social relationships and identity online and offline, in *The television studies reader*, edited by R.C. Robert Allen and A. Hill. London: Routledge.

Waters, M. 1995. *Globalization.* London: Routledge.

Webster, F. 1995. *Theories of the information society.* London: Routledge.

WEBSITES

At the time of writing (October 2006) the following websites were functional. Should they no longer be available, search the web by making use of key words and a search engine such as Google.

BMI-TechKnowledge Group: http://www.bmi-t.co.za

Communication Policy and Research: http://www.benton.org/cpphome.html

Global Fusion 2000: http://www.siu.edu/~gf2000

Global Information Infrastructure Commission: http://www.giic.org

Globalisation Guide: http://www.globalisationguide.org/

Globalisation: http://www.journoz.com/global

Independent Communication Authority of South Africa (ICASA): http://www.icasa.org.za/Default.aspx?Page=2

Independent Media Center: http://www.indymedia.org

Institute for Global Communications: http://www.igc.org/

International Development Research Centre: http://www.idrc.ca

International Telecommunication Union (ITU): http://www.itu.int/

Internet usage: http://www.ams-ix.net

Media Africa – Reading the Mind of the Internet: http://www.mediaafrica.co.za

Medialens: http://www.medialens.org

National Information Technology Forum: http://www.sn.apc.org/nitf

New World Information and Communication Order (NWICO): http://valinor.ca/csyed_libres3.html

OneWorld.net: http://www.oneworld.net

Organisation for Economic Co-operation and Development: http://www.oecd.org

Sangonet: http://www.sangonet.ord.za

(South African) Department of Communications: http://www.doc.org.za/

South African National Information Technology Forum: http://www.sn.apc.org/nitf

State Information Technology Agency: http://sita.pwv.gov.za

United Nations Educational Scientific and Cultural Organisation (UNESCO) http://www.unesco.org
World Bank Development Forum: http://www.worldbank.org/devforum
World Summit on the Information Society (WSIS): http://www.itu/wsis/tunis/index.html
World Wide Worx – http://www.theworx.biz/

References

Addressing the state of the media. 2007. [Online]. Available: http://www.mediamonitoring.org.za/Resources/MediaUpdates/tabid/60/articleType/ArticleView/articleId/88/Addressing-the-state-of-the-media.aspx Accessed on 2007/02/13.

AfricaFocus. 2005. [Online]. Available: http://www.africafocus.org/docs06/econ0601.php. Accessed on 2006/05/02.

Ainslie, R. 1966. *The press in Africa: communications past and present.* London: Victor Gollancz.

Anderson, J. 2000. The 'Third Generation' of the Frankfurt School, in Intellectual History Newsletter. 22: 49–61.

Ang, I. 1998. The performance of the sponge: Mass communication theory enters the postmodern world, in *The media in question: Popular cultures and public interests*, edited by K. Brants, J. Hermes & L. van Zoonen. London: Sage.

Armour, C. 1984. The BBC and the development of broadcasting in British colonial Africa 1946–1956, in African Affairs. 84 (332): 359–402.

Armstrong, J. 2006. Applying critical theory to electronic media history, in *Methods of historical analysis in electronic media*, edited by D.G. Godfrey. Mahwah, NJ: Lawrence Erlbaum: 145–165.

Article 19. 2006. Broadcasting pluralism and diversity: a training manual for African regulators. London: Article 19.

Baker, T.N. 2006. Musings of a Postmodern Negro: decoding The Da Vinci Racial Code. [Online]. Available: http://postmodernegro.wordpress.com/2006/05/20/the-davinci-racial-code/ Accessed on 2006/07/31.

Banda, F. 2003. Community radio broadcasting in Zambia: a policy perspective. PhD thesis, University of South Africa, Pretoria.

Banda, F. 2004. Newspapers and magazines in Zambia: a question of sustainability. Lusaka: Media Institute of Southern Africa (MISA) Zambia.

Banda, F. 2006. Negotiating global influences – globalization and broadcasting policy reforms in Zambia and South Africa, in Canadian Journal of Communication. 31(2): 459–467.

Banda, R. 1999a. It's news, but not all good news, at e.tv. The *Cape Times*, 18 January: 3.

Banda, R. 1999b. IBA, e.tv relations sour over licence. The *Star*, 25 February: 14.

Baran, S.J. & Davis, D.K. 2003. *Mass communication theory: foundations, ferment, and future.* 3rd edition. London: Thomson/Wadsworth.

Bardoel, J. & Brants, K. 2003. Public broadcasters and social responsibility in the Netherlands, in *Broadcasting & convergence: New articulations of the public service remit*, edited by G.F. Lowe & T. Hujanen. Göteborg, Sweden: Nordicom.

Barker, J.M. 2001. Is no policy a policy goal? in *Media, democracy and renewal in Southern Africa*, edited by K.G. Tomaselli & H. Dunn. Colorado Springs: International Academic Publishers: 151–180.

Barnes, F. 2006. The media gets religion. Available on the Internet: http://www.nyu.edu/fas/center/religionandmedia/ Accessed on 2006/10/01.

Barnhurst, K.G. 2005. Bourdieu and political communication: An infrastructure proposal for improving political news. Available on the Internet: http://www.uic.edu/ortgs/politcom. Accessed: 2005/04/05.

Barrel, H., Ngobeni, E., & Kindra, J. 2000. Media are racist ... if you say so. The *Mail & Guardian*, 25–31 August: 4.

References

Barthes, R. 1967. *Elements of semiology*. New York: Hill & Wang.

Barthes, R. 1977. *Image, music, text*. Glasgow: Fontana.

Barton, F. 1979. *The press of Africa: persecution and perseverance*. London and Basingstoke: Macmillan.

Baudrillard, J. 1983 (a). De implottie van de betekenis in de media, in Skrien. 132: 13–15.

Baudrillard, J. 1983 (b). *Simulations*. New York: Semiotext.

Baynes, K. 1998. Habermas, Jürgen. In Routledge Encyclopedia of Philosophy, edited by E. Craig. London: Routledge. Available on the Internet: http://www.rep.routledge.com/article/DD024SECT1. Accessed 2004/07/02.

Bennett, T. 1981. *Popular culture: themes and issues*. Milton Keynes: Open University Press.

Bennett, T. 1982. Theories of the media, theories of society, in *Culture, society and the media*, edited by M. Gurevitch, T. Bennett, J. Curran & J. Woollacott. London: Routledge: 30–55.

Berelson. B. 1949. What missing the newspaper means, in *Communications Research: 1948–1949*, edited by P. Lazarsfeld and F. Stanton. New York: Harper.

Berger, A. 1995. *Essentials of mass communication theory*. Thousand Oaks, California: Sage.

Best, S. & Kellner, D. 1999. Rap, black rage, and racial difference, in Enculturation, Volume 2, Number 2, Spring 1999. Available on the Internet: Electronic version: http://enculturation.gmu.edu/2_2/best-kellner.html Accessed on 2006/06/14.

Bhengu, C. 2000. White editors walk out of HRC hearings. *The Sowetan*, 8 March: 3.

Blankenberg, N. 1999. In search of real freedom: Ubuntu and the media, in Critical Arts, 13 (2): 42–65.

Bloom, K. 2007. Untapped markets. Available on the Internet: http://www.the media.co.za/article.aspx?articleid+200953&area+/media_insightfeatures Accessed: 2007/06/18.

Bonorchis, R. 2005. Glut of tabloids hitting streets must be cause for concern. The *Sunday Tribune*, 9 October: 3.

Bourdieu, P. 1998. *On television*. Translated by P. Ferguson. New York, N.Y.: New Press.

Bourdieu, P. 1992. *Language and symbolic power*. Cambridge: Polity Press.

Bourgault, L.M. 1995. *Mass media in sub-Saharan Africa*. Bloomington & Indianapolis: Indiana University Press.

Boyd-Barrett, O. 1977. Media imperialism: towards an international framework for the analysis of media systems, in *Mass communication and society*, edited by J. Curran, M. Gurevitch & J. Woollacott. London: Edward Arnold.

Braman, S. 1996. Interpenetrated globalisation: scaling, power, and the public sphere, in *Globalisation, communication, and transnational civil society*, edited by S. Braman & A. Sreberny-Mohammadi. Cresskill: Hampton.

Braman, S. 2002. A pandemonic age: The future of international communication theory and research, in *Handbook of international and intercultural communication*. 2nd edition, edited by W.B. Gudykunst & B. Mody. Thousand Oaks, CA.: Sage: 399–413.

Branston, G. & Stafford, R. 1999. *The media student's book*. 2nd edition. London: Routledge.

Brants, K. 1998. With the benefit of hindsight: Old nightmares and new dreams. In K. Brants, J. Hermes & L. van Zooned (Eds.). *The media in question: Popular cultures and public interest*. London: Sage.

Brants, K., Hermes, J. & van Zoonen, L. (eds). 1998. *The media in question: popular cultures and public interests*. London: Sage.

Briggs, A. 1980. Problems and possibilities in the writing of broadcasting history, in Media, Culture & Society 2: 5–13.

Briggs, A. & Burke, P. 2002. *A social history of the media. From Gutenberg to the Internet*. Cambridge: Polity.

Brown-Syed, C. 1993. The New World Order and the geopolitics of information, in LIBRES: Library and Information Science Research. 19 January 1993.

Brown-Syed, C. 1999. The New World Order and the geopolitics of information. [O]. Available on the Internet: http://www.valinor.purdy.wayne.edu/csyed_libres3.html Accessed on 2000/12/04

Brydon, D. 2000. *Postcolonialism: critical concepts in literary and cultural studies*. Volume 2. London and New York: Routledge.

Buchanan, A. 1998. Community and communitarianism. In E. Craig (Ed.). *Routledge Encyclopaedia of Philosophy*. London: Routledge. Available at http://www.rep.routledge.com/article/S010 Accessed: 2005-09-22.

Burgelman, J-C. 1994. Assessing information technologies and telecommunications services: the case of developing countries, in *Communicatio*. 18 (2): 64–79.

Burgelman, J-C. 1995. De 'informatiesameleving' en de toekomstige uitdagingen voor het communicatiebeleid. Referaat naar voor gebracht voor de Parlementaire Commissies Economie & Media van de Vlaamse Raad. Brussel: SMIT, Vrije Universiteit van Brussel.

Burton, G. 2005. *Media and society: critical perspectives*. Berkshire, U.K.: Open University.

Calhoun, C. (ed.) 1992. *Habermas and the Public Sphere*. Cambridge, Mass: MIT Press.

Cantril, H. 1940. *The invasion from Mars*. Princeton: Princeton University Press.

Carey, J. & Moss, M. 1985. The diffusion of new telecommunication technologies, in Telecommunications Policy, June 1985: 145–158.

Castells, M. 1996. The rise of the Network Society. Volume 1: the information age: economy, society and culture. Volume 2 (1997): The power of identity. Volume 3 (1998): End of millennium. Oxford: Blackwell.

Castells, M. 1999. An introduction to the information age, in *The media reader: Continuity and transformation*, edited by H. MacKay and T. O'Sullivan. London: Sage.

Castells, M. 2003. *The Internet galaxy: reflections on the Internet, business, and society*. New York: Oxford University Press.

Charon, J.M. 1979. *Symbolic interactionism*. Englewood Cliffs, NJ: Prentice-Hall.

Christians, C.G. 2004. Ubuntu and communitarianism in media ethics, in Ecquid Novi, 25 (2): 235–256.

Connor, S. 1989. *Postmodern culture: an introduction to theories of the contemporary*. New York: Blackwell.

Corner J., Schlesinger, P., & Silverstone, R. (eds). 1997. *International media research: a critical survey*. London: Routledge.

Croteau, D. & Hoynes, W. 2003. *Media society: industries, images, and audiences*. 3rd edition. Thousand Oaks, California: Pine Forge Press.

Culler, J. 1983. *Structuralist poetics: structuralism, linguistics and the study of literature*. London: Routledge & Kegan Paul.

Curran, J. 2002. *Media and power*. London and New York: Routledge.

Curran, J. & Park, M-J. 2000. *De-westernizing media studies*. London: Routledge.

Curran, J. & Gurevitch, M. 1996. *Mass media and society*. 2nd edition. London: Arnold.

Curran, J., Gurevitch, M. & Woollacott, J (eds). 1977. *Mass communication and society*. London: Open University/Arnold.

Curran, J., Gurevitch, M. & Woollacott, J. 1982. The study of the media: theoretical approaches, in *Culture, society and the media*, edited by M. Gurevitch, T. Bennett, J. Curran & J. Woollacott. London: Methuen: 11–29.

Curtis, J. 2000. The study of popular culture by academia in the United States. Available on the Internet: http://www.msoe.edu/library/dr_who/study_of_popular_culture.htm Accessed on 2006/10/05.

References

Cutten, T.E.G. 1935. *A history of the press in South Africa.* Cape Town: National Union of South African Students.
Dahl, H.F. 1978. The art of writing broadcasting history, in Gazette 24 (2): 130–137.
Dahlgren, P. 1998. Enhancing the civic ideal in television journalism, in *The media in question: Popular cultures and public interests*, edited by K. Brants, J. Hermes & L. van Zoonen. London: Sage.
De Fleur, M.L. & Dennis, E.E. 1994. *Understanding mass communication: a liberal arts perspective.* 5th edition. Boston, USA: Houghton Mifflin.
De Ionno, P. 2000. e.tv tightens empowerment belt. The *Star*, 10 January: 1.
De Kock, W. 1982. *A manner of speaking: the origins of the press in South Africa.* Cape Town: Saayman & Weber.
Dervin, B. 1991. Comparative theory reconceptualised: from entities and states to processes and dynamics, in Communication Theory, 1: 59–69.
Dervin, B. & Shields, P. 1990. Users: the missing link. Conference Paper, IAMCR 1990.
Dethier, H. 1993. Het gesicht en het raadsel: profielen van Plato tot Derrida. Brussel: VUB Pers.
De Villiers, C. 1993. Radio: chameleon of the ether, in *Mass media for the nineties: the South African handbook of mass communication*, edited by A.S. de Beer. Pretoria, S.A.: van Schaik: 125–146.
Diamond, L. & Plattner, M.F. (eds). 1999. *Democratisation in Africa.* Baltimore and London: Johns Hopkins University Press.
Diederichs, P. 1993. Newspapers: the fourth estate – a cornerstone of democracy, in *Mass media for the nineties: the South African handbook of mass communication*, edited by A.S. de Beer. Pretoria: Van Schaik: 71–98.
Dodge, M. & Kitchen, R. 2000. *Mapping cyberspace.* London: Routledge.
Dorfman, A. & Mattelart, A. 1971. Para Leer al pato Donald: Comunicacion de masa y colonialismo. Buenos Aires, Argentina: Siglo Veintuno Argentian Editores.
Downing, J. 1996. *Internationalising media theory.* London: Sage.
Dread, Z. 2001. Arts Festival or Boerfest? The *Mail & Guardian*, 20–25 April.
Dreyfus, H.L. 2001. *On the Internet.* London: Routledge.
Dreyfus, H.L. 2004. Kierkegaard on the Internet: Anonymity versus commitment in the present age. Available: http://ist-socrates.berkeley.edu/~hdreyfus/html/paper_kierkegaard.html. Accessed: 2005/09/02.
Duncan, J. 2000. Talk left, act right: what constitutes transformation in South African media? [O]. Available: http://www.und.ac.za/und/ccms/jane.htm Accessed on 2000/08/08.
Dzidonu, C.K. 2000. Looking back, moving forward: a look at the information 'revolution' from an historical perspective, in *Into or out of the digital divide? Perspectives on ICTs and development in Southern Africa*, edited by D. Lush, H. Rushwayo & F. Banda. Lusaka: Panos Southern Africa.
Editors Notes. 2006. *The Da Vinci Code.* A heretical, pagan indoctrination. Available on the Internet: http:///www.movieguide.org/?s=Books&s1=ViewBook&_id=9 Accessed on 2006/07/31.
Eitzen, D.S. 1989. *Sport in contemporary society.* 3rd edition. New York, N.Y.: St Martin's.
Elliot, P. 1982. Intellectuals, the information society and the disappearance of the public sphere, in Media, Culture and Society 4 (3): 243–53.
Emdon, C. 1998. Ownership and control of media in South Africa, in *Media and democracy in South Africa*, edited by J. Duncan & M. Seleoane. Pretoria: Human Science Research Council and Freedom of Expression Institute.
Émile Durkheim files [O]. Available: http://durkheim.itgo.com/main.html Accessed on 2006/09/30.
Engelbrech, J.C.R. 1972. Die pers as massakommunikasiemedium. (The press as a mass communication medium.) Pretoria: Human Sciences Research Council.

Eurasian Media Forum. Windhoek Declaration on Promoting an Independent and Pluralistic African Press. [0]. Available: http://www.eamedia.org/windhoek.php. Accessed on 2006/08/30.

Fant, G. 2006. How to read 'The Da Vinci Code'. Available on the Internet: http://www.lifeway.com/lwc/article_main_page Accessed on 2006/07/31.

Faringer, G.L. 1991. *Press freedom in Africa*. New York, Westport, Connecticut and London: Praeger.

Faure, C. 1995. Ondersoekende joernalistiek en sosiale verandering: 'n ontleding en evaluering van die agendastellingsrol van Vrye Weekblad. DLitt et Phil thesis, University of South Africa (UNISA): Pretoria.

Faure, C. 1996. The alternative press, in *Introduction to communication – course book 5: journalism, press and radio studies*, edited by L.M. Oosthuizen. Kenwyn: Juta: 264–281.

Ferguson, M. 1990. Electronic media and the redefining of time and space in public communication, in *The new imperatives. Future directions for media research*, edited by M. Ferguson. London: Sage.

Fidler, R.F. 1997. *Mediamorphosis: understanding new media*. Thousand Oaks, California: Pine Forge.

Fieldhouse, D.K. 1981. *Colonialism 1870–1945: an introduction*. London: Weidenfeld and Nicolson.

Finlayson, J.G. 2005. *Habermas: a very short introduction*. Oxford: University Press.

Fishman, M. 1978. Crime waves as ideology, in Social Problems, 25 (5): 531–543.

Fiske, J. [sa]. Pluralism and polysemy. Available on the Internet: http://www.indigogroup.co.uk/foamycustard/fc041.htm. Accessed on 200/06/08.

Fiske, J. 1987. *Television culture*. London: Methuen.

Fiske, J. 1987. British cultural studies and television, in *Channels of discourse: Television and contemporary criticism*, edited by R.C. Allen. London: Methuen.

Fiske, J. 1990. *Introduction to communication studies*. London: Routledge.

Forbes, D. 2005. *A watchdog's guide to investigative reporting*. Johannesburg: Konrad Adenauer Stiftung.

Fore, W.F. 1987. *Television and religion: the shaping of faith, values and culture*. Minneapolis: Augsburg.

Fouhy, E.M. 2001. Civic journalism: rebuilding the foundations of democracy. Available on the Internet: http://www.cpn.org/cpn/pew_partnership/civic_partners_journalism.html Accessed on 2001/03/08.

Fourie, P.J. 1983. Van Jerusalem na Hollywood: 'n Parallel tussen godsdiens en massvermaak. Professorale intrerede (inaugural lecture), Universiteit van Suid-Afrika (UNISA), Pretoria.

Fourie, P.J. 1988. *Aspects of film and television communication*. Cape Town: Juta.

Fourie, P.J. 1994. Zuid-Afrika, in *Nederlandstalige en Afrikaanstalige media*, 2nd edition, edited by N. van Zutphen & J. Nootens. Brussels: Vlaamse Raad: 279–341.

Fourie, P.J. (ed). 1996. *Introduction to communication – course book 3: communication and the production of meaning*. Cape Town: Juta.

Fourie, P.J. (ed). 1997. *Introduction to communication – course book 6: film and television studies*. Cape Town: Juta.

Fourie, P.J. 2001. Globalisation, the information superhighway, and development, in *Media studies. Volume 1: institutions, theories and issues*, edited by P.J. Fourie. Lansdowne: Juta: 593–625.

Fourie, P.J. 2001. The role and functions of the media: functionalism, in *Media studies. Volume 1:Institutions, theories and issues*, edited by P.J. Fourie. Lansdowne: Juta: 264–289.

Fourie, P.J. (ed.) 2001. *Media Studies. Volume 1: Institutions, theories and issues*. Cape Town: Juta.

References

Fourie, P.J. 2002. Rethinking the role of the media in South Africa, in Communicare 21 (1): 17–41.

Fourie, P.J. 2003. The future of public service broadcasting in South Africa: the need to return to basic principles. Communicatio, 29 (1 & 2): 148–182.

Fourie, P.J. 2004. The market paradigm and the loss of public service broadcasting (television) for development and nation building, in Communitas: Journal for Community Communication and Information Impact, Volume 9 2004: 1–19.

Fourie, P.J. 2005. Finding a new policy model for public service broadcasting (PSB): From PSB as an institution to PSB as a genre, in Communitas, Volume 10: 21–37.

Fourie, P.J. 2007. Moral philosophy as the foundation of normative media theory: The case of African ubuntuism. Communications: European Journal of Communication Research, 1/2007: 1–29.

Fourie, P.J. & Oosthuizen, L.M. 2001. Media imperialism: the New World Information and Communication Order, in *Media studies. Volume 1: Institutions, theories and issues*, edited by P.J. Fourie. Lansdowne: Juta: 415–446.

Fowler, R. 1991. *Language in the news: Discourse and ideology in the press.* London: Routledge.

Freeden, M. 2003. *Ideology: A very short introduction.* Oxford: Oxford University Press.

Freedom of Expression Institute. 1998. Roundup. FXI Update December: 11–15.

Friedland, W.H. & Rosberg, C.G. 1964. Anatomy of African socialism, in *African socialism*, edited by W.H. Friedland & C.G. Rosberg. Stanford: Stanford University Press.

Galtung, J. 1981. A structural theory of imperialism, in Perspectives on world politics. London: Croom Helm in association with the Open University Press.

Galtung, J. & Vincent, R.C. 1992. *Global glasnost. Toward a New World Information and Communication Order.* Cresskill, NJ: Hampton.

Gauntlett. D. 1998. Ten things wrong with the 'effects model', in *Approaches to audiences – a reader*, edited by R. Dickinson, R. Harindranath & O. Linné. London: Arnold.

Gecau, K. 1996. The press and society in Kenya: a re-appraisal, in *Media and democracy*, edited by Bruun Andersen. Oslo: University of Oslo: 183–212.

Geertz, C (ed.). 1973. *The interpretation of cultures: selected essays.* New York: Basic.

Gernber, G. 1967. Mass media and human communication theory, in *Human communication theory*, edited by F. Dance. New York: Holt, Rinehart & Winston.

Geus, R. 1981. The idea of critical theory: Habermas and the Frankfurt School. Cambridge: Cambridge.

Giddens, A. 1990. *The consequences of modernity.* Cambridge: Polity Press.

Giddens, A. 1999. Globalisation: a runaway world. BBC Reith Lectures 1999. Available on the Internet: http://www.news.bbc.co.uk/hi/english/static/events/reith_99/week1.htm Accessed on 1999/07/28.

Giddens, A. 2000. Globalisation: Giddens' dilemma. 2000. Available on the Internet: http://www.sociologyonline.f9.co.uk/GlobalGiddens1.htm Accessed on 2000/11/14.

Gitlin, T. 1978. Media sociology: the dominant paradigm, in Theory and Society 6: 205–253.

Gitlin. T. 1989. Television screens: hegemony in transition, in *Cultural and economic reproduction in education: essays on class, ideology and the state*, edited by M. Apple. London: Routledge.

Glaser, D. 2000. The media inquiry reports of the South African Human Rights Commission: a critique. African Affairs 99 (396): 373–393.

Gombrich, E. 1977. *Art and illusion.* London: Phaidon.

Gore, A. 1994. Speech to the International Telecommunication Union Conference in Buenos Aires, Argentina. Available on the Internet: http://www.friends-partners.org/oldfriends/telecomm/al.gore.speech.html. Accessed 2007/08/07

Greven, M. 1987. Power and communication in Habermas and Luhmann, in *Political Discourse*, edited by B. Parekh. London: Sage.

Griffin, E. 2003. *A first look at communication theory*. 5th edition. Boston: McGraw-Hill.

Grogan, J. & Barker, G. 1993. Media law: to tread cautiously on different beats, in *Mass media for the nineties: the South African handbook of mass communication*, edited by A.S. de Beer. Pretoria: Van Schaik: 229–244.

Grossberg, L., Wartella, E., & Whitney D. 1998. *Media Making: mass media in a popular culture*. London and Thousand Oaks, California: Sage.

Grote, D. 1983. *The end of comedy: the sit-com and the comedic tradition*. Connecticut: Archon.

Gumede, W. 2006. Is the SABC the 'pulse of the nation'? *The Witness*, 8 November: 14.

Gunaratne, S.A. 2002. Theory of communication outlets and free expression. A humanocentric exploration. Paper presented at the 2002 Conference of the International Association of Media and Communication Research, Barcelona. Available: http://www.Portalcommunication.com/bcn2002/N_eng/programme/prog_ind/paper/g/pdf/go14_gunar.pdf Accessed: 2006/06/28.

Gunaratne, S.A. 2005. *The dao of the press: a humanocentric theory*. Cresskill, N.J.: Hampton Press.

Habermas, J. 1968. *Erkenntnis und Interesse*. Frankfurt: Suhrkamp.

Habermas, J. 1976a. *Zur Rekonstruktion des historischen Materialismus*. Frankfurt: Suhrkamp.

Habermas, J. 1976b. Was heißt Universalpragmatik? In K.O. Apel (ed): *Sprachpragmatik und Philosophie*. Frankfurt: Suhrkamp.

Habermas, J. 1981. *Theorie des kommunikativen Handelns*. Volumes 1 to 2. Frankfurt: Suhrkamp.

Habermas, J. 1984. *The theory of communicative action: reason and rationalization of society*. Boston, MA: Beacon Press.

Habermas, J. 1989. *The Structural Transformation of the Public Sphere*. Cambridge: Polity. (Originally in German, 1962.)

Habermas, J. 1996. *Between Facts and Norms: contributions to a Discourse Theory of Law and Democracy*. Cambridge: Polity Press. (Originally in German, 1992.)

Habermas, J. 2004. "Public Space and Political public sphere – The biographical roots of two motifs in my thought." Unpublished commemorative lecture, Kyoto, Japan. 11 November.

Habermas, J. 2006. "Political Communication in Media Society – Does Democracy still enjoy an epistemic dimension? The impact of normative theory on empirical research." Unpublished paper presented at the International Communication Association Conference, Dresden, 20 June.

Habermas, J. and Luhmann, N. 1971. *Theorie der Gesellschaft oder Sozialtechnologie*. Frankfurt: Suhrkamp.

Hachten, W.A. 1971. *Muffled drums: the news media in Africa*. Ames, Iowa: Iowa State University Press.

Hachten, W.A. 1974. Mass media in Africa, in *Mass communications: a world view*, edited by A. Wells. California: National Press Books: 91–111.

Haffajee, F. & Shapshak, D. 1999. Gloves off in the battle of the paperweights. The *Mail & Guardian*, 5–11 March: 4.

Hagen, H. 1999. e.tv news at last. The *Citizen*, 18 January: 1.

Hall, S. 1982. The rediscovery of ideology: the return of the repressed in media studies, in *Culture, society and the media*, edited by M. Gurevitch, T. Bennett, J. Curran & J. Woollacott. London: Methuen.

Hall, S. 1980. Encoding/decoding, in *Culture, media language*, edited by S. Hall, D. Hobson, A. Lowe and P. Willis. London: Hutchingson: 128–138.

Hamelink, C.J. 1994. *The politics of world communication*. London: Sage.

References

Hamelink, C.J. 1997. World communication: business as usual? in *Democratizing communication? Comparative perspectives on information and power*, edited by M. Bailie & D. Winseck. Cresskill, NJ: Hampton Press.

Hamelink, C.J. 2004. Did WSIS achieve anything at all? In Gazette: The International Journal for Communication Studies, 66 (3–4): 281–290.

Hammer, R. & Kellner, D. [sine anno]. Critical Reflections on Mel Gibson's "The Passion of the Christ". Available on the Internet: http://enculturation.gmu.edu/2_2/best-kellner.html Accessed on 2006/08/19.

Hamminga, B. 2005. Epistemology from the African point of view. Available on the Internet: http://mindphiles.com/floor/philes/epistemo/epistemo_f.htm Accessed: 2005/04/15.

Harber, A. 2003. SA's press becomes a table for empowerment pinball. The *Business Day*, 28 November: 31.

Harber, A. 2005. Bicycles still best in race to reach daily readers. The *Business Day*, 2 November: 11.

Harber, A. 2006. SABC should encourage openness, not obeisance to political will. The *Cape Argus*, 3 August: 18.

Hartley, J. 1999. *Uses of television*. London: Routledge.

Hartley, J. 2004. Television, nation and indigenous media, in Television & New Media. 5 (1): 7–25.

Hartley, J., Goulden, H. & O'Sullivan, T. 1985. *Making sense of the media: popular culture and the teaching of media studies*. London: Comedia.

Heard, J. 1998. What a rush as e.tv goes into orbit. The *Sunday Times*, 4 October: 5.

Held, D. & McGrew, A. 2002. *Globalization/Anti-Globalization*. Cambridge: Polity Press.

Hlophe, N. 1999. e.tv invests R100m in news shows. The *Star*, 12 January: 6.

Hoeane, T. 2005. The great debate around the slush media. *Weekend Post*, 3 September: 8.

Hohendahl, P. 1979. Critical Theory, Public Sphere, and Culture: Jürgen Habermas and his Critics, in New German Critique. 16: 89–118.

Honneth, A. 1989. Vom Zentrum zur Periferie einer Denktradition in Kölner Zeitschrift für Soziologie und Sozialpsychologie. 41: 1–32.

Hoover, F. 2006. 'Da Vinci Code' becomes Sunday-sermon fodder. Available on the Internet: http://www.columbusdispatch.com/religion/religion.php?story=185972 Accessed on 2006/ 07/31.

Howitt, D. & Cumberbatch, G. 1977. *Massamedia en geweld*. Utrecht: Spectrum.

Huizenga, J. 1950. *Homo ludens: a study of the play element in culture*. London: Temple Smith.

Hujanen, T. & Lowe, G.F. (eds). 2003. *Broadcasting & convergence: New articulations of the public service remit*. Göteborg, Sweden: Nordicom.

Hunter, Cheryl. 2001. RSG explores converging frontiers. The *Business Report*, 24 February: 16.

Huntington, S.P. 1991. *The third wave: democratization in the late twentieth century*. Norman and London: University of Oklahoma Press.

Huteau, J. 2000. Media self-control, the south's new option. UNESCO Courier April: 43–45.

Hyden, G. & Leslie, M. 2002. Communications and democratization in Africa, in *Media and democracy in Africa*, edited by G. Hyden, M. Leslie & Folu F. Ogundimu. New Brunswick, N.J. (U.S.A) and London (U.K.): Transaction Publishers: 1–27.

Hyden, G. & Okigbo, C. 2002. The media and the two waves of democracy, in *Media and democracy in Africa*, edited by G. Hyden, M. Leslie & F.F. Ogundimu. New Brunswick, N.J. (U.S.A) and London (U.K.): Transaction Publishers: 29–53.

Independent Broadcasting Authority. 1995. Report on the protection and viability of public broadcasting services, cross media control of broadcasting services, local television content and South African music (Triple inquiry report). Johannesburg.

Independent Broadcasting Authority. 2000. Annual report for the financial year ending 31 March 1999. Sandton, Gauteng.
Inglis, F. 1990. Media theory: an introduction. London: Blackwell.
ISAD. 1996. Information Society and Development conference: Conclusions. Midrand, Gauteng.
Jacka, E. 2003. Democracy as defeat: the impotence of arguments for public service broadcasting. *Television and New Media*, 4 (2): 177–191.
Jackson, G.S. 1993. *Breaking story: the South African press*. Boulder, Colorado: Westview.
Jackson-Opoku, S. & West, M. [sa]. From homeland to township: rap music and the South African choral tradition. Available on the Internet: http://www.worldandi.com/public/1994/april/cl1.cfm Accessed on 2006/05/23.
James, T. (ed). 2001. *An information policy handbook for Southern Africa: a knowledge base for decision-makers*. Johannesburg: International Development Research Centre.
Jayiya, E. 1999. e.tv owners embroiled in squabbles. The *Star*, 24 September: 3.
Johnson, S. 1991. An historical overview of the black press, in *The alternative press in South Africa*, edited by K. Tomaselli & P.E. Louw. Bellville: Anthropos: 15–32.
Kamwangamalu, N. 1999. Ubuntu in South Africa: a sociolinguistic perspective to a Pan-African concept, in Critical Arts, 13 (2): 24–41.
Kasoma, F.P. 1986. *The press in Zambia*. Lusaka: Multimedia.
Kasoma, F.P. 1994. Journalism ethics in Africa. Nairobi, Kenya: African Council for Communication Education (ACCE).
Kasoma, F.P. 1996. The foundations of African ethics (Afriethics) and the professional practice of journalism: the case for society-centred media morality, in Africa Media Review, 10 (3): 93–116.
Keane, J. 1991. *The media and democracy*. Cambridge: Polity.
Kellner. D. 1989. *Baudrillard: from Marxism to postmodernism and beyond*. Cambridge: Polity.
Kellner, D. (a) [sine anno]. Communications vs. Cultural Studies: overcoming the divide. Available on the Internet: http://www.gseis.ucla.edu/faculty/kellner/kellner.html Accessed on 2006/08/20.
Kellner, D. (b) [sa]. Cultural Marxism and Cultural Studies. Available on the Internet: http://www.gseis.ucla.edu/faculty/kellner/ Accessed on 2006/08/20.
Kerckhove, D. 1996. De huid van onze cultuur. Een onderzoek naar de nieuwe elektronische realiteit. Amsterdam: Addison-Wesley.
Keulartz, J. 1986. Over Kunst en Kultuur in het werk van Habermas, in *Filosofie en Maatskapijkritiek* edited by F. van Doorne and J. Korthals. Amsterdam: Boom.
Kipnis, L. 1986. 'Refunctioning' reconsidered: towards a left popular culture, in *High theory/low culture: analysing popular television and film*, edited by C. MacCabe. Manchester, University Press: 11–36.
Kitchen, H. (ed). 1956. *The press in Africa*. Washington: Ruth Sloan.
Klapper, J. 1960. *The effects of mass communication*. New York: Free Press.
Klein, M. 1999a. Midi's e.tv says it is catching up with competitors. The *Sunday Times*, 18 April: 3.
Klein, M. 1999b. Lean and mean is the new motto at cash-strapped e.tv. The *Sunday Times Business Times*, 4 July: 3.
Klein, M. 1999c. We're doing best thing for e.tv, says Golding. The *Sunday Times*, 19 September: 4.
Kobokoane, T. 1999a. Funds crisis drives e.tv parent into a corner. The *Sunday Times Business Times*, 2 May: 1.

References

Kobokoane, T. 1999b. Midi row about 'bull-in-kraal' Marcel Golding. The *Sunday Times Business Times*, 23 May: 1.

Kobokoane, T. 1999c. Legal row looms over e.tv shake-up. The *Sunday Times*, 13 June: 1.

Koenderman, T. 1999a. Circulation bloodbath. The *Financial Mail*, 152 (7): 123.

Koenderman, T. 1999b. e.tv begins to make headway. The *Financial Mail* 152 (7): 124.

Koenderman, T. 1999c. Now for some stability. The *Financial Mail* 153 (10): 33.

Koenderman, T. 2000a. The last word … . The *Financial Mail* 1 September: 94.

Koenderman, T. 2000b. Print circulation in trouble. *The Financial Mail* 18 August: 75.

Kornhauser, W. 1949. *The politics of mass society.* New York: Free Press.

Kovecses, Z. 1990. Sport and semiotics, in *Semiotics in the individual sciences*, edited by W.A. Koch. Bochum: Brockmeyer: 35–48.

Krippendorf, K. 1993. Conversation or intellectual imperialism in comparing communication (theories) in Communication Theory, 3: 252–266.

Kubey, R. & Csikszentmihalyi, M. 1990. *Television and the quality of life: how viewing shapes everyday experience.* Hillsday, N.J.: Lawrence Erlbaum.

Kunczik, M. 1984. *Communication and social change.* Bonn: Friedrich-Ebert-Stiftung.

Lang, K. 1980. The critical functions of empirical communication research: observations on the German-American influences, in *Mass Communication* Review Year Book, Volume 1, edited by G.C. Wilhout & H. de Bock. Beverly Hills, CA: Sage.

Lasswell, H. 1948. The structure and function of communication in society, in *The Communication of ideas*, edited by L. Bryson. New York: Institute for Religious and Social Studies/Harper & Row.

Laurence, P. 2000. Racism in media neither quantified nor specified. The *Financial Mail* 1 September: 36.

Lazersfeld, P. & Merton, R. 1948. Mass communication, popular taste and organised social action in *The process and effects of mass communication* (1971), edited by W. Schramm & D. Roberts. Champaign, Ill: University of Illinois Press.

Leahy, P.E. & Voice, P. 1992. *The media book, 1991–2: your guide to getting the most from media: for marketing, advertising, public relations and media professionals.* Bryanston: W.T.H.

Lemon, L.T. 2001. Media and culture, in *Media studies. Volume one: institutions, theories and issues*, edited by P.J. Fourie. Juta: Landsdowne: 354–381.

Leonard, W.M. 1994. *A sociological perspective on sport.* 2nd edition. Minneapolis, USA: Burgess.

Lesame, N.C. (ed). 2005. *New media: technology and policy in developing countries.* Pretoria: Van Schaik.

Lind, P. 1990. *Computerization in Developing Countries.* London: Routledge.

Lindgren, E. 1963. *The art of the film.* London: Allen & Unwin.

Littlejohn, S.W. 1992. *Theories of human communication.* 4th edition. Belmont, California: Wadsworth.

Lloyd, T. 2000. And may they all live happily ever after … The *Financial Mail* 14 January: 32.

Lotman, Y. 1990. *The universe of the mind: a semiotic theory of culture.* Translated by Ann Shukman. Bloomington and Indianapolis: Indiana University Press.

Louw, D.J. 2004. Ubuntu: An African assessment of the religious other. Available: www.bu.edu/wcp/Papers/Afri/AfriLouw.htm Accessed: 2005-07-26.

Louw, P.E. 1989. The emergence of a progressive-alternative press in South Africa with specific reference to Grassroots, in Communicatio 15 (2): 26–32.

Louw, P.E. 1993. *South African media policy: debates of the 1990s.* Bellville: Anthropos.

Louw, P.E. & Tomaselli K.G. 1991. Developments in the conventional and alternate presses, 1980–1989, in *The alternative press in South Africa*, edited by K.G. Tomaselli & P.E. Louw. Bellville: Anthropos: 5–4.

Lovink, G. 2002. The network society and its reality romantics. Review of Hubert L. Dreyfus' On the Internet. Available on the Internet: http://amsterdam.nettime.org/List-Archives/nettime-1-0204/msg00197.html Accessed 2005/02/09.

Lowe, G.F. & Hujanen, T. (eds). 2003. *Broadcasting & convergence: New articulations of the public service remit*. Göteborg, Sweden: Nordicom.

Lowery, S. & de Fleur, M.L. 1983. *Milestones in mass communications research: media effects*. New York: Longman.

Lull, J. (ed). 1992. *Popular music and communication*. 2nd edition. London: Sage.

Mackay, H., Maples, W. & Reynolds, P. 2001. *Investigating the information society*. London: Routledge.

Magardie, K. 2000. e.tv has to find local content. The *Mail & Guardian*, 7–13 January: 7.

Makoe, A. 1999. Black Wednesday – a day of bannings, a day to remember. The *Star*, 18 October: 11.

Malefane, M. 1999. SAUJ warns e.tv of channel collapse. The *Citizen*, 15 January: 8.

Manoim, I. 1996. *You have been warned: the first ten years of the Mail and Guardian*. London: Viking.

Mansell, R. & Wehn, U. 1998. *Knowledge societies: information technology for sustainable development*. Oxford: Oxford University Press.

Maples, W. 2001. Culture, representation and identities, in *Investigating the information society*, edited by H. Mackay, W. Maples & P. Reynolds, London: Routledge.

Marshall, T. & Bottomore T. (eds.). 1992. *Citizenship and Social Class*. London: Pluto Press.

Masango, G. 2004. ThisDay suspended until Monday. The *Star*, 27 October: 3.

Mathiane, N. 2000. Self-scrutiny needed, forum told. *The Business Day*, 25 August: 5.

Matloff, J. 1996. Issue of free press now divides old allies who fought apartheid. The Christian Science Monitor 10 July: 9.

Mazama, A (ed). 2003. *The Afrocentric paradigm*. Trenton/Asmar: Africa World Press.

McLuhan, E. & Zingrone, F. 1997. *Essential McLuhan*. London: Routledge.

McLuhan, M. 1987 (1964, 1965). *Understanding media: the extensions of man*. London: Abacus/Routledge.

McNair, B. 2002. *Public service broadcasting in the UK: the case of political access TV and radio*. Paper presented to the working session on Broadcasting in Europe, Conference of the International Association for Media and Communication Research (IAMCR), Barcelona, 2002-07-10.

McNeil, T. 2006. Roland Barthes: Mythologies (1957). Available on the Internet: http://orac.sund.ac.uk/~os0tmc/myth.htm. Accessed: 2006-05-31.

McPhail, T.L. 2002. *Global communication: theories, stakeholders, and trends*. Boston: Allyn & Bacon.

McQuail, D. 1984. *Communication*. 2nd edition. London: Longman.

McQuail, D. 1987. *Theories of mass communication*. 2nd edition. London: Sage.

McQuail, D. 1992. *Media performance: mass communication and the public interest*. London: Sage.

McQuail, D. 1994. *Mass communication theory: an introduction*. 3rd edition. (4th edition: 2000; 5th edition: 2005) London: Sage.

References

McQuail, D. 1995. Mass communication and the public interest: Towards social theory for media structure and performance, in *Communication theory today*, edited by D. Crowley & D. Mitchell. Cambridge: Polity Press.

McQuail, D. & Windahl, S. 1993. *Communication models*. 2nd edition. London: Longman.

McQueen, D. 1998. *Television: a media student's guide*. London: Arnold.

Mda, Z. 1998. On the small screen: e.tv offers nothing to tempt viewers away from the SABC. The *Sunday Times*, 4 October: 20.

Media Development and Diversity Agency. 2000. A draft position paper. [0]. Available. http://www.gov.za/documents/2000/mdda/mddaintro.pdf. Accessed on 2002/10/12.

Media Institute of Southern Africa (MISA). 2004a. African Charter on Broadcasting. [0]. Available: http://www.misa.org/broadcasting/acb.html. Accessed on 2006/08/30.

Media Institute of Southern Africa (MISA). 2004b. Campaign to abolish 'insult laws' in Africa. [0]. Available: http://www.misa.org/insultlaws.html. Accessed on 2006/08/31.

Media Institute of Southern Africa (MISA). 2006. So this is democracy? Windhoek, Namibia: MISA.

Melody, W. 1991. The information society: the transnational economic context and its implications, in *Transnational communications. Wiring the Third World*, edited by G. Sussman & J. Lent. London: Sage.

Mersham, G.M. 1993. Television: a fascinating window on an unfolding world, in *Mass media for the nineties: the South African handbook of mass communication*, edited by A.S. de Beer. Pretoria: Van Schaik: 173–197.

Merton, R. 1957. *Social theory and social structure*. New York: Free Press.

Metoyer-Duran, C. 1991. Information-seeking behaviour of gatekeepers in ethnolinguistic communities: overview of a taxonomy. LISR. 13: 319–346.

Meyer, W.H. 1988. *Transnational media and Third World development: the structure and impact of imperialism*. New York: Greenwood Press.

Mills, J.S. 1964 (first published in 1859). *On Liberty*. Harmondsworth: Penguin.

Moerdyk, C. 1999a. IBA will get egg on its face over e.tv. The *Saturday Star*, 11 September: 15.

Moerdyk, C. 1999b. Publications get boldface economics lesson. The *Saturday Star*, 20 February: 15.

Moerdyk, C. 1999c. Sales of papers rise in Gauteng. The *Saturday Star*, 7 August: 15.

Mohammadi, A. 1997. *International communication and globalization: a critical introduction*. London: Sage.

Morley, D. 1980. *The 'nationwide' audience: structure and decoding*. London: British Film Institute.

Mosco, V. & Reddick A. 1997. Political economy, communication and policy, in *Democratizing communication? Comparative perspectives on information and power*, edited by M. Bailie & D. Winseck. Cresskill, NJ: Hampton Press: 11–32.

Mosco, V. & Rideout V. 1997. Media policy in North America, in *International Media Research: a critical survey*, edited by J. Corner, P. Schlesinger & R. Silverstone. London: Routledge.

Mosia, L., Riddle, C. & Zaffiro, J. 1994. From revolutionary to regime radio: three decades of nationalist broadcasting in Southern Africa, in African Media Review. 8 (1): 1–24.

Mowlana, H. 1997. *Global information and world communication: New frontiers in international relations*. London: Sage.

Moyo, D. 2006. Broadcasting policy reform and democratisation in Zambia and Zimbabwe, 1990–2005: Global pressures, national responses. PhD thesis, University of Oslo, Oslo.

Muller, J. 1987. Press houses at war: a brief history of Nasionale Pers and Perskor, in *Narrating the crisis: hegemony and the South African press*, edited by K. Tomaselli, R. Tomaselli & J. Muller. Johannesburg: Richard Lyon: 118–140.

Murdock, G. & P. 1977. Capitalism, communication and class relations. In: *Mass communication and society*, edited by Murdock, G., Golding, P., Curran, J. and Gurevitch, M. London: Edward Arnold.

Mwanakatwe, J. 1994. *End of Kaunda era*. Lusaka: Multimedia.

Myers, M. 2000. Community radio and development: issues & examples from Francophone West Africa, in *African broadcast cultures: radio in transition*, edited by R. Fardon & G. Furniss. Harare: Baobab.

Mytton, G. 1983. *Mass communication in Africa*. London: Edward Arnold.

Nain, Z. 2000. Globalized theories and national controls: the state, the market, and the Malaysian media, in *Communication theory today*, edited by D. Crowley & D. Mitchell. Cambridge: Polity Press.

Naspers. 2000. Available on the Internet: http://www.fm.co.za/reports/giant2000/naspers.htm Accessed on 2001/03/22.

National Institute of Cuban Architects and Engineers [sa]. Available on the Internet: http://www.louisville.edu/org/sun/sustain/articles/1999/cuba/architecture/index.html Accessed on 2006/06/07.

Navasky, V. 2000. Is big really bad? Well, yes. *Time*, 24 January: 39–50.

Negt, O., and Kluge, A. 1972. *Öffentlichkeit und Erfahrung*. Frankfurt: Suhrkamp.

Nkutha, Z. 2000. HRC says SA media is racist. The *Sowetan*, 25 August: 2.

Nordenstreng, K. 1997. Beyond the four theories of the press, in *Media and politics in transition. Cultural identity in the age of globalization*, edited by J. Servaes & R. Lie, Leuven: Acco.

Nulens, G. 1997. Socio-cultural aspects of information technology in Africa: the policy of the World Bank studies on media information and telecommunications (SMIT), in Communicatio. 23 (2): 15–23. Available on the Internet: http://www.unisa.ac.za/dept/press/comca/222/nulens.htm. Accessed on 1998/12/12.

Nussbaum, B. 2003. African culture and ubuntu: reflections of a South African in America, in World Business Academy, Perspectives, 17 (1): 1–12.

Nxumalo, F. & Hlophe, N. 1999. e.tv newsdesk may face staff walkout. The *Saturday Star*, 16 January: 13.

Nyamnjoh, F. 2005. *Africa's media: democracy & the politics of belonging*. London, New York & Pretoria: Zed Books & UNISA Press.

Okigbo, C. 1996. Contextualising Freire in African sustainable development, in Africa Media Review 10 (1): 31–54.

Oosthuizen, L.M. 1989. *Media policy and ethics*. Cape Town: Juta.

Oosthuizen, L.M. 1991. Suid-Afrikaanse mediabeleid: die media se bondgenoot is soek. Communicatio 17 (1):38–47.

Oppelt, P. 1999. The ecstasy and the agony. The *Sunday Times*, 3 October: 19.

O'Sullivan, T., Hartley, J., Saunders, D., Montgomery, M., & Fiske, J. 1994. *Key concepts in communication and cultural studies*. 2nd edition. London: Routledge.

O'Sullivan, T. & Jewkes, Y. 1997. *The media studies reader*. London: Arnold.

Pacatte, R. 2006. *The Da Vinci Code*: Alas, No Heroes. Available on the Internet: http://www.daughtersofstpaul.com/mediastudies/reviews/filmdavincicode.html Accessed on 2006/07/31.

Palmer, J. 1999. Weeklies grow while dailies' figures drop. *The Business Day*, 24 August: 21.

Parker, J. 1999a. News comes too late to help e.tv's case. *The Business Day*, 12 January: 2.

References

Parker, J. 1999b. Internal disputes at e.tv denied by Midi Television. *The Business Day*, 21 January: 4.

Perry, D.K. 1996. *Theory and research in mass communication: context and consequences*. Mahwah, NJ: Lawrence Erlbaum.

Philp, R. 1998. Grooming the couch potato. The *Sunday Times Lifestyle*, 25 November: 21–23.

Pieterse, J.N. (sa) Wit over zwart. Beelden van Afrika en Zwarten in de Westerse Populaire Cultuur. Amsterdam: Koninklijk Instituut voor de Tropen.

Pityana, B. 2000. South Africa's inquiry into racism in the media: the role of national institutions in the promotion and protection of human rights. African Affairs 99 (397): 525–532.

Pluralism and polysemy. Available on the Internet: http://www.indigogroup.co.uk/foamycustard/fc041.htm Accessed on 2006/06/08.

Pokwana, V. 1998. e.tv line-up fails to satisfy viewers. *City Press Showbiz*, 11 October: 3.

Pollak, R. 1981. *Up against apartheid: the role and the plight of the press in South Africa*. Carbondale, Illinois: Southern Illinois University Press.

Pople, L. 2000. Europa gaan nie Kersvader speel. *Naweek-Beeld*, 11 November: 3.

Poster, M. 1995. CyberDemocracy: Internet and the public sphere. Available on the Internet: http:www.hnet.uci.edu/mposter/writings/democ.html Accessed on 2005/02/10.

Poster, M. 2001. *What's the matter with the Internet?* Minnesota: University of Minnesota Press.

Postman, N. 1985. *Amusing ourselves to death: public discourse in the age of show business*. London: Methuen.

Postman, N. 1992. *Technopoly: the surrender of culture to technology*. New York: Knopf.

Potter, W.J. 1998. *Media literacy*. Thousand Oaks, CA: Sage.

Prinsloo, I. 1990. South African syntheses – architecture. Available on the Internet: http://www.findarticles.com/p/articles/mi_m3575/is_n1177_v197/ai_16788119 Accessed on 2006/08/19.

Ramose, M.B. 2002. The philosophy of ubuntu and ubuntu as a philosophy, in *Philosophy from Africa: a text with readings* (2nd edition), edited by P.H. Coetzee & A.P.J. Roux. Oxford: Oxford University Press.

Real, M. 1998. MediaSport: technology and the commodification of postmodern sport, in *MediaSport* edited by L. Wenner. London: Routledge: 50–75.

Reynolds, J. 2006. Jacques Derrida. The Internet encyclopedia of philosophy, available: http://www.iep.utm.edu/d/derrida.htm#Trace Accessed: 2006/06/01.

Rheingold, H. 1994. *The virtual community: Homesteading on the electronic frontier*. New York, N.Y.: Harper Perennial.

Rheingold, H. 1997. Disinformocracy, in *The media studies reader*, edited by T. O'Sullivan & Y. Jewkes. London: Arnold.

Roach, C. 1990. The movement for a New World Information and Communication Order: a second wave, in Media, Culture and Society. 12 (3): 283–307.

Roelofse, J.J. 1983. Towards rational discourse: an analysis of the report of the Steyn commission of inquiry into the media. Pretoria: van Schaik.

Roelofse, K. 1996. The history of the South African Press, in *Introduction to communication – course book 5: journalism, press and radio studies*, edited by L.M. Oosthuizen. Kenwyn: Juta: 66–118.

Rosenfield, L. and Mader, T. 1984. The functions of human communication, in *Handbook of rhetorical and communication theory*, edited by C. Arnold & J. Bowers. Boston: Allyn & Bacon.

Rosenthal, E. 1974. *You have been listening … The early days of history of radio in South Africa*. Cape Town: Purnell.

Rowe, D. 2004. *Sport, culture and the media*. Berkshire, England: Open University Press.

Ruben, R.W. & Soleri, P. 1979. Architecture: medium and message, in *Beyond media: new approaches to mass communication,* edited by R.W. Budd & B.R. Ruben. New Jersey, USA: Hayden: 106–115.

Sage, G.H. 1990. *Power and ideology in American sport: a critical perspective.* Champaign, Illinois: Human Kinetics.

Scambler, G. and Martin, L. 2001. Civil Society, the Public Sphere and Deliberative Democracy, in *Habermas, Critical Theory and Health,* edited by G. Scambler. London: Routledge.

Scannell, P. 1990. Public service broadcasting: the history of a concept, in *Understanding television,* edited by A. Goodwin & G. Whannell. London: Routledge.

Senghor, L.S. 2000. Negritude and African socialism, in *Postcolonialism: critical concepts in literary and cultural studies,* volume 3, edited by D. Brydon. London and New York: Routledge.

Servaes, J. 2004. Multiple perspectives on development communication, in *Development and communication in Africa,* edited by C.C. Okigbo & F. Eribo. Lanham, Boulder, New York, Toronto and Oxford: Rowman & Littlefield Publishers: 55–64.

Shannon, C.E. & Weaver, W. 1949. *The mathematical theory of communication.* Illinois: University of Illinois Press.

Shome, R. and Hegde, R.S. 2002. Postcolonial approaches to communication: Charting the terrain, engaging the intersections, in Communication Theory, 12 (3): 249–270.

Shutte, A. 2001. *Ubuntu: An ethic for a new South Africa.* Pietermaritzburg, KZN: Cluster Publications.

Siebert, F., Peterson, T. & Schramm, W. 1956. *Four theories of the press.* Urbana, IL: University of Illinois Press.

Silverstone, R. 1999. *Why study the media?* London: Sage.

Slater, D. 2004. Social relationships and identity online and offline, in *The television studies reader,* edited by R.C. Robert Allen and A. Hill. London: Routledge.

Sonderling, S. 2006. Communication theory from an African perspective. Tutorial Letter 101/2006 HKMTHE: Advanced Communication Theory. Department of Communication Science: University of South Africa.

South Africa. 1981. Report of the commission of inquiry into the mass media. Pretoria: Government Printer. Chairman: M. Steyn.

South Africa. 1993. Independent Broadcasting Authority Act, no 153, 1993. Pretoria: Government Printer.

South Africa. 1995. Report of the Arts and Culture Task Group. Pretoria: Government Printer.

South Africa. 1996. Telecommunications Act, no 103, 1996. Pretoria: Government Printer.

South Africa. 1998. Government Communications. The media. [O]. Available: http://www.gov.za/yearbook/media.htm Accessed on 2000/06/26.

South Africa. 1999. Broadcasting Act, no 4, 1999. [O]. Available: http://www.polity.org.za/govdocs/legislation/1999/act99-004.html Accessed on 1999/09/03.

South Africa. 2000. Independent Communication Authority of South Africa Act, no 13, 2000. Pretoria. Government Printer.

South African Advertising Research Foundation. 2000. Readership of newspapers in 1000's [O]. Available: http://www/saarf.co.za/topnewspapers.htm Accessed on 2001/01/15.

South African Broadcasting Corporation. 1996. Annual report and financial statements, 1995/96. Johannesburg.

South African Broadcasting Corporation. 1999. Annual report and financial statements, 1998/99. Johannesburg.

References

South African Human Rights Commission. 2000. Research Report commissioned by the South African Human Rights Commission as part of its Inquiry into Race and the Media. Johannesburg: HRC.

South African music ... Available on the Internet: http://www.english-theatre.org/et_new/html/main.php?nav=46&url=3Kat.html Accessed on 2006/10/05.

South African Task Group, Broadcasting in South and Southern Africa. 1991. Report of the task group on broadcasting in Southern Africa. Pretoria: Government Printer: Chairman: C. Viljoen.

Sowaga, D. 2003. Battle lines drawn in daily newspaper wars. The *City Press*, 24 August: 4.

Spitulnik, D. 2002. Alternative small media and communicative spaces, in *Media and democracy in Africa*, edited by G. Hyden, M. Leslie & F. F. Ogundimu. New Brunswick (U.S.A) and London (U.K.): Transaction Publishers: 177–205.

Steyn, R. 1994. *The transition process and the South African media*. Editor & Publisher 127 (2): 44.

Stillo M. [sa]. The life and work of Antonio Gramsci. Available on the Internet: www.theory.org.uk/ctr-gram.htm Accessed on 2006/09/04.

Stöber, R. 2004. Media evolution is: a theoretical approach to the history of new media. European Journal of Communication 19 (4): 483–505.

Stoke, O. (ed). 1971. *Reporting Africa*. Uppsala: The Scandinavian Institute of African Studies.

Strinati, D. 1995. *An introduction to theories of culture*. Routledge: London.

Sussman, G. 1997. *Communication, technology, and politics in the information age*. London: Sage.

Sussman, G. & Lent, J. 1991. Introduction: critical perspectives on communication and Third World development, in *Transnational Communications: wiring the Third World*, edited by G. Sussman and J. Lent. London: Sage.

Switzer, L.S. & Switzer, D. 1979. *The black press in South Africa and Lesotho*. Boston: GK Hall.

Szeman, I. 2005 (a). Fast thinking, slow thoughts: Pierre Bourdieu on journalism. [Online]. http://www.humanities.mcamaster.ca/~szeman/fast.htm. Accessed: 2005/04/05.

Szeman, I. 2005 (b). Szeman's review on Bourdieu. [Online]. http://eserver.org/clogic/1-2/szeman.html. Accessed: 2005/04/05.

Tabane, J.J. Editors are mirror versions of Snuki. The *City Press*, 12 November: 4.

Talero, E. & Gaudette, P. 1995. Harnessing information for development: a proposal for a World Bank Group vision and strategy. The World Bank.

Taunyane, M. 2006. Poor distribution and marketing killed Nova. The *City Press*, 12 February: 7.

Taunyane, M. 2006. KZN papers ahamba phambili. The *City Press*, 4 June: 4.

Tehranian, M. 1991. Is comparative communication theory possible/desirable? In Communication theory, 1: 44–59.

Thomass, B. 2003. Knowledge society and public sphere: two concepts for the remit, in *Broadcasting & convergence: New articulations of the public service remit*, edited by G.F. Lowe & T. Hujanen. Göteborg, Sweden: Nordicom.

Thompson, J.B. 1984. *Studies in the theory of ideology*. Cambridge: Polity.

Thompson, J.B. 1990. *Ideology and Modern Culture: critical social theory in the era of mass communication*. Cambridge: Polity Press.

Thompson, J.B. 1995. *The Media and Modernity: a social theory of the media*. Cambridge: Polity Press.

Thompson, K. (ed). 1997. *Media and cultural regulation*. London: Sage Publications in association with the Open University.

Tolson, A. 1996. *Mediations: texts and discourse in media studies*. London: Arnold.

Tomaselli, K., Tomaselli, R. & Muller, J. 1987. *Narrating the crisis: hegemony and the South African press*. Johannesburg: Richard Lyon.

Tomaselli, R., Tomaselli, K. & Muller, J. 1989. *Currents of power: state broadcasting in South Africa*. Bellville: Anthropos.

Tomaselli, K. & Louw, P.E. (eds). 1991. *The alternative press in South Africa*. Bellville: Anthropos.

Traber, M. 1993. Changes of communication needs and rights in social revolution, in *Communication and democracy*, edited by Slavko Splichal & Janet Wasko. Westport, Connecticut & London: Ablex Publishing: 19–31.

Tracey, M. 1998. *The decline and fall of public service broadcasting*. Oxford: Oxford University Press.

Tuchman, G. 1973. Making news by doing work: routinizing the unexpected, in the American Journal of Sociology, 79 (1): 110–131.

Turkle, S. 1995. *Life on the screen: Identity in the age of the Internet*. New York: Simon & Schuster.

Turner, G. 2000. *British Cultural Studies: an introduction*. 2nd edition. New York, NY: Routledge.

Underwood, M. 2005. The Internet as public sphere. Available on the Internet: http://www.zip.com.au/~athornto//links.htm Accessed 2005/03/07.

United Nations Economic Commission for Africa (UNECA). 2006. African Information Society Initiative. [Online]. Available: http://www.uneca.org/aisi/abtaisi.htm. Accessed on 2006/08/01.

Van Cuilenburg, J. & McQuail, D. 2003. Towards a new communications policy paradigm, in European Journal of Communication, 18 (2): 181–207.

Van Cuilenburg, J., Scholten, O. & Noomen, G. 1992. Communicatiewetenschap. Muiderberg: Coutinho.

Van den Brink, R. 1987. Informatie over de informatie: handboek over de informatiemedia in Nederland 1938–1985. Leiden: Stenfert Kroese.

Van der Merwe, C. 1995. Electronic media management. Johannesburg: Africa Growth Network.

Van Driel, H. 2003. Identiteit in een digitale kultuur. [O] Available on the Internet: http:/comcom.uvt.nl/e-view/inhoud.htm. Accessed on 17 November 2003/11/17.

Van Graan, A. & Winberg, C. 2003. *Communication for architecture*. Cape Town, South Africa: Oxford University Press.

Van Poecke, L. 1994. Mediacultuur en identiteitsconstitutie in het licht van de postmoderne swakke classificatie en framing. *Communicatie. Tijdschrift voor Massamedia en Cultuur* 23(3_): 1–27.

Vermeulen, A. 1999. Rembrandt and e.tv minorities in talks on funding. *Sunday Times Business Times*, 10 October: 1.

Vincent, R.C. 1997. The future of the debate: setting an agenda for a new world information and communication order, ten proposals, in *Beyond cultural imperialism: globalization, communication and the new international order*, edited by P. Golding & P. Harris. London: Sage.

Vincent, R.C. 1997. The new world information and communication order (NWICO) in the context of the information super highway, in *Democratizing communication? Comparative perspectives on information and power*, edited by M. Bailie & D. Winseck. Cresskill, N.J.: Hampton Press.

Wang, G. & Shen, V. 2000. East, West, communication and theory: Searching for the meaning of searching for Asian communication theories, in the Asian Journal of Communication, 10 (2): 14–32.

References

Wasserman, H. & de Beer, A.S. 2004. Covering HIV/ Aids: towards a heuristic comparison between communitarian and utilitarian ethics, in Communicatio 30 (2): 84–97.
Watson, J. & Hill, A. 1984. A dictionary of communication and media studies. London: Edward Arnold.
Webster, F. 1995. *Theories of the information society.* London: Routledge.
Westley, B.H. & MacLean, M.S. 1957. A conceptual model for communication research, in Journalism Quarterly 34: 31–38.
White, M. 1987. Ideological analysis and television, in Channels of discourse: television and contemporary criticism, edited by R.C. Allen. London: Methuen: 73–81.
Wigston, D.J. 1996. A historical overview of radio, in *Introduction to communication – course book 5: journalism, press and radio studies,* edited by L.M. Oosthuizen. Kenwyn: Juta: 283–326.
Wigston, D.J. 2001. A South African media map, in *Media studies. Volume 1: institutions, theories and issues,* edited by P.J. Fourie. Lansdowne: Juta.
Wikipedia, the free encyclopedia. Available on the Internet: http://www.wikipedia.org/ Accessed on 2006/09/04.
Wikipedia. 2006. African nationalism. Available on the Internet: http://en.wikipedia.org/wiki/African_nationalism. Accessed on 2006/08/25.
Wilcox, D.L. 1975. *Mass media in black Africa: philosophy and control.* New York: Praeger.
Williams, R. 1977. *Marxism and Literature.* Oxford University Press: Oxford.
Williams, R. 1981. *The sociology of culture.* New York: Schocken.
Winfield, B.H., Mizuno, T. & Beaudoin, C.E. 2000. Confucianism, collectivism and constitutions: Press systems in China and Japan. Communication Law & Policy, 5: 323–347.
Wood, J.T. 2000. *Communication theories in action.* 2nd edition. Belmont, CA: Wadsworth.
World Association for Christian Communication (WACC). 2002. Is the 'information society' a useful concept for civil society? In Media Development. Available on the Internet: http://www.wacc.org.uk/publications/md/md2002-4/infosociety.html. Accessed on 2002/12/11.
Wright, C. 1975. Mass communications: a sociological approach. New York: Random House.
Waters, M. 1995. *Globalization.* London: Routledge.
Wrottesley, S. 1999. Nice e.studio, shame about the news content. The *Cape Argus,* 18 January: 5.
Yew, L. 2002. *Notes on colonialism.* Available on the Internet: http://www.postcolonialweb.org/poldiscourse/colonialismnotes.html. Accessed on 2006/08/28.
Young, R.J.C. 2001. *Postcolonialism: an historical introduction.* Oxford: Blackwell Publishers Ltd.
Zambia. Ministry of Transport and Communications. 2005. National information and communication policy. Lusaka: Ministry of Transport and Communications.

Index

5FM 23

A
A Programme 9
Abantu-Batho 38
ability 217
Access to Information and Protection of Privacy Act 77
Accra Evening News 65–66
accumulation theory 238–239
active audience 172
administrative
　paradigm 202
　power 352
Adorno, Theodor 127, 326, 334
advertisements 261
advertising and the media 50
aesthetic barren culture 272–273
affective media effects 230
Africa
　Anglophone 63
　anti-communism in 68–70
　capitalist expansion in 68
　colonial period in 61–70
　colonialist federalism in 67
　Francophone 64
　functions of media in colonial 65–70
　liberation of 61
　media in 60–85
　missionary activity in 66
　post-colonial media in 70
　United Nations Economic Commission for 81
　African Broadcasting Company 8
　Broadcasting Corporation 55
　Charter on Broadcasting 78
　Consolidated Film 55
　Consolidated Theatres 55
　Information Society Initiative 81, 82
　language radio services 14
　media and globalisation 74-82
　National Congress 18, 38, 41,133, 275
　nationalism 63, 65–66
　Peer Review Mechanism 83
　Union 83
African Drum 39
African Lodestar, The 41
Afrikaans
　broadcasts in 9–10
　press 33–38
　press groups 35–36
　Service 12
Afrikaanse Patriot, Die 34, 35
Afrikanerbond 34
Afrikaner, Die 49
Afrocentric approach to theory 174–178

agency 114
Agenda Feminist Media Project 199
agenda-setting theory 244–245
Al Qalaam 42
alphabets, phonetic 92
alternative press 40–44
Althusser, Louis 132, 133, 274, 279, 313, 315
Amazwi Writers 199
Angola 64
Anima 258
Animus 258
anomie 234
anthropological historical accounts 61
AOL/Time Warner 393
apartheid 45, 55
　Afrikaans newspapers and 45
　press and 44–52
apathy 346
archetype 257–258
architecture and built environment 292–293
　history of 302–303
Arendt, Hannah 125, 126
Argus
　Company 38
　Group 68
Arnold, Matthew 125, 126, 273
Ashante, Molefi Kete 177
Associated Scientific and Technical Societies 7
Astrasat 23
audience 100–101
　active 173
　media 100
Austin, John Langshaw 327
authoritarian theory 191–192
automation, station 13
Azikiwe, Nnamdi 63, 65, 66, 69, 70

B
B Programme 9
Bacon, Francis 131
Baily, Abe 39
Baily, Jim 39
Bamako Declaration on Radio Pluralism 79
Bantu
　Press Ltd 38
　Programmes Control Board 14
Bantu World 38
Barthes, Roland 162, 164, 252, 253, 254, 255, 274
battleground 280
Baudrillard, Jean 162, 170–173
Beeld 190
behavioural media effects 230

behaviourism 109, 118–119
belief systems 285, 307
Ben, Babsie en Familie 254
Bénin 79
Benjamin, Walter 127
Berelson, Bernard 120, 122–123
Berlusconi, Silvio 347
Bertelsmann 393
Biko, Steve 42
binary oppositions, theory of 249–251
black
　consciousness 41
　empowerment, role of, in broadcasting 23–26
　listeners, programming for 11–12
Black Economic Empowerment 55, 56
black press
　development of 36–40
　independent élitist period 37–38
　missionary period 37
　multiracial period 40
　white-owned period 38–39
Black Review 42
Black Viewpoint 42
blacklisting 26
blogs 137
Blue Free Voucher Scheme 8
Blumler, Herbert 148
Bonaparte, Napoléon 310
Boniface, Charles Etienne 31
Bop-TV 15
Botha, PW 18
Botma, Gabriël 138
Botswana 79
　Telecommunications Authority 79
Bourdieu, Pierre 162, 168–169, 274
bourgeois public sphere 329
bourgeoisie 328
Bourke, Richard 30
braaivleis 253, 254
Brand, Christoffel Joseph 34
Breteuil, Charles de 64
Breteuil, Michel de 64
British
　Broadcasting Corporation 8, 69, 195
　cultural studies 316–317
　settlers 30
　Sky Broadcasting 393
broadcasting 6–27
　black empowerment and 23–26
　commercial 22
　community 22
　establishment of radio in South Africa 6–8
　legislation, changes to 27
　post-apartheid 26–27

428

Index

public 21
  rationalisation of 17
  regulators, independent 82
  in South Africa 5
Broadcasting
  Act 8, 21, 55, 366
  African Charter on 78
  Authority of Zimbabwe 77
  Complaints Commission of South Africa 194
broadcasts
  amateur 6–7, 55
  experimental 7, 55
  Railway 7
  first regular 7–8
Brown, Dan 288, 300
Brussels Summit 380
Burger, De 33, 35, 36
Burger, Die 35, 36
Burke, Edmund 178
Burkina Faso 79
Business Day 190

C

Canal Plus 393
Cantril, Hadley 233
CanWest 393
Cape Argus, The 31
Cape Peninsula Publicity Association 7
Cape Times, The 31
Cape Town Gazette and African Advertiser 28
Capital Radio 13, 16
capitalism 136, 352
capitalist system, world 355
Carey, James 274
Castells, Manuel 398
catharsis theory 265
Central African Mail 64
Central African Post 67, 68
Centre for Contemporary Cultural Studies 274
Chiluba, Frederick 76
China 100
Chomsky, Noam 138
Christians, Clifford 201, 202
church 286
  electronic 287
Citizen, The 46, 190
civic journalism 200–201
civil society, media and 347–348
class struggle 132
Clegg, Johnny 296
codes 148, 149, 150, 151
codes of conduct 264
coercive power 140
cognitive media effects 230
collaborative media role 202
collectivism 211
Colonial Office 68, 69
colonial period in Africa 61–70

colonialism 65
  definition 62
  reversed, globalisation and 360–361
combination 160
commercial broadcasting 22
commercialisation 368
  of state media 77–78
communication 101–102
  culture and 271–272
Communication
  Authority of South Africa 367
  Problems, International Commission for the Study of 377
communicative action 337–342
  theory of 339–341
communicator 97–98
  identifying a single 97–98
  intention of 262
communitarianism 79–80
community
  broadcasting 22
  media 83
  print 199
  radio 19, 79–80, 199
  TV 199
comparative theory 208
concentration 363
conflict of interpretation 318
Congo, Democratic Republic of 82
consciousness, false 278, 311
constructive criticism 73
consumption 160
contemporary society, public sphere in 325–348
Contemporary Studies, Centre for 142
content 204
convergence 364–366
"cool" media 172
cosmopolitan society, globalisation and 361–362
Cradocksche-Afrikaner 34
crime waves 319
critical paradigm 202
critical/dialectical media role 203
Cronjé, Hansie 241
critical approach to mass communication 124–146
  cultural and feminist studies 142–143
  criticism of 143–145
  ideology 130–133
  Frankfurt School 127
  mass/popular culture 127–130
  mass society theory 124–126
  political economy 135–139
  public sphere 139–141
cultural
  expression 277
  forms of expression 271
  identities, local 358–359
  negotiation paradigm 202
  studies 142, 274–276

culture
  aesthetic barren 272–273
  and communication 271–272
  definition 276–277
  future development 298
  high, popular and mass 272–274
  industry 355–356
  organic folk 272
  popular 128, 129
  research on 297–298
currency, national 354
cyberspace 397

D

Da Vinci Code, The 288, 300–301
Daily Graphic 68
Daily Mail 68
Daily Mirror 38
Daily Mirror group 68
Daily News, The 33, 77
Daily Sun, The 32, 52
Daily Times 68
Daily Voice 52
Dallas 15
Davidson, Donald 327
De Klerk, FW 18, 50, 241
De Waal, JHH 35
deconstruction 167–168
"Deep-drilling" 5
deliberation 345
democracy 205
  and the public sphere 342–348
  Internet and 402–403
democratic participant theory 199–201
dependency 394–395
Derrida, Jacques 162, 167–168
Destutt de Tracy, Antoine-Louis-Claude 131, 310
determinism 106
determinism, technological 151–154
  criticism of 153–154
Dethier, Herbert 171
development theory 198–199
Dewey, John 326, 327
diffusion of innovation theory 239–240
Digger's News 32
digital
  culture 91
  divide 397, 404
Digital Satellite Television (DStv) 74
Dilthey, Wilhelm 122, 123, 327
discourse 164–166
discourses, texts as 271
discursive practices 319
disembedment 353
Disney 393
dissimulation 317
distance 221
distanciation, time-space 352
distortion of reality 311
distraction 236

429

diversion 236
diversity 206
dominant reading 282, 318
Dormer, Joseph 31
Drum 39
DStv 366
Du Preez, Max 43
Du Toit, Daniel François 34
Du Toit, Stephanus Jacobus 34, 35
dubbing 15
Dube, John 38
Durban City Corporation 7
Durkheim, Émile 120, 126, 185, 326
Dutch East India Company 28

E
e-tv 22, 24, 25, 366
    news bulletins 24
    near bankruptcy 25
East Coast Radio 13
Eastern philosophies 208
Eastern Star, The 32
economic
    downturn 51
    power 140
Editorial Charter 26
education, mass 72
effect theories and research, caution about 264–266
effects model 265–266
Eid 288
Electronic Communications Act 20, 27, 366
electronic public mass communication culture 91, 94–95
Emerging Communication Industry Media Paradigm 370
Emigrant, De 31
empiricism 118
employment policy 263–264
Engels, Friedrich 131, 259
English
    press 28–33
    Service 12
Enlightenment 159–160, 192, 327, 333
entertainment 216–225
    behavioural perspective 219–222
    rhetorical motifs 216–218
    sociological perspective 222–224
    as a value judgement 224
epistemology 107–108
    postmodern 159
Equity 15
Ethiopia 72
Eurocentrism 177
evaluating a theory 110–112
expert systems 354
Express en Oranje Vrijstaats Advertensieblad, De 33

expression, freedom of 178
    ubuntu and 212, 214–215
expression, social and cultural forms of 285–297

F
facilitative media role 203
Fairbairn, John 29, 30, 33, 34
Fakkel 33
false consciousness 278, 311
family series 217
fantasy 160
Faure, Abraham 29, 35
feedback 101
feminist
    history 61
    studies 143
Ferguson, Jennifer 296
Festival Radio 19
feudal
    era 328
    society 328
Fichte, Johan Gottlieb 327
FIFA World Cup Soccer 290
Fighting Talk 41
film 94
Financial Mail 190
Fishkin, James 343
Fiske, John 283
FM *see* frequency modulation
folk culture, organic 272
force 308
Ford, Henry 157
Forte Community Radio 199
Foucault, Michel 162, 164–166, 274
Fouhy, Edward 200
"fourth estate" 17
fragmentation 160, 161–162, 317
framing 245–246
Franco, Francisco 192
Francophone Africa 64
Frankfurt School 126, 127, 326
freedom of expression 82, 178
    ubuntu and 212, 214–215
Freedom of Expression in Africa, Declaration of Principles on 77, 78
freedom of the media 193
freedom of the press, struggle for 29–30
French Socialist Party 64
frequency modulation (FM) 12–13
Freud, Sigmund 130, 326, 327
Friend of the Free State, The 32
Friend of the Sovereignty and Bloemfontein Gazette, The 32
Friend, The 32
Fromm, Erich 127
functionalism 119–120, 185–188
    objections to 187

G
G–7 81
Gadamer, Hans-Georg 326, 327
Gaudet, Hazel 122
Gauntlett's criticism 265–266
Geertz, Clifford 274
Gemeinschaft 125
General Agreement on Tariffs and Trade 368
Genootskap van Regte Afrikaners 34
genre of a media text 261
German idealism 327
Gesellschaft 125
Ghana 63, 65, 66, 68
    independence of 69
Ghana News Agency 66
Ghandi, MK 38
Gibson, Mel 298, 299
Giddens, Anthony 351, 352, 353, 354, 355, 357, 360, 361
Giddens' theory of globalisation 351–362
    criticism of 356
Glasser, Theodore 201, 202
global communication research, media imperialism 392–396
Global Information Infrastructure Project 380–382
    criticism of 383–387
    liberal critique 384
    Luddite critique 384
    participation in 386
    quality concerns 385–386
    and South Africa 381–382
"global village" 94
globalisation 84, 197
    affecting personal lives 358
    African media and 74–82
    characteristics of 357–362
    and cosmopolitan society 361–362
    disembedment a characteristic of 353–354
    Giddens' theory of 351–362
    impact of, on the media 362–372
    and inequalities 359–360
    and the media 351–407
    and the nation-state 361
    outstanding features of 355–356
    as product of human inspiration 359
    researching 393–405
    and reversed colonialism 360–361
    and revival of local cultural identities 358–359
    as a social process 352
goals of mass media theory 112–115
Goethe, Johann Wolfgang von 330
Golden City Post 39
Gore, Al 380
Gouvernements Courant 33
Gouvernements Courant der ZAR 31
Government Gazette 31

Index

Grahamstown National Arts Festival 19
Gramsci, Antonio 132, 274, 279, 280, 315
Grassroots 42
Great Trek, re-enactment of 9
Greig, George 29
Group Areas Act 292
Group of Seven 81, 380
Guardian, The 41, 44
Guinea 79
Gunaratne, Shelton 208
Gutenberg, Johann 93

H

Habermas, Jürgen 127, 139, 325, 326, 328, 329, 330, 331, 332, 333, 334, 337, 338, 339, 340, 341, 342, 343, 344, 345, 346, 347, 348
   criticism of early 334–337
   and critical theory 339
   and hermeneutics 338
   and Marxism 337
   and modernity 340
   and politics 341–342
   and pragmatism 338
   and social rationalisation 340
   and speech-act theory 330–340
   and technology and science 338
   and theory of communicative action 339–341
"hailing" 315
Hall, Stuart 142, 173, 274, 281, 282, 318
Hall's theory 281–283
Ham, children of 259
Hamelink, Cees 384, 385, 386
Harber, Anton 43
Havenga, NC 36
HCI 25
Hegel, Georg Wilhelm Friedrich 130, 208, 259, 327
hegemonic
   forces 275
   reproduction 275
hegemony 279–281, 315–316
   sport and 291
Heidegger, Martin 327
Herman, Edward 138
hermeneutics 327
Hertzog, JBM 36
Hitler, Adolf 192, 325
Hobbes, Thomas 208, 259
Hoggart, Richard 142, 274
Home Affairs, Department of 19
homelands, independent 15, 16
homosexuality 166
Hopkins, Reginald 6
Hopkinson, Tom 39
Horkheimer, Max 127, 334
Human and People's Rights, African Commission on 77
humanism 106, 109
humanocentric theory 208, 209

Hussein, Saddam 316
Huxley, Aldous 157
hypodermic needle theory 232–233

I

IBA 55
ICASA Amendment Act 27
ICASA *see* Independent Communications Authority of South Africa
ideas 307
identification 219
identifiability of characters 219
identity 216
   on-line 401
Ideological State Apparatuses 279, 313
ideological struggles 318–322
ideologies, conflicting 275
ideology 130–133, 275, 278–279, 308
   critical theories of 310–317
   definition 130–131
   history 131
   Marx's realist theory of 311–313
   mass media promotion of 321–322
   neutral theory of 309–310
   neo-Marxist critical theories of 313–315
   popular view of 308–309
   professional 319
   sport and 291
   theories of 309–317
Ihorin 66
Ikwezi 37
Ilanga 53, 190
Ilanga Lase Natal 38
imperialism, media/cultural 73
Imvo Zabantsundu 37, 38
Indaba 37
Independent Broadcasting Authority (Zambia) 77
Independent Broadcasting Authority (IBA) 18, 19, 20, 23
   Act 19, 21
Independent Communication Authority of South Africa (ICASA) 77, 194
independent radio 15–16
Independent, The 33
Indian Opinion 38
Industrial Revolution 132
industrialisation 352
inequalities, globalisation and 359–360
information and communication technology 95, 102, 153, 155–156, 362
   access to 385
   control of 384
   impact of, on culture, identity and democracy 400–405
   and the media 351–407
   new 80–82
   and popular culture 298
information and technology policy
   achieving balance 390–391

ensuring needs are met 388–390
guaranteeing cultural preservation 388
monitoring of 387–392
prevention of employment inequities 388
prevention of misallocation of scarce resources 387–388
provision for financial management 387
supporting sustainable development 391–392
Information Scandal 46–47
Information Society and Development Conference 81
Information Society, World Summit on 382–383
   criticism of 383–387
   liberal critique 384
   Luddite critique 384
information superhighway 379, 380
Information, Department of 46, 47
Inkundla 41
Innes, Arthur Sydney 7
Innis, Harold Adams 151
inspiration, human, globalisation as product of 359
"insult laws" 82
intended media effects 230
International Telecommunications Union 380, 382
internationalisation 367–368
internationalism 160
Internet 137
Internet 81, 99, 100, 102, 137
   access 396–405
   applications 399
   communicative nature of 397–398
   and democracy 402–403
   global participation 400
   and identity 400
   interconnectivity 398
   newspapers available on 365–366
   and on-line identity 401
   participation 399
   policy research 397
   politics and identity 401–402
   regulation 403–404
   timeless-time 398
   usage 382
interpellation 315
interpretations 279
   alternative 283–284
   conflict of 318
intertextuality 284–285
introjection 220
Isigisdimi Sama Xhosa 37, 38
Isolezwe 53, 190
Izwi la Bantu 38

Media Studies: Volume 1

J
Jabavu, John Tengo 37, 38
Jefferson, Thomas 208
Jeffries, Charles 69
Jeppe, Fredrich 32
journalism, civic 200–201
journalist skills, scarcity of 53
Journalistic Ethics, UNESCO Statement on 377
journalists, professional ideology of 319–321
Jung, Karl 258

K
Kaapsche Stads Courant en Afrikaansche Berigte 28
Kafir Express, The 37
Kagiso Media 56
Kant, Immanuel 325, 327
Kapwepwe, Simon 73
Kasoma, Francis Peter 176
Katz, Elihu 122
Kaunda, Kenneth 70, 71
Kerckhove, Derrick de 153
Kerkorrel, Johannes 296
Kgalagadi Community Radio 199
Kierkegaard, Søren 402
Kipling, Rudyard 32
Klapper, J.T. 122, 234, 235
knowledge 217
Kombuis, Koos 296
Kramer, David 296
Kruger, Paul 34

L
Lacan, Jacques 274
laissez-faire 332
language
　analytical theory 327
　as a sign system 150
Lasswell, Harold 122, 186
Latekgomo, Joe 40
latent media effects 230
Lazarsfeld, Paul F. 120, 122, 186
legitimation 317
Lerner, Daniel 376
Lévi-Strauss, Claude 163, 249, 250, 251, 252, 274
Lewin, Kurt 120
liberal
　history 61
　pluralists 144
liberal-individualist paradigm 202
liberalisation 366–367
libertarian
　historical accounts 61
　press theory 193
　theory 192–193
Lippmann, Walter 121, 122
LM Radio 15

localisation 356
Locke, John 208, 259
London Missionary Society 37
long-term theories 237–247
Lovedale Missionary Institute 37
Luther, Martin 286
Luthuli, Albert 41
Lyotard, Jean François 159

M
M-Net 15, 17, 22, 50, 366
MacBride Commission 377–378
MacBride, Sean 377
Machiavelli, Niccolò 131, 208
macro-plurality 189, 190
Madam & Eve 254, 261
Mail & Guardian 44, 53, 100, 190, 254, 262
Mail & Guardian Online 366
Malawi 67, 76, 83
Malawi Communications Regulatory Authority 77
Malawi Media Council 83
male gaze 143
Mali 64, 79
Mandela, Nelson 63, 292, 357
Mani, Lara 175
manifest media effects 230
Manoim, Irwin 43
Marcuse, Herbert 127
marginal discourses 275
market-orientated philosophy 196
market, oversaturation of 52–53
Marx, Karl 130, 131, 132, 208, 259, 278–279, 310, 311, 312, 313, 325, 327, 238
Marx's realist theory of ideology 311–313
Marxism 278–279
mass
　education 72
　media 312, 333
　society theory 124–126
mass communication
　and considered public opinion 344–346
　critical approach to 124–146
　effects of 228–268
　ethical importance 229
　positivism and 120–121
　scientific importance 229
　strategic importance 229
mass communication culture 90, 91
　definition 95, 96–97
　questions related to definition of 97–103
Mass Democratic Movement 42, 51
mass/popular culture criticism 127–130
material base of society 311
Matsepe-Casaburri, Ivy 77
Mattelart, Armand 138
Mauritania 79
Mbeki, Thabo 26
McChesney, Robert Waterman 138

McKinsey and Associates 23
McLuhan, Marshall 94, 151, 152, 153, 171, 172
McQuail, Denis 187, 201, 202
McQuail's typology of functions 188
Mead, George Herbert 148, 326
meaning 149, 150, 151
　construction theory 242–243
　production theory 146–151
meanings
　potential 283
　struggle for 277
media
　in Africa, challenges 82–84
　audience 100
　big business 372
　campaigns 231
　and capitalism 136, 137
　and civil society 347–348
　collaborative role of 202
　critical/dialectical role of 203
　culture 270–304
　describing new 154–155
　environment, new 204
　evolution, theory of 54
　facilitative role of 203
　free 144
　freedom of 193
　functions of 185–215
　globalisation and 351–407
　history of South African 4–58
　"hot" and "cool" 152
　as ideological agent 130
　ideological power of 307–323
　impact of globalisation on 362–372
　imperialism 392–396
　independence 347
　information communication technology and 351–407
　limited ownership of 145
　message exposure 230, 231
　most advanced in sub-Saharan Africa 4
　ownership 138
　pluralism 189
　political functions of 188–190
　production 134
　relationships 115, 116
　representations, contextualising of 260–263
　role and functions of 185–225
　role of, in society 178
　as show business 169–170
　as simulation 170–173
　surveillance role of 202
　as symbolic form of expression 133–134
　as text 134
Media
　Development and Diversity Agency 79–80, 198, 199

Index

Foundation for West Africa 77
and Information Commission 77
Institute of Southern Africa 77
Monitoring Project 52
Tenor Institute for Media Analysis 122
media effects
    categorising 229–232
    behavioural 230
media history
    recent phenomenon 5
    approaches to 5
media-culturalist perspective on mass communication 95–96
media-materialist perspective on mass communication 96
Media24 145
Mediaset 393
medium 98–99
    nature of 260
memory 92
Merton, Robert 122, 186
meso-plurality 189, 190
message 99–100
    levels of 99–100
Metro FM 23
Meyer Commission 14
micro-plurality 189, 190
Middle Ages 128
Midi group 23, 25
militarism 352
Mill, John Stuart 125, 178, 208, 402
Milton, John 208
mimesis theory 265
Mining Argus, The 32
missionary activity in Africa 66
MixIt 137
Mlambo-Nquka, Phumzile 26
Mlenga, Kelvin 64, 68
modelling theory 240–241
modern society, pre-modern society compared to 353
modernisation 352
modernity 328
Molière 128
moral panic 234
Morisa Oa Molemo 37
Mozambique 64, 76
Mozart, Wolfgang Amadeus 273
Mugabe, Robert 76
Mukupo, Titus 64
Mulder, CP 47
Multichoice Africa 74
Murray, RW 31
music 293–297
    hip hop 294–295
    popular 294
    rap 295, 296
Mussolini, Benito 192
myths 251–252

N
Namibia 60
Nasionale Pers 18, 35, 47
Naspers 364, 393
Natal Mercantile Advertiser 31
Natal Mercury, The 31
Natal Witness, The 31
Natalier, Die 31
nation-building 71
nation-state, globalisation and 361
National Education, Department of 17
National Party
    and control of the press 45–46
    formation of 35
national unity 71–72
nationalism, African, definition 63
nationalist newspapers 65
Neblo, Michael 343
Nederduitsch Zuid-Afrikaansch Tijdschrift, Het 29
negotiated reading 282, 318
negotiation 280
neo-colonialism 175
neo-Marxist critical theories of ideology 313–315
Neolithic society 128
New Africa 43
New Africa Investments Limited 40
New Age 41
New Communication Policy Paradigm 371
New Nation 43
New World Economic Order 74
New World Information and Communication Order 74, 373–380
    basic premises of 374–375
    changing emphasis 378
    history of 373–374
    liberal school 376
    main documents of 376–378
    structuralist school 375–376
news
    sources 320–321
    theme 320
news bulletin
    first radio 10
    television 149
News Corporation 393
Newspaper Press Union 30–31, 49
newsworthiness 320
Nichols, John 138
Nietzsche, Friedrich 171
Nigeria 63, 64, 65, 66, 68
Nkomo, Joshua 65, 66, 70
Noomen, G.W. 188, 189
Nordenstreng, Kaarle 201, 202
normative questions 179–180
normative theory 178–180, 190–191
    questioning 205–206
    rethinking 201–207
    in South Africa 209–215

Northern News 67
Nova 53
Nyerere, Julius 70

O
objectivity 123, 124
Ombudsman, Press 194
ontology 106–107
oppositional reading 282, 318
oral mass communication culture 91–92
Ordinance No. 60 29, 36
organic folk culture 272
Organisation of African Unity 74
orientation 223
Orkney Snork Nie 261
Ortega y Gasset, José 125, 402
Oude Emigrant, De 31
oversaturation of market 52–53

P
Paine, Thomas 178, 208
Pan-African News Agency 74
Park, Robert E. 120
parsimony 112
Parsons, Talcott 120, 185, 326
Passion of the Christ, The 287, 298–300
pastiche 160, 161
Pathé 393
Patriot, Die 49
Pavarotti, Luciano 297
Paver, Bertram 38
Pearson 393
Peirce, Charles Sanders 326, 327
perception 263
Perskor 47
personal
    identity 236
    relations 236
Petersen, Taliep 296
Peterson, Theodore 208, 209
phenomenology 146
photography 94
Pienaar, François 292
pirate viewing 23
Plato 208
play 222
pluralism 144, 206
    media 189
plurality, social 189
police and action dramas 217
policy research 156
political
    functions of the media 188–190
    opinion, truth-tracking potential of 343
    power 140
political communication
    pathologies of 347
political economy 135–139
    definition 135

433

Media Studies: Volume 1

politics
  deliberative 341
  Habermas and 341–342
  and Internet identity 401–402
polysemy 283–284, 318
Pool, Ithiel de Sola 120, 376
popular culture 204
popularity 160
positivism 117–118, 145
  criticism of 122–124
  and mass communication 120–121
Post 40
Post Office 10
post-Saussurian semiotics 369
postcolonial
  perspective 207–209
  research 176
  theory 174–178
postcolonialism, definition 663
Postman, Neil 169–170
postmodern
  epistemology 159
  society 203–207
  postmodernstyle 160–162
postmodernism 157–174
postmodern society 157–160
poststructuralism 157–174
power 140–141, 311
  unequal 316
  forms of 346
pragmatism 327
pre-modern society compared to modern society 353
preferred reading 281–283, 318
  dominant 318
  negotiated 318
  oppositional 318
press 28–57
  Afrikaans 33–36
  in Afrikaans 9–10
  alternative 40–44, 51
  during the apartheid years 44–52
  black 36–40
  English 28–33
  pressures on 49–52
  in South Africa 5
  struggle for freedom of 29–30
Press Ombudsman 194
Pretoria News 190
Primedia 56
Pringle, Thomas 29, 30
printing press 286
  invention of 93
privatisation 367
  of state media 77–78
professional ideology 319
  of journalists 319–321
projection 219
propaganda 231
Prophets of the City 295, 296

public
  broadcasting 22
  pressure 51–52
  reason 337–342
public service broadcasting
  in South Africa 195–197
  manifesto for 195–196
Public Service Media Policy Paradigm 370
public opinion, considered 342
  mass-communication and 344–346
public sphere 139–141, 325–348
  transformation of 328–334
  practices and institutions in 329–332
  bourgeois 329
  rational 329–330
  institutions of 330–331
  decline of 332–334
  democracy and 342–348

Q
Qoboza, Percy 39

R
racial structuring 276
racism 250
radical narrative 61
Radio 702 13, 16
Radio Bantu 14
Radio Bop 13, 16
Radio Good Hope 13
Radio Highveld 13
Radio Pluralism, Bamako Declaration on 79
Radio Port Natal 13
Radiosondergrense 9, 99, 365
Radio Thohoyandou 16
Radio Tsonga 13
Radio Venda 13
radio
  African language services 14
  amateur broadcasts 6–7
  black listeners, programming for 11–12
  community 19, 79–80
  establishment of, in South Africa 6–8
  independent 15–16
  introduction of frequency modulation 12–13
  invention of 94
  receivers, building own 7
  sets, leasing 8
  stations, automation of 13
Railway
  broadcasts 7
  Institutes 7
Ramadaan 288
Rand Daily Mail 40, 43, 51
Rand Easter Show 19
rap music 295, 296
Rapport 190, 254

rational public sphere 329–330
reading
  dominant 282
  negotiated 282
  oppositional 282
  preferred 281–283, 318
Reagan, Ronald 49, 359
reality 217
  false 311
rediffusion service 12
refeudalism 332
regional newspapers 53–54
regulatory
  bodies 194
  paradigm, new 369–372
regulatory system 4
  forces that shape 4
reification 317
Reith Report 11
Reith, Sir John 8, 195, 196
relationships, media 115, 116
religion 285–289, 309
  belief system 285
  definition 285
  as mass entertainment 287–288
  mass marketed 287
  rituals 286
Renaissance 128
representations, system of 313
Repressive State Apparatuses 313
rhetorical motifs 216–218
  in popular television genres 217–218
Rhodes, Cecil John 34
Richardson, Samuel 330, 334
rituals 286
Robertson, John 28
Roelofse, J.J. 190
Roos TJ 36
Roos, Gideon 12
Rorty, Richard 327
Rousseau, Jean-Jacques 259, 330
Royal Gazette 63
Royal Gold Coast Gazette 64
Rugby World Cup 291

S
Saamstaan 42
SABC *see also* South African Broadcasting Corporation
SABC 1 22, 23
SABC 2 22
SABC 3 22
SABC 4 27
SABC 5 27
SABC tower 13
Said, Edward 175
sales tax 51
Sampson, Anthony 39
Santa Barbara 15
SASO Newsletter 41, 42
"saucepan special" 66

Index

Saussure, Ferdinand de 162, 167, 252, 274
Schelling, Friedrich 327
schizophrenia 160
Schleiermacher, Friedrich 327
Schlesinger, Isidore William 8, 55
Schoch Commission 10–11
Scholten, Otto 188, 189
Schramm, Wilbur 208, 209
Schubert, AF 31
Schutz, Alfred 146
Scott, Alexander 67
Searle, John 327
Second Conference of African Journalists 70
Seditious Offences Bill 64
semiosphere 369
semiotics 148–151
    post-Saussurian 369
Sénégal 64, 79
Senghor, Léopold 210
sensitivity 263
Sentec tower 13
sexual divisions 276
Shakespeare, William 128
Siebert, Fred 208, 2009
Sierra Leone 63, 65, 68,
signs 148, 149–150, 151
silence, spiral of 246–247
Siswe media 56
situation comedies 217
Smith, Adam 208
Smith, Ian 69
Smuts, General Jan 9
social
    expectation theory 241–242
    myth theory 252–256
    plurality 189
    position 312
    rationality 326
    relations 113–114
    responsibility paradigm 202
    responsibility theory 194–197
social-culturalist perspective on mass communication 96
social-materialist perspective on mass communication 96
society,
    material base of 311
    needs of 331–332
    structures in 113
Soga, AK 38
Soleil, Le 64
Somerset, Lord Charles 29, 30
Son, Die 52, 190
South 43
South Africa 60, 63, 76
South African
    Associated Newspapers 46
    Communist Party 275
    National Editors Forum 194
    Native National Congress 38
    Press Association 10
    Students Organisation 41
    Telecommunication Regulatory Authority 20
South African Broadcasting Corporation 5, 6, 55, 195–197
    broadcasts in Afrikaans 9–10
    formation of 8–9
    introduction of news services 10
    introduction of television services 14
    restructuring of 22–23
    role of, as public broadcaster 26–27
South African Commercial Advertiser, The 29, 33, 34
South African Journal, The 29
Southern African Development Community 367
Soviet communist theory 197–198
Sowetan 40, 52
Sowetan Mirror 40
Sowetan, The 32
Soweto Community Television 22
Spark 41
spectator-centred technology 289
spiral of silence 246–247
Spivak, Gayatri Chakravorty 175
sport 289–292
    as cultural phenomenon 290
    as ritualised experience 290
    politics endemic in 291–292
Springbok Radio 11, 12, 368
Springboks 291
Staats Courant 31
Stalin, Joseph 126, 208
Standard and Transvaal Mining Chronicle, The 32
STAR TV 393
Star, The 32, 51, 52, 190
state media, privatisation and commercialisation 77–78
State of Emergency 50
Station JB 7, 10
stereotype theory 243–244
stereotypes 255
    changing 263–264
    characteristics and working of 256–258
    origins of 258–260
stereotyping 247–264
    definition 248
Steyn Commission of Enquiry 17, 47–49
Steyn, Marthinus 48
Streeter, John Samuel 6
structural limitations 168–169
structuralism 162–164
structuralist school 375–376
structure 114
Suasso de Lima, Josephus 33
subjectivity 123, 124
subscription services 17–18
Sun, The 52, 190
Sunday Independent 190
Sunday Times 190
surveillance 236
    media role 202
survival 217
Swazi Music radio 15
Swaziland 83
symbolic
    interactionism 147–148
    power 141
    token 354
    universe 313

T

tabloid journalism, rise of 52
tabloids 52
Tanzania 70, 72, 83
Tanzania Media Council 83
technological determinism 151–154
technologies, new information and communication 80–82
technology 98, 102, 357
telegraph, discovery of 94
television 152
    advent of 94–95
    advertising on 50
    licence fees 23
    introduction of 14–15
    news bulletin 149
    opposition to introduction of 14
television genres, rhetorical motifs in popular 217–218
Telkom 367
textual devices 284
Thatcher, Margaret 17, 359
theory 103–115
    accumulation 238–239
    Afrocentric approach 174–178
    agenda-setting 244–245
    authoritarian 191–192
    behaviourism 118–119
    binary oppositions 249–251
    building blocks of 105–110
    catharsis 265
    comparative 208
    critical approach 124–146
    cultural and feminist studies 142–143
    democratic participant 199–201
    development 198–199
    diffusion of innovation 239–240
    empiricism 118
    epistemology 107–108
    evaluating 110–112
    focus of 109–110
    formulating 106
    framing 245–246
    functionalism 119–120
    goals of 104–105
    goals of mass media 112–115
    human account 104
    hypodermic needle 232–233
    ideology 130–133

of ideology, critical 310–317
of ideology, neutral 309–310
information society approach 154–156
libertarian 192–193
libertarian press 193
long-term 237–247
macro and micro 115
mass society 124–127
mass/popular culture criticism 127–130
meaning construction 242–243
meaning production 146–151
mimesis 265
modelling 240–241
normative 178–180, 190–191
normative, questioning 205–26
normative, rethinking 201–207
ontology 106–107
phenomenology 146–147
political economy 135–139
positivism 117–118, 120–121
postcolonial 174–178
postcolonial 207–209
poststructuralist/postmodern approach 157–174
practical value of 103–104
public sphere 139–142
purpose of 108
scientific value of 103
scope of 111
semiotics 148–151
simplicity of 112
social expectation 241–242
social myth 252–256
social responsibility 194–197
Soviet communist 197–198
speech-act 339–340
spiral of silence 246–247
stereotype 243–244
symbolic interactionism 147–138
technological determinism 151–154
testability of 111–112
two-step-flow 234–236
uses and gratifications 236
utility of 112
value of 103–104
ThisDay 53
Thompson, Edward Palmer 274
three tier system 21–22
Tijd, De 33
Time Warner 363
time-scale media effects 230
time-space distanciation 352
timeless-time 398

To The Point 46
Tocqueville, Alexis de 178, 402
Togo 72
Tönnies, Ferdinand 125
Transvaal Argus 32
Transvaal Observer, The 32
Transvaler, Die 36
Treatment Action Campaign 280
Trinity Broadcasting Network 15
Triple Inquiry Report 20–21, 55
Tuchman, Gaye 147
Tunis Summit 383
two-step-flow theory 234–236

U

Ubuntu 176, 210–215
   and freedom of expression 214–215
   journalism 213
   as a normative media theory 210–215
UmAfrika 53, 190
Umshumayeli Wendaba 37
unequal power 316
UNESCO
   Media Declaration 377
   Statement of Journalistic Ethics 377
unification 317
unintended media effects 230
United Democratic Front 42
United Nations
   Administrative Committee on Coordination 382
   Economic Commission for Africa 81
   Educational, Scientific and Cultural Organisation 74, 75, 377
   System Chief Executive Board 382–383
United Party 9
United Press International Television News 47
United States Commission on Freedom of the Press 208
uses and gratifications theory 236–237
Utopian society 127

V

Vaderland, Die 36
Vaderland, Ons 36
Van Cuilenborg, Jan 188, 189
Van Riebeeck, Jan 28
vernacular, regional newspapers in 53–54
Verwoerd, Hendrik 36, 241
Verzamelaar, De 33
Viacom 393
Viljoen Commission 17, 18–19
violence 308

visual impact 219–220
Vivendi Universal 393
Volksblad, Het 35
Volkstem, De 32
Volkstem, Die 32
Vorster, B.J. (John) 47, 241
Vrye Weekblad 43, 44

W

Walker, Alexander 28
"warm" media 172
Washington Star 47
Weber, Alfred 326
Weber, Max 122, 123
Weekly Mail 43, 44
Welles, Orson 233
Wells, H.G. 233
Wesleyan Missionary Society 37
West African Pilot 65
Western Electric 7
Williams, Raymond 142, 171, 274
Windhoek Declaration 75–76
Wittgenstein, Ludwig 326, 327
World Association for Community Radio Broadcasters
World Bank 81
world economic order, new 357
World Summit on the Information Society 382–383
   criticism of 383–387
   liberal critique of 384
   Luddite critique of 384
World Vision Botswana 79
World, The 39, 40
Wright, Charles 186
Wright's model of functions 186, 187
writing 92–93
written and printed mass communication culture 91, 92–94

Y

YouTube 137

Z

Zambia 60, 64, 67, 70, 72, 73, 83, 84
   National Broadcasting Corporation 76
   National Broadcasting Corporation (Licensing) Regulations 76
Zambian Mail 68
Zimbabwe 60, 67, 69, 76, 79, 347
Zionist church 280
Zuid-Afrikaan, De 31, 34
Zuid-Afrikaanse Republiek 31, 34
Zuma, Jacob 246, 284